MARK COHEN

RESPASS

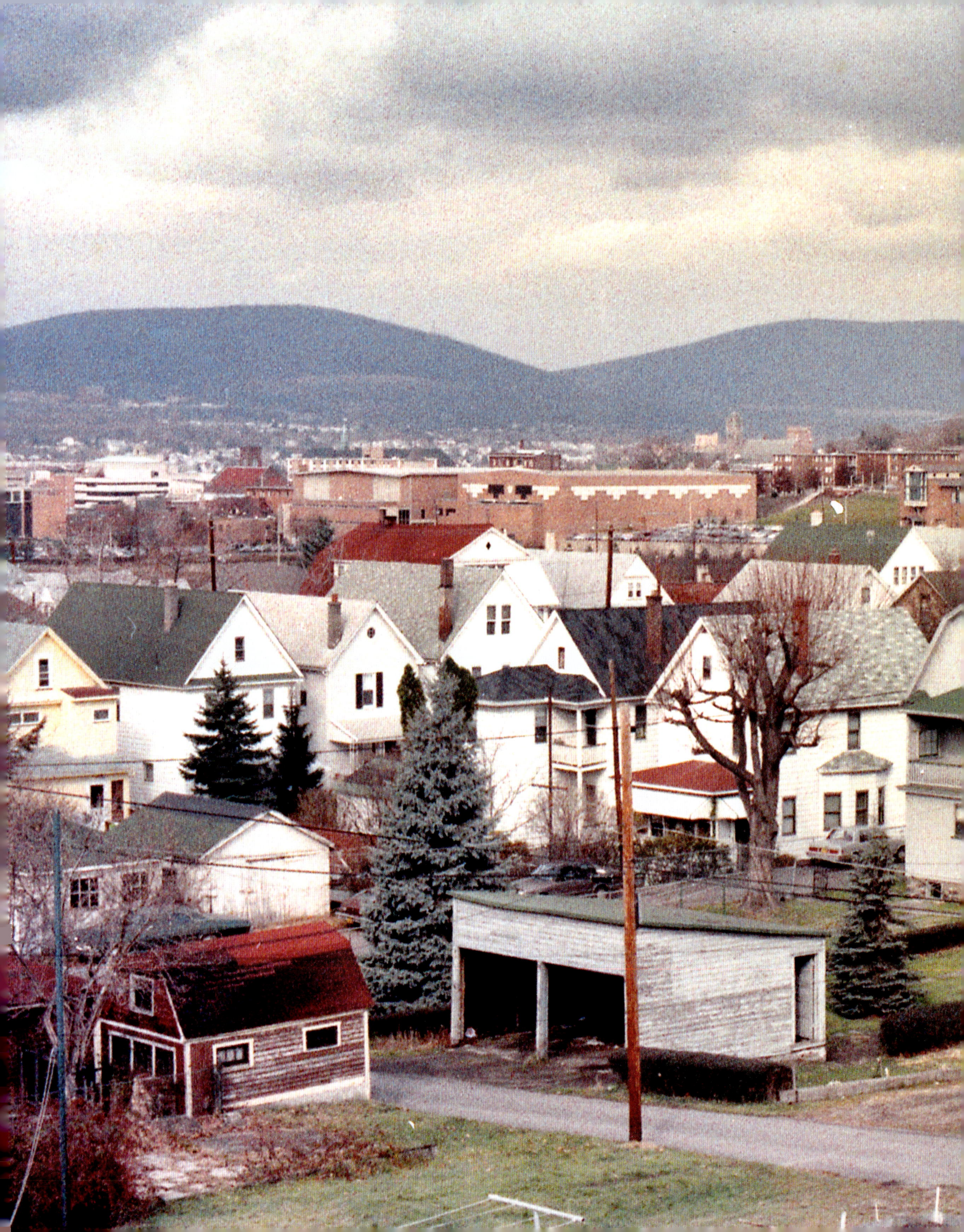

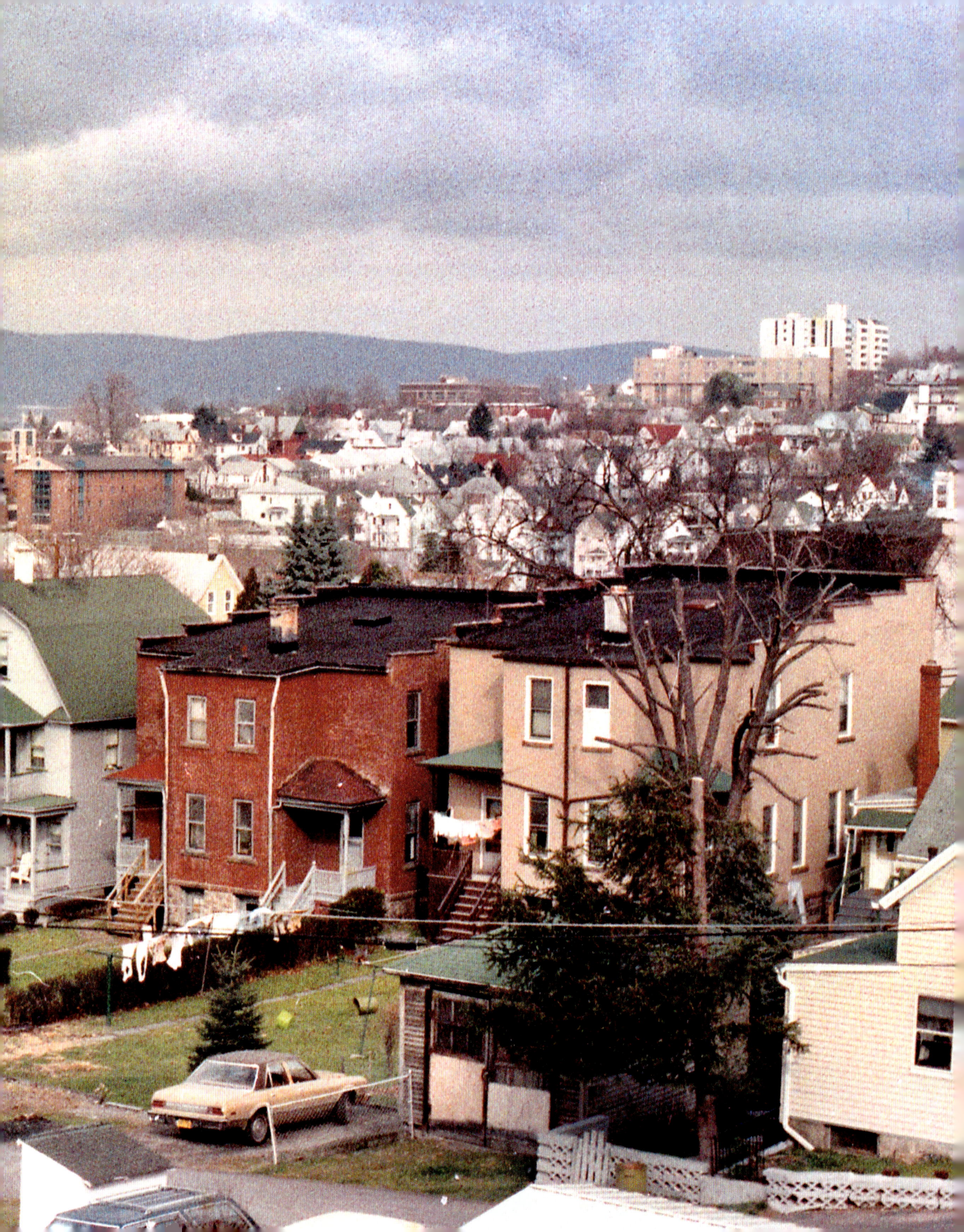

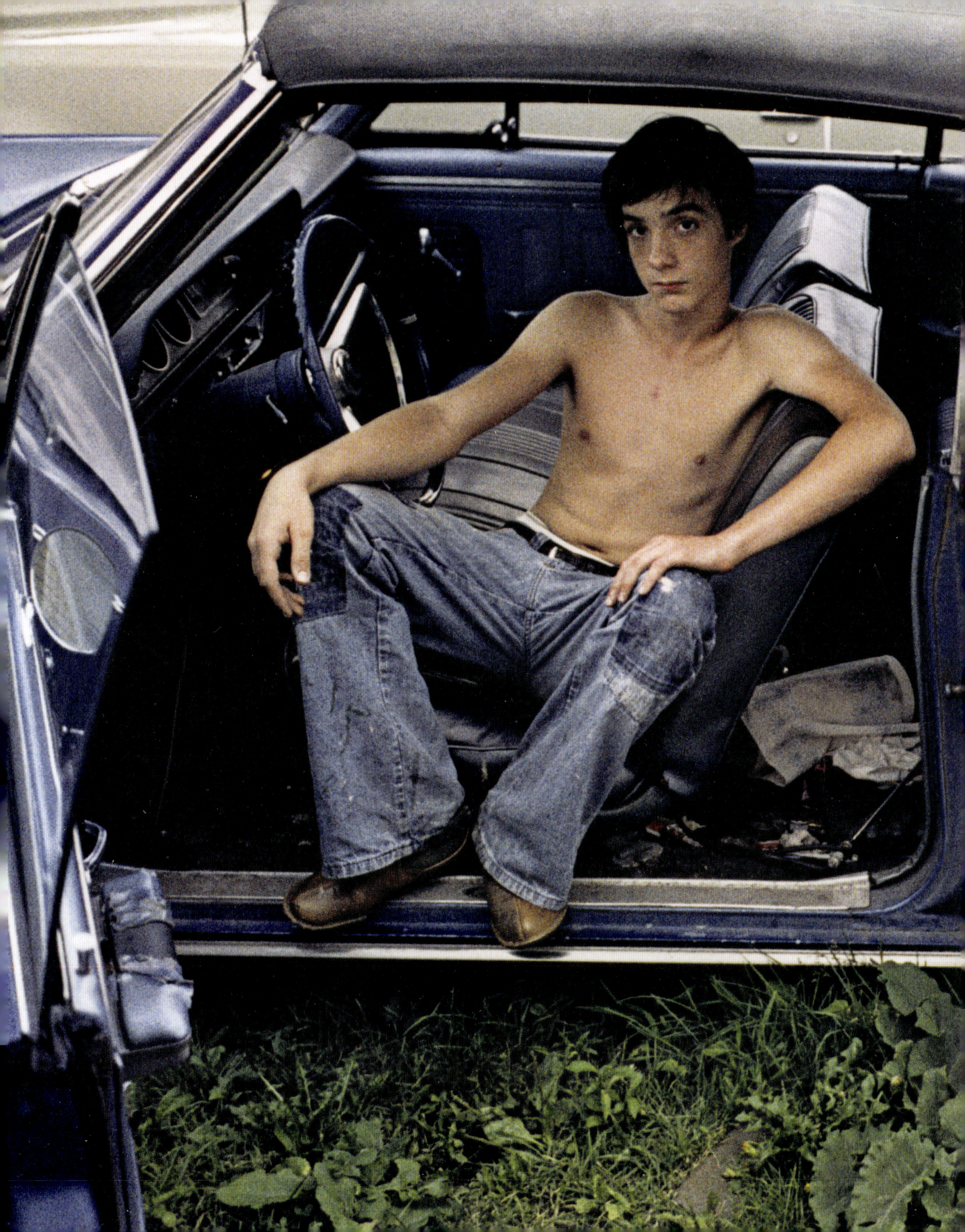

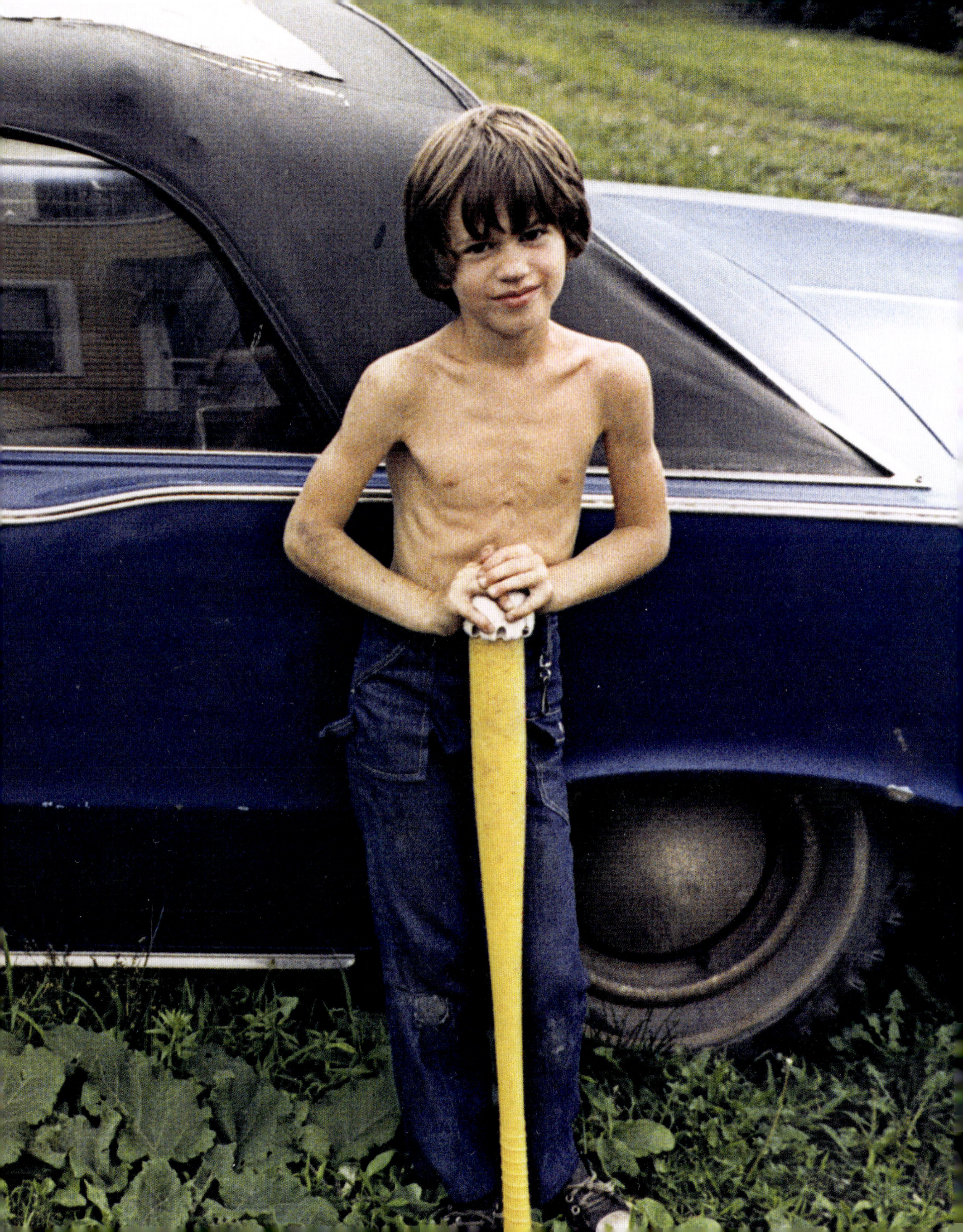

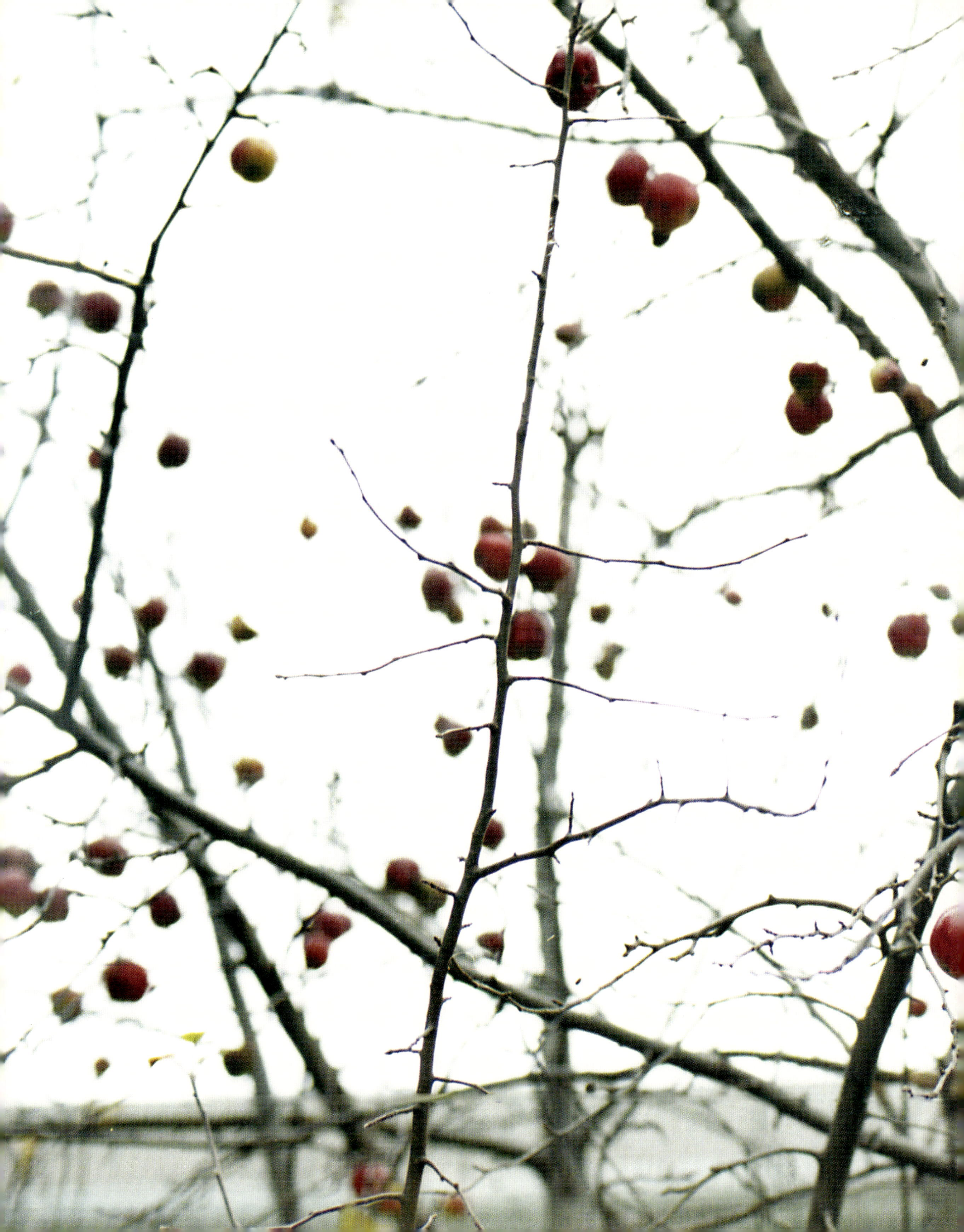

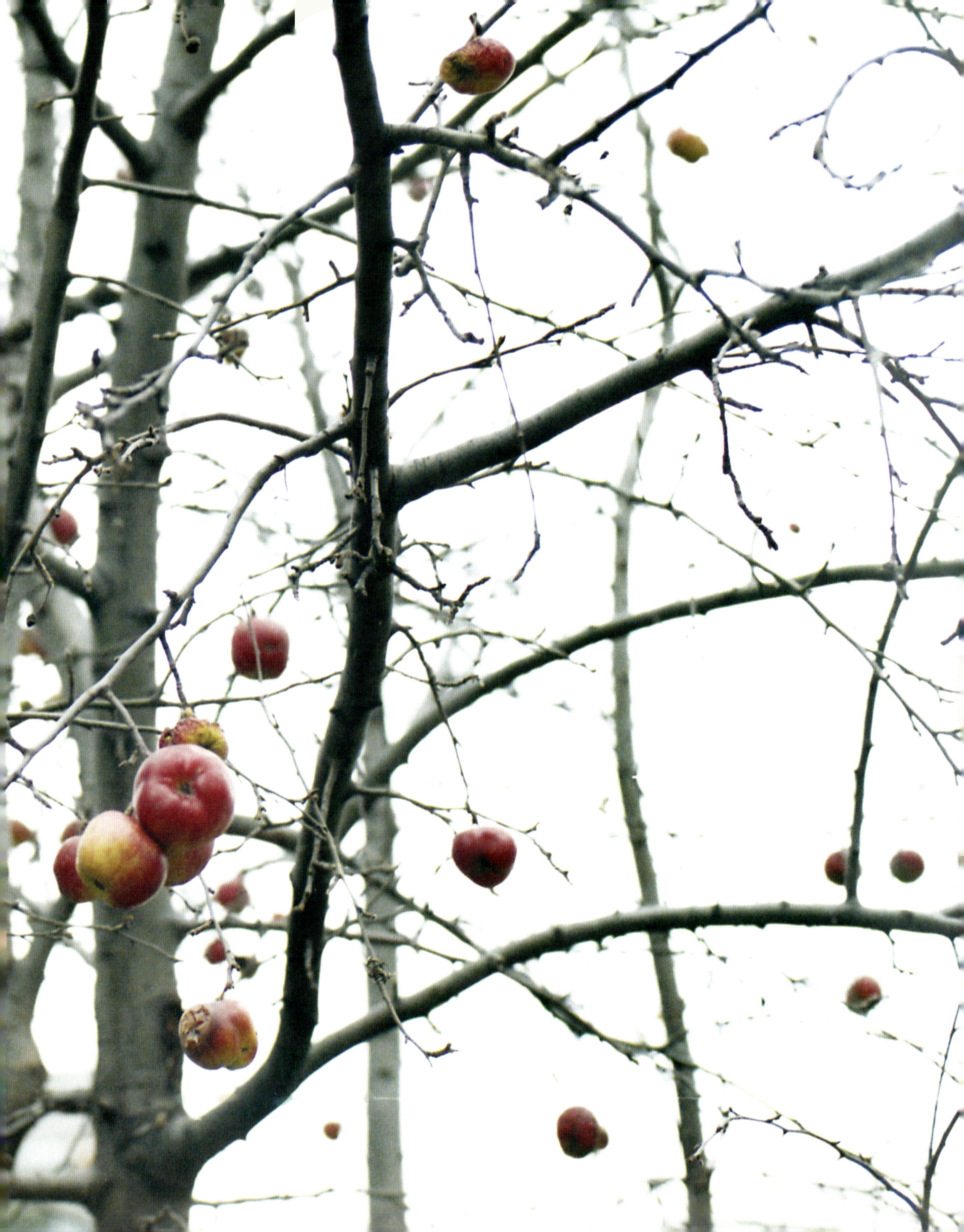

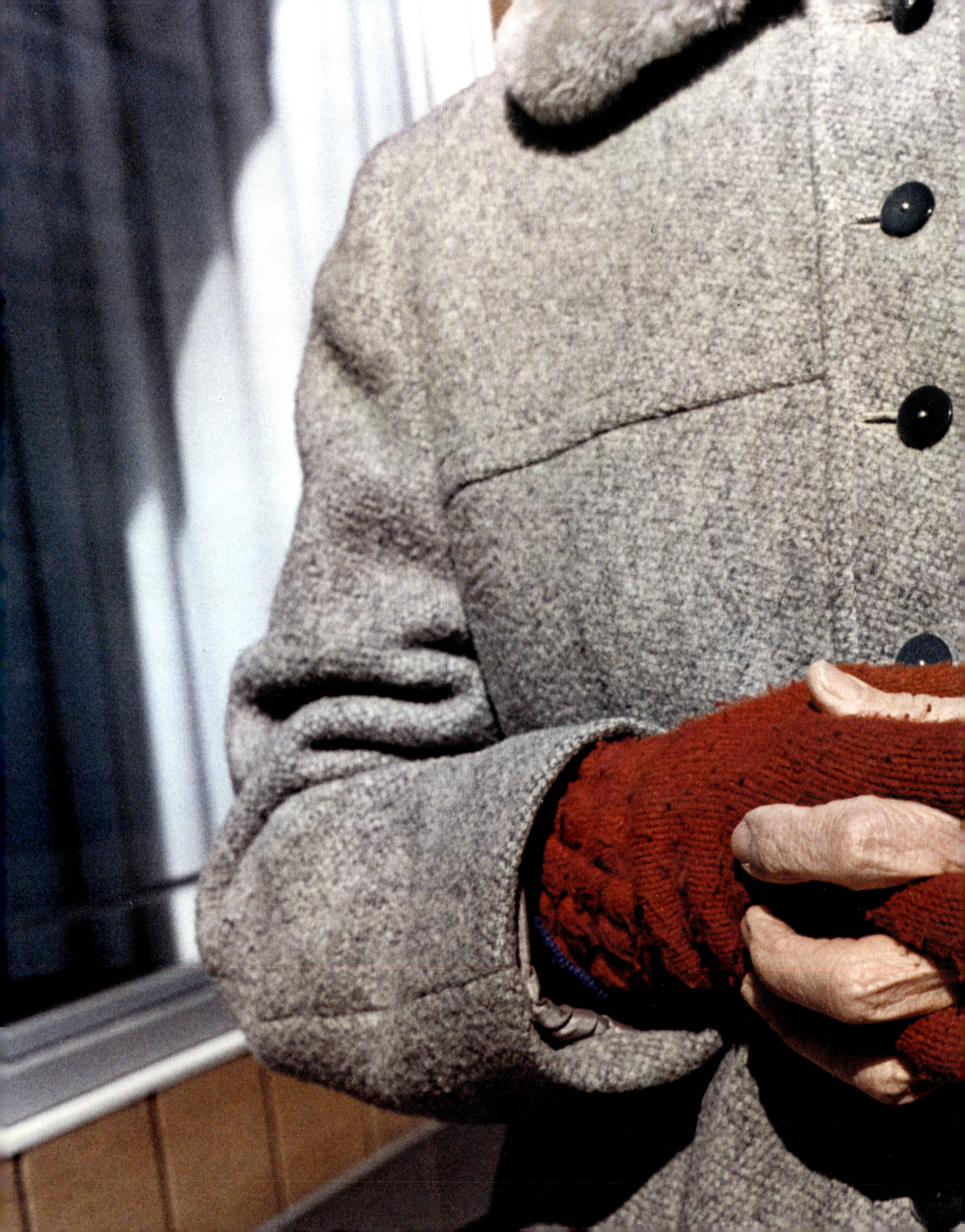

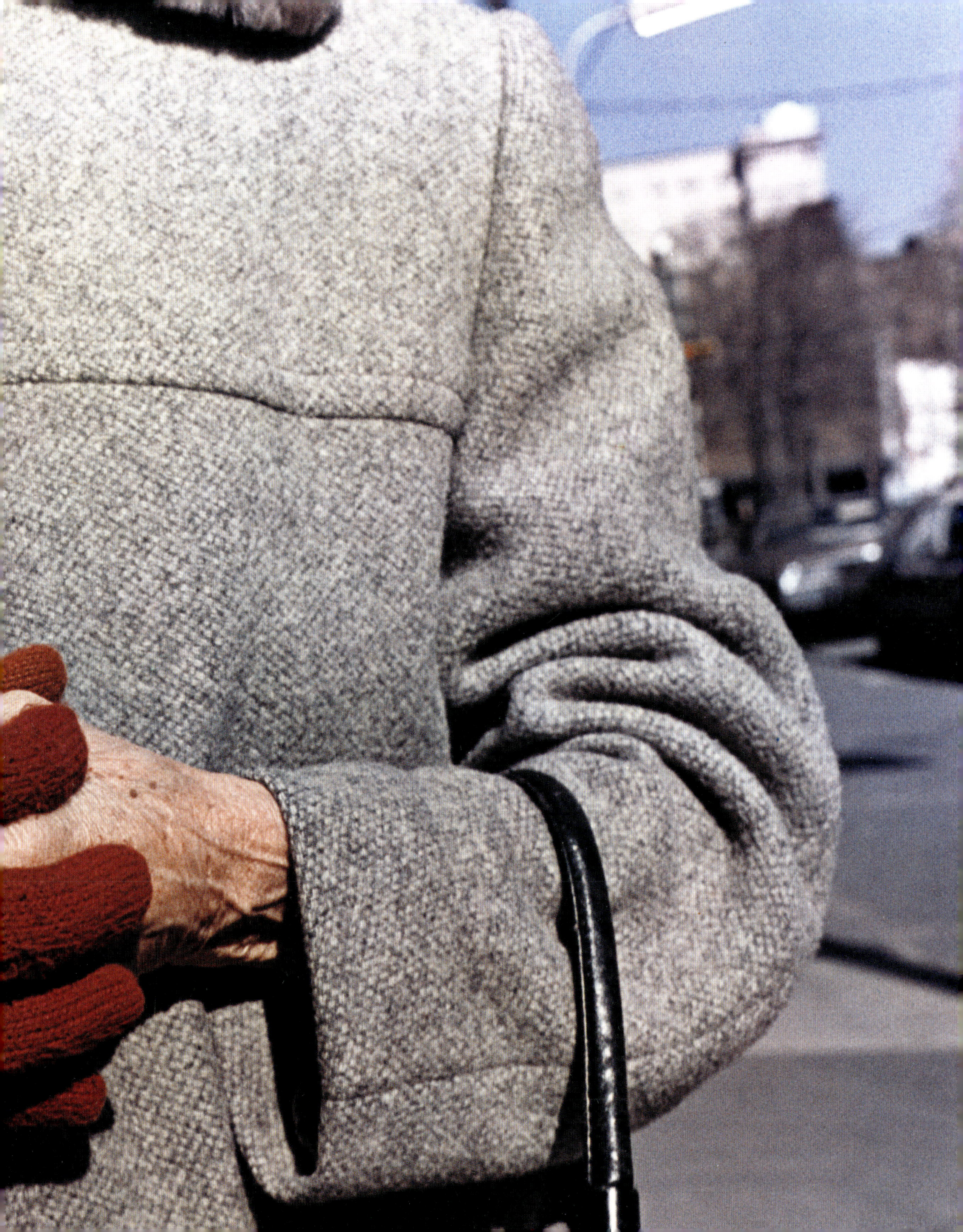

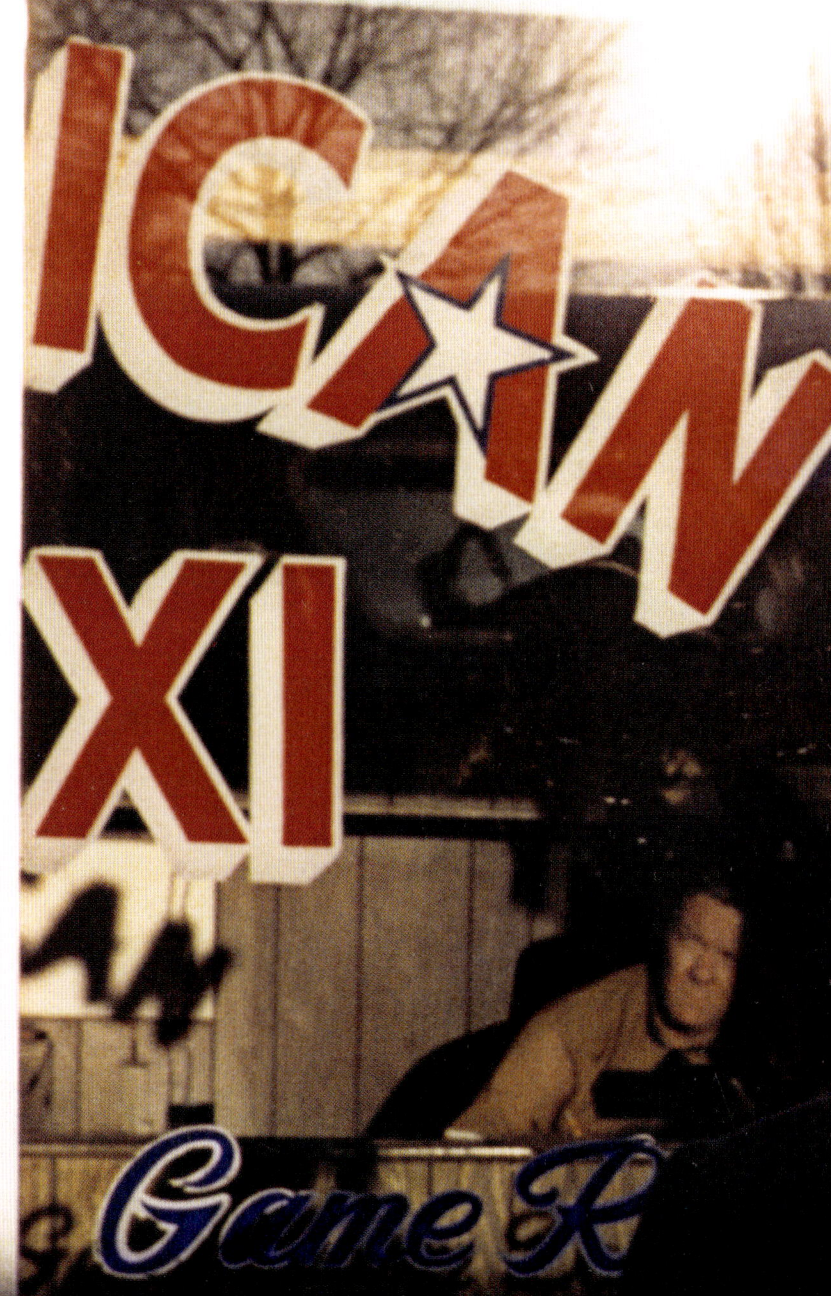
MERICAN
TAXI
3·3186
Game R

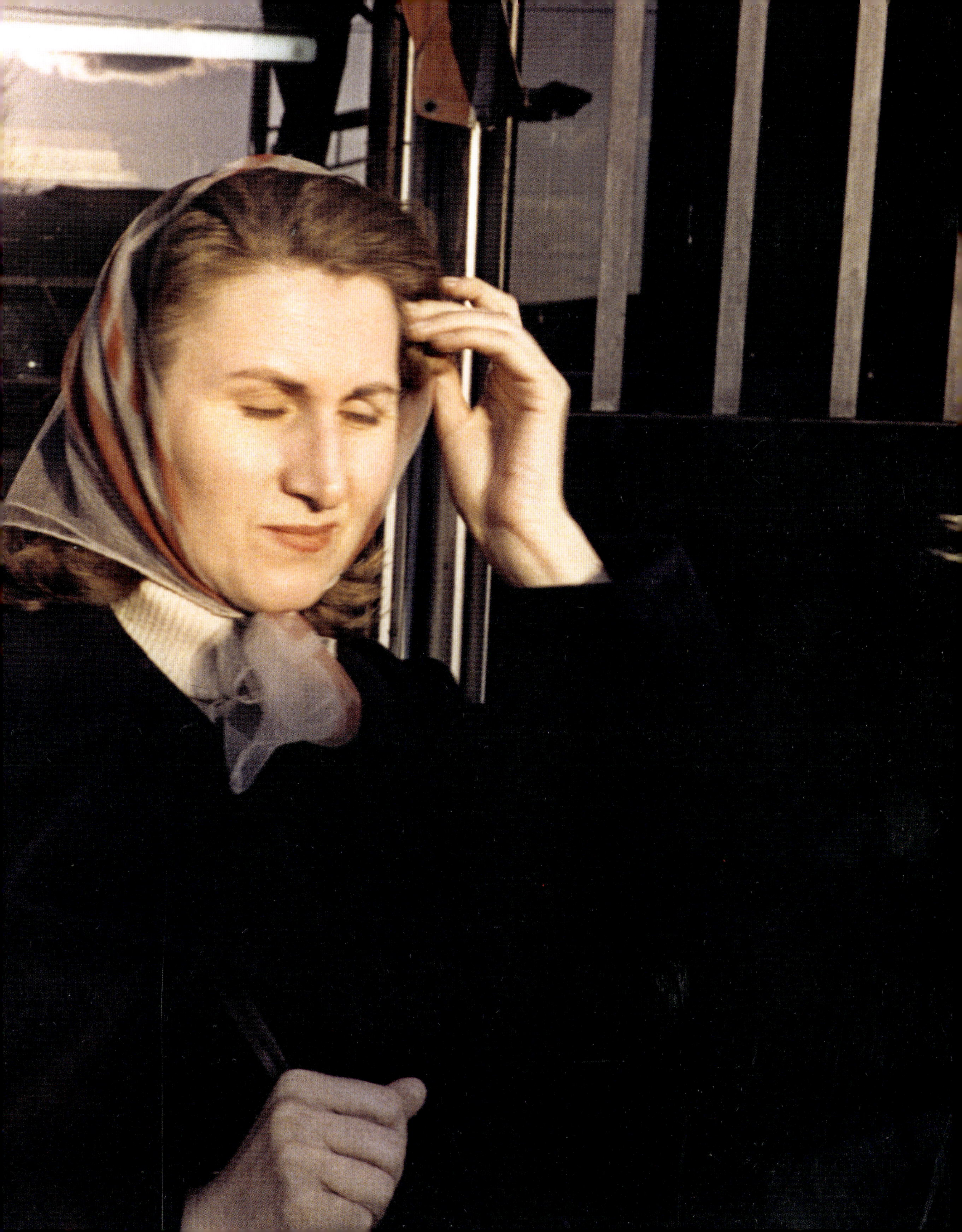

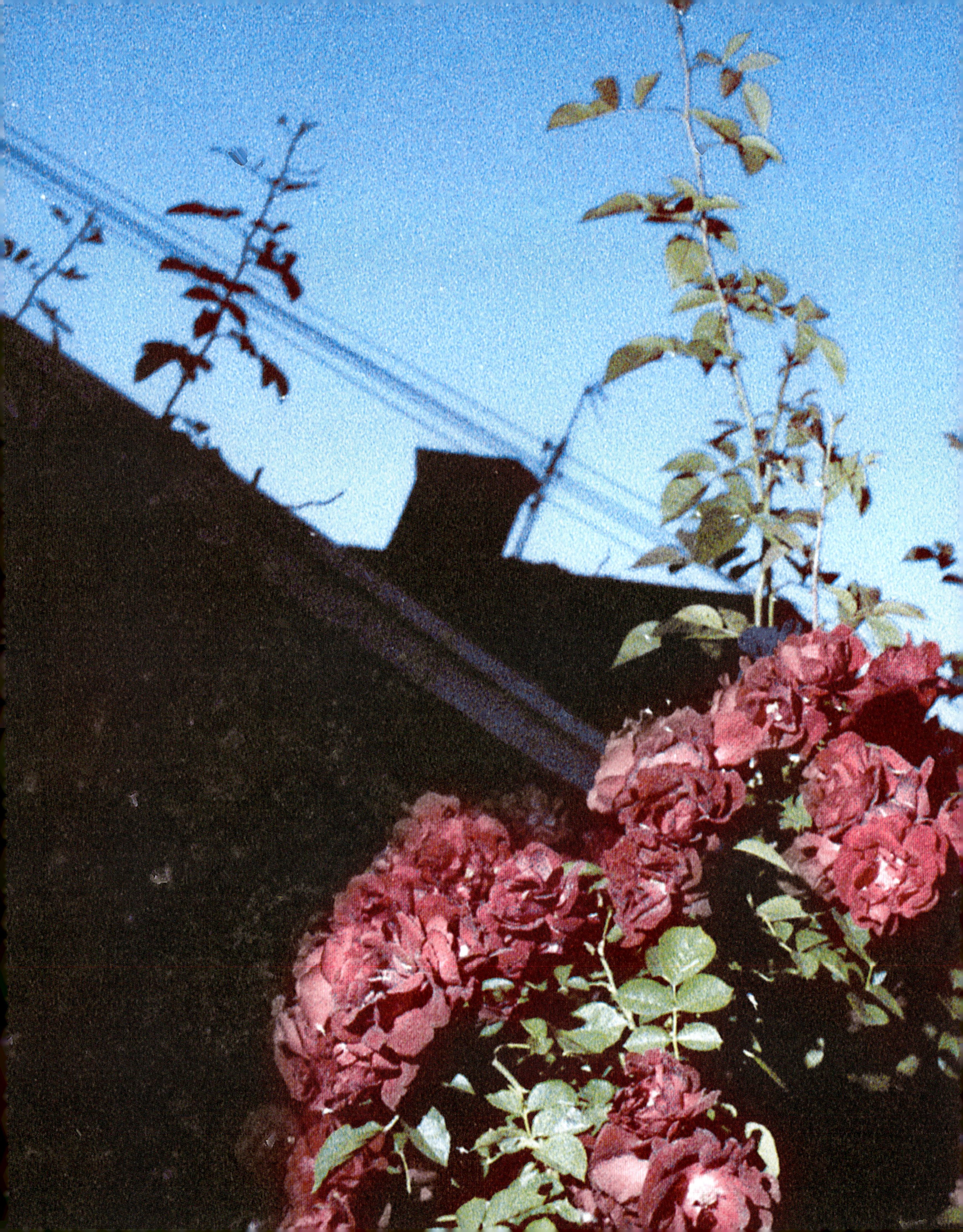

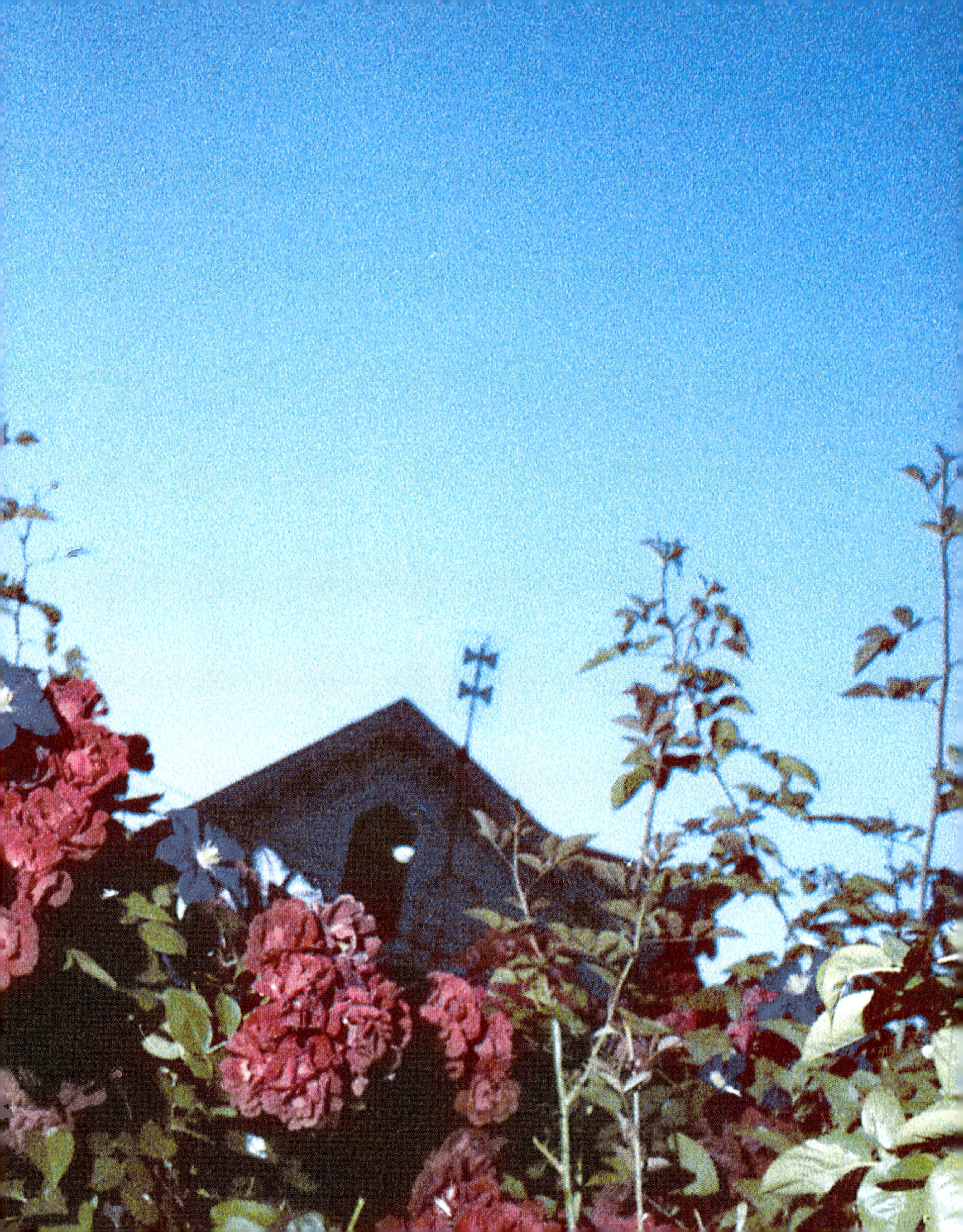

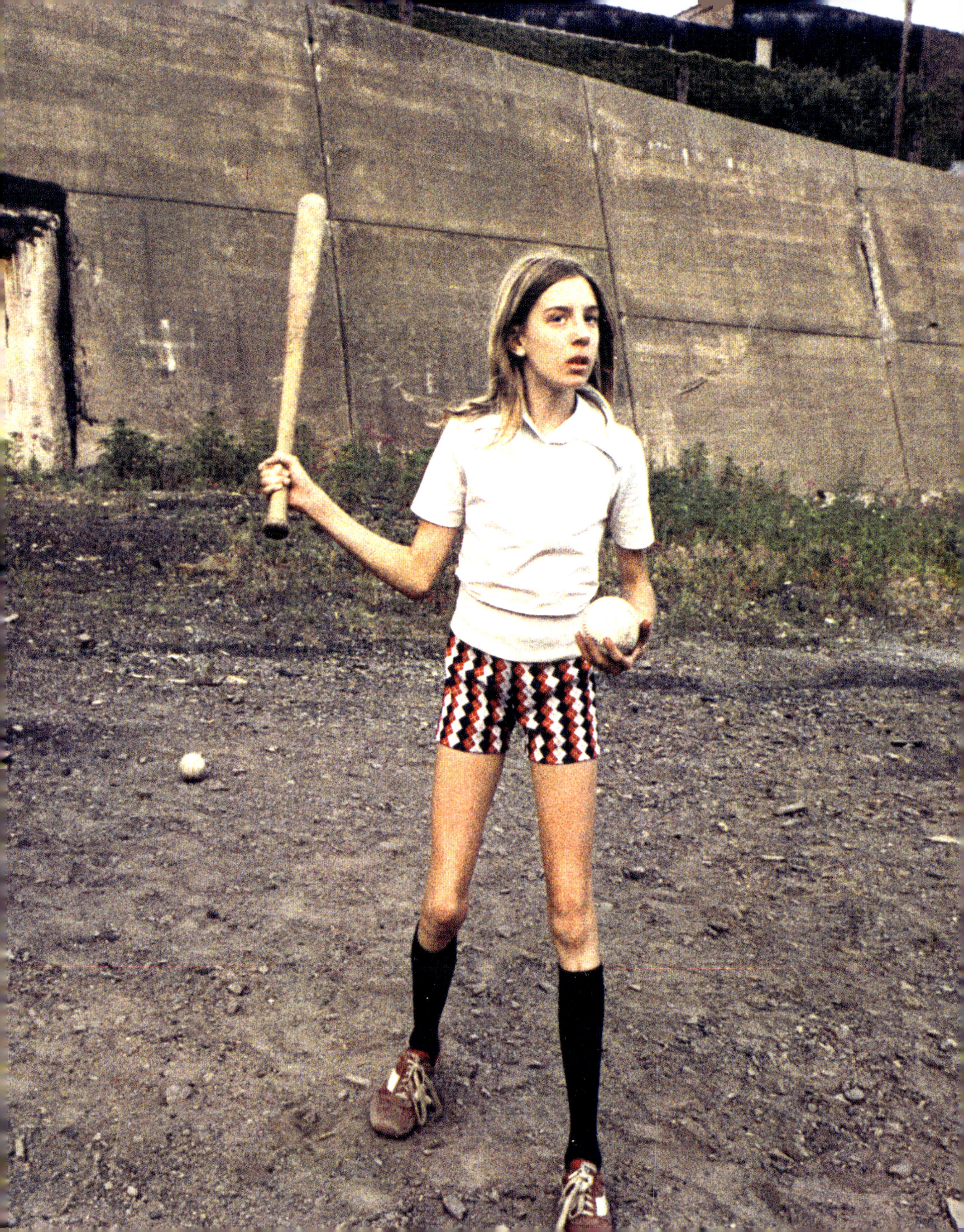

MARK COHEN

TRESPASS

Phillip Prodger

PRESTEL
MUNICH · LONDON · NEW YORK

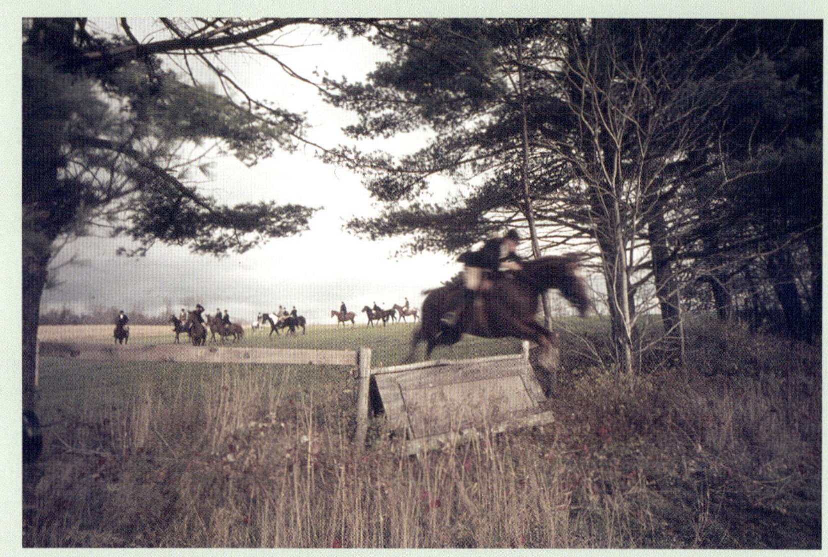

2 Mark Cohen, *Horse Jump, Scranton*, 1967

MARK COHEN: ANONYMOUS

PHILLIP PRODGER

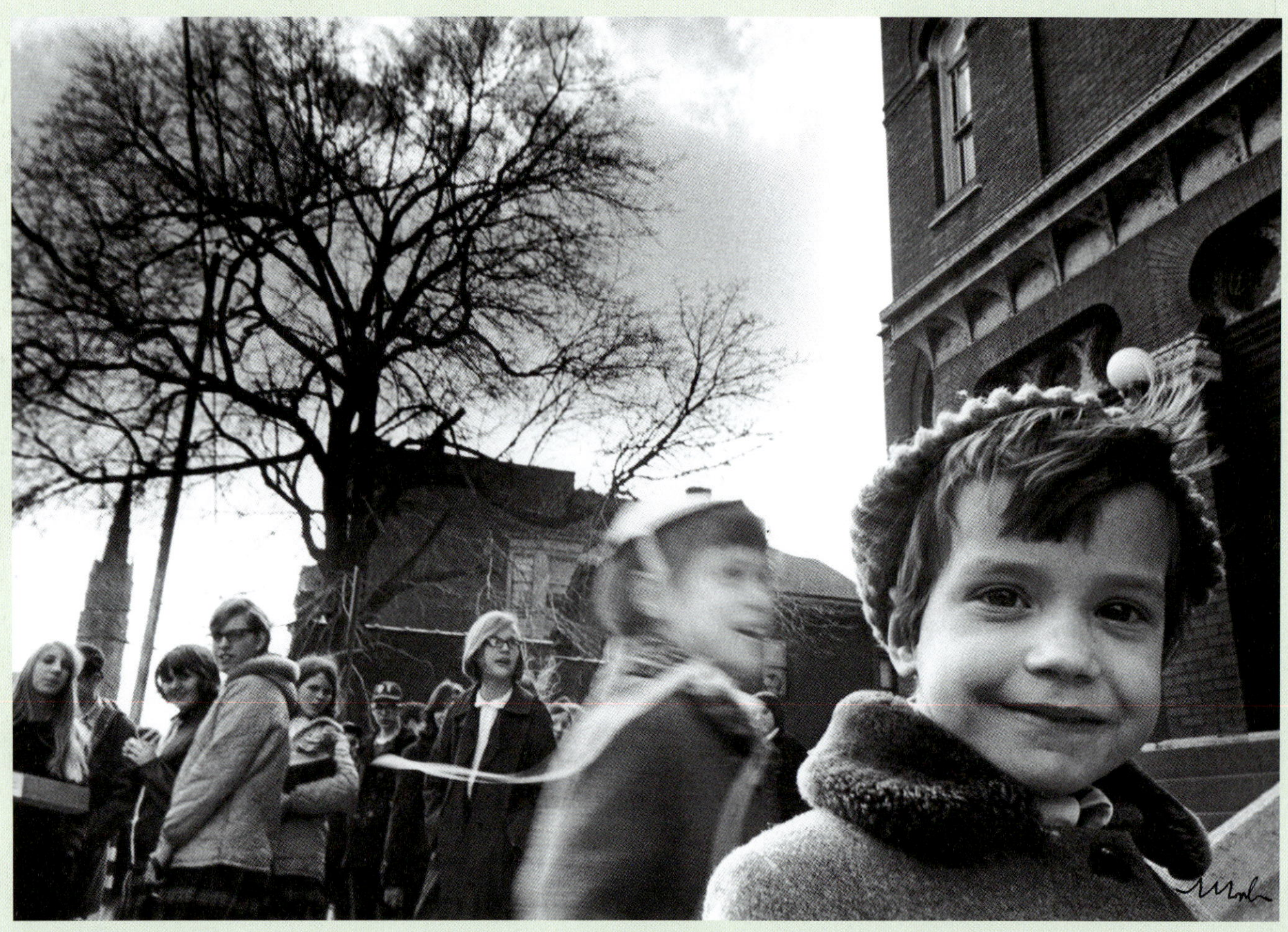

1 Mark Cohen, *Untitled*, May 1969

Wilkes-Barre, Pennsylvania, is an unlikely place for a revolution. Yet as the birthplace and longtime home of Mark Cohen, one of the most original voices in contemporary photography, it became the epicenter of a groundbreaking new approach to the medium. It was here, beginning in the 1960s, that Cohen developed his signature brand of street photography, bringing his camera uncomfortably close to his subjects, usually with flash and often without consent, invading personal space to create fragmented portrait vignettes, studies of found objects, and haunting landscapes. Initially, Cohen photographed almost entirely in black and white (fig. 1). But in the 1970s, his work increasingly turned to color, placing him at the forefront of pioneering "new color" photographers who were then experimenting with newly available materials and equipment.

Cohen's photographs first came to public prominence in 1973 with the solo exhibition *Photographs by Mark Cohen* at New York's Museum of Modern Art (MoMA). Although Cohen had already begun experimenting in color, the 1973 exhibition featured only black-and-white works. It was not the first time he had been shown in MoMA's photography galleries; in 1969, the museum had acquired two works by the then twenty-five-year-old artist for its permanent collection. These were included in a *New Acquisitions* group show the following year, dedicated, in part, to the "reshaping of the documentary tradition based on the artists' own fascination with the snapshot, the most personal, reticent, and ambiguous of documents."[1]

Cohen's solo show opened at a pivotal time for MoMA's photography department. Its director John Szarkowski was in the process of publishing his landmark book *Looking at Photographs* (also 1973) and was beginning to feature a new wave of young color photographers in the galleries. These included William Eggleston, whose landmark exhibition *Photographs by William Eggleston* (1976) and its accompanying publication, *William Eggleston's Guide*, would soon transform color practice (fig. 3).

Had the timing been slightly different, the history of color art photography in America might have been radically altered. Since Cohen's color work was still in an exploratory phase, the museum did not include it. As a result, Cohen became known primarily as a black-and-white photographer, and it was not until years later that the scope and importance of his contributions to color photography were acknowledged, with the inclusion of five pictures in Sally Eauclaire's influential *The New Color Photography* (1981) and the later monograph *Mark Cohen: True Color* (2007).

Cohen was one of dozens of serious photographic artists experimenting with color materials at the time. In the early 1970s, technical improvements in color film, printing, and processing had begun to open new creative possibilities for color photography. Kodachrome slide film (and its rival, the German Agfacolor) had been around since 1936, but its limitations made it impractical for many uses.

When embarking on his professional career, Cohen tried out both Kodak and Agfa materials, producing works such as *Horse Jump, Scranton* (1967; fig. 2). The results held promise, but were ultimately unsatisfying. For one thing, slide films were slow—the original Kodachrome had a rating of 25 ISO, eventually joined by a later, faster 64 ISO version. This was much slower than color negative films, which could be used at the same speeds as the black-and-white films Cohen favored. Kodachrome was too insensitive for sharp action photography, and required bright lighting to expose reliably. In *Horse Jump, Scranton*, Cohen used this quality to good effect, showing the leaping horse and rider in an explosive moment of blur, a gesture reminiscent of another pioneering color photographer of a generation earlier, Ernst Haas. Haas, whose *Color Photography* became, in 1961, one of the first such exhibitions staged at MoMA, enjoyed widespread popularity at the time, both for his legendary work with *Life* magazine and his television broadcast *The Art of Seeing* (1962), as well as the accompanying exhibition of the same name (1966). Nevertheless, the materials Haas had pioneered for his own brand of photography were not a great fit for the young Cohen.

Cost was another important issue. Kodachrome film was too complicated to process locally, so once exposed it had to be mailed to a central lab for development. And since Kodachrome resulted in direct color positives on film—known as transparencies, or slides—either an intermediate negative (called an internegative) had to be produced, or special papers were needed, capable of printing from a positive original to a positive print. So-called reversal products such as Cibachrome, Ilfochrome, and others like them could be printed directly from slides, but they had a distinctive (if undeniably beautiful) cast, were comparatively high in contrast, and their surfaces were easily scratched. Eggleston famously solved this problem by printing in dye transfer, a luminous, hands-on method usually used only for high-end commercial work, which Ernst Haas had also used. Cohen, who made ends meet by working as a local studio photographer doing yearbook and class pictures, did not have ready access to such luxurious materials.[2]

Mass-market photography presented an affordable alternative. The spread of color drugstore printing and drive-through photo kiosks made economical color photography widely available, while the arrival of self-contained minilabs in the 1980s accelerated the process. Most professionals avoided these comparatively inexpensive setups, which were designed to satisfy the popular appetite for homemade pictures. But to a growing number of photographers, including Cohen, the availability of these new materials made color photography more accessible. Moreover, the growing aesthetic of "snapshot" color photography suggested new ways of thinking about photography itself.

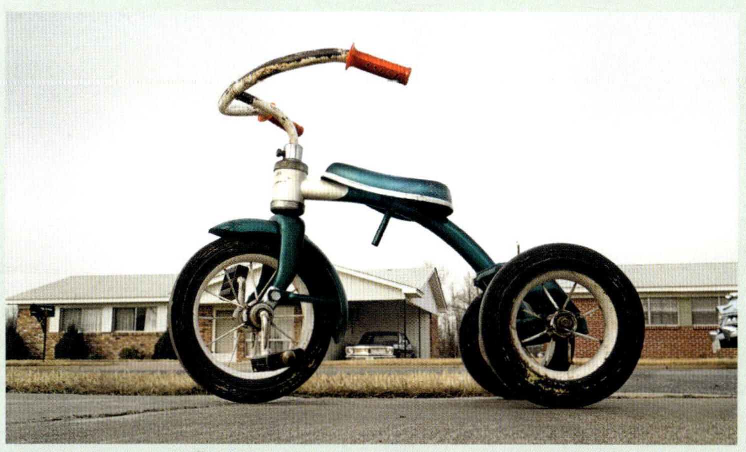

3 William Eggleston, *Memphis*, ca. 1969

Cohen used film that he could buy and process locally. This inevitably meant color negative film, which was widely available and easily processed at cheap photo finishers, using the ubiquitous C-41 process. This somewhat unusual choice of materials for art photography had a pronounced effect on how his pictures look. Unlike slide films, which have comparatively fine grain, with negative films grain can be strongly pronounced, especially when enlarged. The palettes of negative films vary but tend toward blue and yellow compared to the punchy warmth of Kodachrome. In addition, the quality of processing and printing was very much hit-or-miss, since with machine-made prints specialists were not laboring over every frame, making minute corrections.

From a technical perspective, Cohen's photographs break every rule. Some are completely out of focus, they are grainy, and colors shift from one picture to the next. Films fail and blow out in bright light, dark backgrounds disappear into nothingness. They are blurry, otherworldly, with deep shadows and halo lighting effects. Superficially, these resemble common failures of routine snapshot photography. They are meant to.

Looking closely at Cohen's photographs from this period, it is easy to see why he was so attracted to color. The brown tweeds and gray herringbones of businessmen and commuters pacing the sidewalk perfectly convey the mood of a downtown rush hour; vivid red and yellow flowers and grassy greens and russets track the change of season from spring to summer to autumn. Skin tones vary from vibrant rosy pink to sallow and withdrawn, while cheerfully patterned shirts and dresses, dilapidated red upholstery, and aqua-colored swimsuits paint personality. Faded color hints at loss, while the garish synthetic tints of polyester wigs and hair dye reflect the strained vanity of shoppers.

Cohen started using color materials in high school, but he did not explore them seriously until around 1973–74. About a year earlier, in 1972, he had begun using color in his commercial studio, making school portraits using a medium-format Hasselblad camera and sending the results out for processing and printing. Encouraged by the results, he tried making street photographs using Kodak Vericolor materials but was quickly waylaid by cost considerations, since he habitually printed his black-and-white prints in a sixteen-by-twenty-inch size and wanted his color prints to match. This was not just a matter of vanity; for Cohen, the immersive experience of viewing an exhibition print at large scale was critical to its impact.

In 1976, George Eastman House (today the George Eastman Museum) curator William Jenkins provided a catalyst that would prove decisive. Brokering a deal with the Kodak Company in Rochester, New York, Jenkins arranged for Cohen to receive a generous supply of Kodacolor film, which he exposed and the company processed. Cohen then selected a hundred of the best pictures to be printed. Kodak printed two sets of these, one of which was donated to the Eastman House collection, where it remains, and another which Cohen kept in his studio. A number of these images, which date from 1976–77, are reproduced in this book.

Whether in color or black and white, the precise meaning of Cohen's photographs is hard to define; this was doubly true in the late 1960s and early 1970s, when viewers first encountered them. Perhaps struggling to defend them to a general audience, MoMA highlighted the importance of Wilkes-Barre as the location of the work. In the press release for the show, assistant curator Dennis Longwell took a poetic line, describing the artist creating from "the 'fact' of a Wilkes-Barre the 'reality' of an Illyria—a new world existing solely in the tonalities of these photographic pictures.... romantic, intuitive, irreverent, and technically innovative."[3] Longwell went on, continuing to reference Shakespeare's *Twelfth Night*:

> Illumined by twin suns, it [the world of Cohen's pictures] is furnished with quiet gardens and people with beautiful maidens and entranced princes. It is blessed with dogs. Quite simply, this is a world of natural goodness, bounty, mystery, and noble aspiration.[4]

In retrospect, it may seem strange that MoMA chose to single out Wilkes-Barre as a way of helping audiences to understand the work. The point of Longwell's text, of course, was not that Wilkes-Barre was actually an American utopia, but that through his photography Cohen had managed to transform a typical small American city into an escapist fantasy. But do Cohen's photographs really convey an ideal of "quiet gardens, beautiful maidens, and entranced princes?" Are the dogs with which the city is "blessed" really noble, inspiring creatures, or scruffy and neglected—even menacing? Cohen's genius lies in part in leaving such questions unanswered, allowing the viewer to decide the inference of each picture.

Longwell was correct in noting Wilkes-Barre as an important factor in Cohen's work. Large enough to be interesting but intimate enough to be approachable, its people and problems reflect the highs and lows of a sort of mythic middle America. It could be whatever one wanted it to be. Cohen knew it well and, working in and around the city, could explore it in relative safety. Photographing in large cities like New York and Philadelphia (where he would eventually settle) carried an increased risk of angry reactions, violence, or even robbery.

Nestled in an area known as the Wyoming Valley and ringed by the Appalachian Mountains, prior to industrialization Wilkes-Barre must indeed have been idyllic. Most visitors now know it merely as a rest stop on I-81, one of the main arteries for traffic traveling from Virginia to upstate New York. The city of Wilkes-Barre itself, along with neighboring Scranton and the areas that surround them, nevertheless became the primary setting for Cohen's photography.

The Wilkes-Barre that Cohen knew was nearing the end of a long economic cycle. After the discovery of anthracite in the nineteenth century, mines pockmarked the land. Financially, the region thrived for a century or more, but large-scale coal production effectively came to an end in 1959, when the owners of the cash-strapped River Slope Mine dug too deep under the Susquehanna River, just a few miles outside of town. The roof of the mine gave way and flooded, killing twelve workers and causing the river to shift its banks. That accident would prove decisive, but, in truth, commercial decline had been apparent for some time. By the 1950s, many of the local mines had been stripped out, and several exhausted coal beds spontaneously caught fire and had to be capped. Like much of rust-belt America after World War II, the economy foundered.

Regeneration programs in the 1970s and 1980s met with modest success; however, it was never Cohen's aim to highlight Wilkes-

Barre's socioeconomic situation or document its history. He was democratic in his choice of subjects. Seemingly wealthier individuals appear more frequently in private spaces, whereas less wealthy people are seen outside in streets and alleys. The distinction is not always easy to make, since many of the people and places depicted in his photographs are neither obviously affluent nor poverty-stricken. Frequently made close up and nearly always horizonless, his pictures defy conventions of reportage, providing little in the way of context or political commentary.

Cohen's subjects are ordinary people in ordinary situations, going about their daily business and performing simple tasks. Many, especially the children he often photographs, are grimy—their clothes tired, tattered, and ill-fitting. But the grass stains, mud, and worn-out knees they display are not so much a matter of hardship as they are the natural traces of work and play.

Although frequently described as a "street" photographer, Cohen is notoriously difficult to categorize. Early on, he devised a method of making pictures using flash lighting, separating the flash unit from the camera body to enable camera and flash to move independently. Cohen credits the photographer Lee Friedlander with introducing him to this technique around 1970; however, Cohen made it his own.

At the time, most photographers who worked outdoors with flash would mount the flash unit directly on the camera body, using a grooved connector with an electronic trigger called a hot shoe. This was a convenient way to operate, since the equipment functioned as a single unit, and the photographer did not have to give too much thought to how flash and camera synched. Cohen, though, used two hands to control the flash and camera independently—pushing the camera in close while holding back the flash and directing it to illuminate the subject. The two were still connected, tethered using a long, coiled wire called a sync cable. Photographing in this way required intuition and skill, as Cohen had to quickly choreograph the position of each element on the fly.

In 1982, the German documentary filmmaker Michael Engler recorded how this worked (figs. 4 and 5). Cohen would take daily excursions through certain neighborhoods looking for people and situations of visual interest, moving in rapidly to catch them unawares. When he found a likely subject, no introduction was made and no permission requested; Cohen simply brought his camera in close to the subject, held the flash at a slight remove, and then snapped the shutter. Having briefly invaded the sitter's space, he would immediately move on to the next subject, so that his social interactions, such as they were, remained largely anonymous.

Photographing with flash had a number of advantages. It made exposure and depth of field predictable, so Cohen did not have to constantly adjust shutter speed and focus, instead presetting camera and lens for a range of likely conditions. This also meant that he did not have to look through his camera's viewfinder to compose the scene, so many of his photographs were made "blind," based purely on experience and a well-honed sense of what the camera would capture. As skilled as Cohen became at judging his camera's field of view, surprises were an inevitable and desirable part of the process.

In Cohen's hands, photographing became a kind of performance, with the results often jaunty and irregular. People are shown at awkward moments and extreme angles, with arms, necks, and

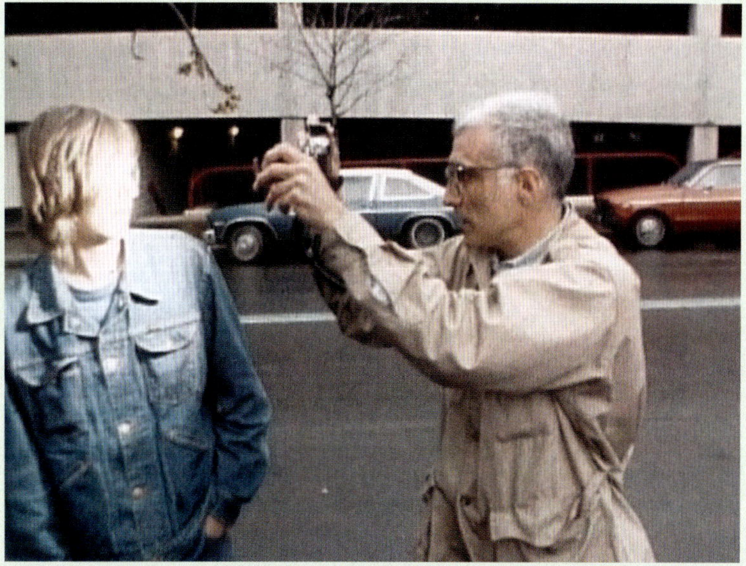

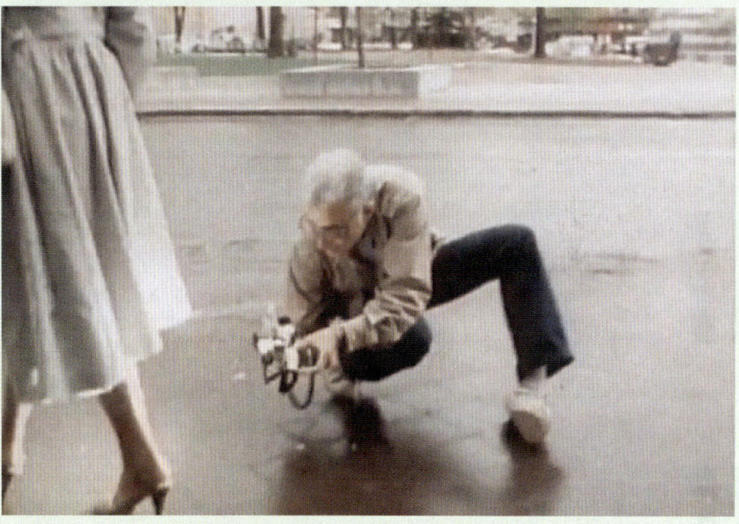

4 and 5 Mark Cohen photographing, Wilkes-Barre, Pennsylvania, still from Michael Engler's documentary film *Mark Cohen: Fotograf*

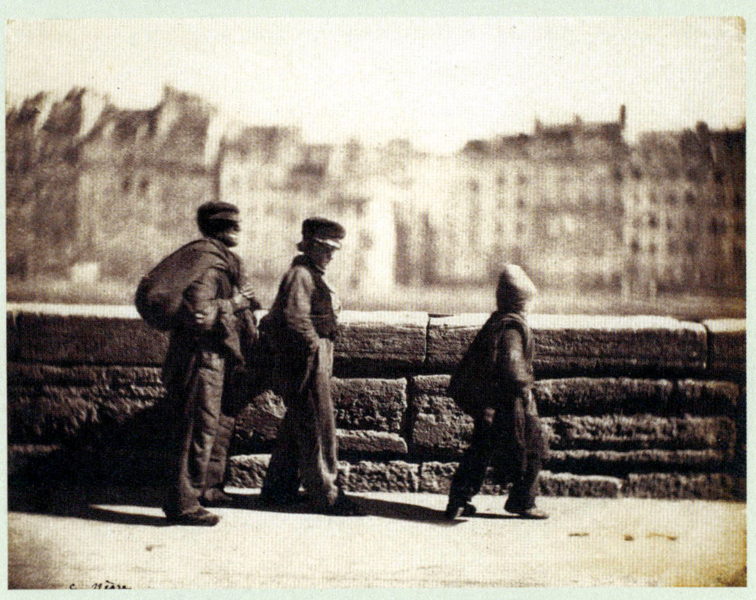

6 Charles Nègre, *Les ramoneurs en marche* (Chimney Sweeps Walking), 1851–52. Musée Carnavalet

elbows variously dominating the frame. Such moments, raw and unfiltered, can be more revealing than even the most carefully conceived photograph. Like a photographic Mars probe, he used his camera to explore and retrieve information beyond the usual horizon of human interaction. What his camera brought back is an equal blend of skill, control, and accident.

Cohen draws on a long tradition of photographing surreptitiously. As early as 1851, the French photographer Charles Nègre caused an uproar with his candid photographs of workers seen on the streets of Paris. The ethics of his *Les ramoneurs en marche* (Chimney Sweeps Walking) of 1851–52 (fig. 6), for example, were hotly debated at the time, and were said to have inspired legislation temporarily forbidding the practice. It is instructive to compare Nègre's iconic picture with Cohen's flash photograph taken on the streets of Paris some 137 years later (fig. 7).

Under American law, persons seen in any public place, or indeed easily seen from a public place, may be photographed legally without permission. There are limits to this rule, such as street photographs cannot be used in advertising campaigns without a signature release (but may, however, be used in artworks). This has inspired generations of photographers to capture their subjects secretly, including, for example, Paul Strand with his famous close-up of a blind woman peeking at a passerby (1915), or Walker Evans's "Subway Portraits" of the late 1930s and early 1940s, which he made (accompanied, on occasion, by Helen Levitt) by concealing his camera under his coat, attaching an angled viewfinder to make it look as though he were pointing the camera at someone else, and running a cable release up his sleeve so the sitter could not tell exactly when the shutter fired (fig. 8). In 1950, photographer Harry Callahan joined this tradition with his *Women Lost in Thought*, photographed on the streets of Chicago with a telephoto lens. Cohen's pictures of subjects caught furtively in Wilkes-Barre and Scranton are in this sense nothing new; rather, they are the logical extension of a tendency nearly as old as photography itself.

Cohen worked so fast that he was often able to make pictures before the subject even knew they were being photographed. Moreover, the brief burst of light emitted by the flash temporarily disoriented the subject, creating a distraction that either helped the artist make good his escape, or drew unwanted attention. In addition, with flash-based exposure times of hundredths or even thousandths of a second, Cohen could not only photograph subjects while they were in motion, he could photograph while *he* was in motion himself, enabling him to make pictures even as he walked by, or retreated.

The flash also gave Cohen extraordinary freedom, as he could bring the camera to within inches of the subject, far closer than social norms would customarily allow. As a result, blur and extremes of focus became part of the vocabulary of his pictures. The implied perspective of the viewer is immersive and experiential. Cohen's photographs convey the chaotic energy of encountering others at close quarters, like incomplete memories recalled from broken narratives. If the camera isolates the weathered skin of an old lady, or lingers on other details of dress and demeanor, it is only doing what right-thinking persons cannot normally do, except in their imaginations. Accordingly, Cohen's photographs can have a transgressive, even at times erotic, quality. The tightrope they walk between acute observation and unseemliness is part of the point.

Photographic portraits, and in their own way so-called documentary photographs, follow certain established conventions. In the case of portraiture, sitters are usually given time to gather

7 Mark Cohen, *Paris*, 1988

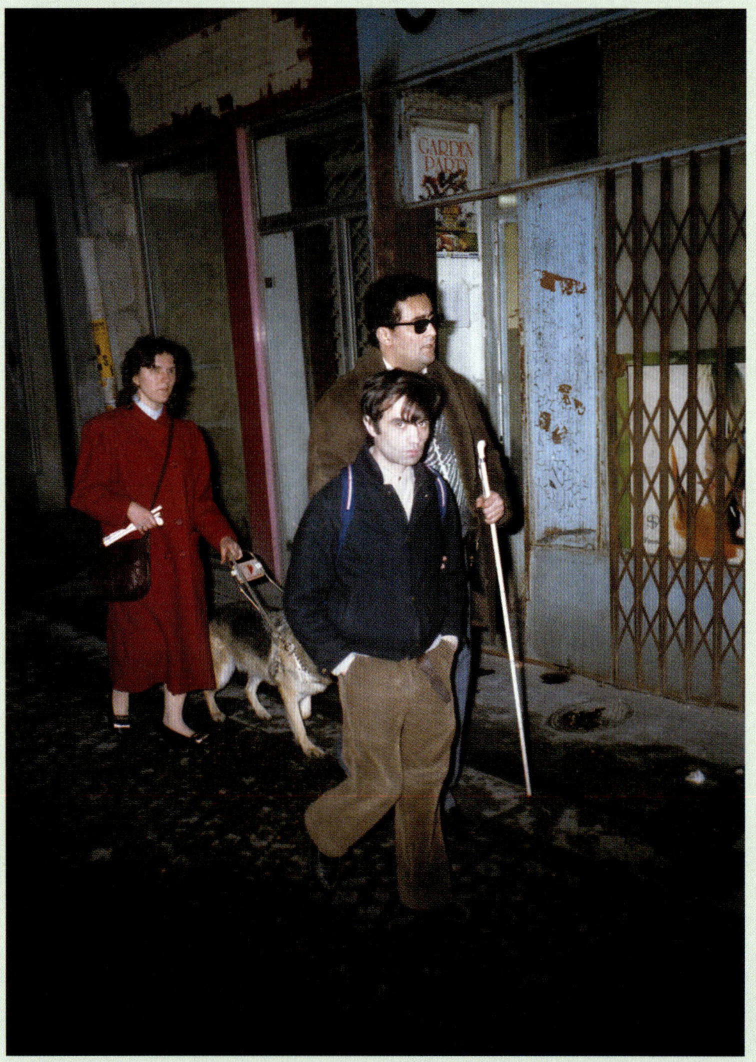

themselves in order to present their best face to the camera. This may involve fashioning a smile, or at the very least an intentionally neutral expression. Without this socially prescribed step, "sitters" may be caught off guard. In daily life, our brains have a tendency to fill in awkward moments to create a somewhat balanced view. The camera, however, has no such filter. Capturing subjects slack-jawed or mid-blink, it is completely agnostic, and the results are seldom flattering. It is as if Cohen had absorbed the lessons of Henri Cartier-Bresson's famous "decisive moment" (the English title of his celebrated 1952 book) and pushed it to an absurd conclusion. Cohen's photographs are indeed moments, but they are far from decisive. Or if they are, then the "decisiveness" they represent is one grounded in confusion and disorder.

In his review of Cohen's MoMA show in 1973, *New York Times* critic Gene Thornton wrote positively, but with reservations, about the photographs on display.

> In photographing people he cuts off legs and heads, or everything except the legs and heads. He shows us odd corners of backyards or vacant lots of a slightly seedy residential neighborhood, half city, half country, but he studiously avoids centering on any one thing. Huge objects loom in the foreground, often out of focus, with violent contrasts of dark and light, blurry motion and unnaturally diminished background perspectives. When he does center on something it is a stone, or a tangle of rope on a fence, or one flower looming out of focus, or a scattering of dead leaves. Time and again I had the impression that in these immense pictures Cohen is showing us only a fraction of what he has seen, and I was frustrated by my inability to get into the picture myself and see the rest.... I felt they must mean something, just the way they are. The question is, what?[5]

Thornton's question is not unreasonable; others have described Cohen's photographs variously as enigmatic, baffling, and bereft of obvious meaning.[6] In Thornton's case, he concludes that the pictures are about the photographic process itself.

There is, undoubtedly, an element of that. However, if Cohen's photographs were merely about process, then their appeal would be limited primarily to insiders interested in issues surrounding the materials and methods of photography. Yet they are no more "about" photographic process than Abstract Expressionist painting is "about" paint. Deeper meaning lies below the surface.

Photographs are distinct from other media in that they derive from the things they depict. Light bounces off a scene and is captured by camera and lens. This process is mechanical and determinative. For this reason, straight photographs have often been described as "indexical," since they have an unbreakable connection to the things they represent. This idea is closely tied to the concept of mimesis—that photographs resemble how things actually look in the real world to such an extent that viewers may start to project on them qualities usually associated with the original thing photographed.

Cohen's photographs ask us to set this idea aside. The subjects of his pictures are indeed real, made in specific locations at certain points in time, and the effects of focus and blur, perspective and color, are both chemical and optic in nature. This means that, in the end, they are both more and less than what they seem.

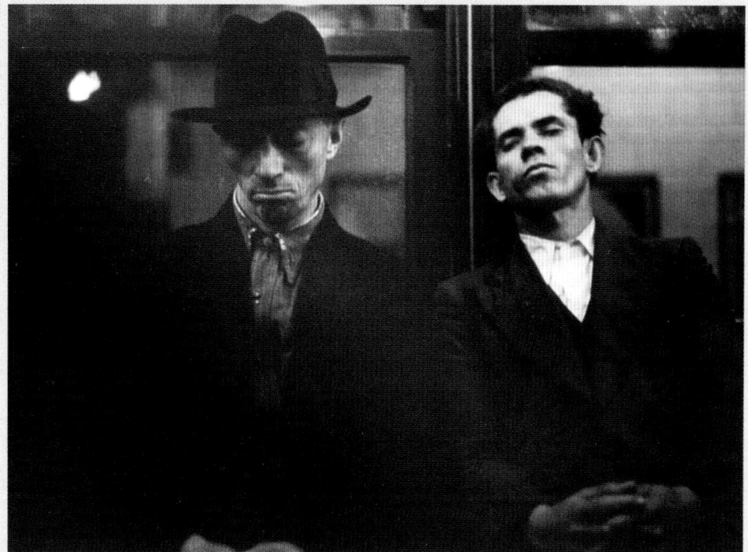

8 Walker Evans, *Subway Portrait*, May 27, 1938, The Museum of Modern Art, New York

In the 1970s, creative color photography was a radical notion in itself. Color was widely derided as vulgar, since it was believed to afford no room for mystery or contemplation, as black-and-white photographs supposedly did. The very thing that distinguished photography from other media—the question of mimesis—disqualified it from being of artistic value. But what if we think of Cohen's photographs differently? Their very refusal to resolve easily to our eyes is precisely what gives them power. We may think of them as provocations, resolute in their incompleteness. Their fractured immediacy is that of a split-second recollection, or a quick glimpse caught side-eye. A color may hit us in the gut; the nape of a neck may remind us of childhood, a parent, or a lover. That such things might hit us on a visceral rather than an intellectual level renders them subconscious.

As intimate as they are, Cohen's photographs lie forever out of reach, beyond our easy comprehension. They refuse to resolve into unambiguous messages. They are organic, unpredictable, and bursting with energy. In this way, they are stand-ins for ourselves, for all of us, for the in-between moments of our lives. We may think of them as snippets of thought and memory—frustrated fragments of realization—synapses firing between neurons. Such is the currency of awareness.

1 John Szarkowski, as quoted in "Photography: New Acquisitions," press release, No. 40, April 15, 1970. The Museum of Modern Art Archives, New York.

2 Initially, Cohen was not even aware of the dye transfer process. Years later, in 2008, this history would converge as Cohen printed a portfolio of thirty dye transfer prints with Eggleston printer Guy Stricherz in conjunction with Rose Gallery, Santa Monica, and the Michael and Jane Wilson Centre of Photography, London.

3 Dennis Longwell, as quoted in "Photographs by Mark Cohen," Press release, No. 21, March 21, 1973. MoMA Archives, NY.

4 Ibid.

5 Gene Thornton, "They Must Mean Something," *New York Times*, April 1, 1973, pp. 18, 32. With "these immense pictures," Thornton is commenting on what he considered to be the large size of his pictures: 16 × 20 in.

6 Carol Squiers, "Mark Cohen: Recognized Moments," *Art Forum* 16, no. 7 (March 1978), p. 22.

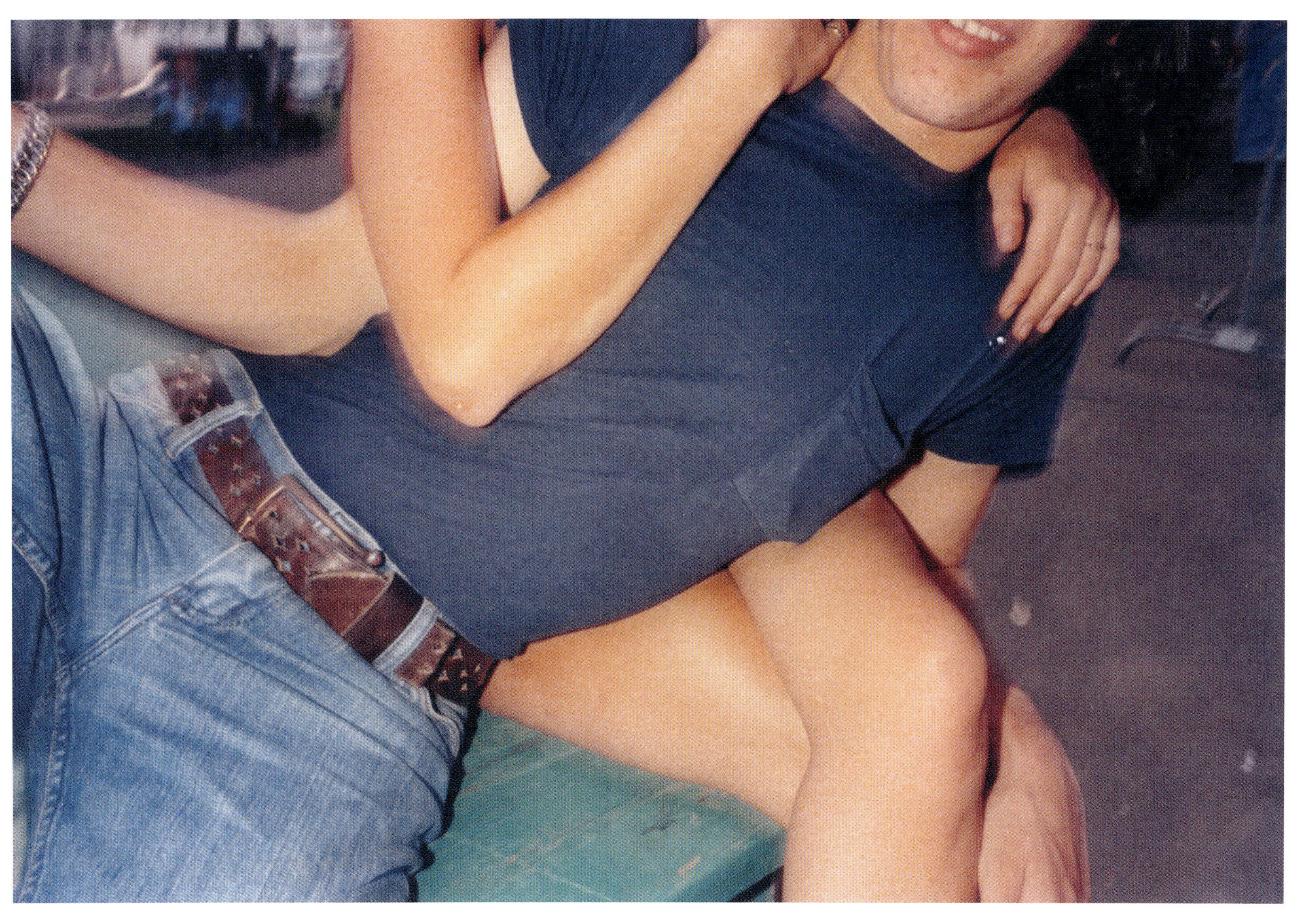

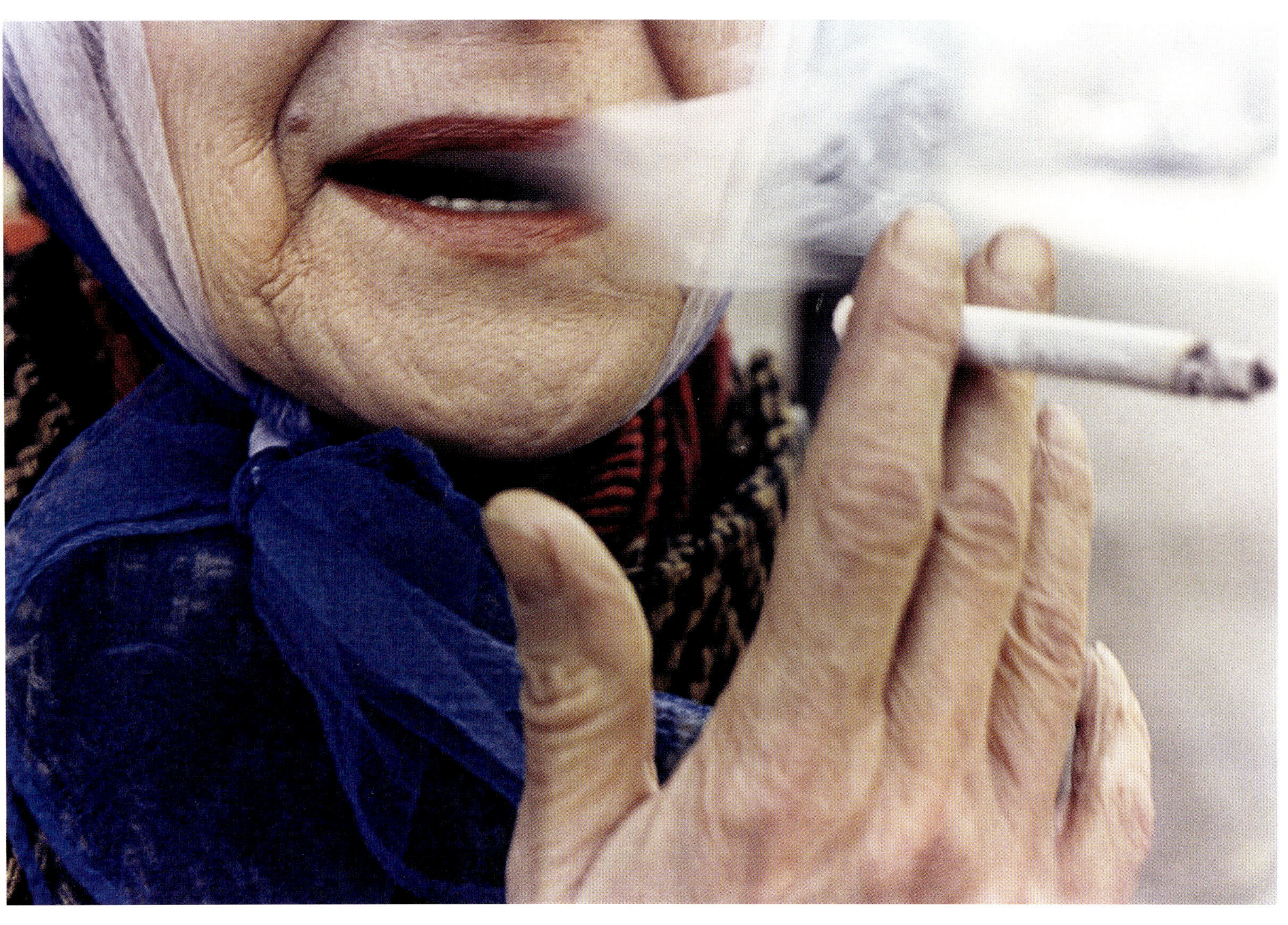

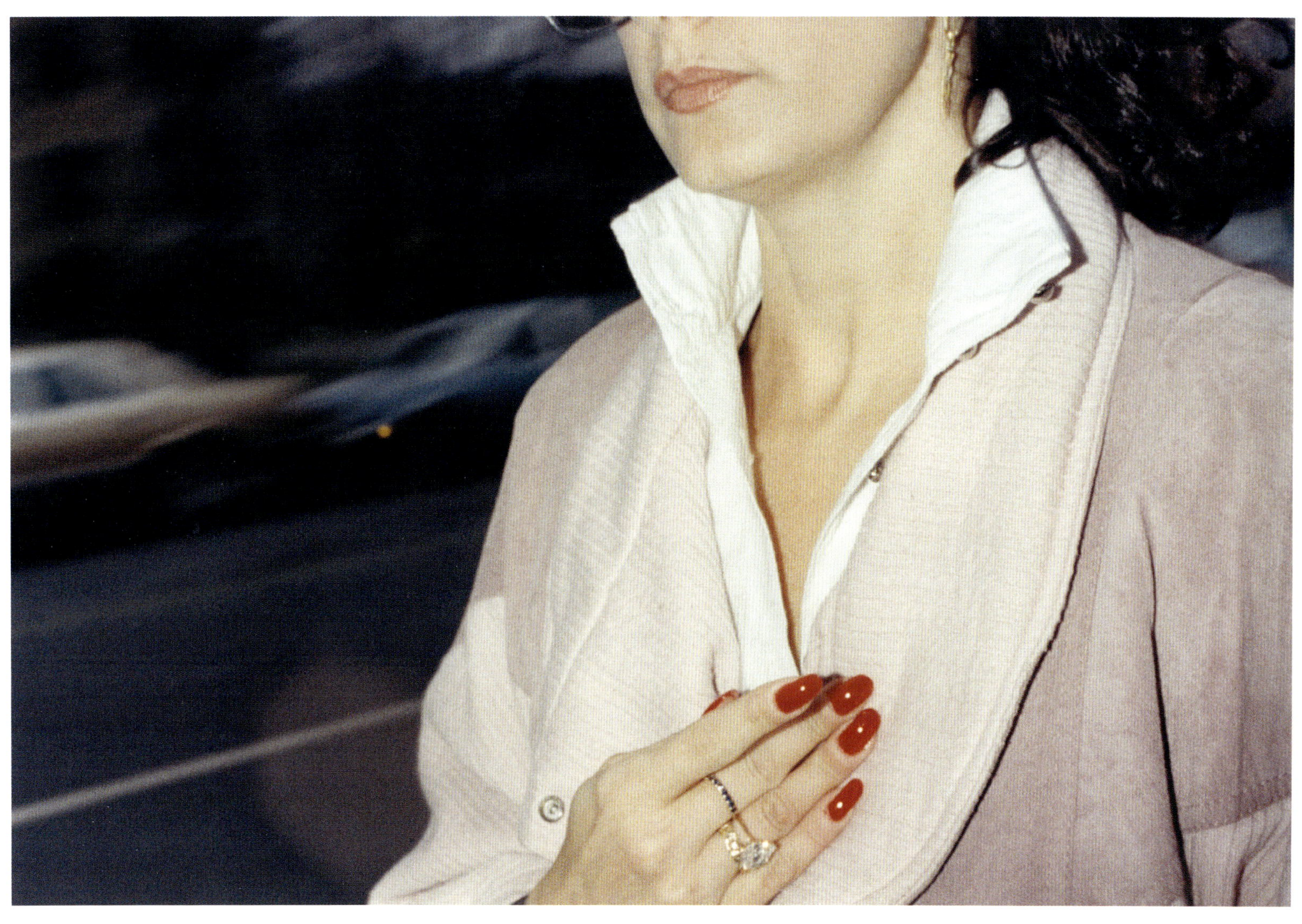

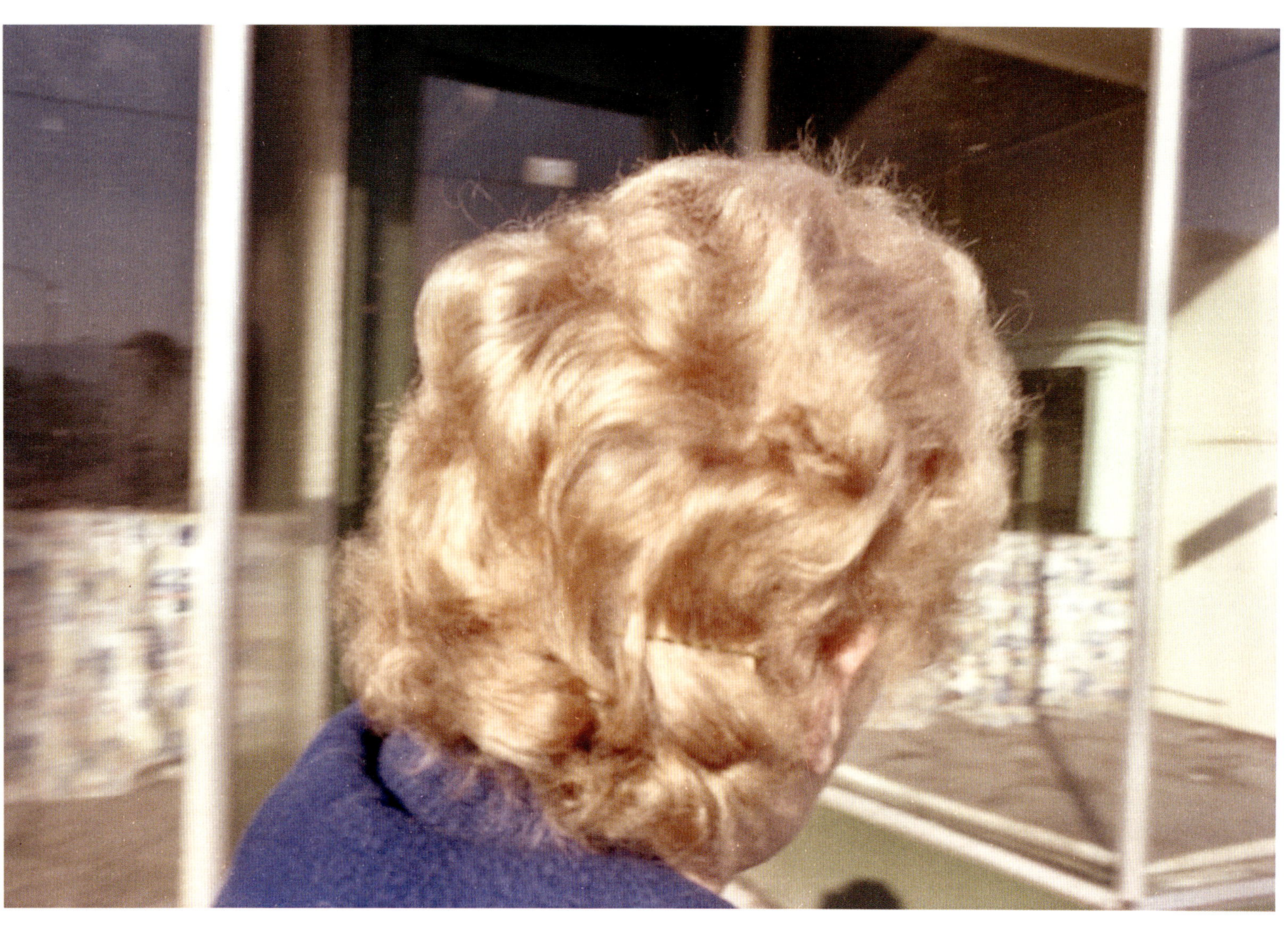

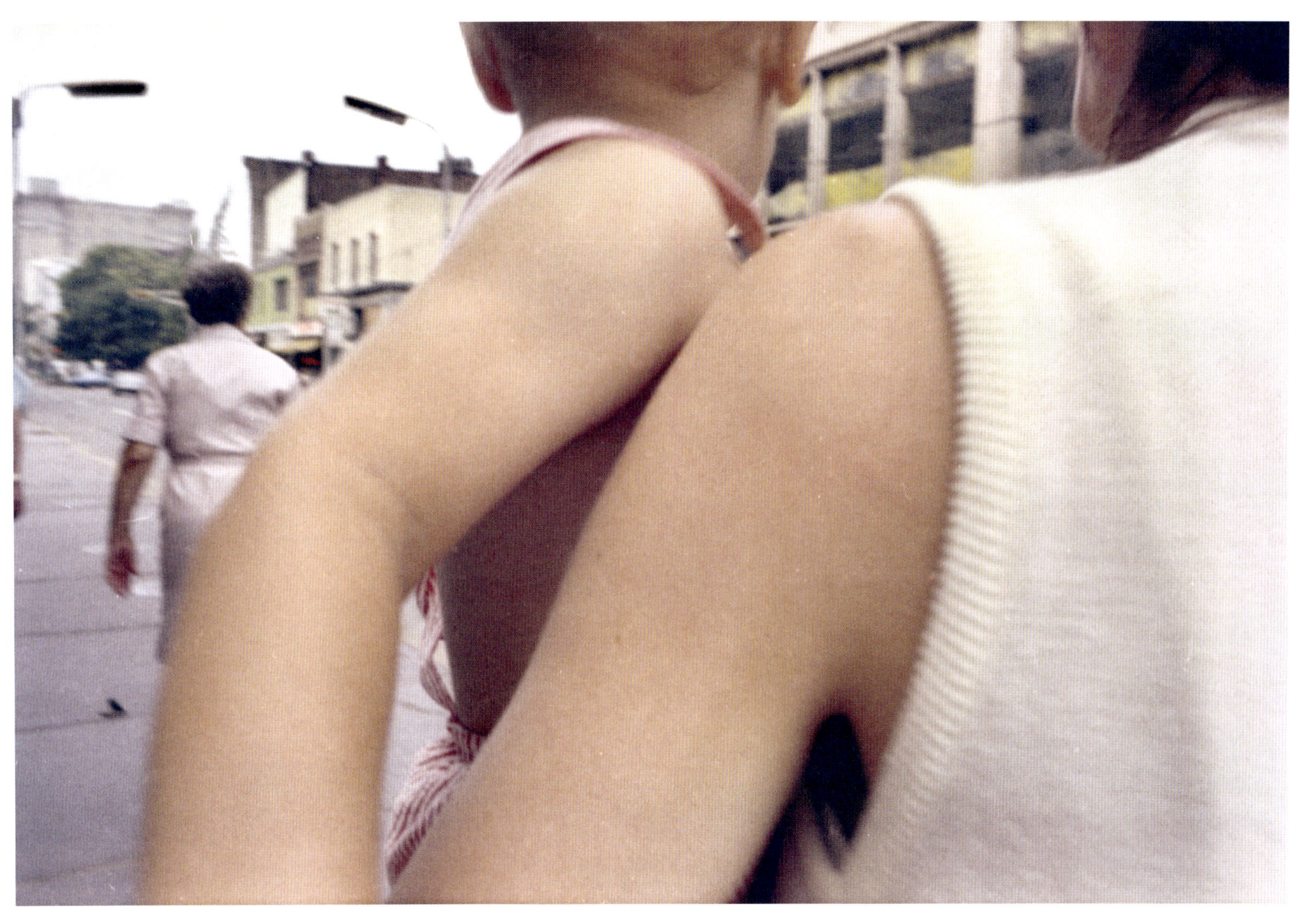

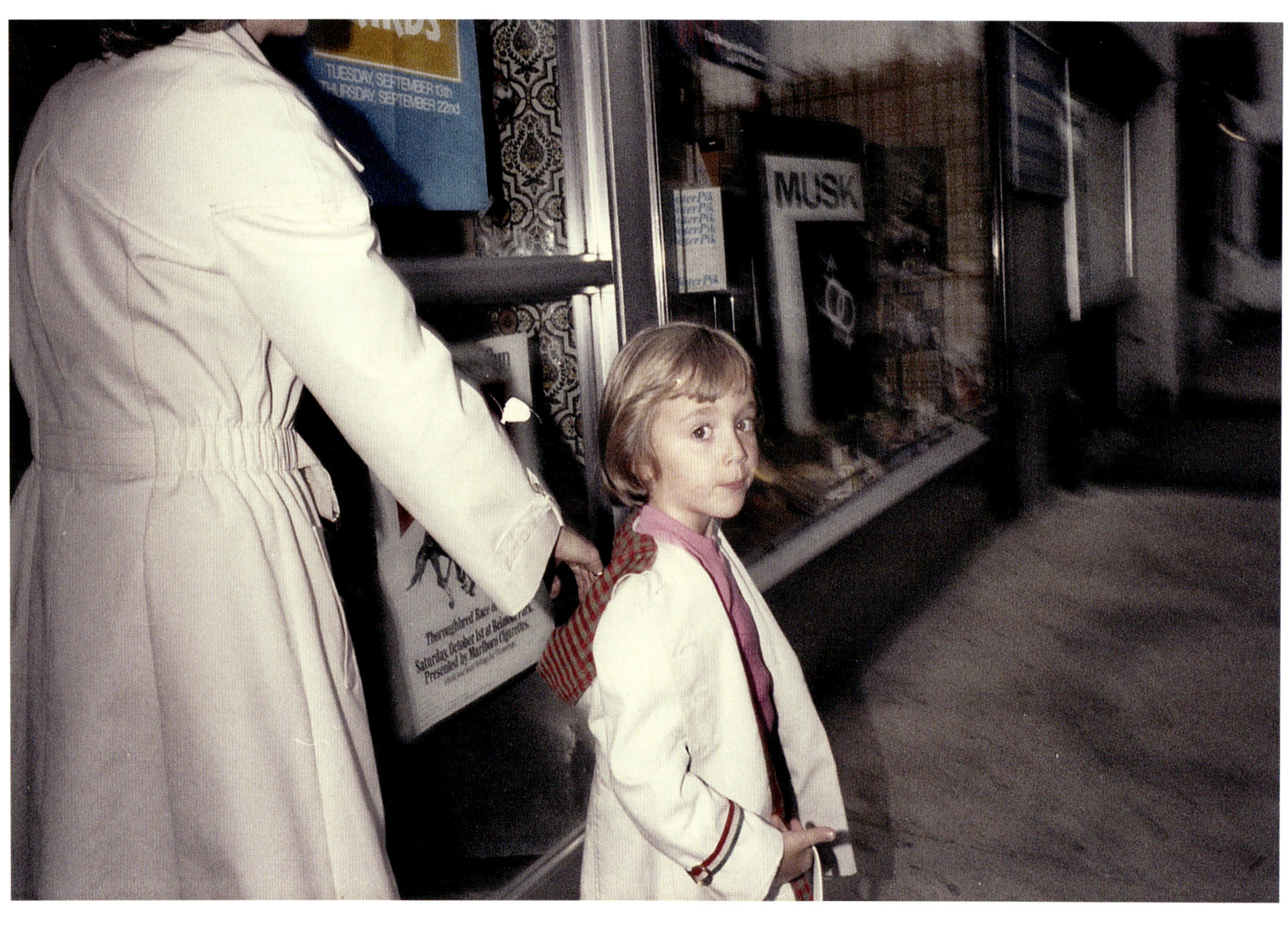
TUESDAY, SEPTEMBER 13th
MUSK
Saturday, October 1st at
Presented by Marlboro Cigarettes

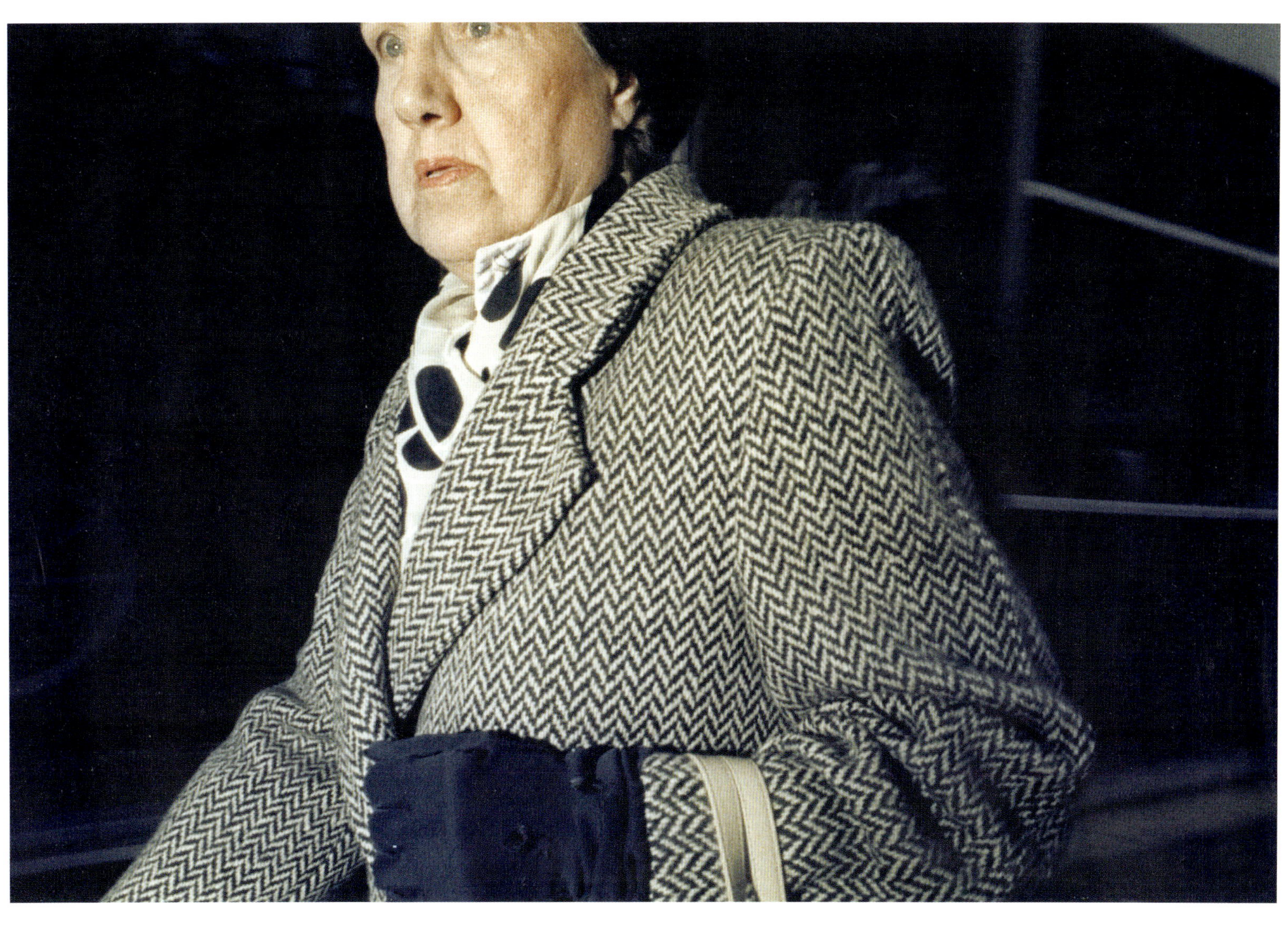

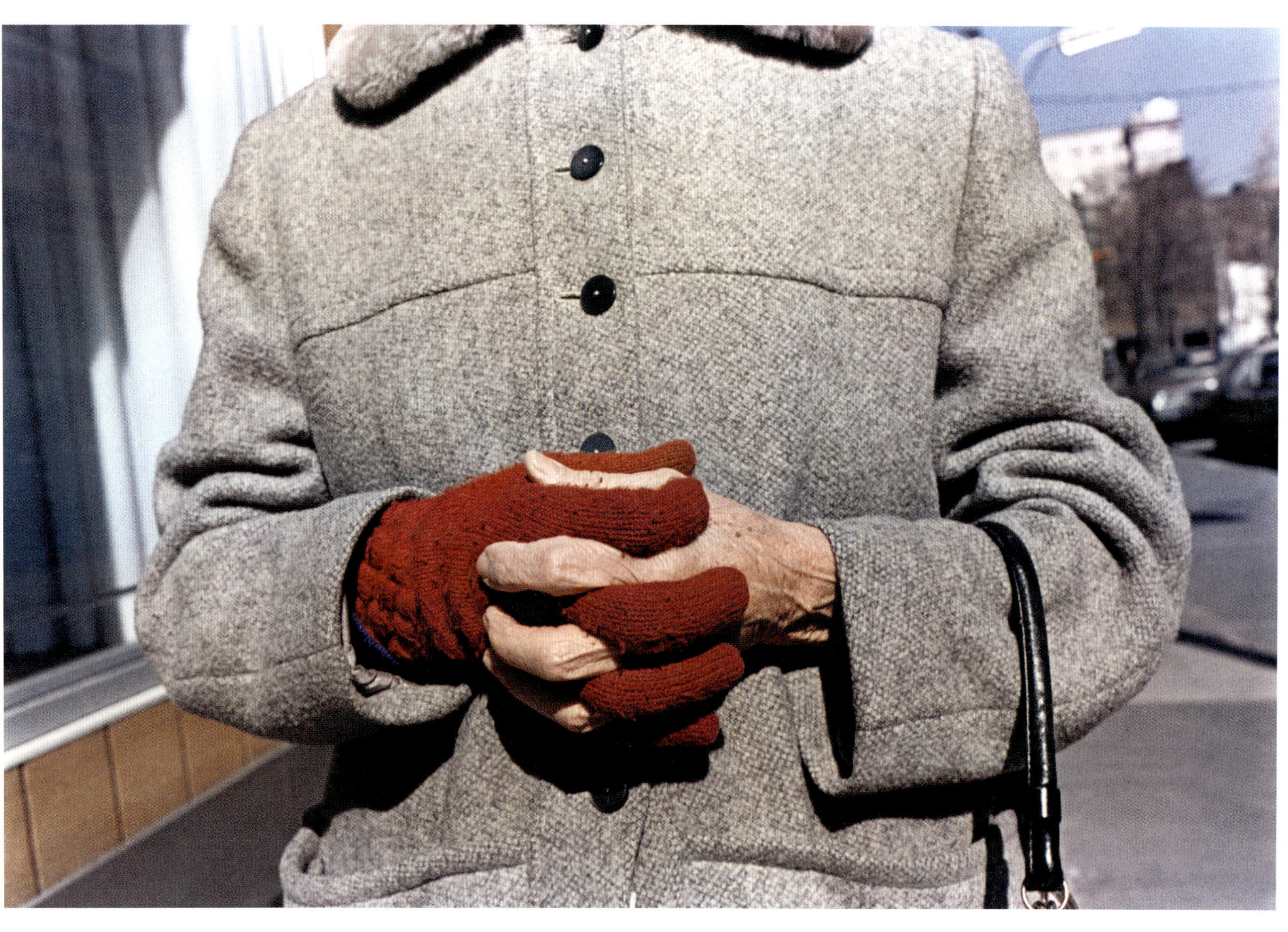

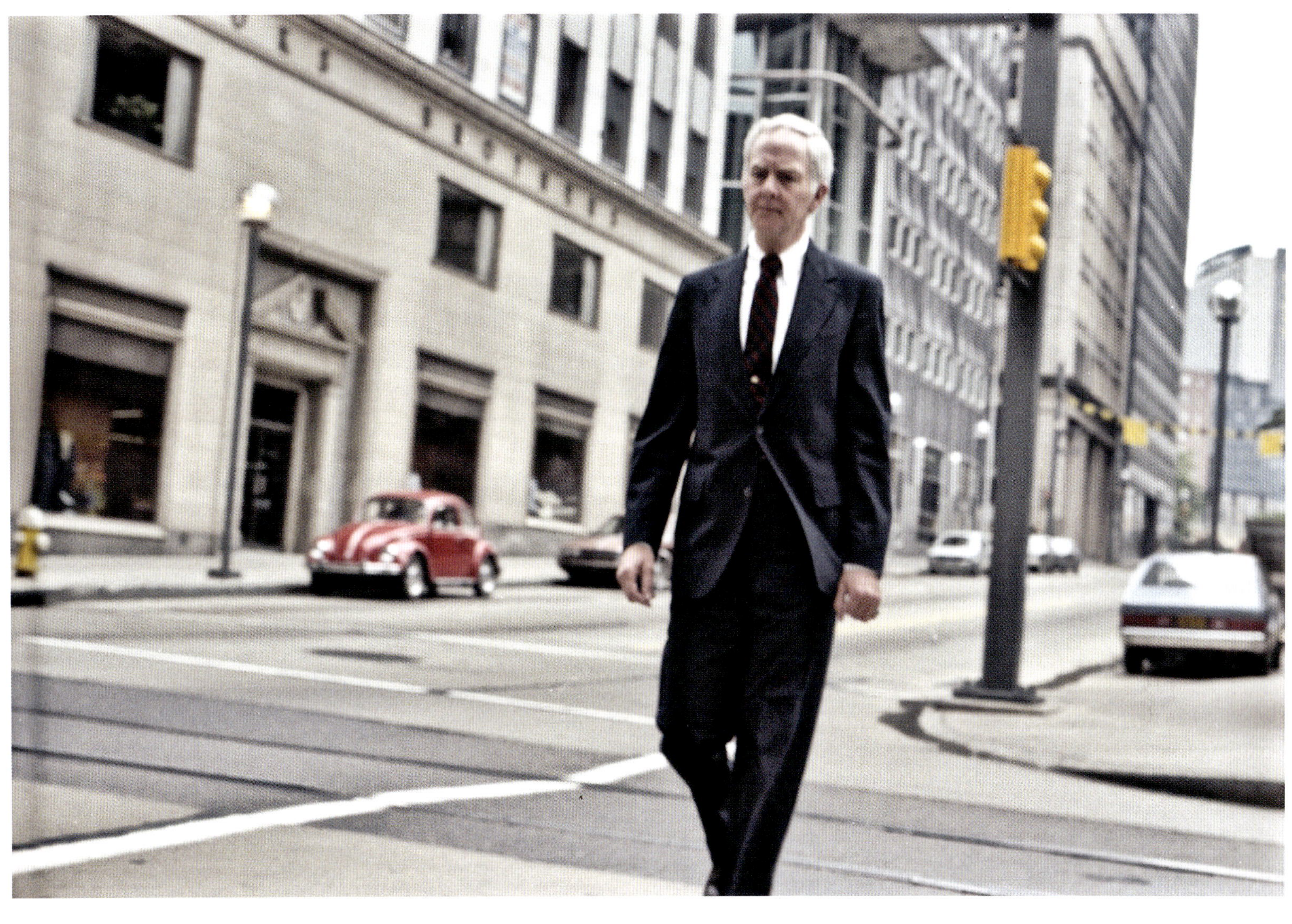

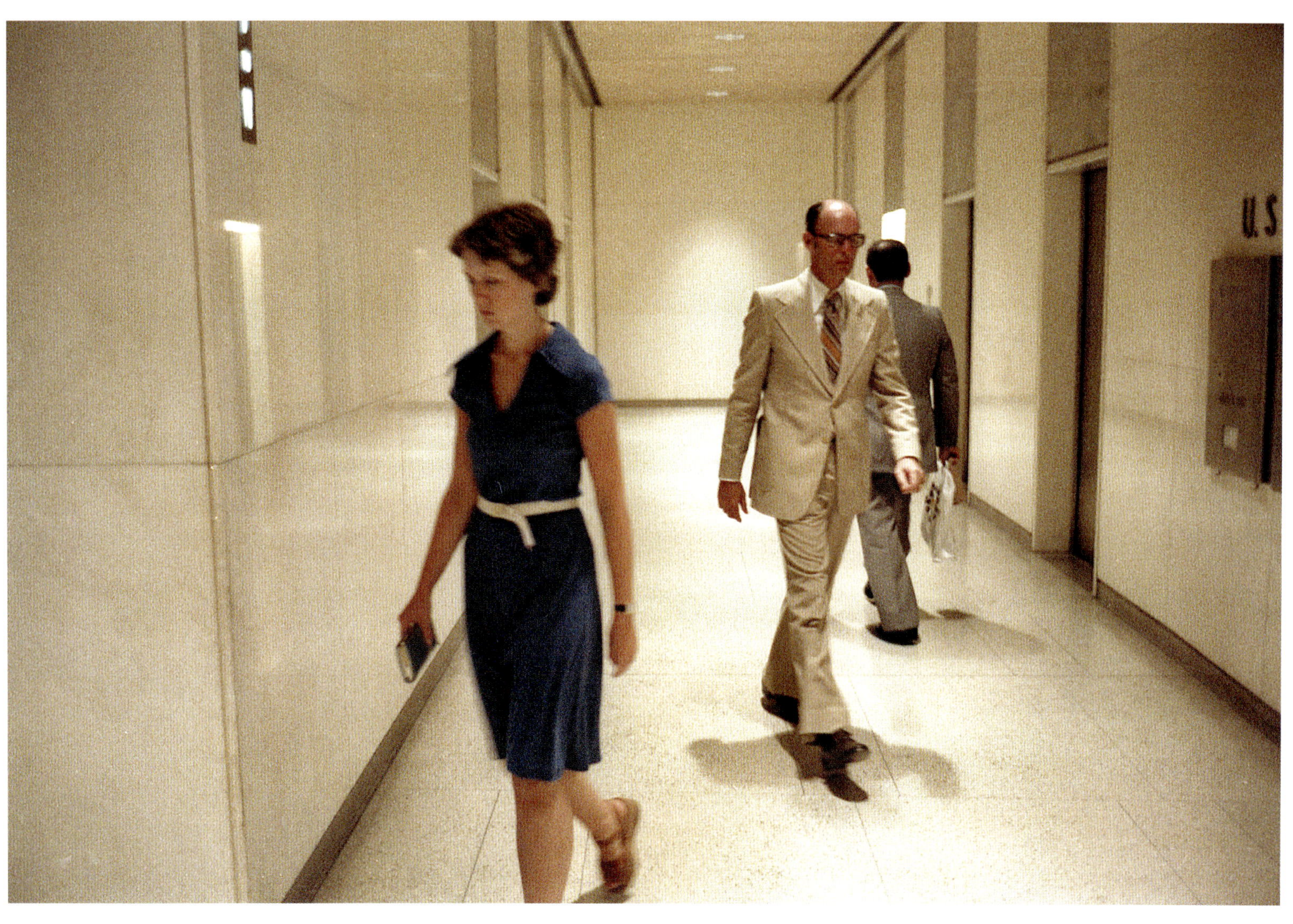

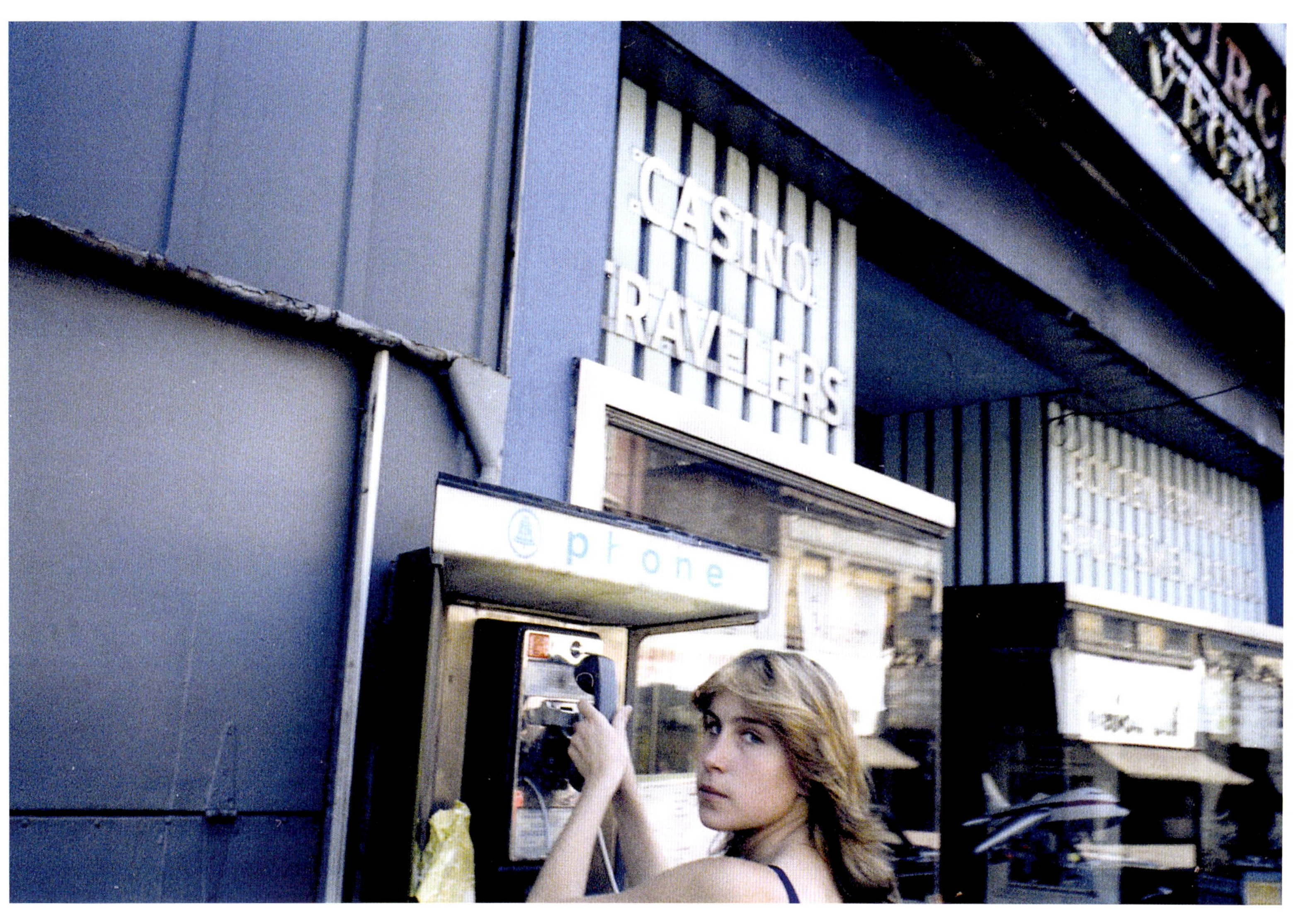
CASINO
TRAVELERS
phone

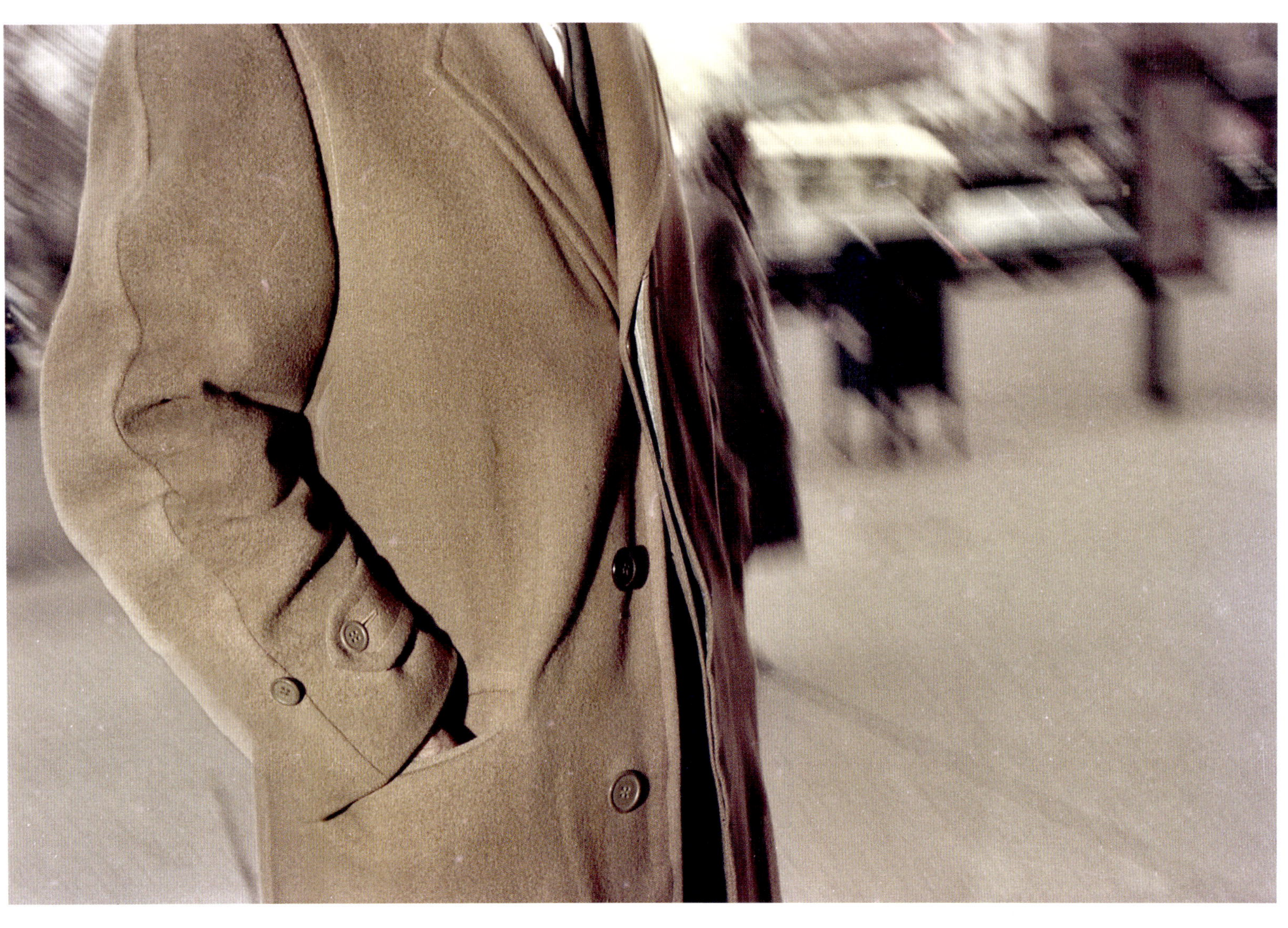

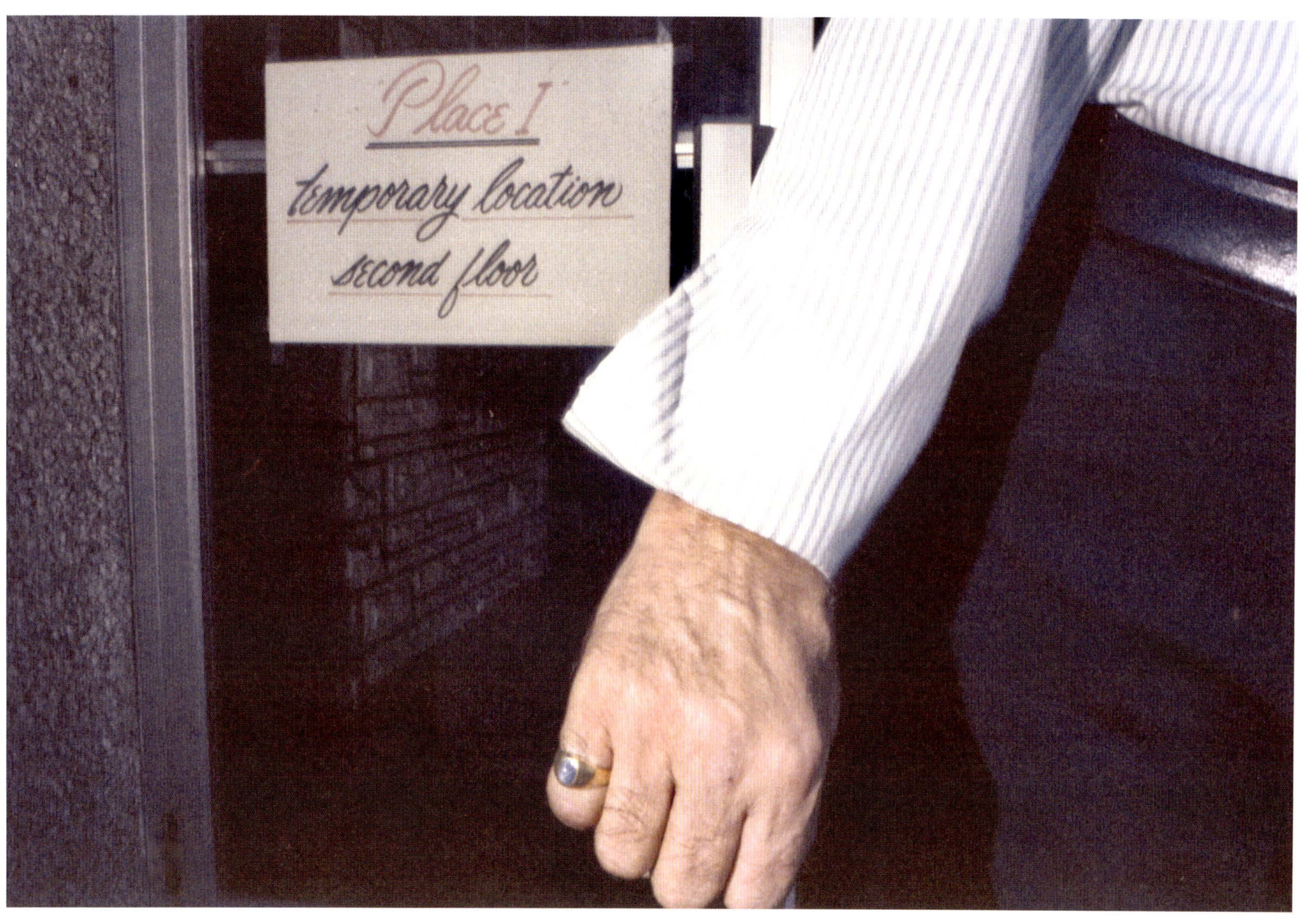
Place I
temporary location
second floor

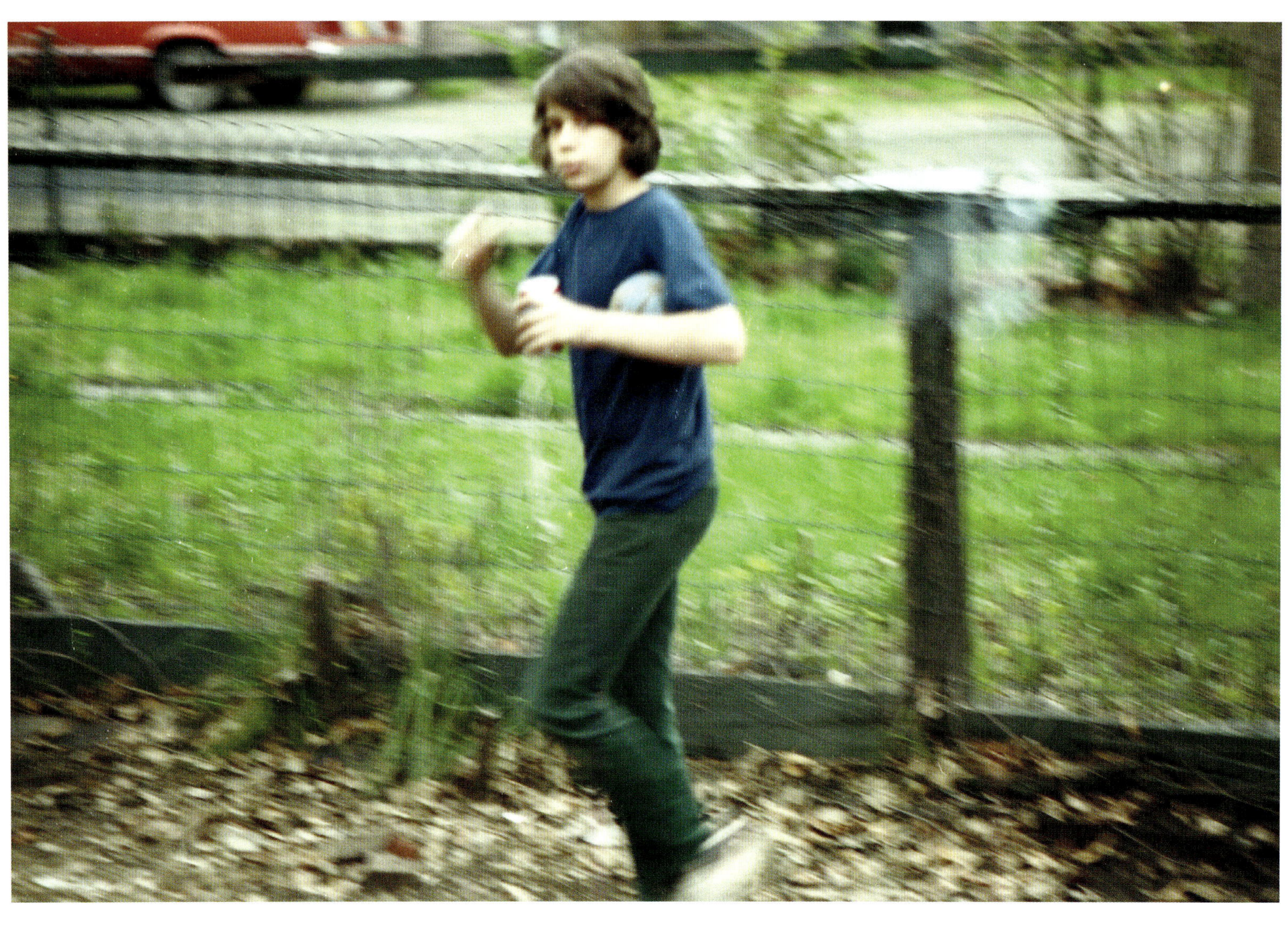

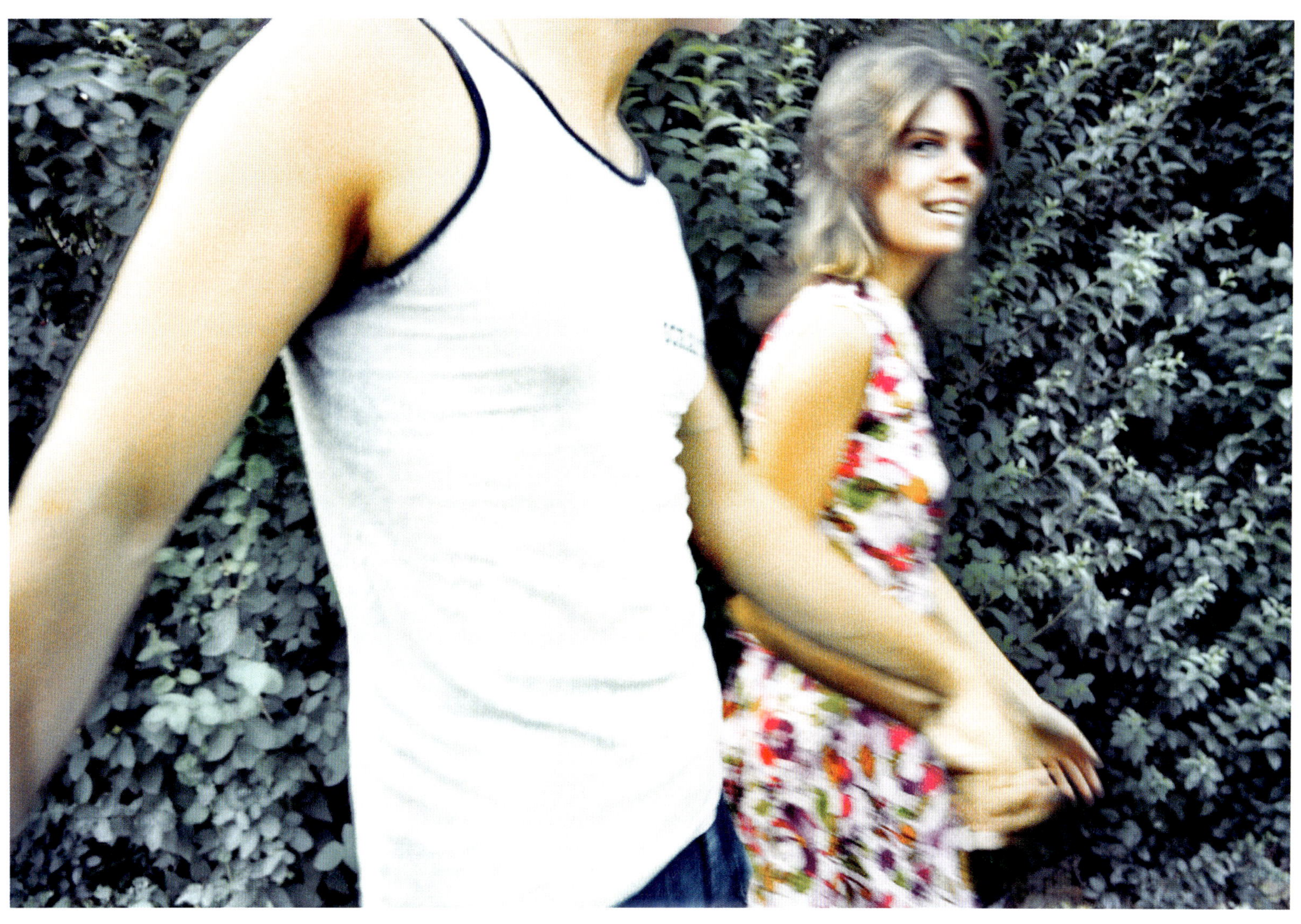

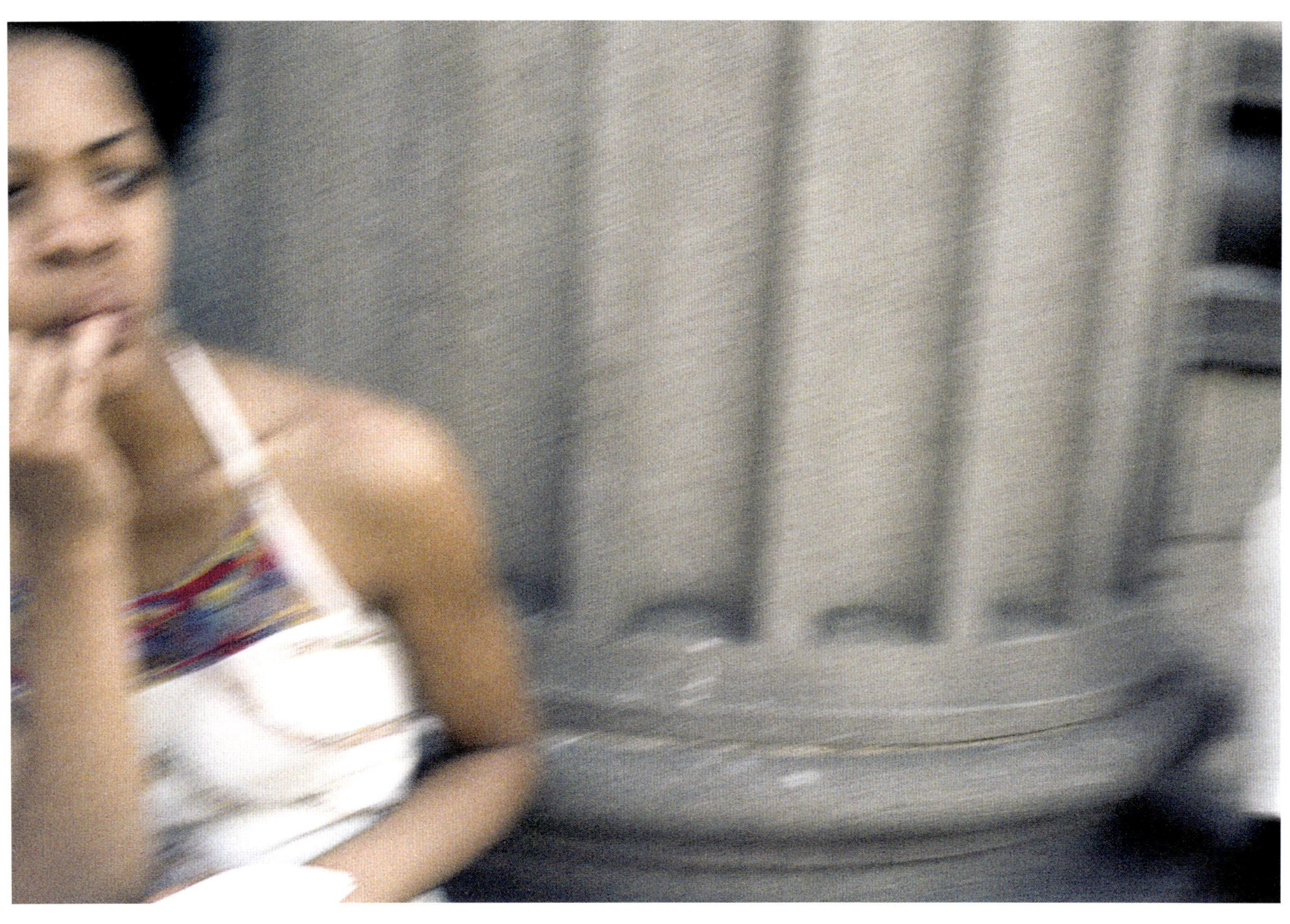

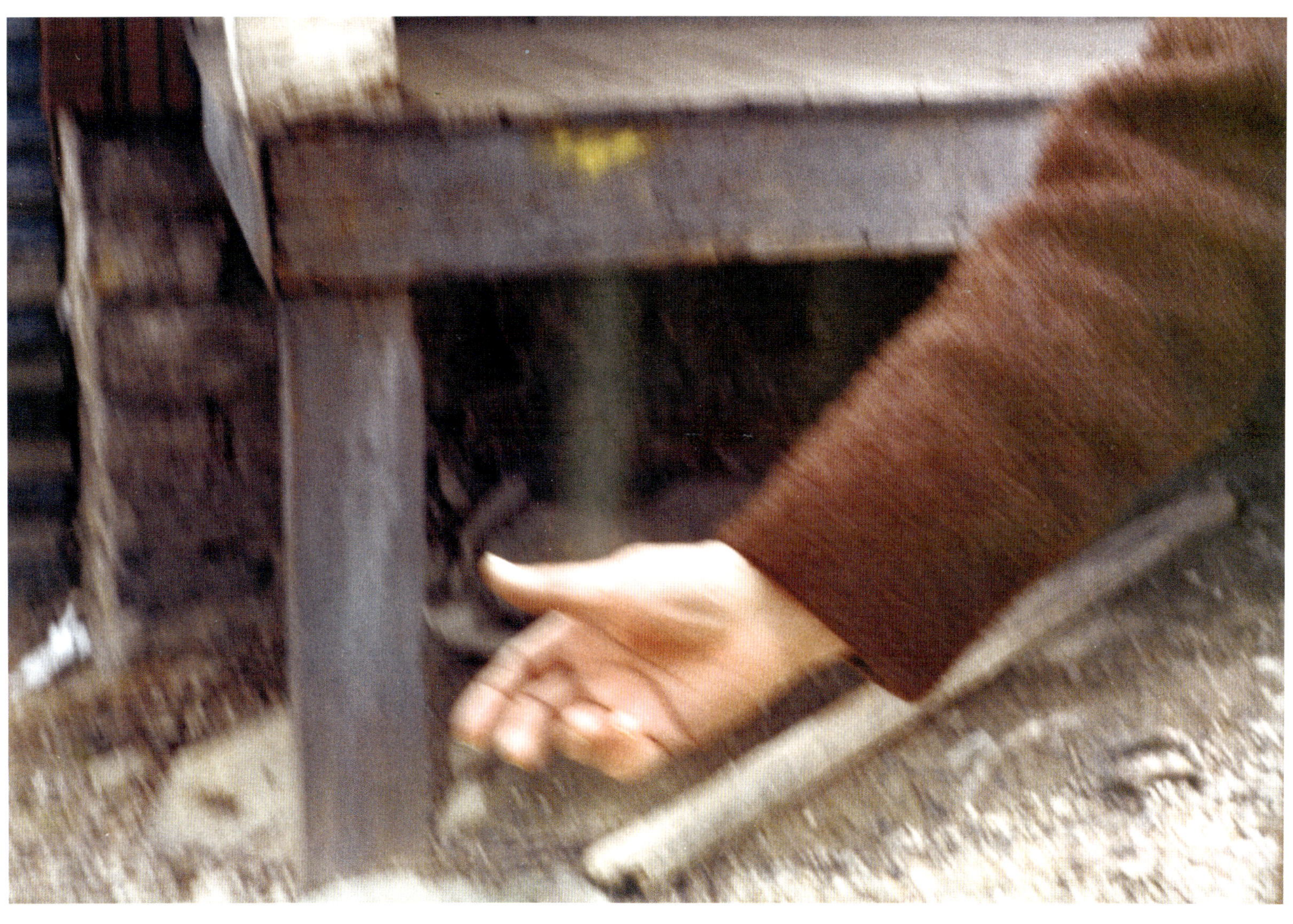

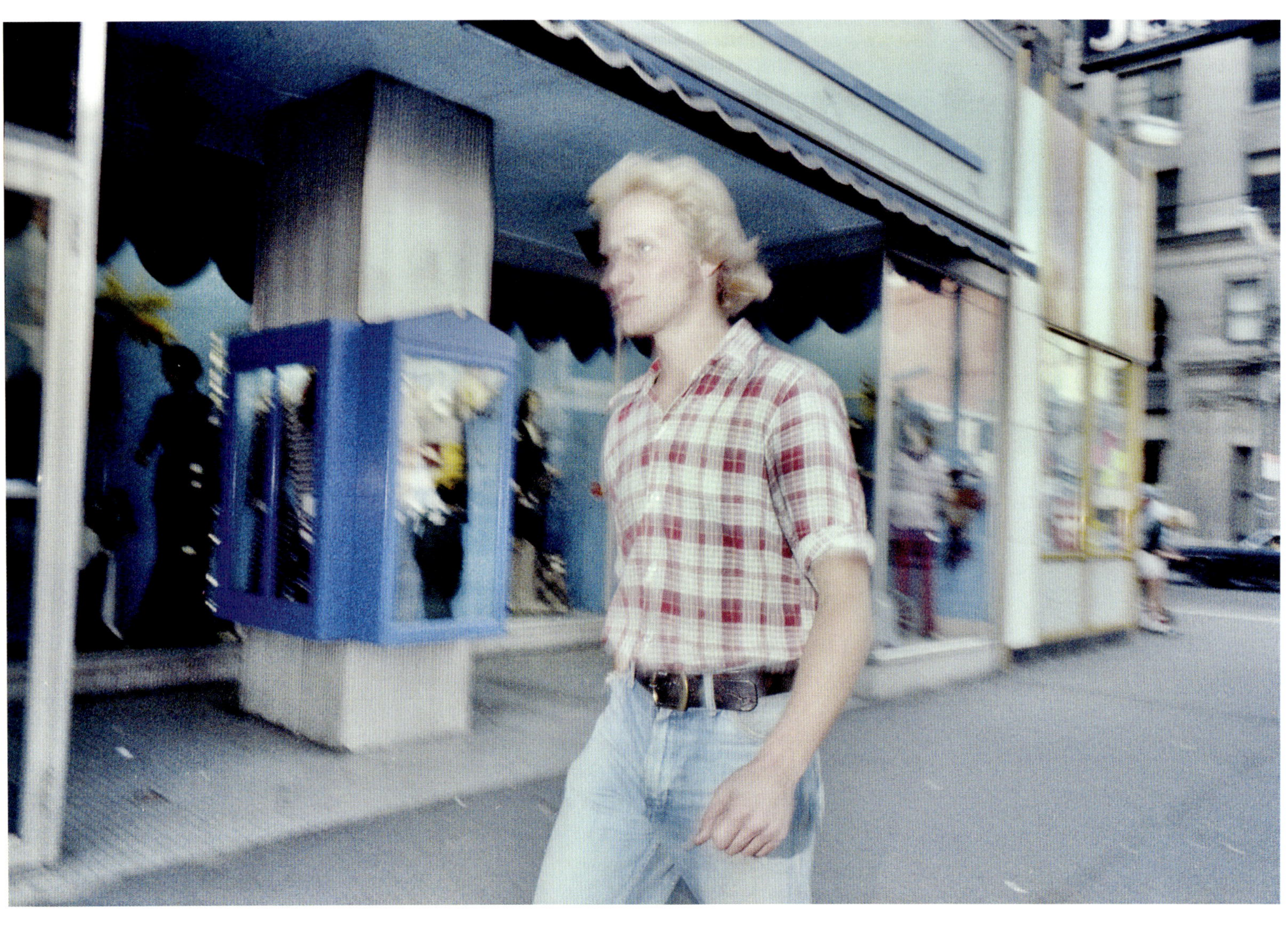

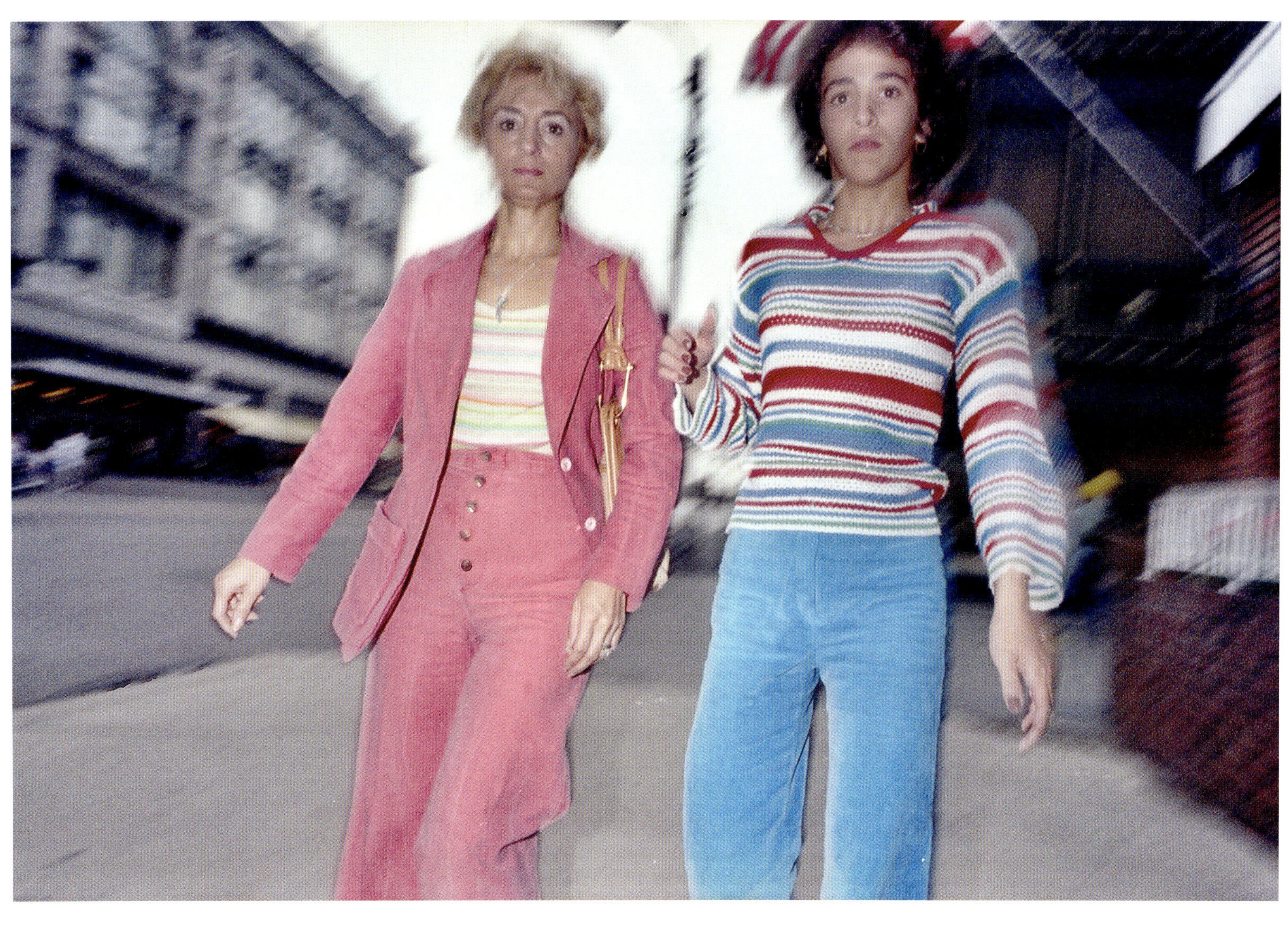

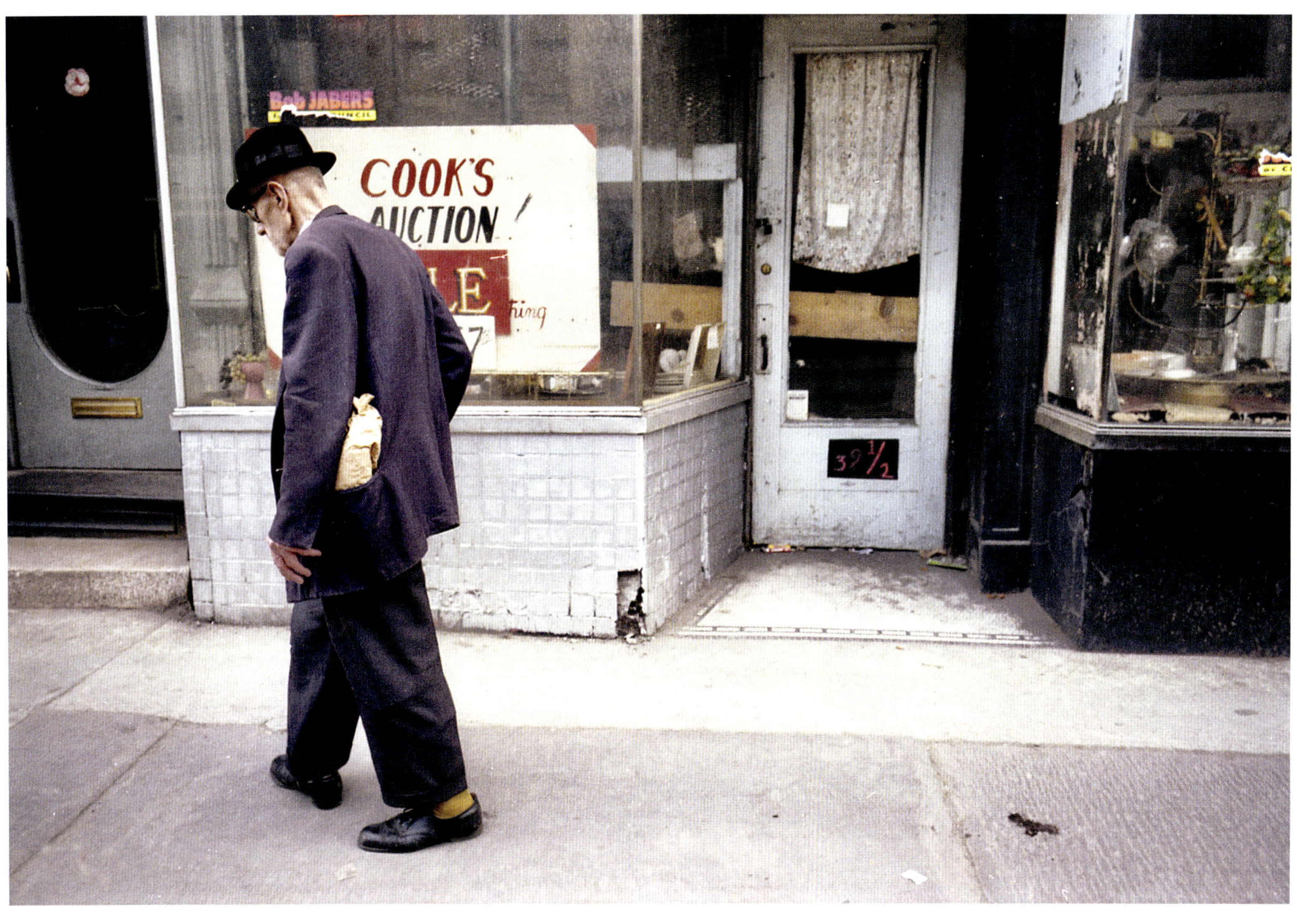
Bob JABERS
COOK'S
AUCTION!
39 1/2

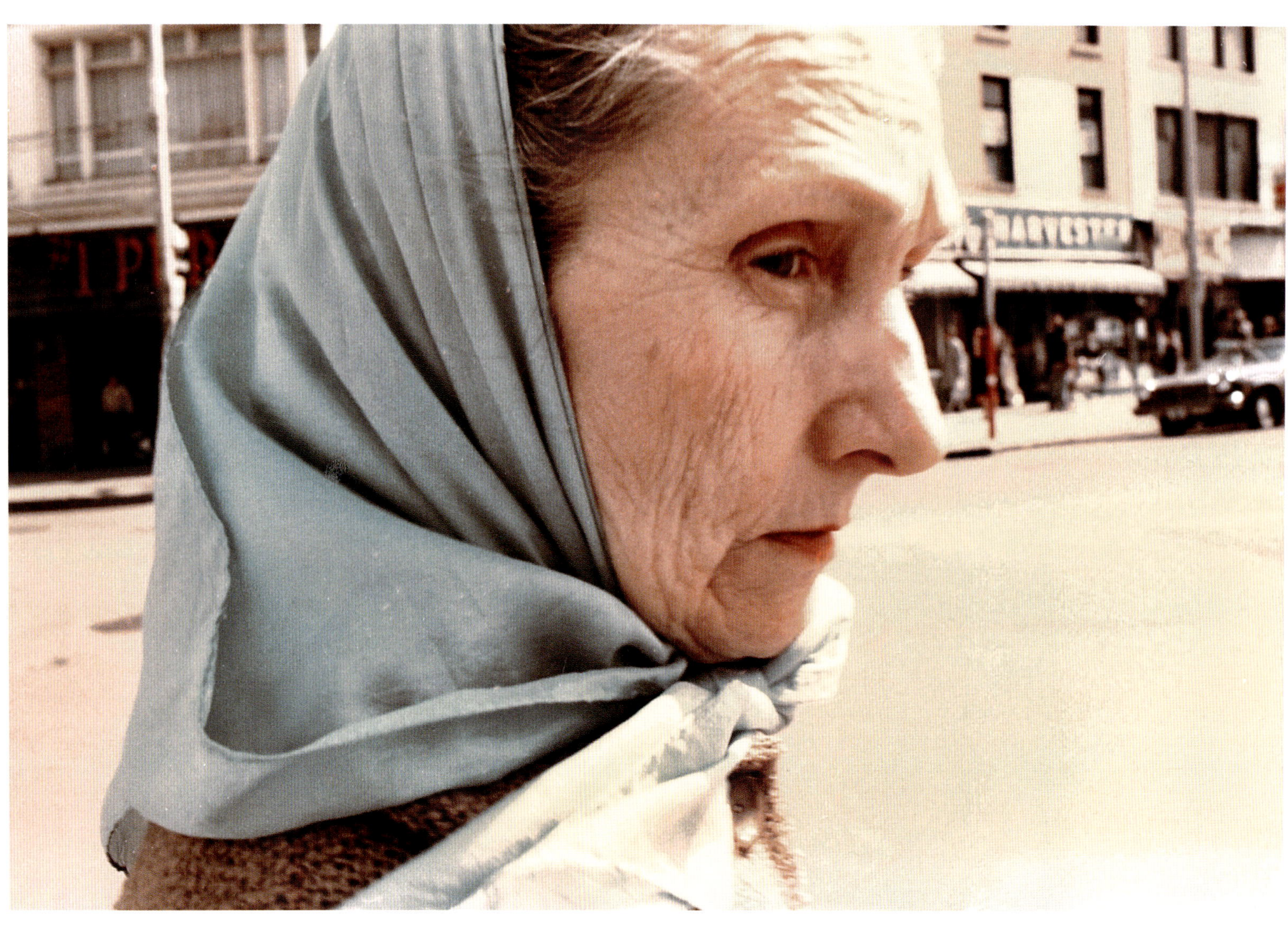

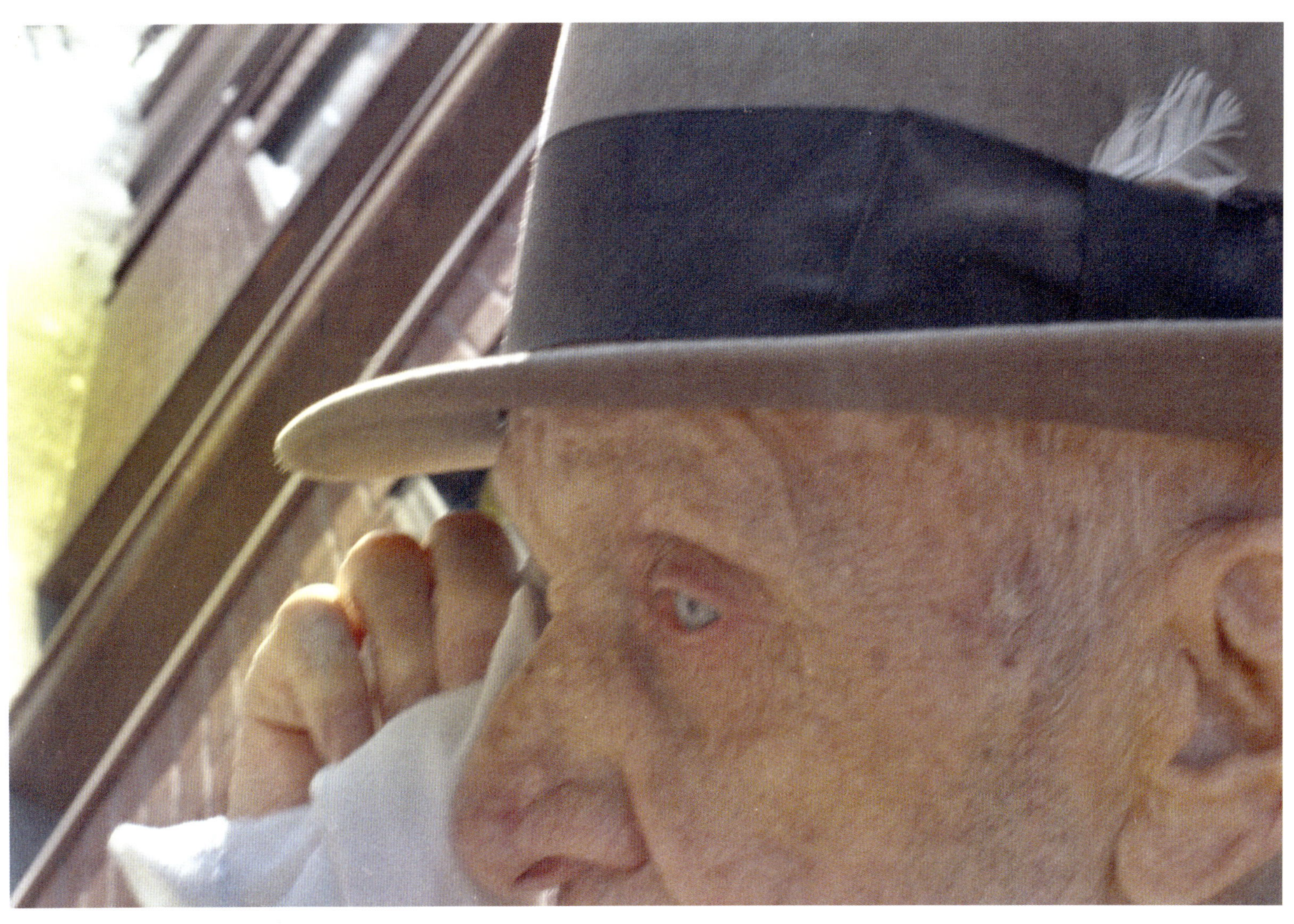

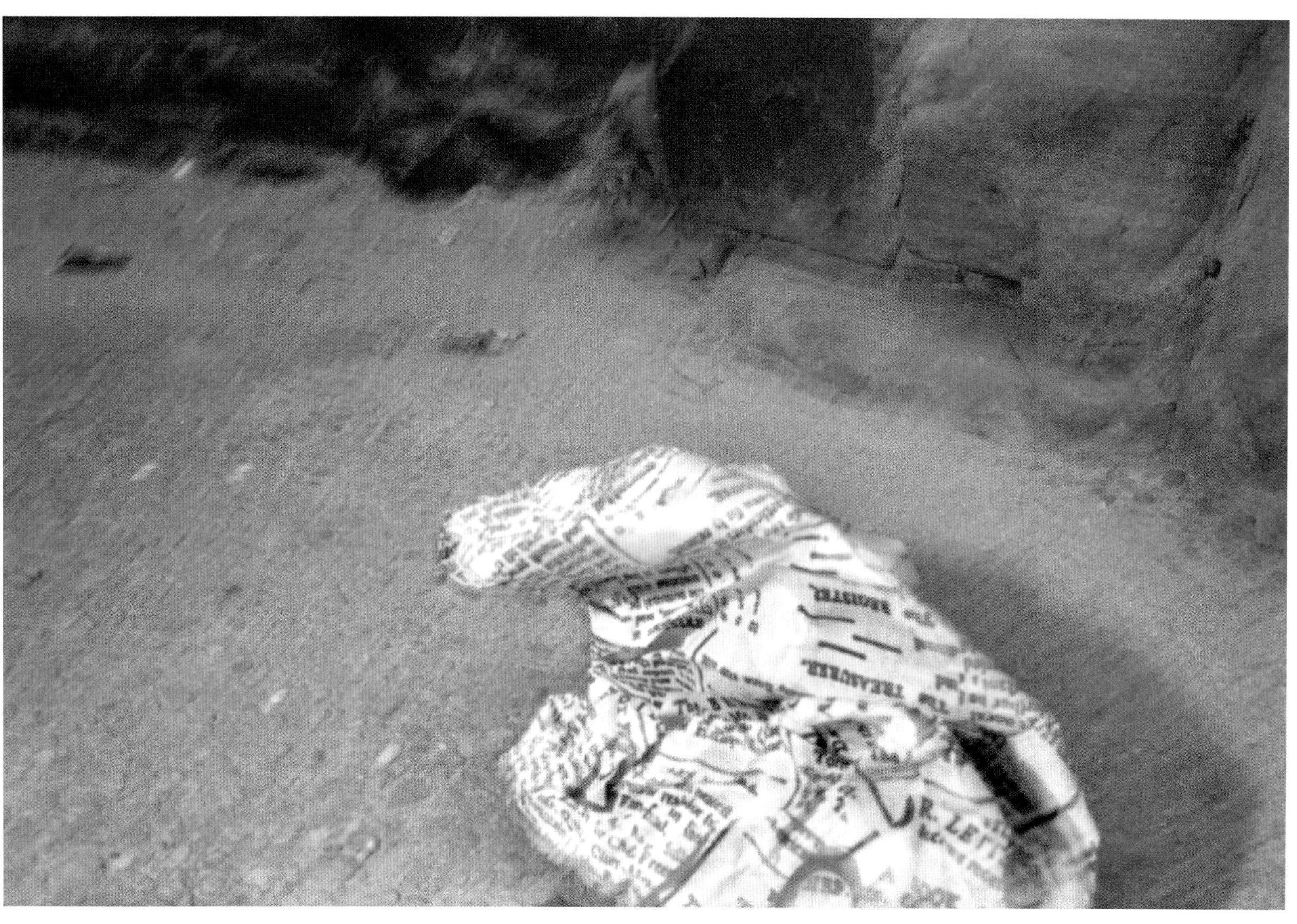

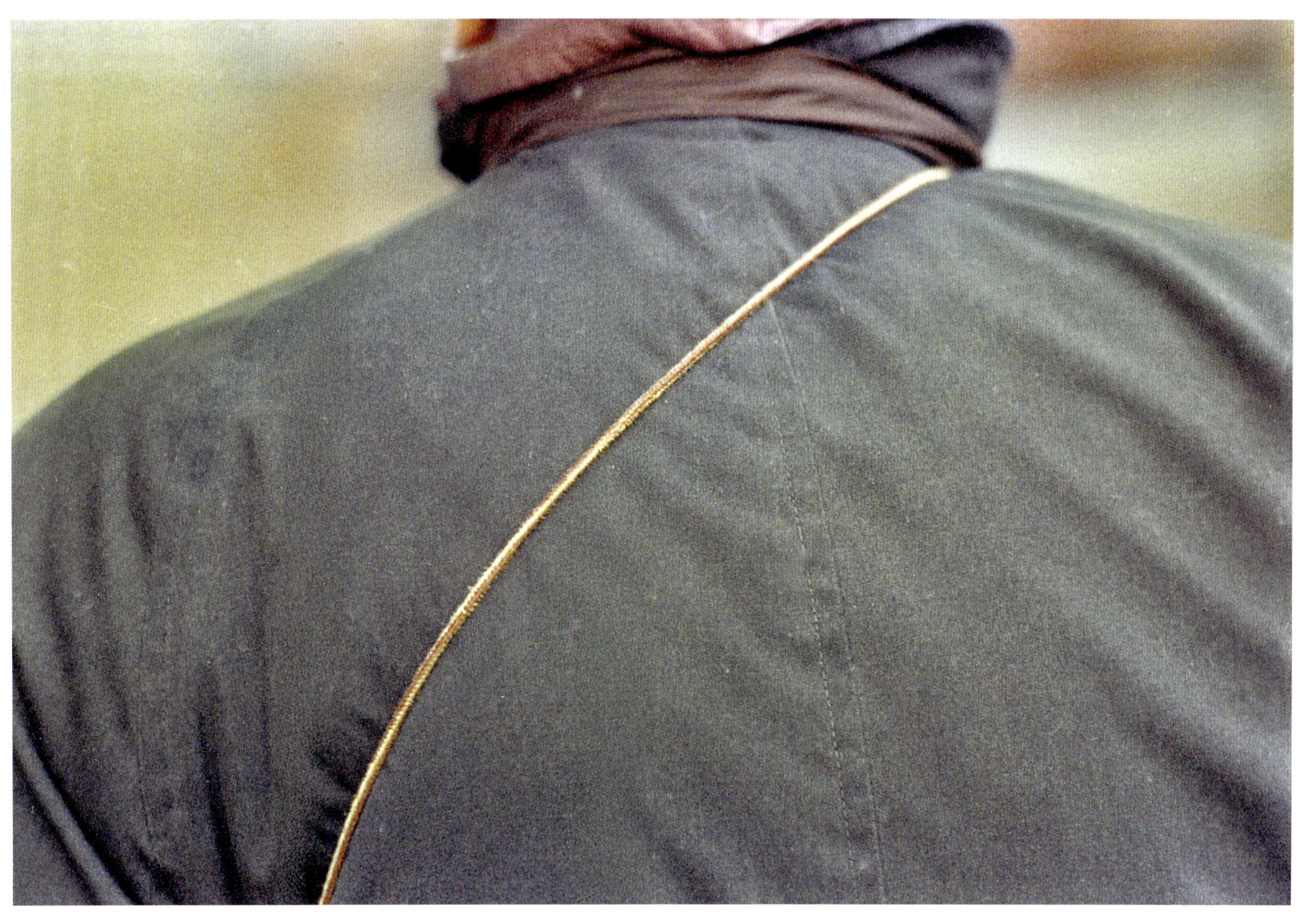

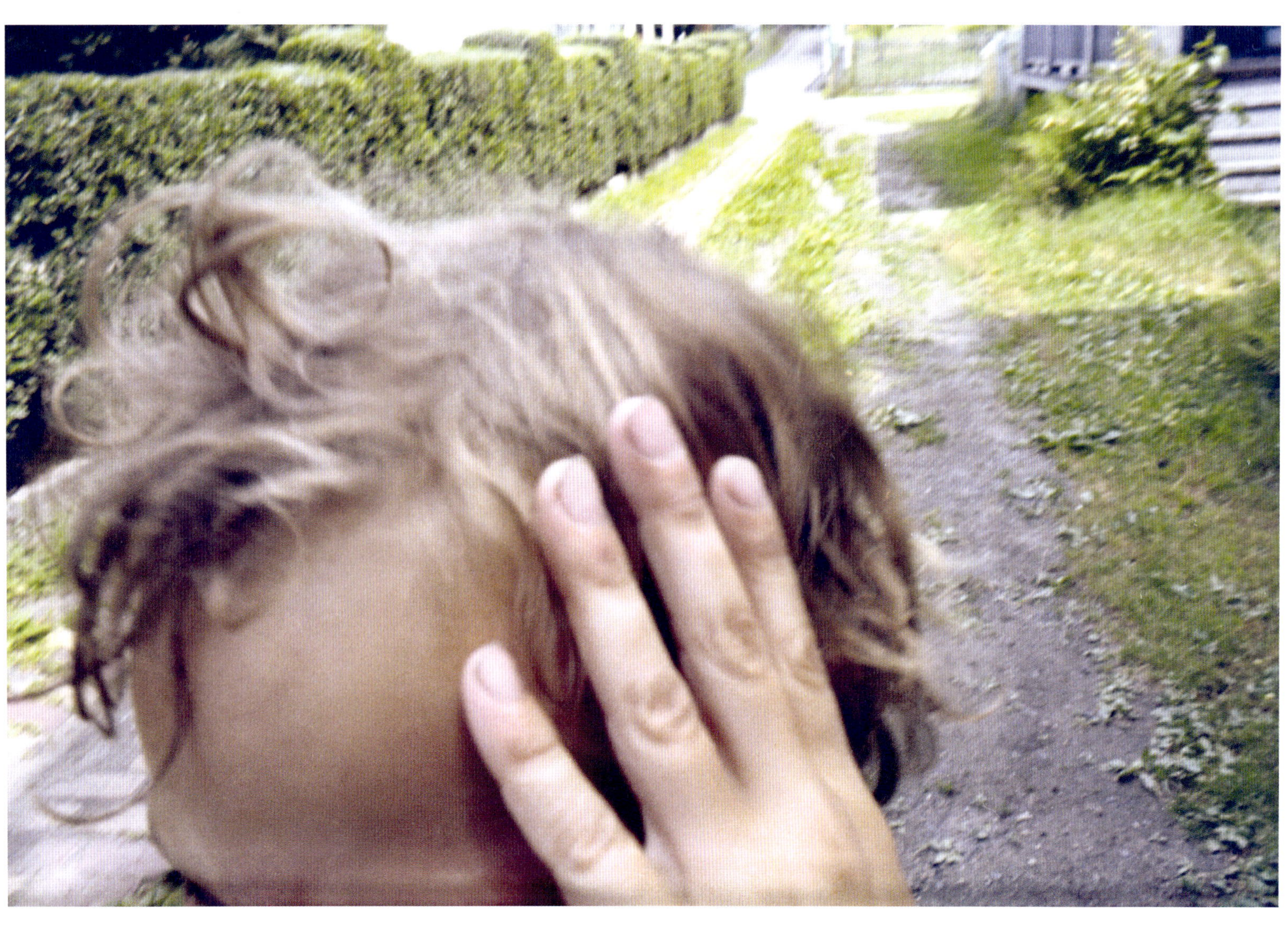

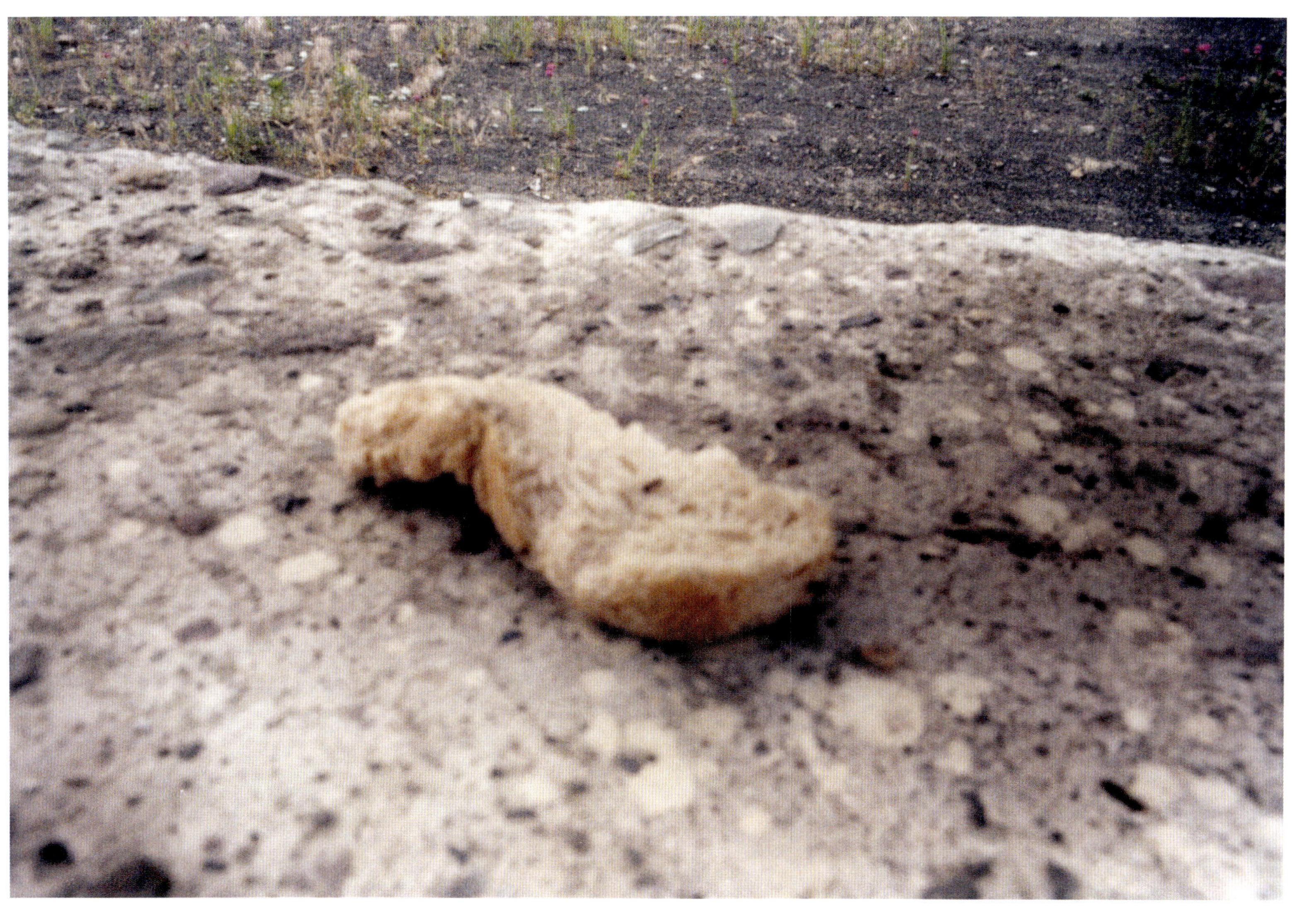

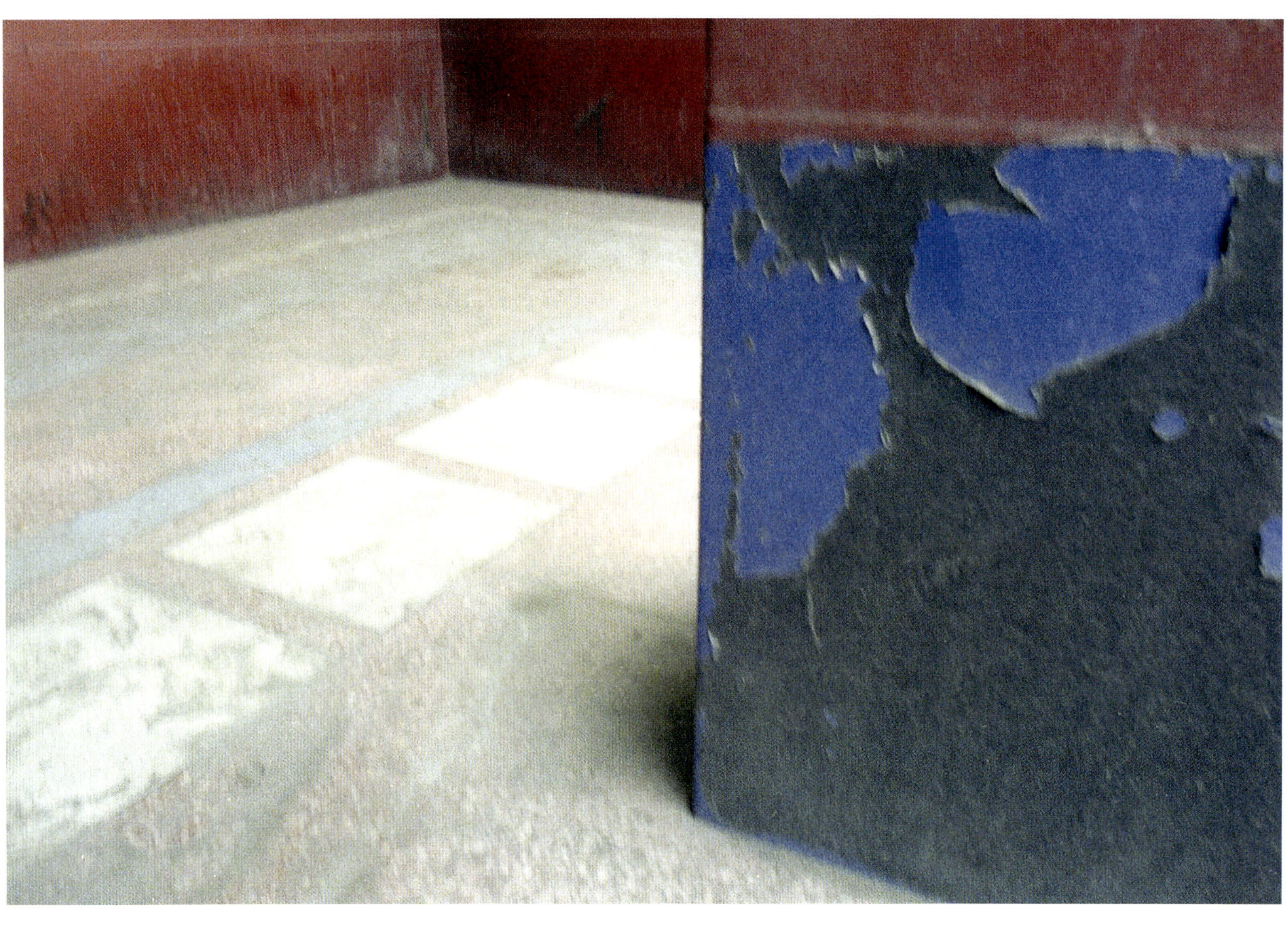

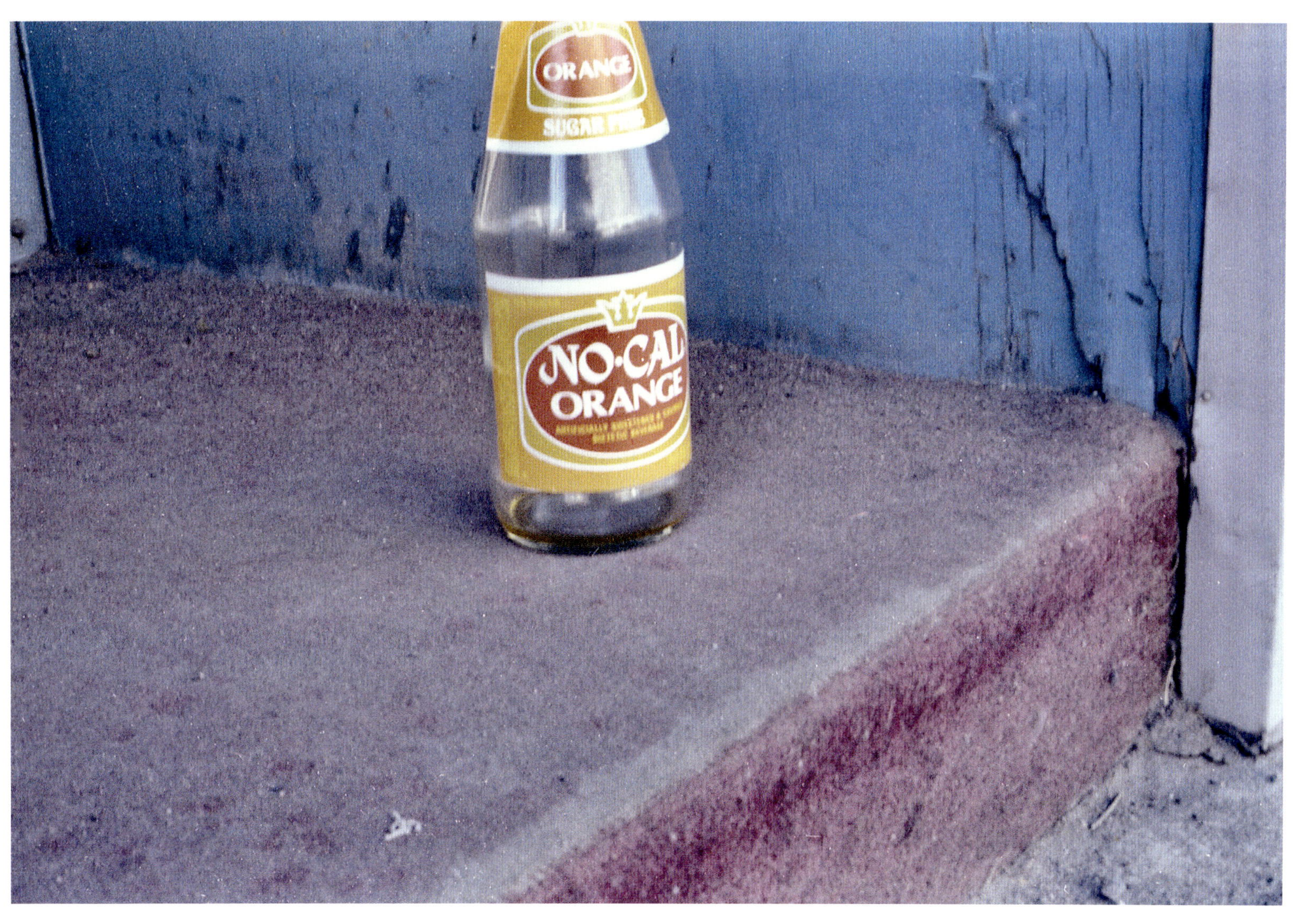
ORANGE
SUGAR FREE
NO·CAL
ORANGE

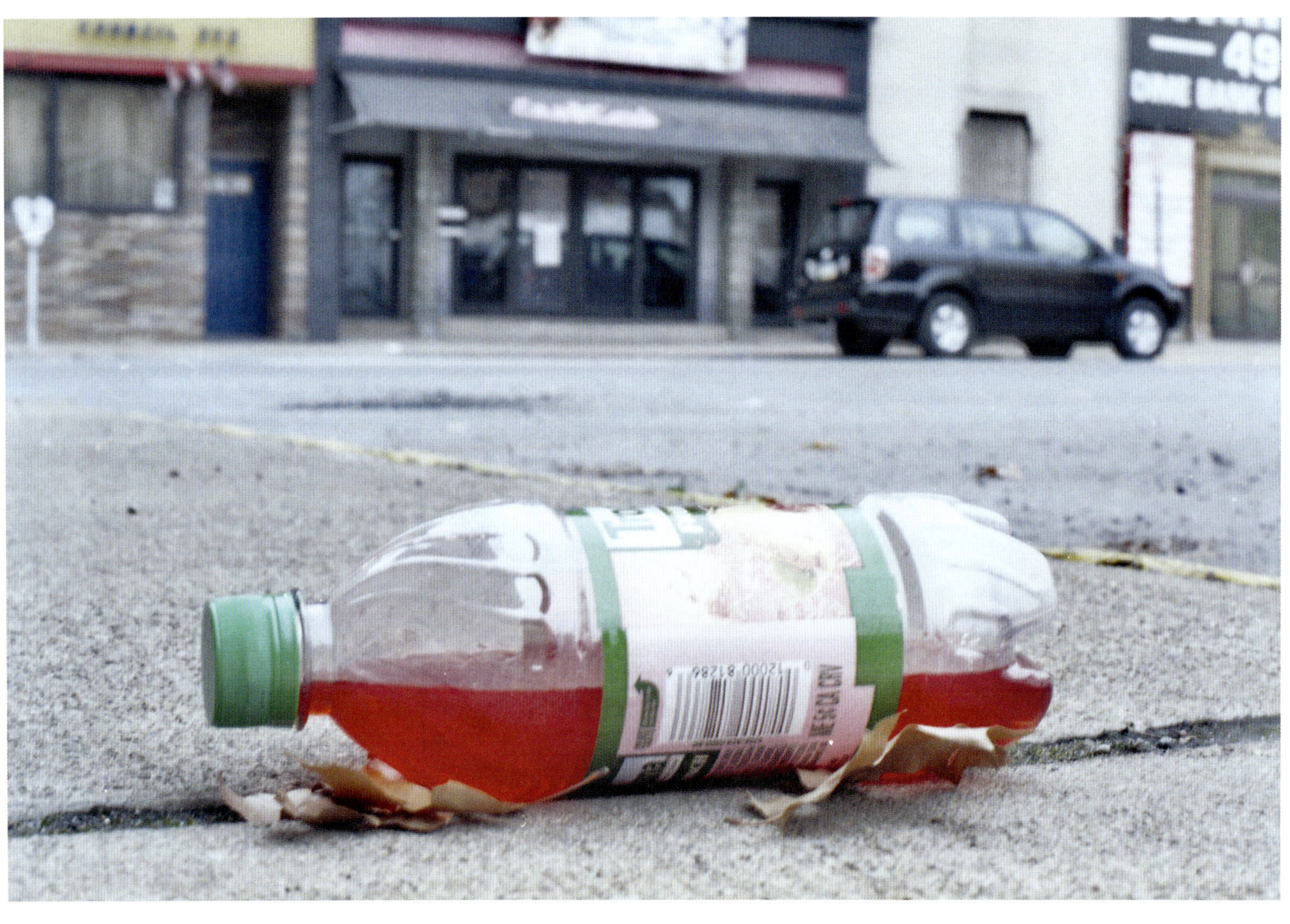

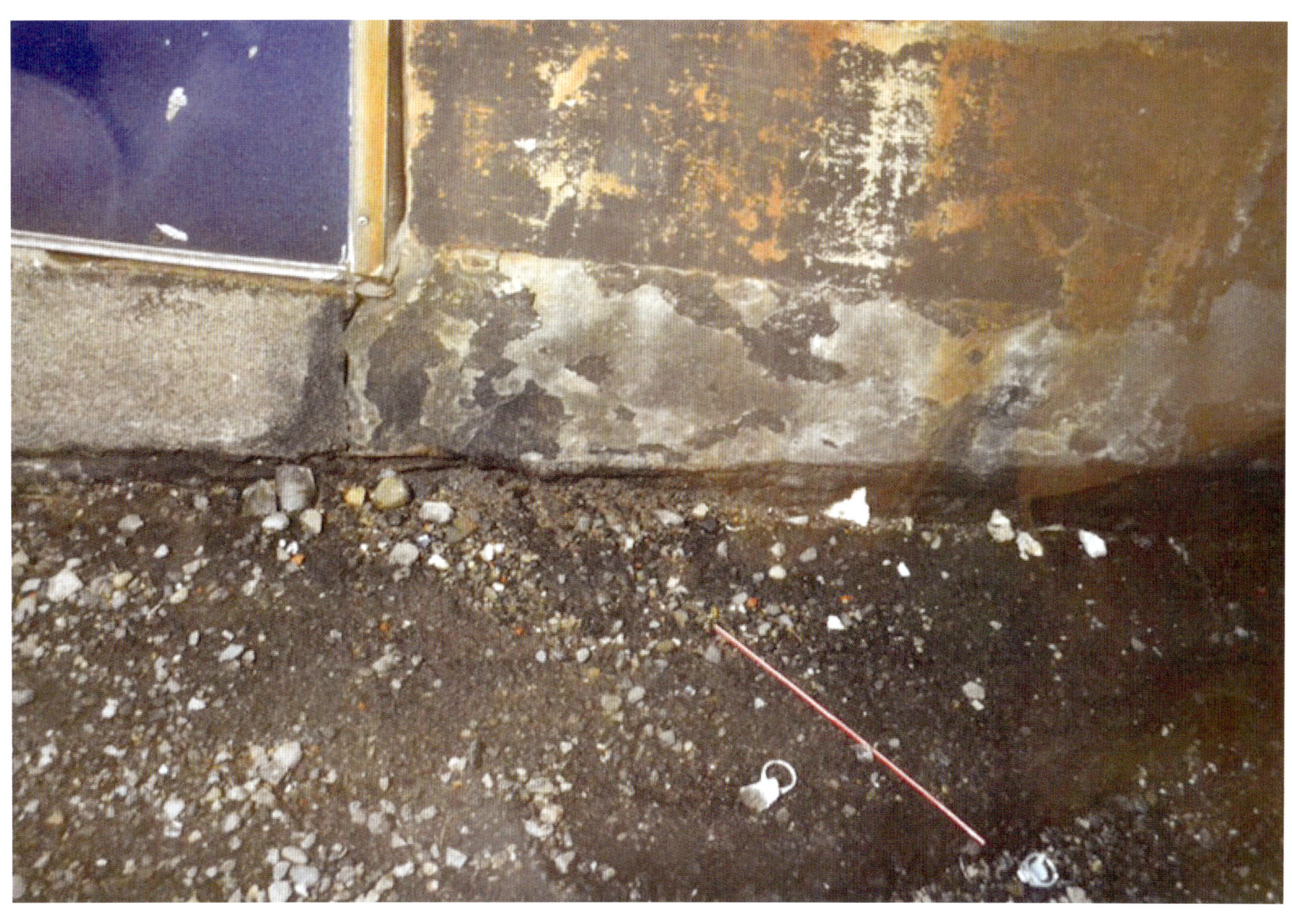

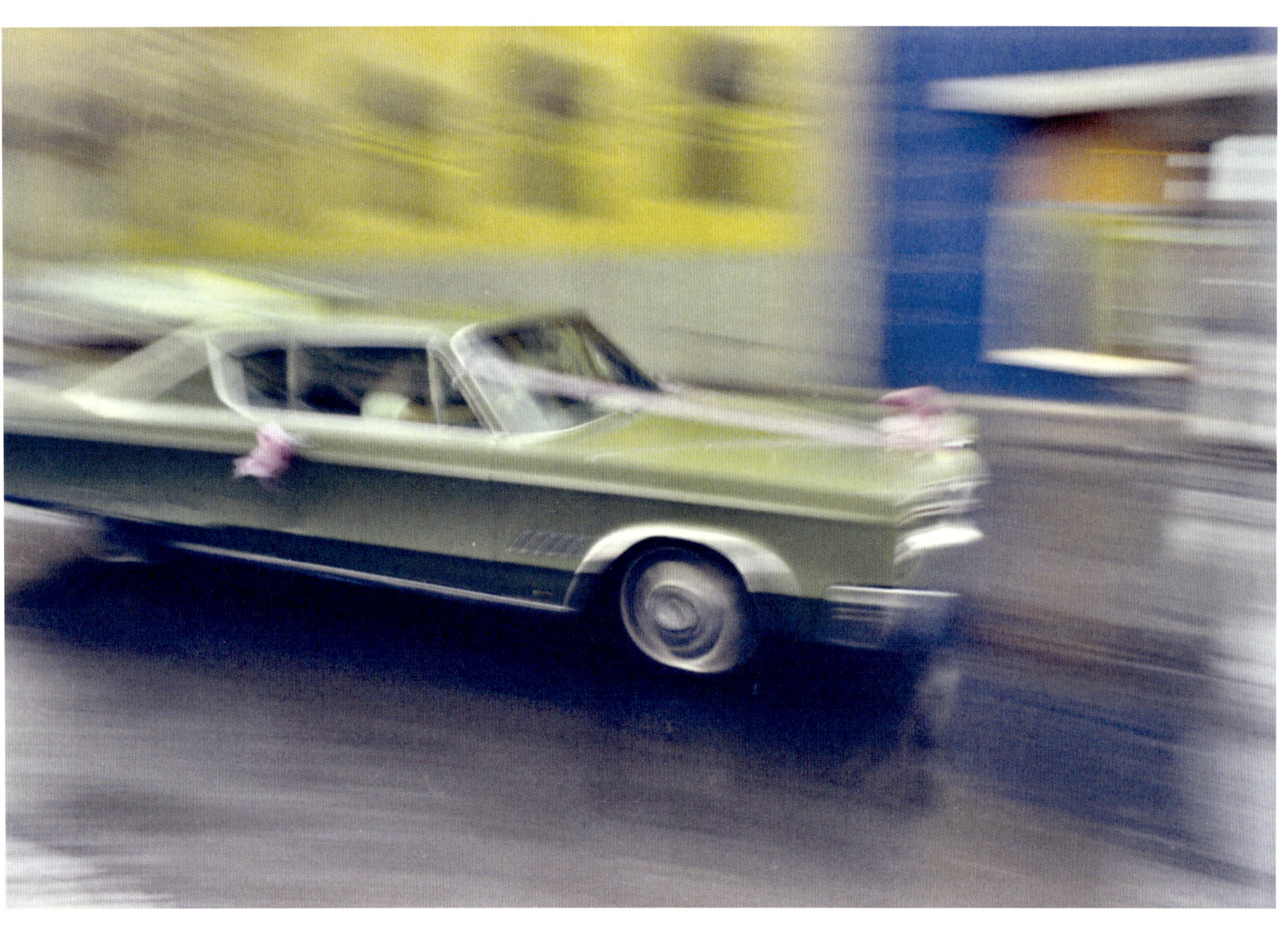

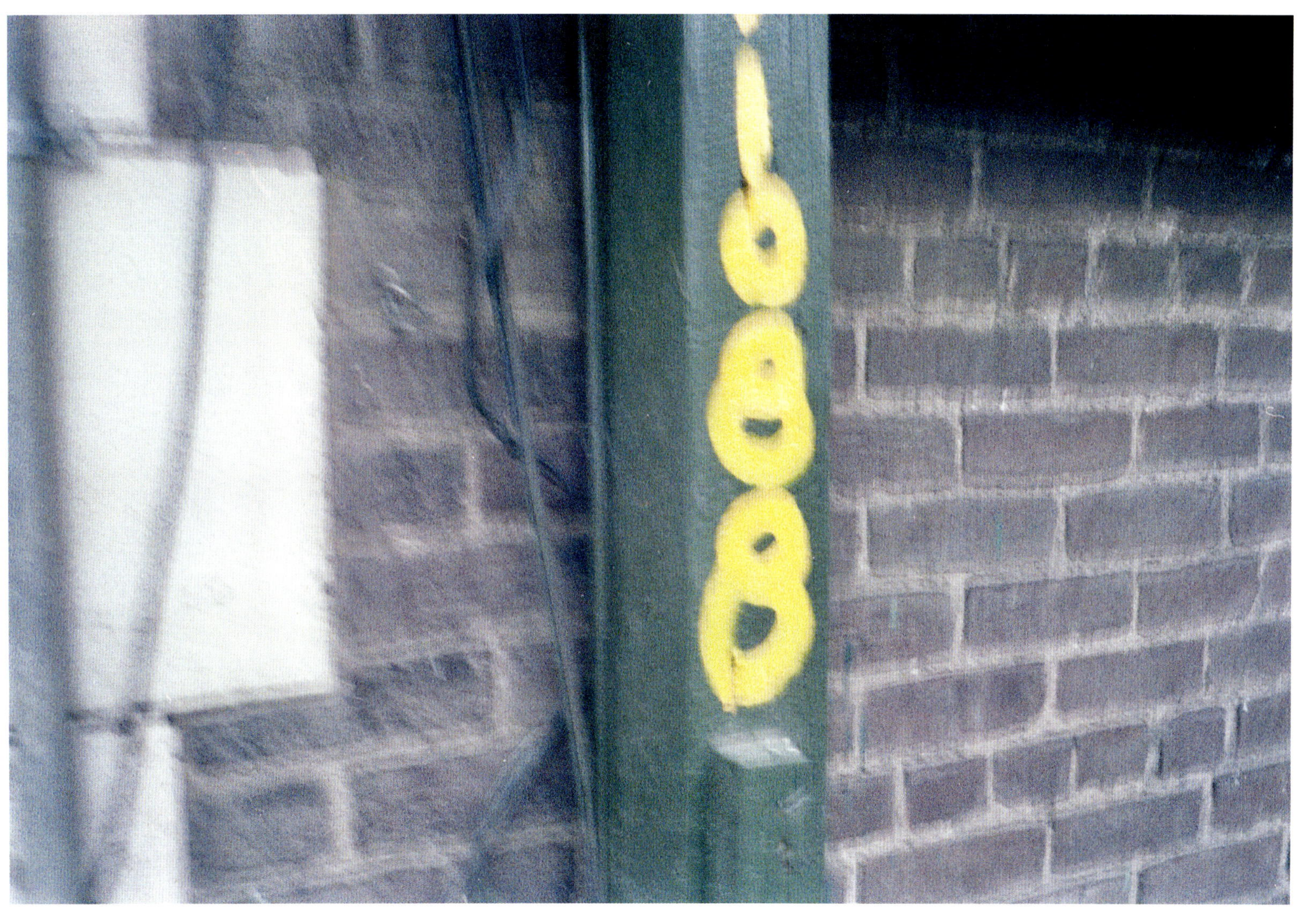

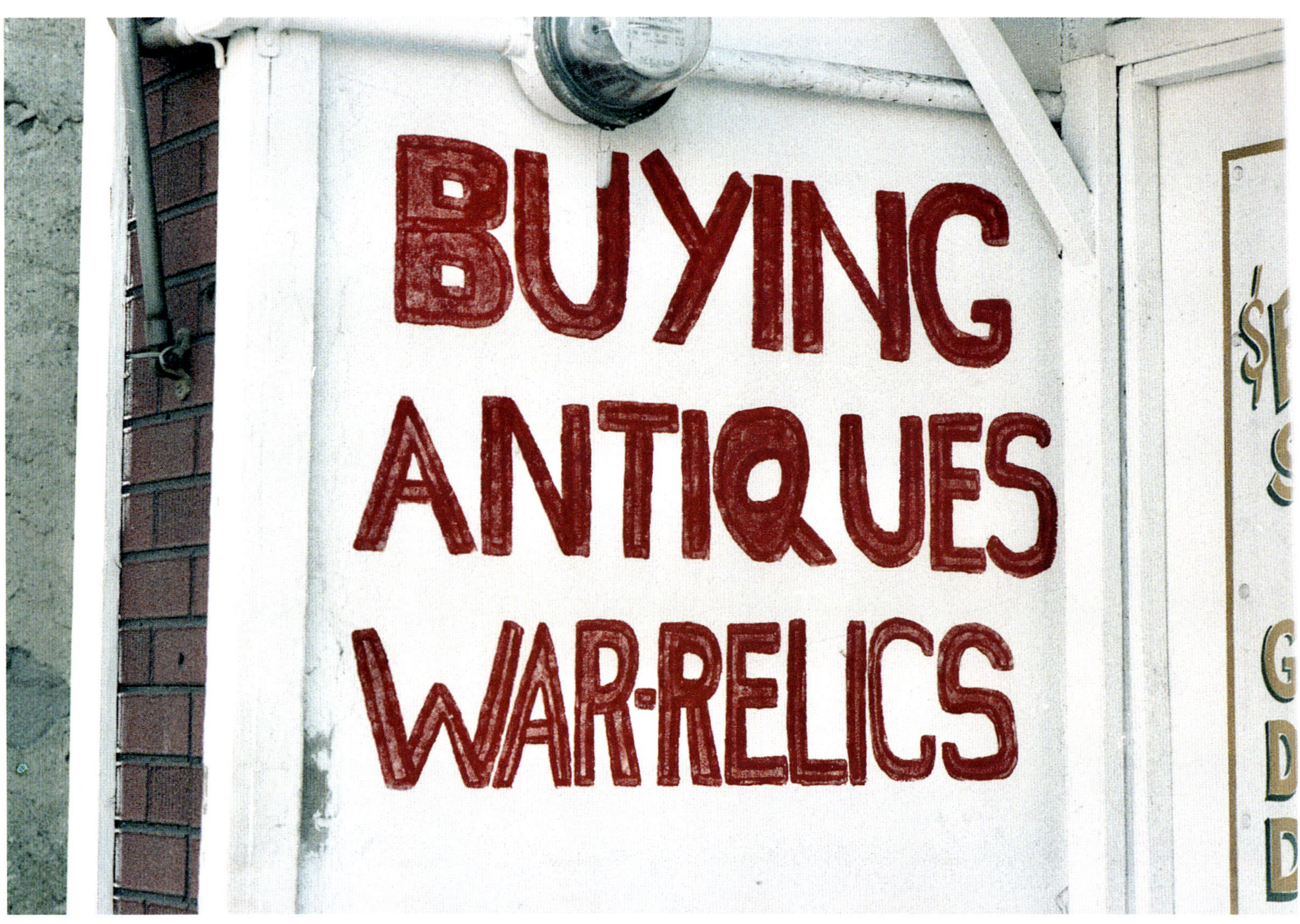
BUYING
ANTIQUES
WAR-RELICS

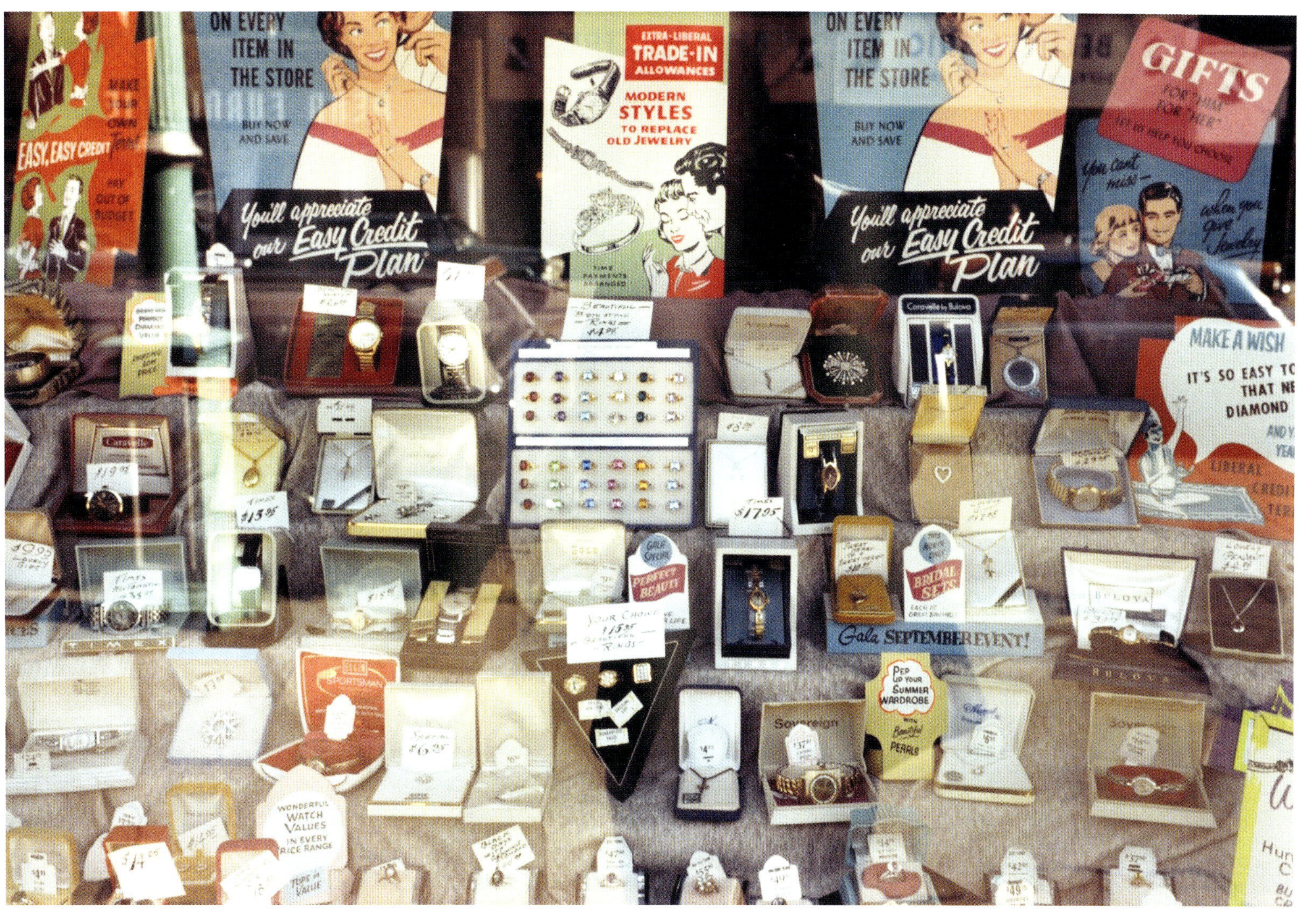

EASY, EASY CREDIT
ON EVERY ITEM IN THE STORE
BUY NOW AND SAVE
You'll appreciate our Easy Credit Plan
EXTRA-LIBERAL TRADE-IN ALLOWANCES
MODERN STYLES TO REPLACE OLD JEWELRY
TIME PAYMENTS ARRANGED
ON EVERY ITEM IN THE STORE
BUY NOW AND SAVE
You'll appreciate our Easy Credit Plan
GIFTS
You can't miss — when you give Jewelry
MAKE A WISH
Caravelle by Bulova
$17.95
GALA SPECIAL PERFECT BEAUTY
BRIDAL SETS
Gala SEPTEMBER EVENT!
BULOVA
TIMEX
SPORTSMAN
PEP UP YOUR SUMMER WARDROBE
PEARLS
Sovereign
WONDERFUL WATCH VALUES IN EVERY

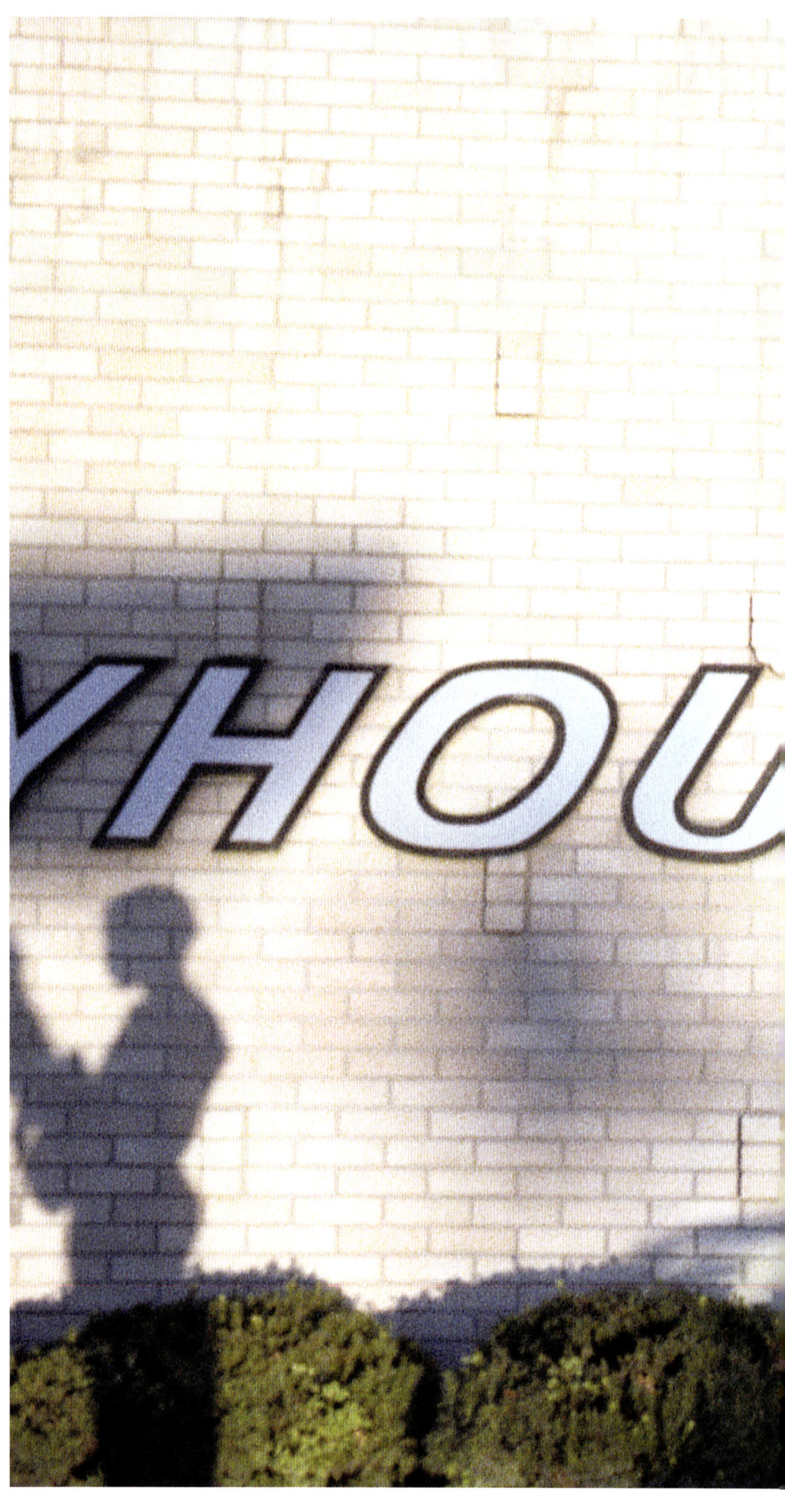
YHOU

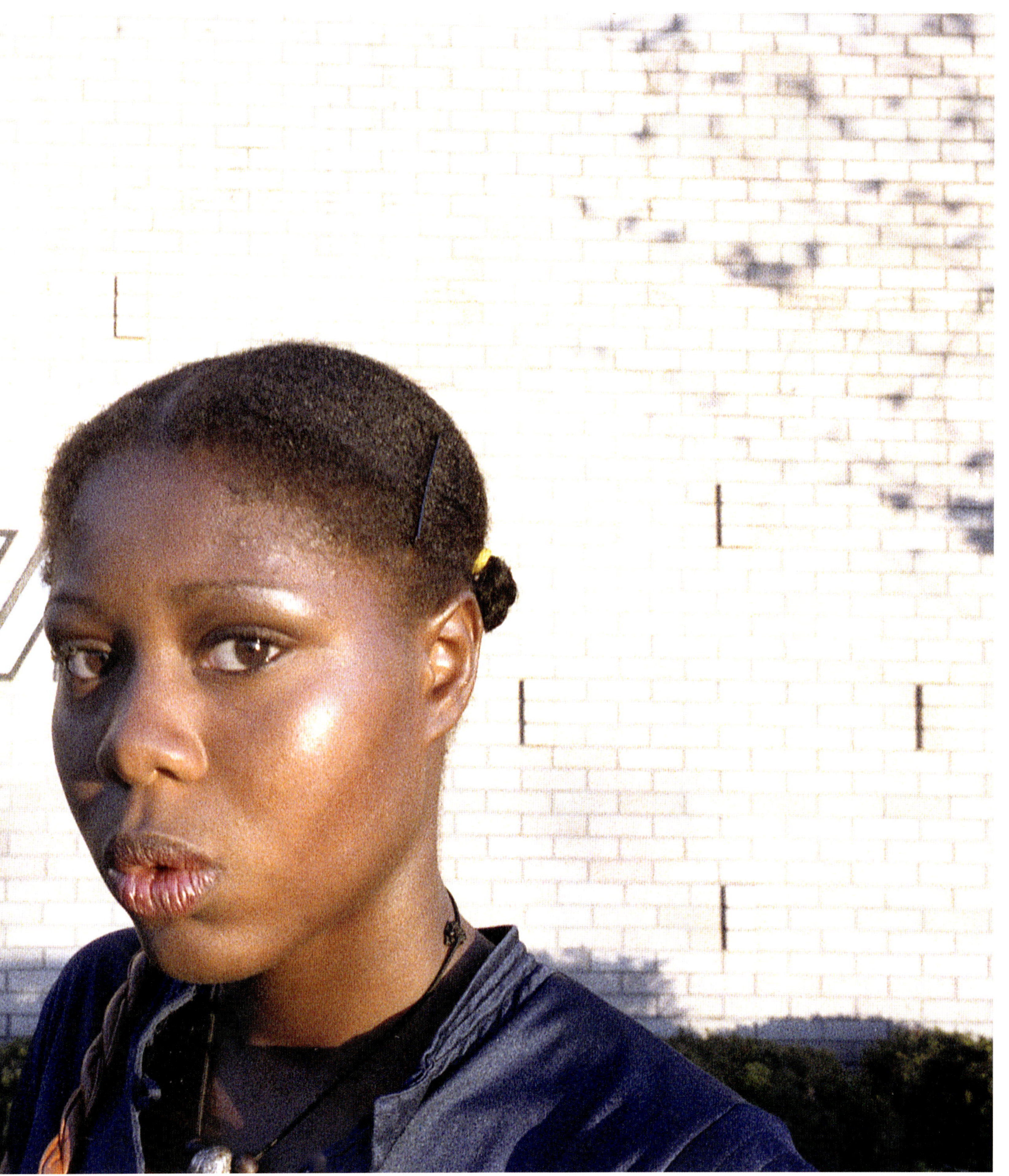

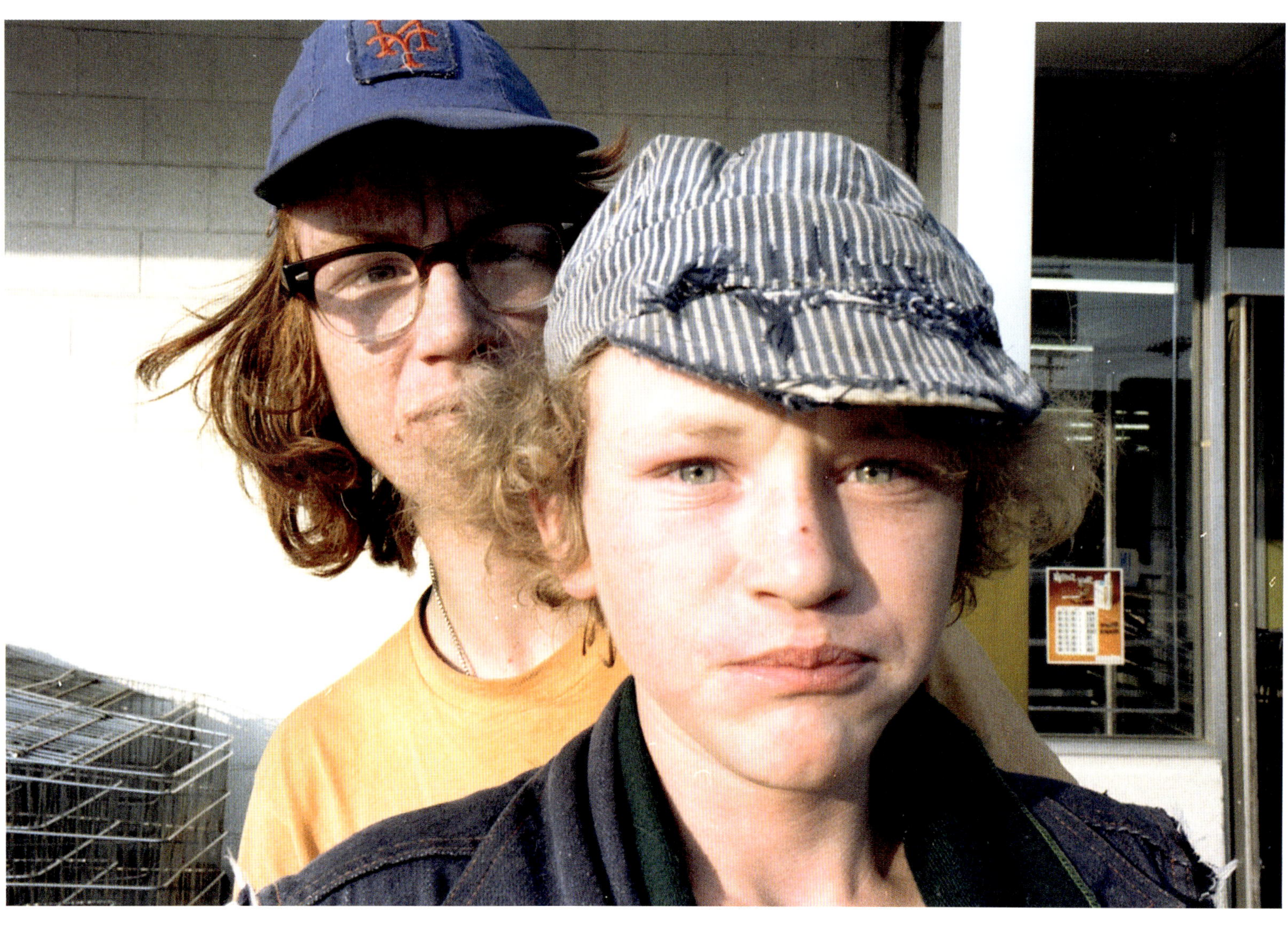

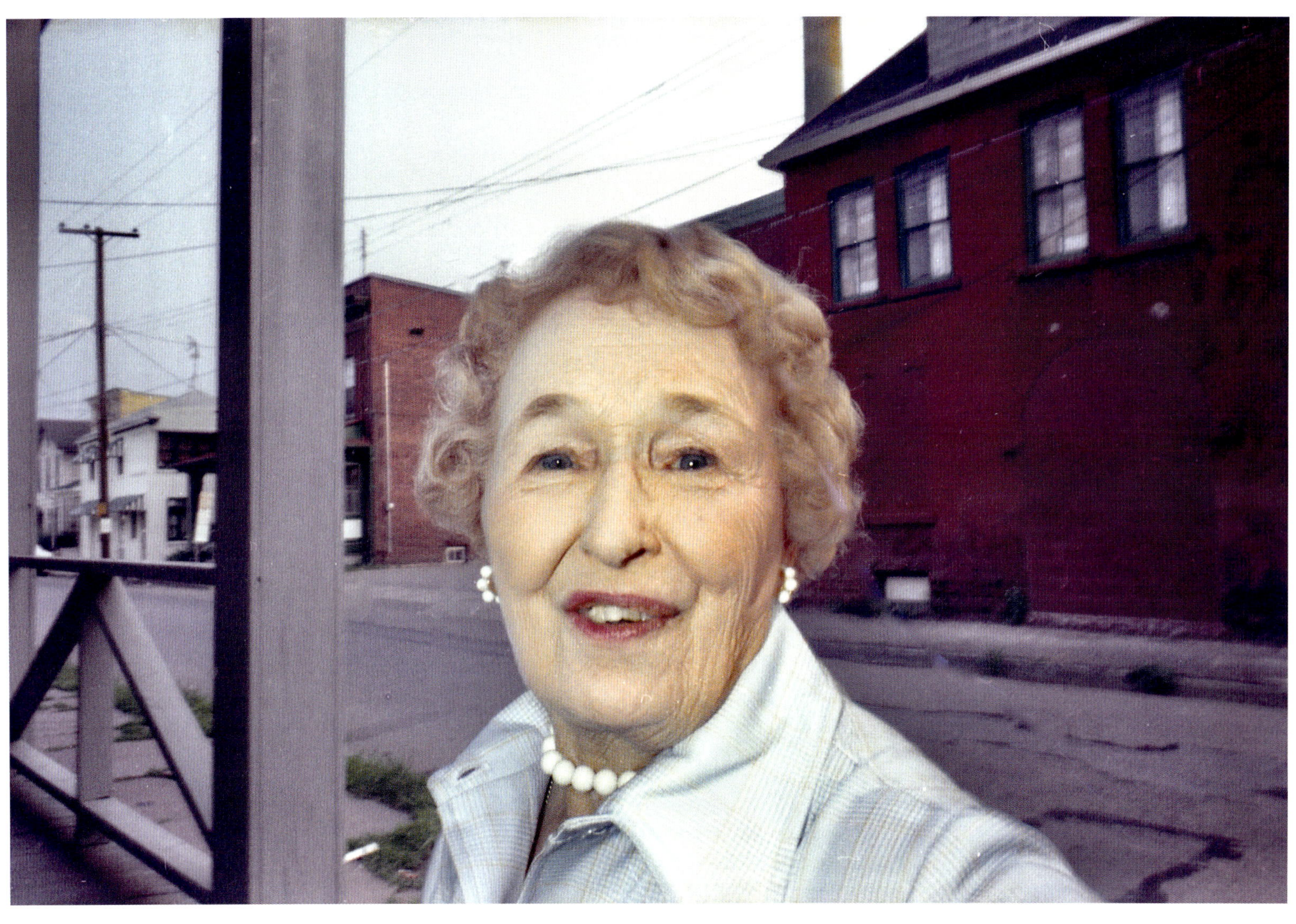

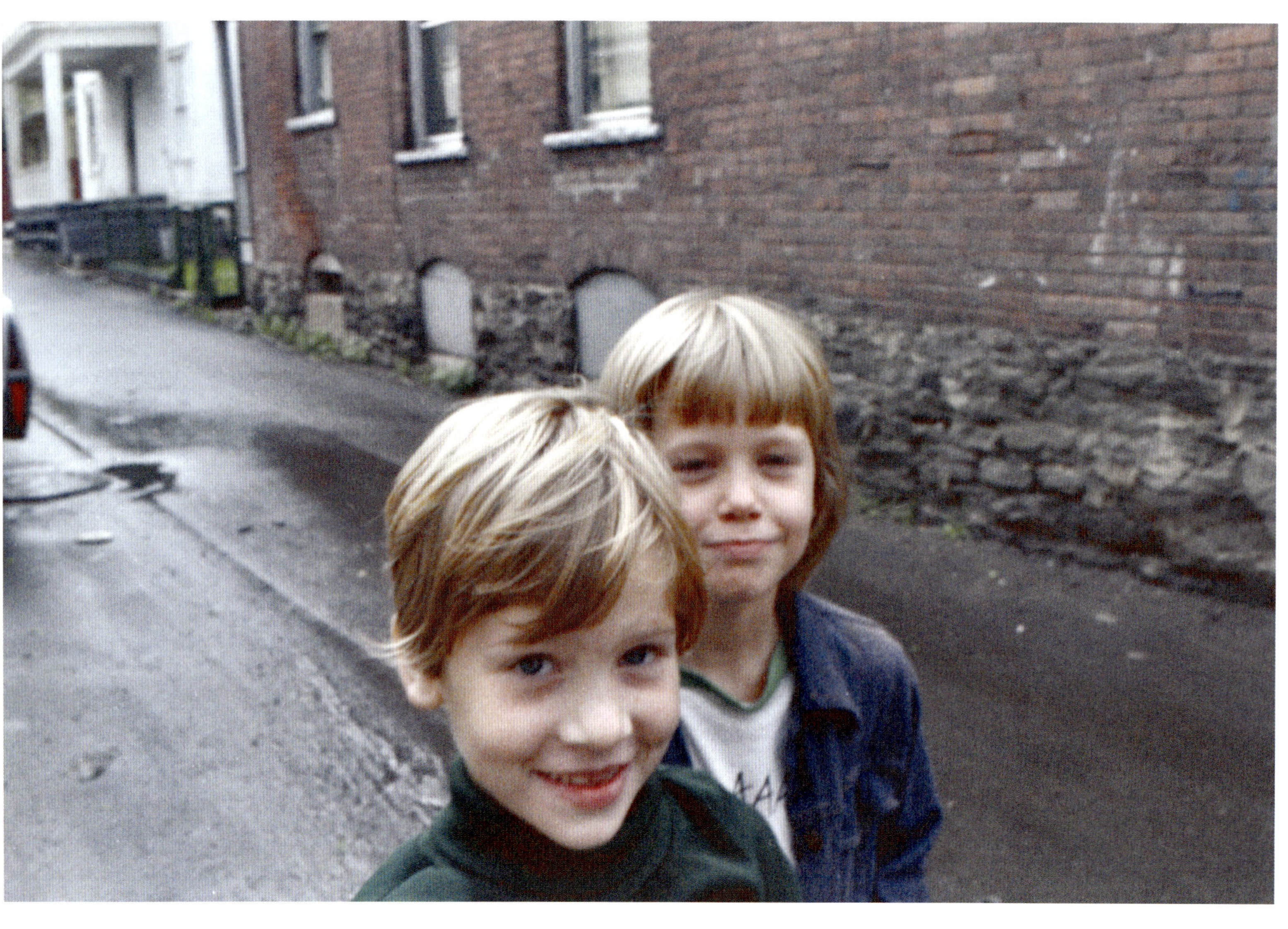

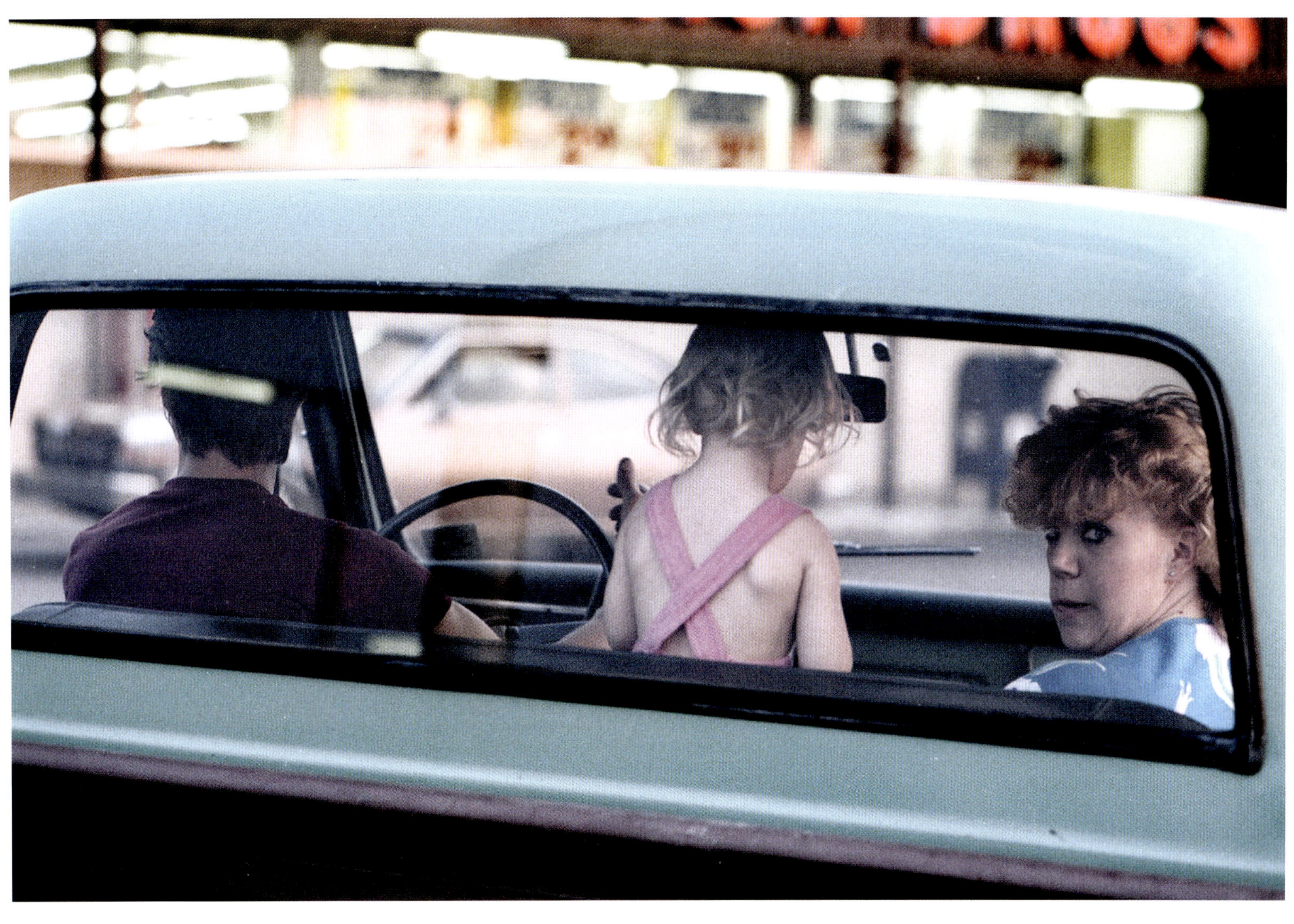

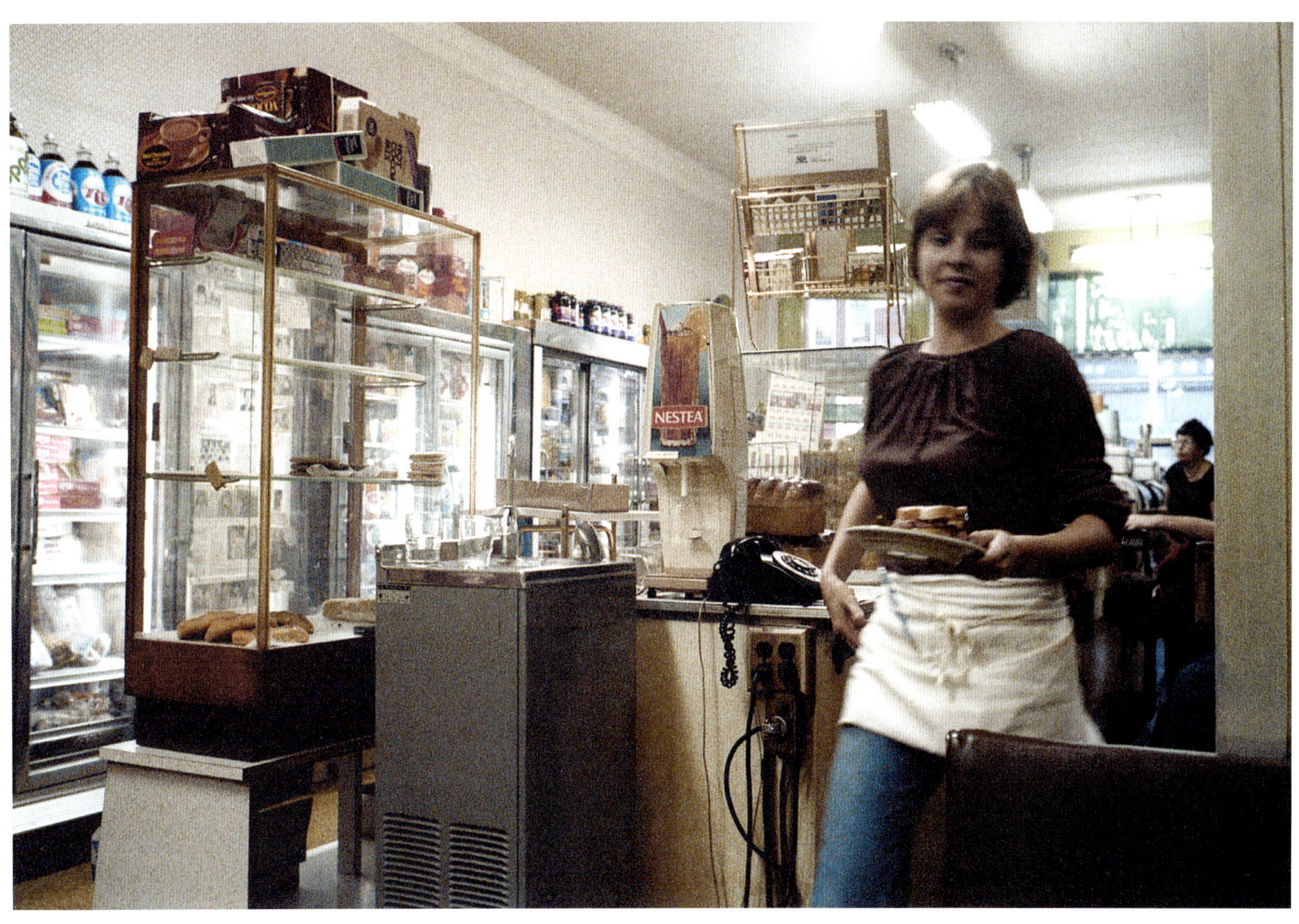
NESTEA

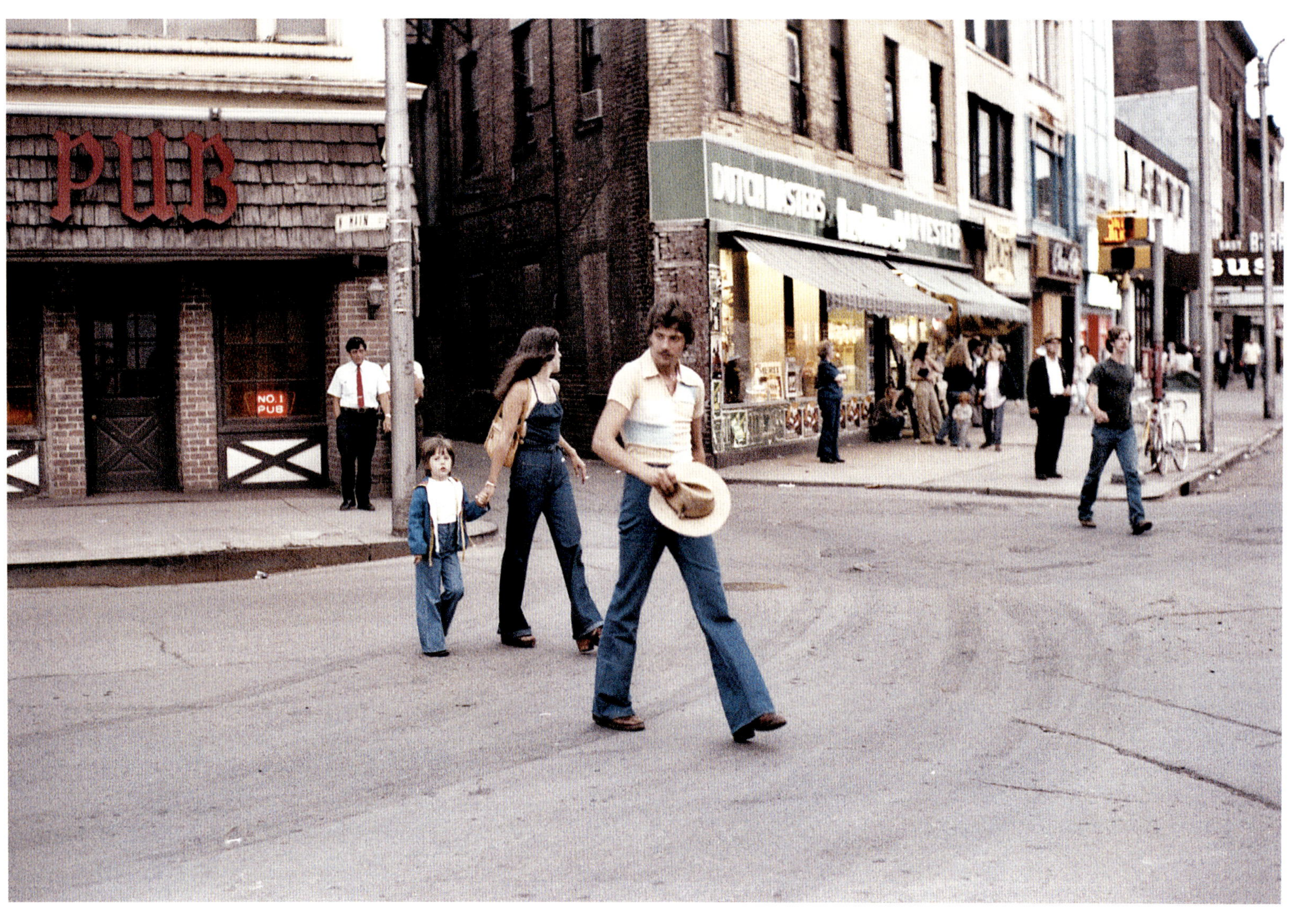
PUB
NO. 1 PUB
DUTCH MASTERS

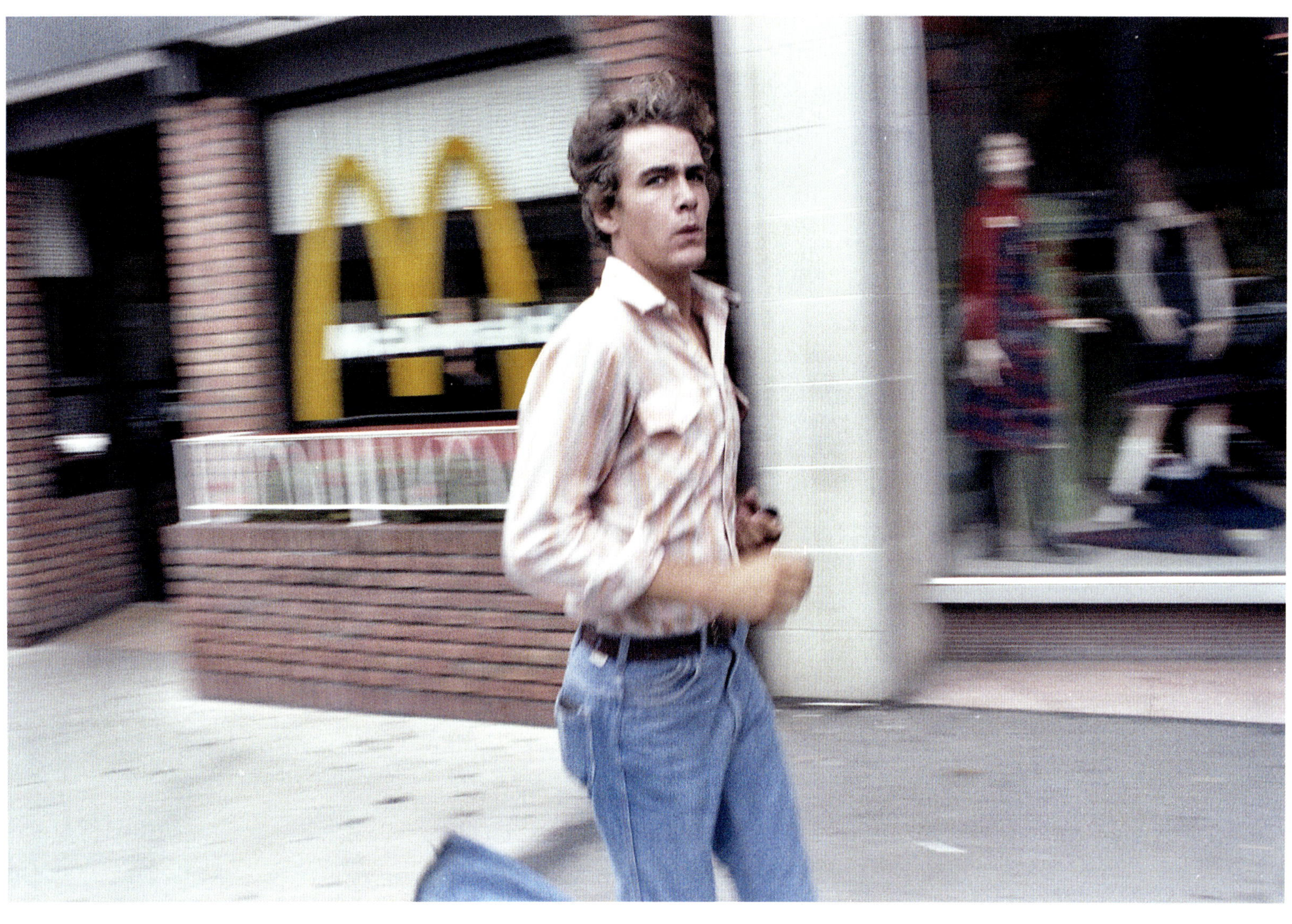

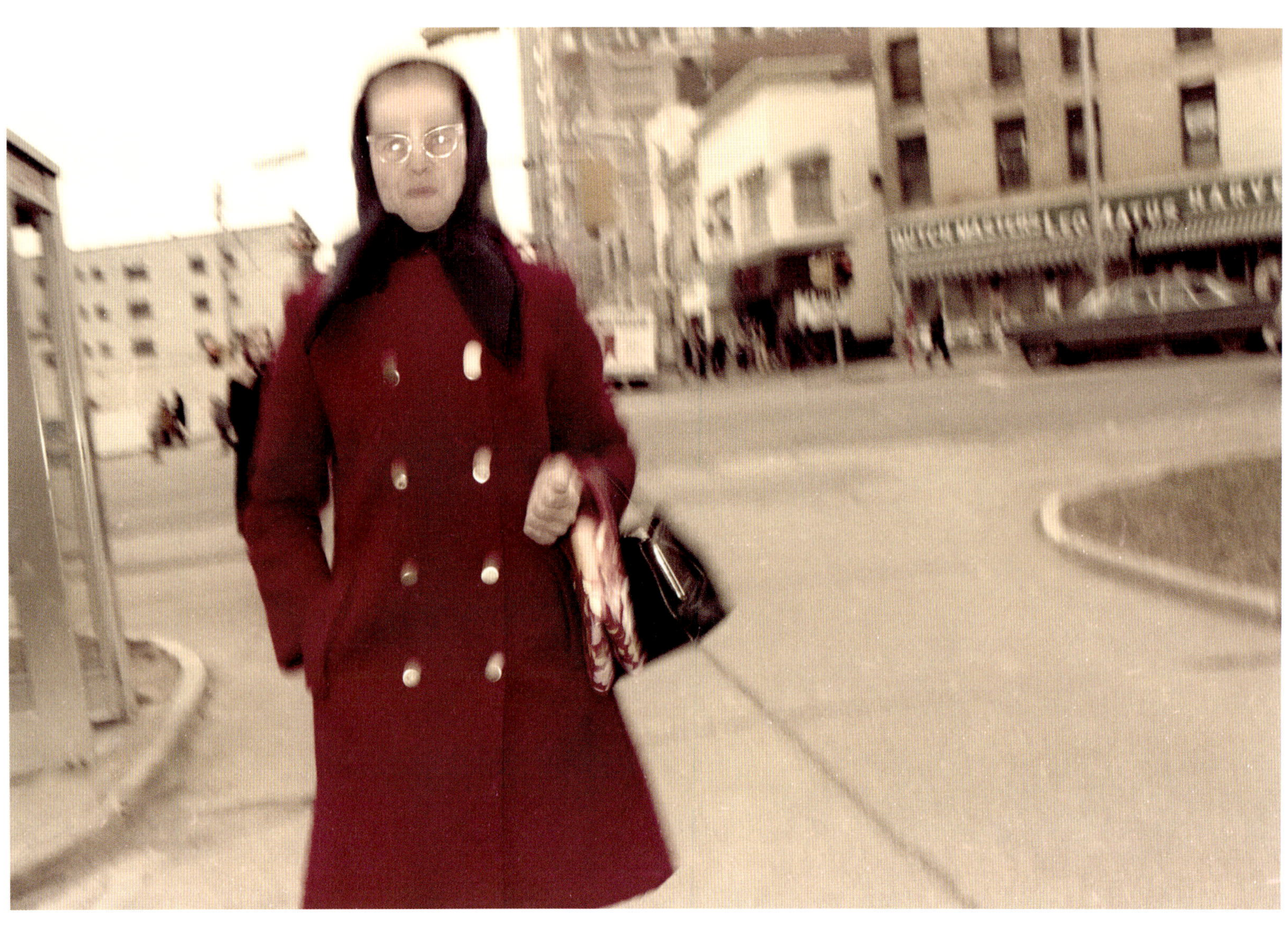

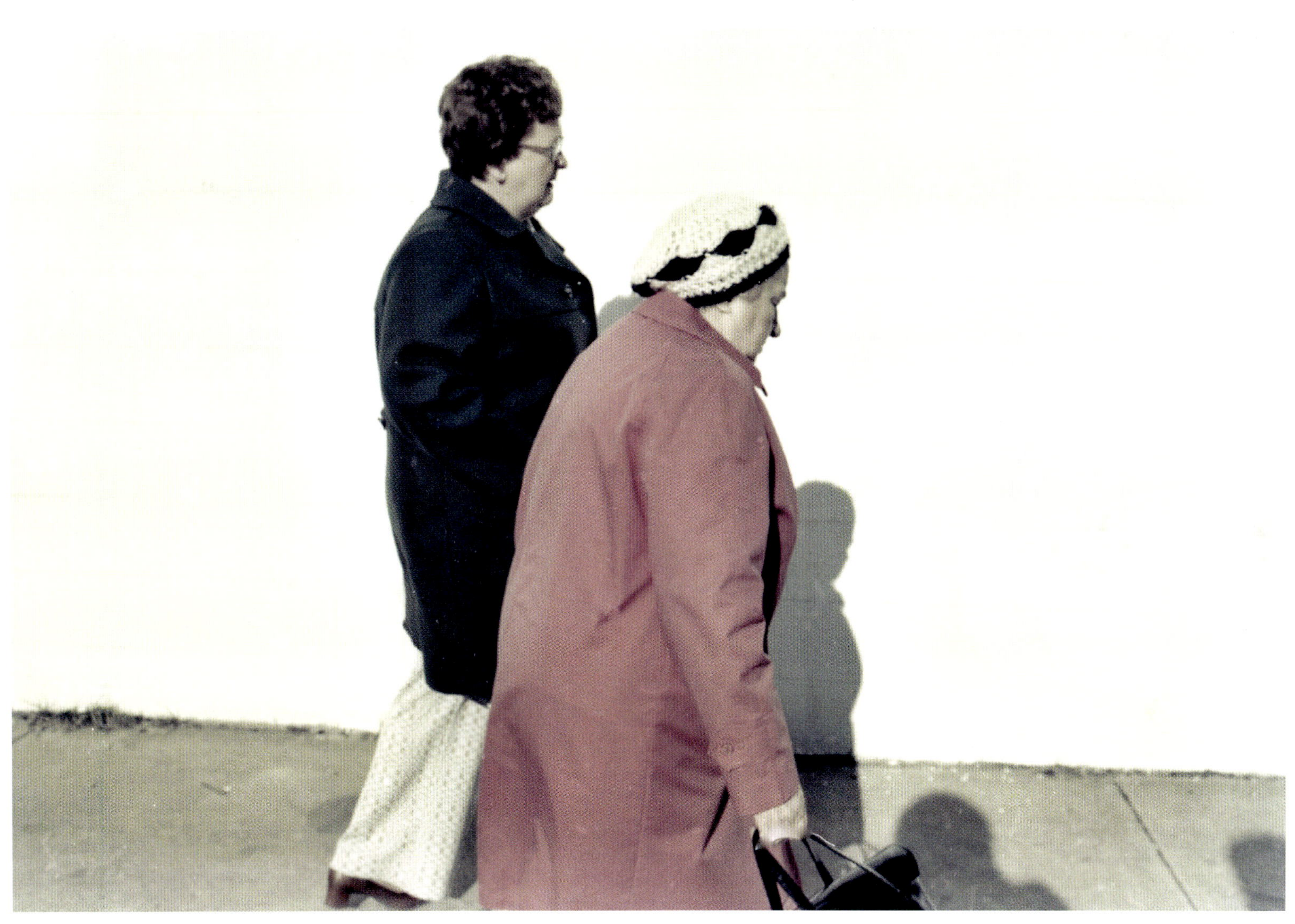

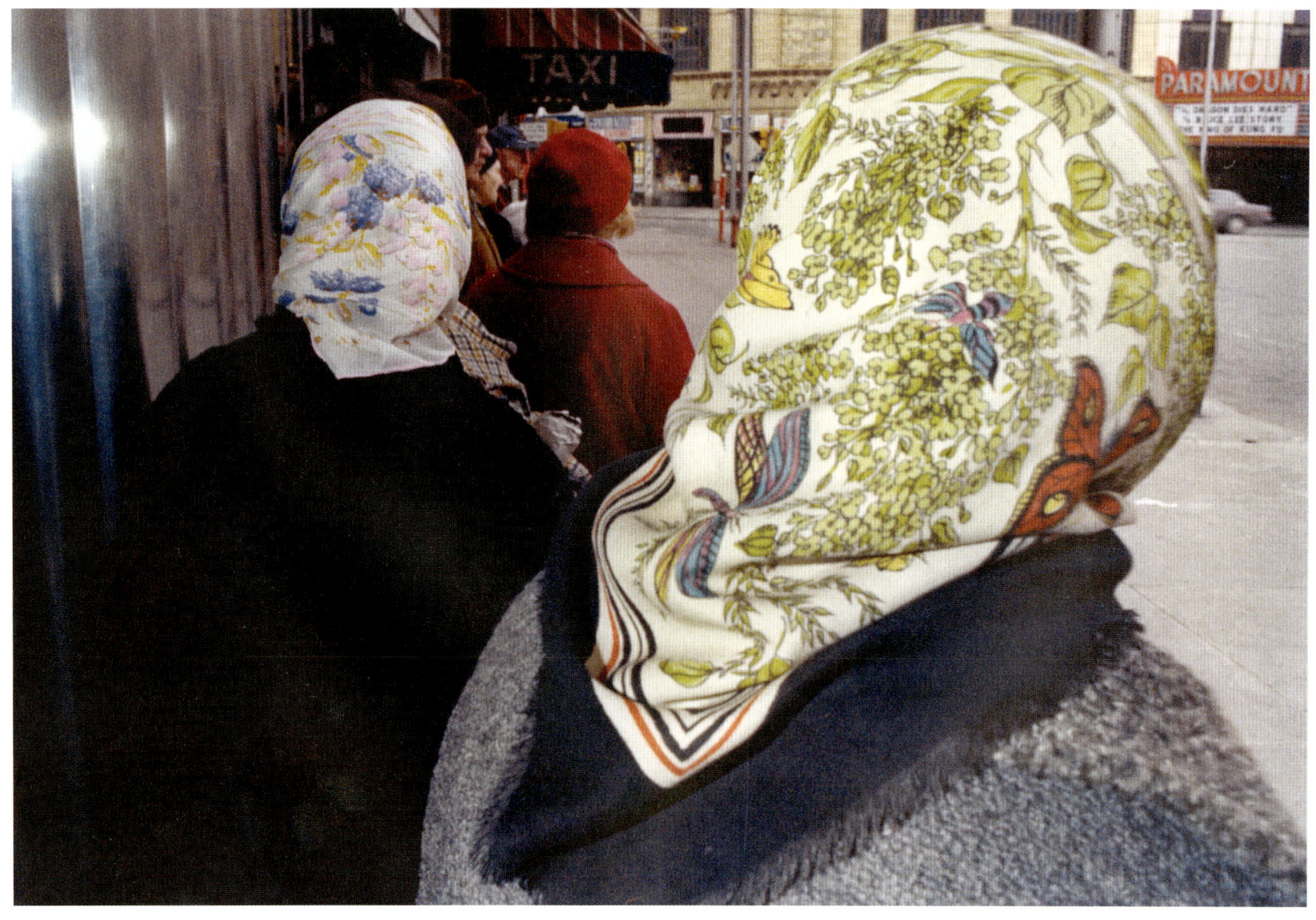
TAXI
PARAMOUNT

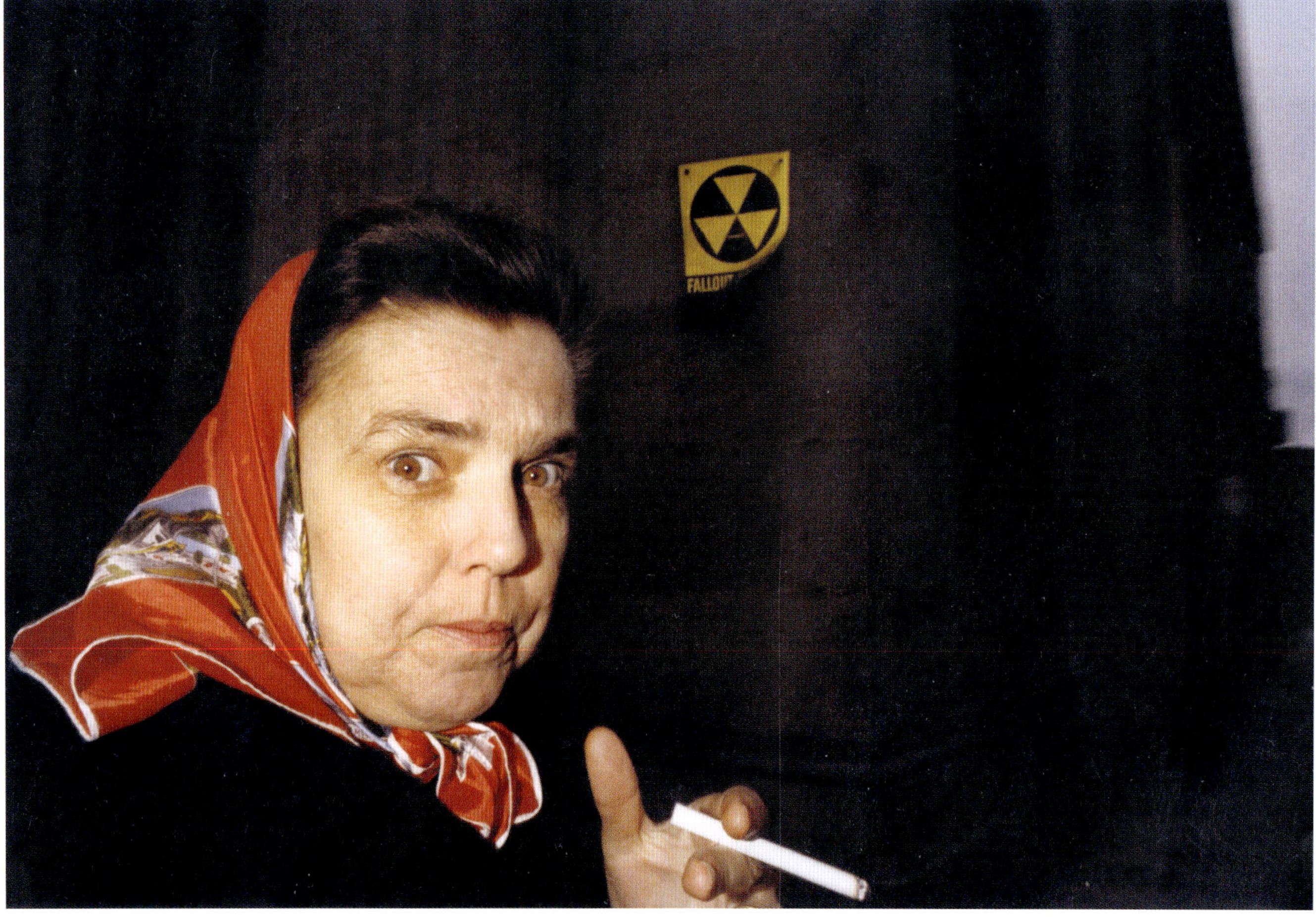

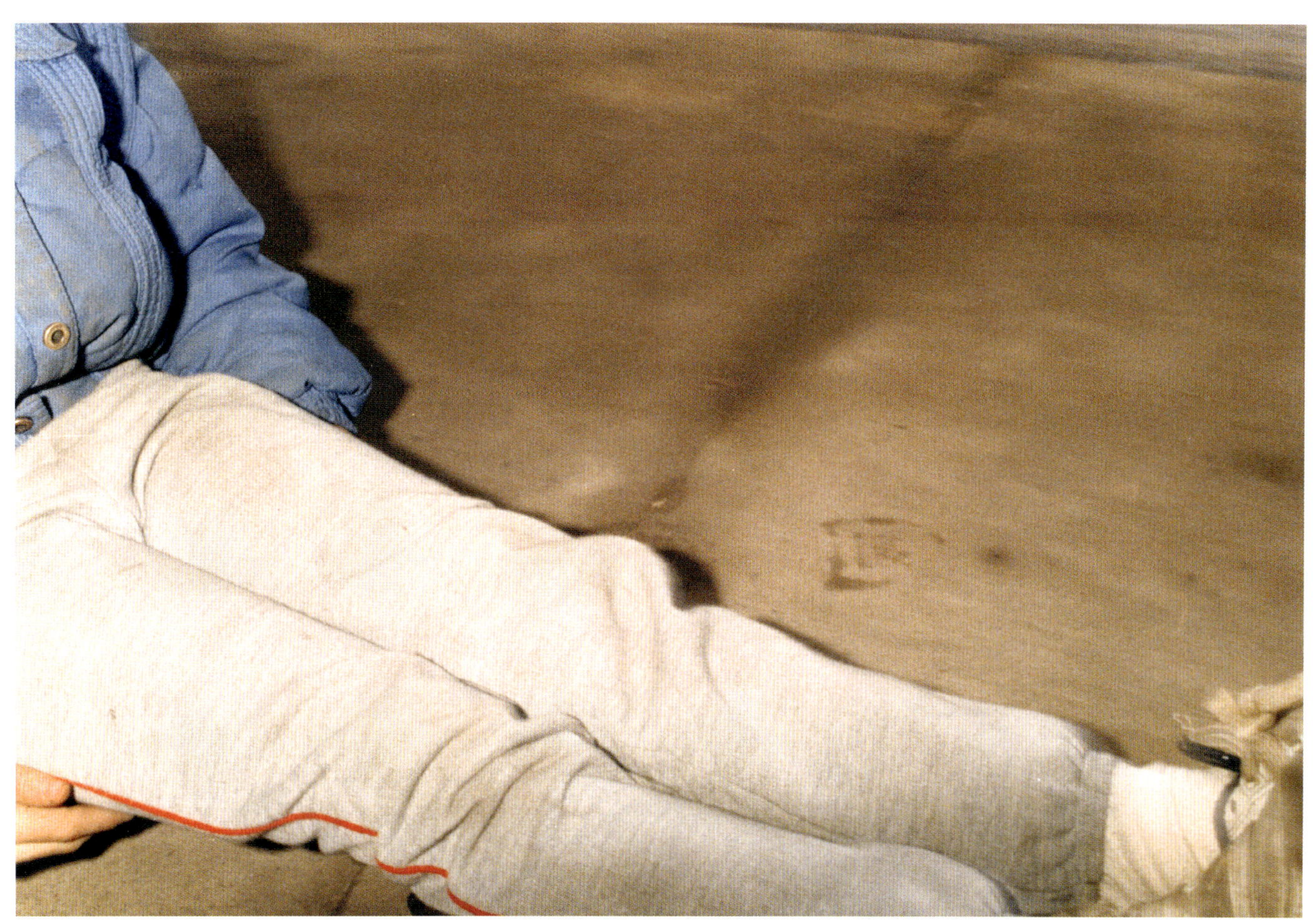

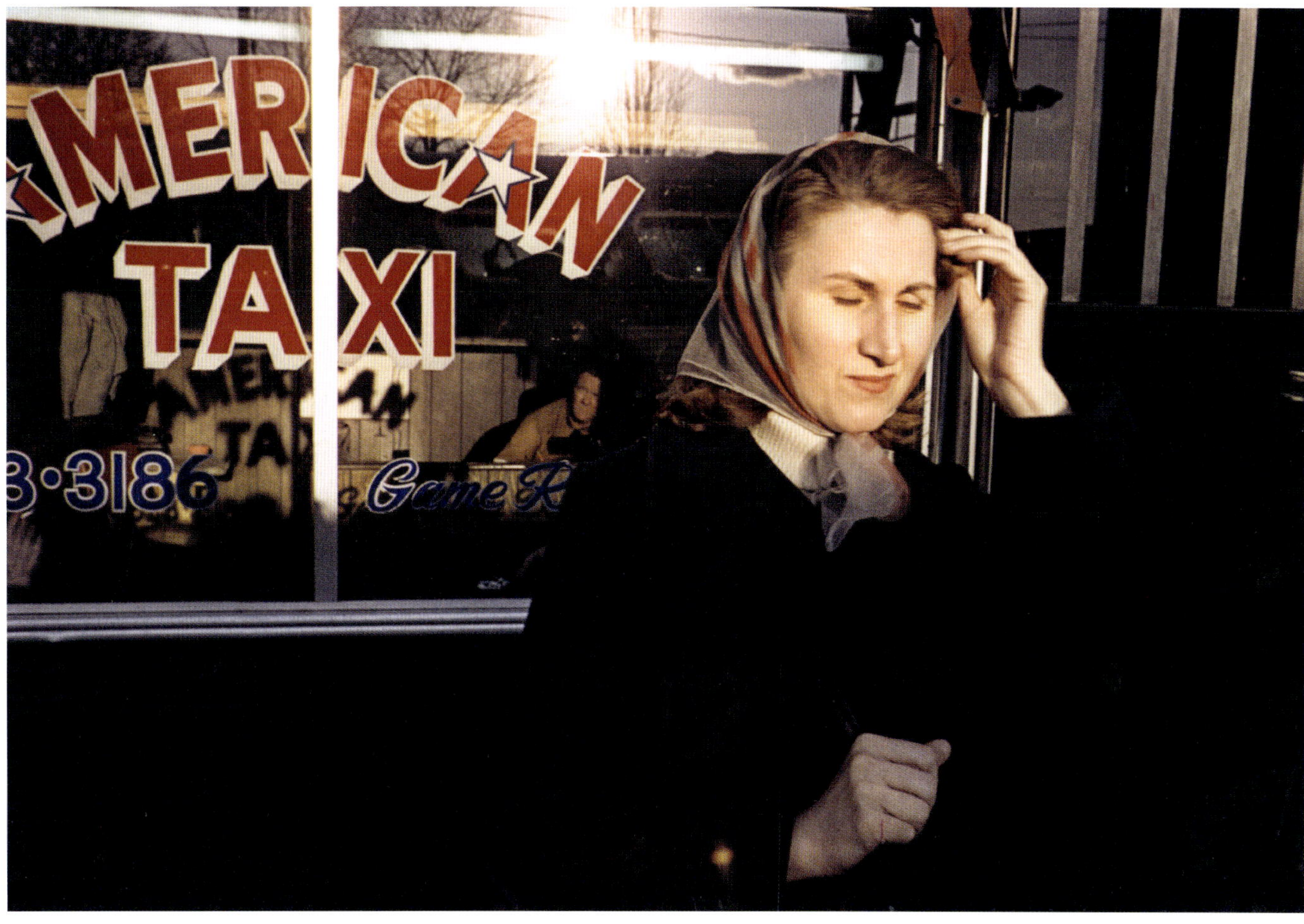
MERICAN
TAXI
3·3186
Game

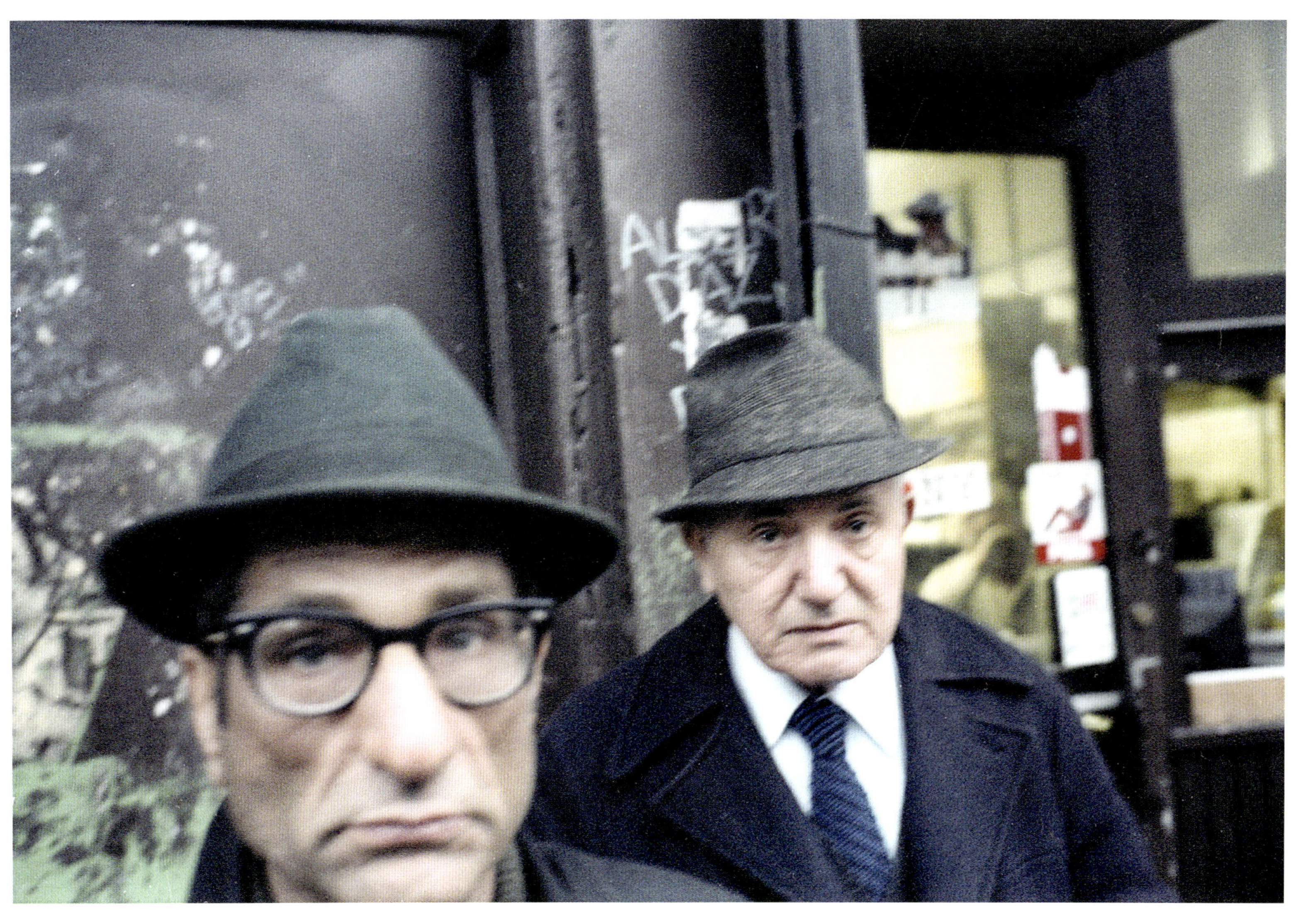

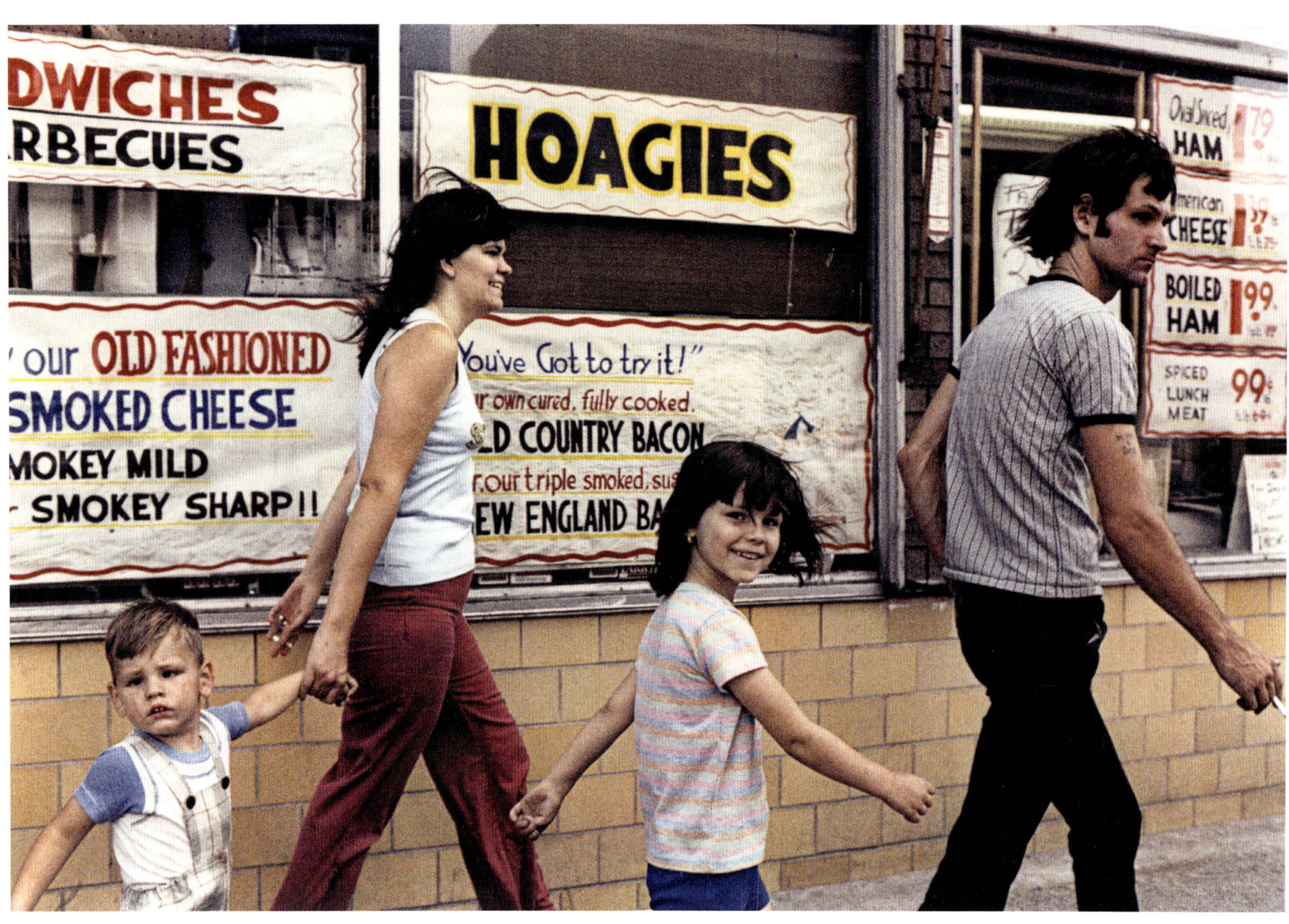
DWICHES
RBECUES
HOAGIES
our OLD FASHIONED
SMOKED CHEESE
MOKEY MILD
SMOKEY SHARP!!
"You've Got to try it!"
r own cured, fully cooked.
LD COUNTRY BACON
r, our triple smoked, su
EW ENGLAND BA
Oval Sliced HAM
merican CHEESE
BOILED HAM
SPICED LUNCH MEAT 99¢

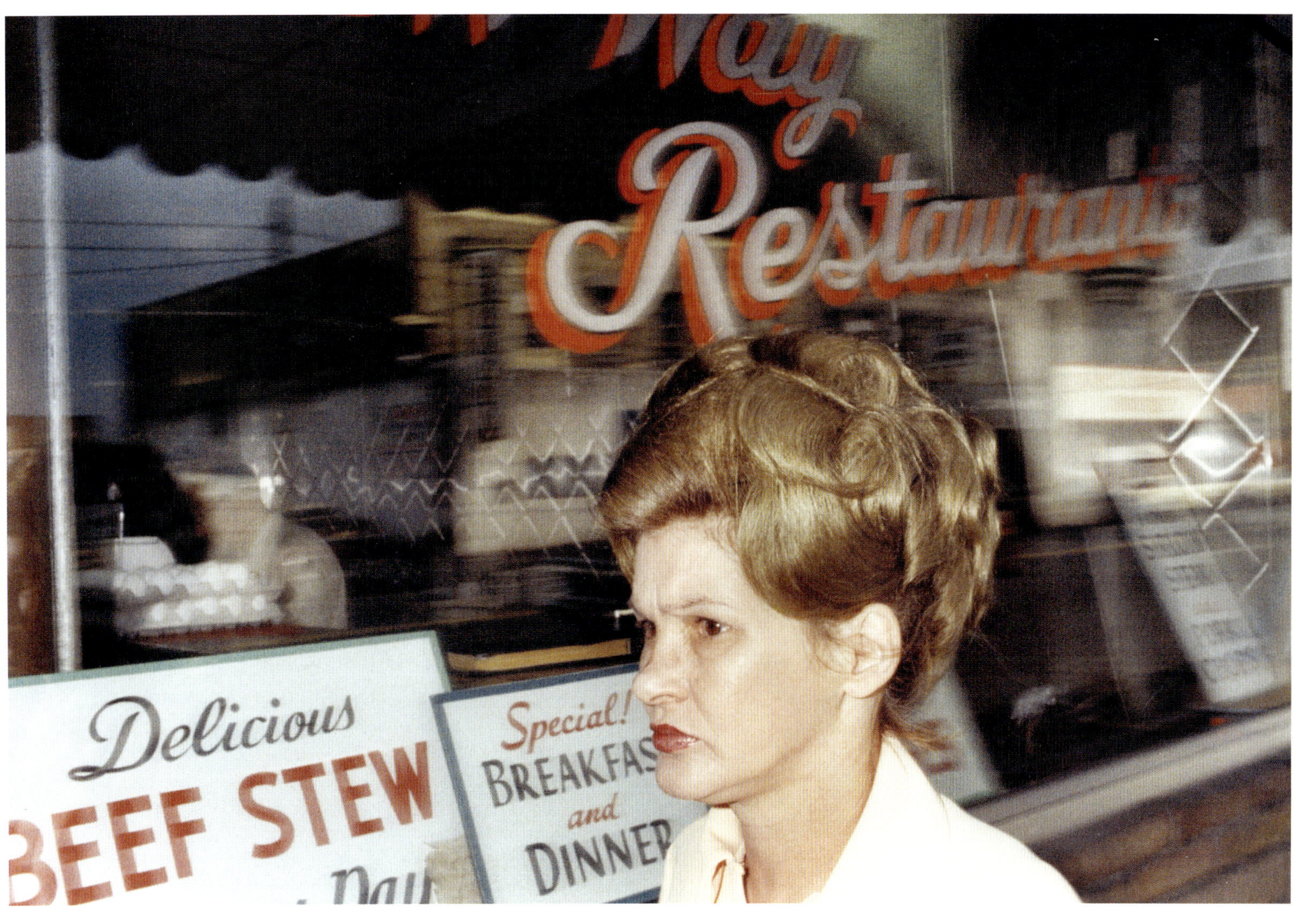
Way
Restaurant
Delicious
BEEF STEW
Special!
BREAKFAS
and
DINNER

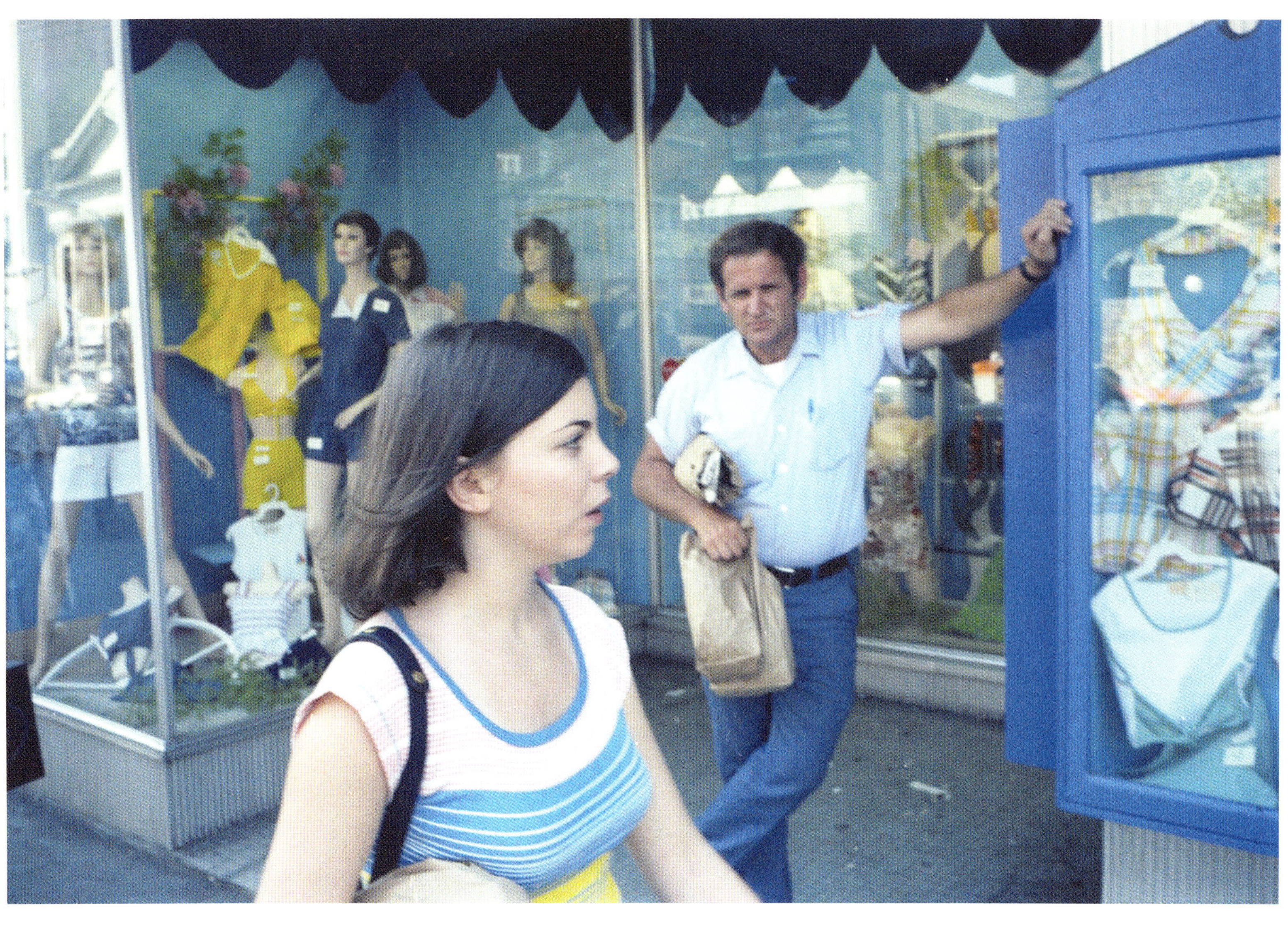

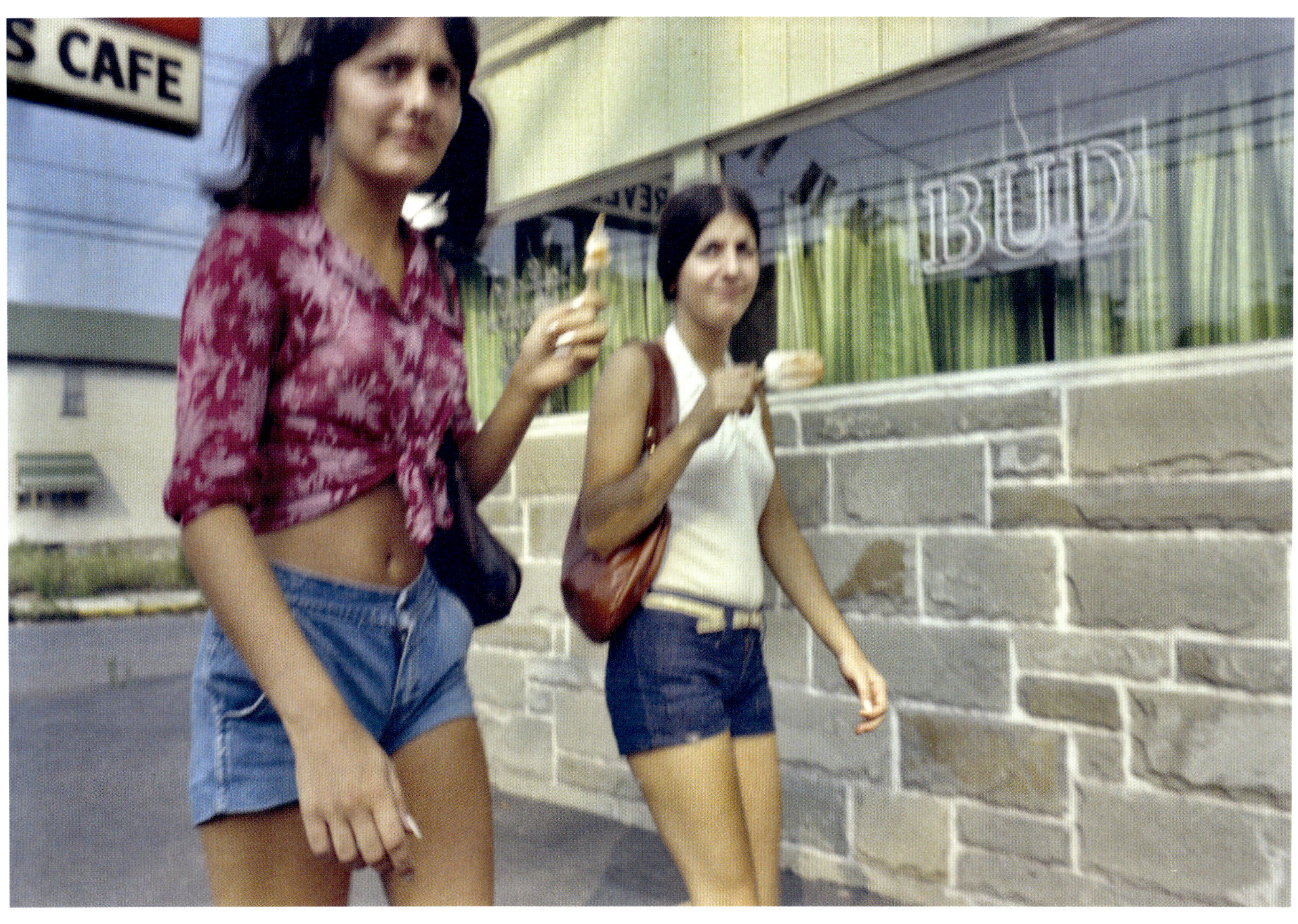
S CAFE
BUD

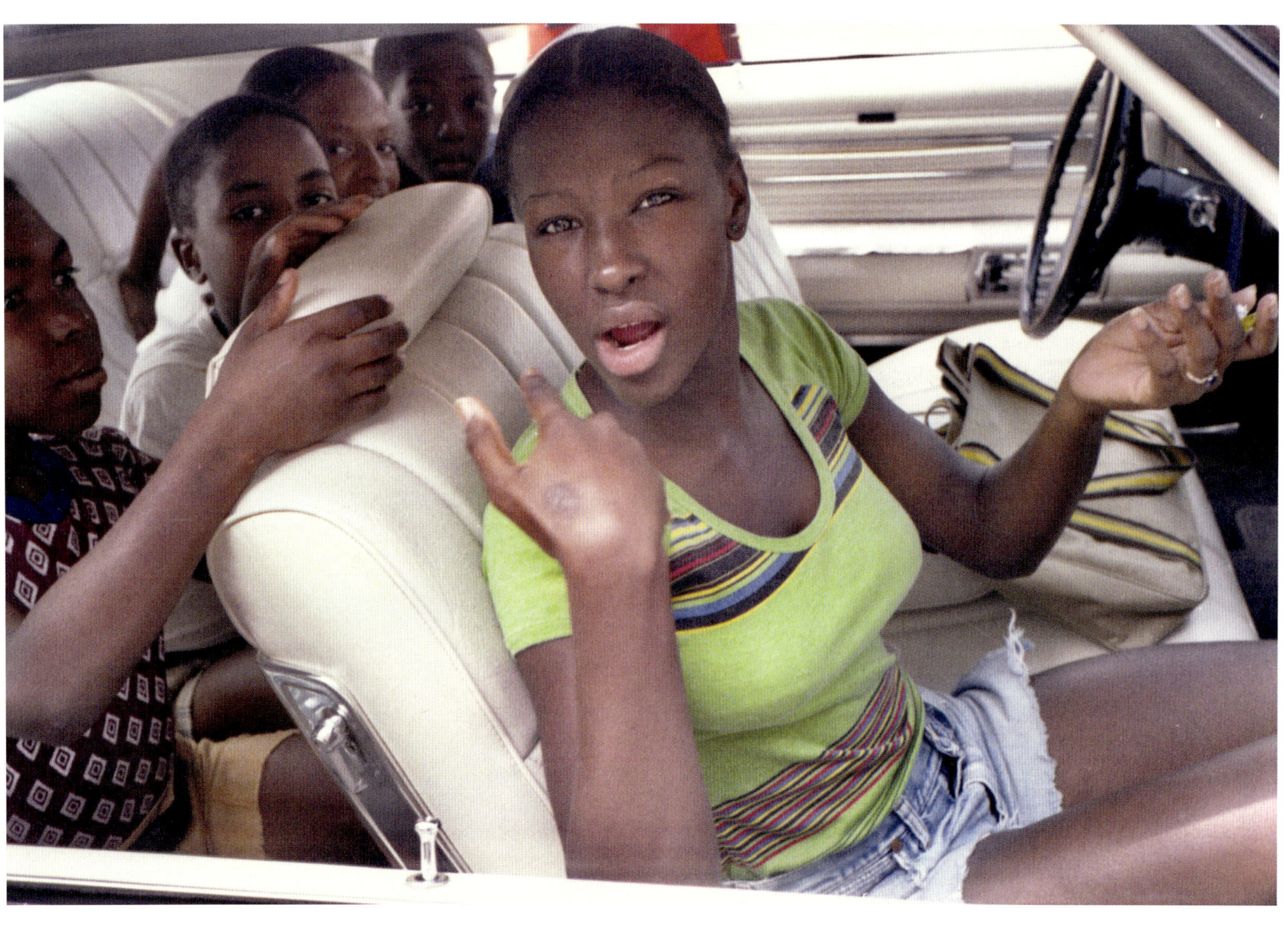

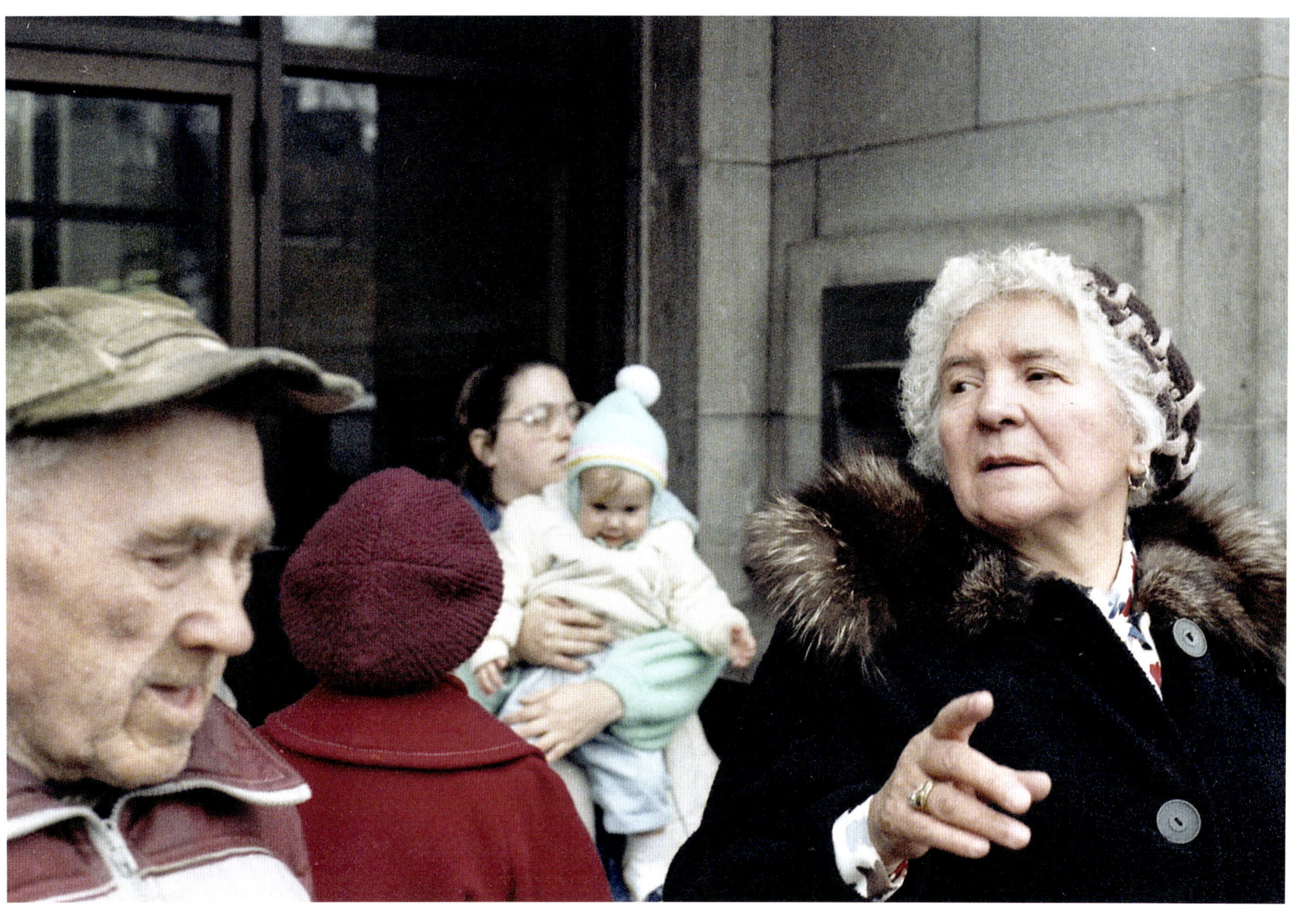

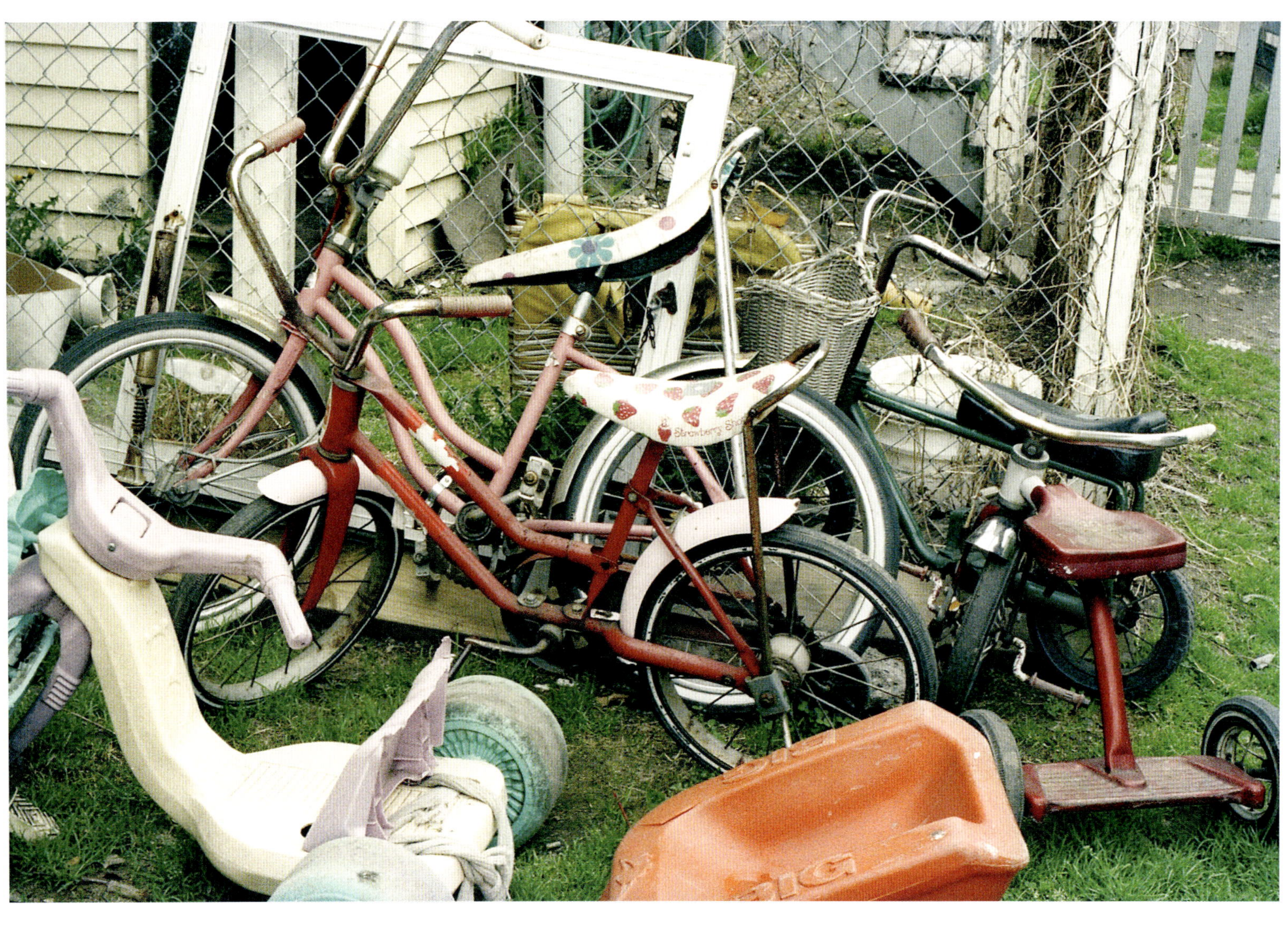
Strawberry

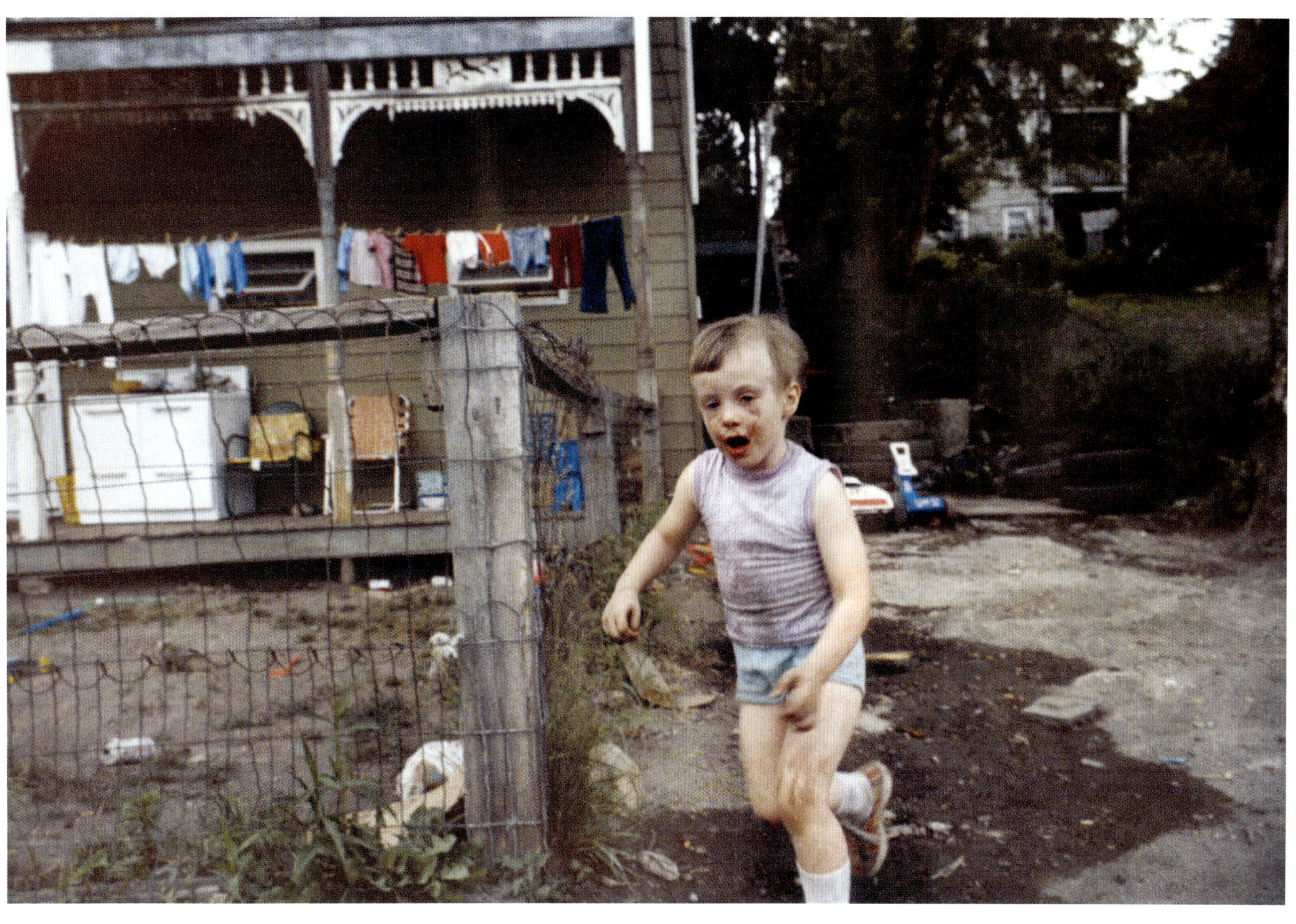

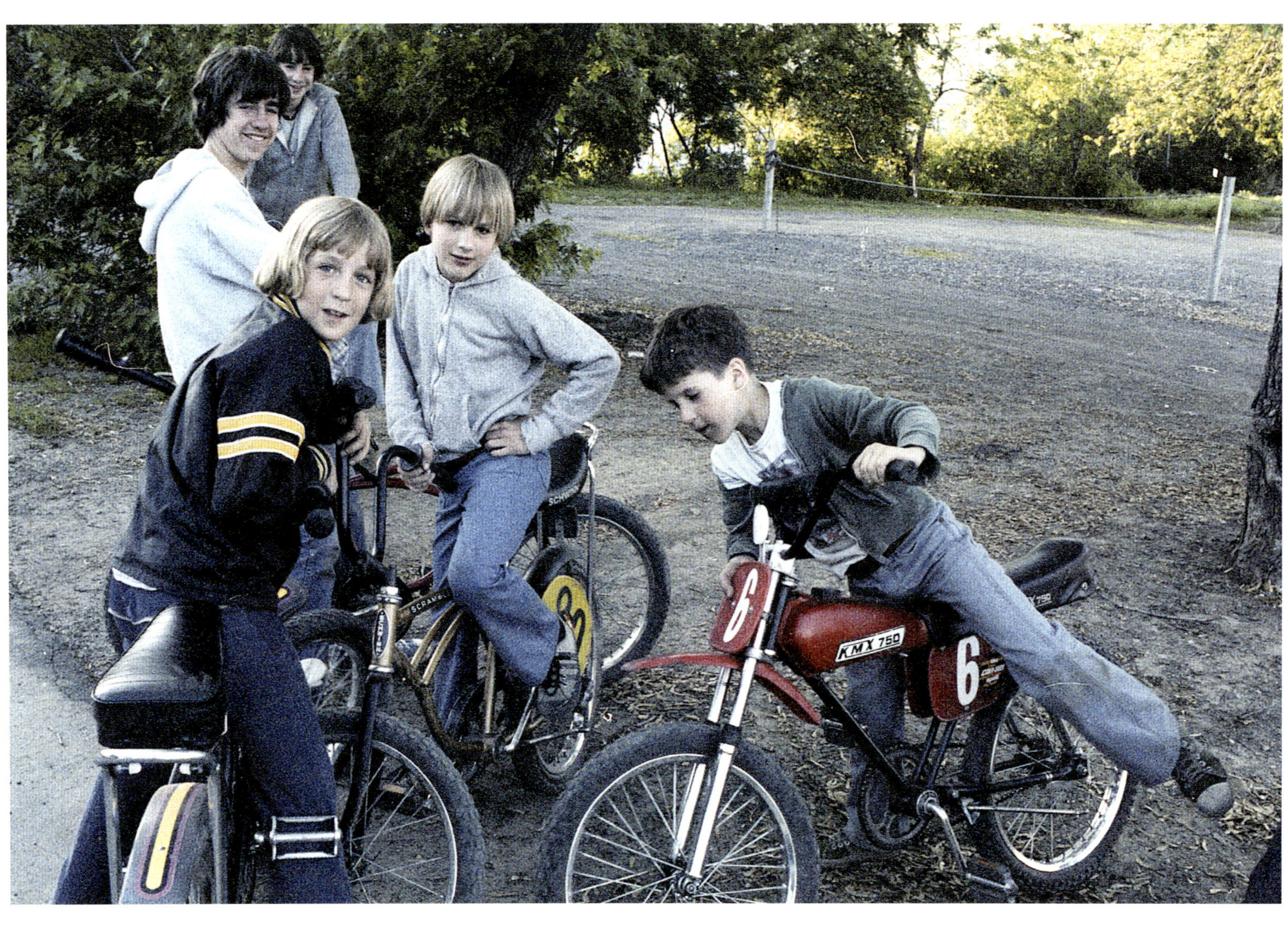
6
KMX 750
6

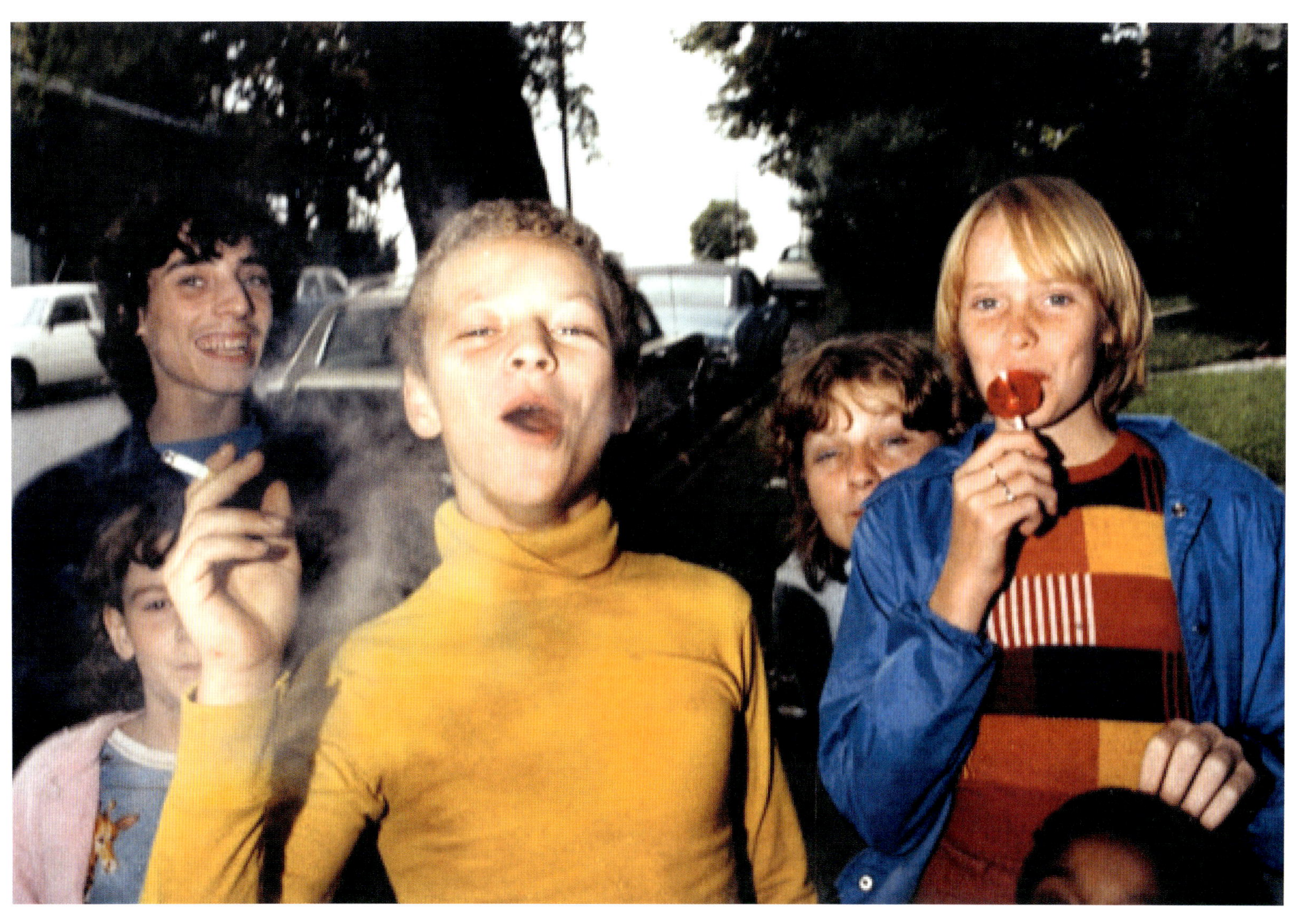

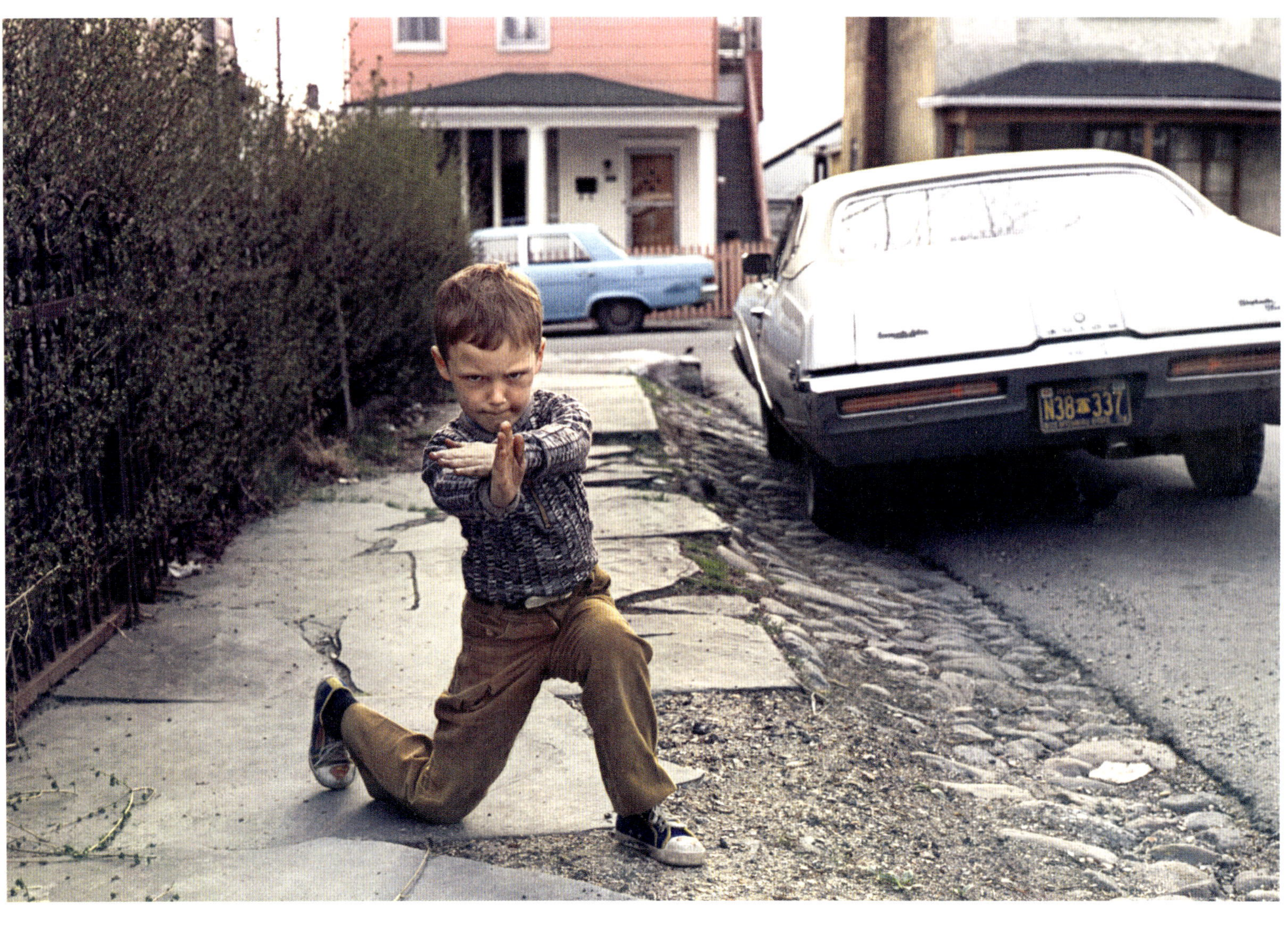
N38 337

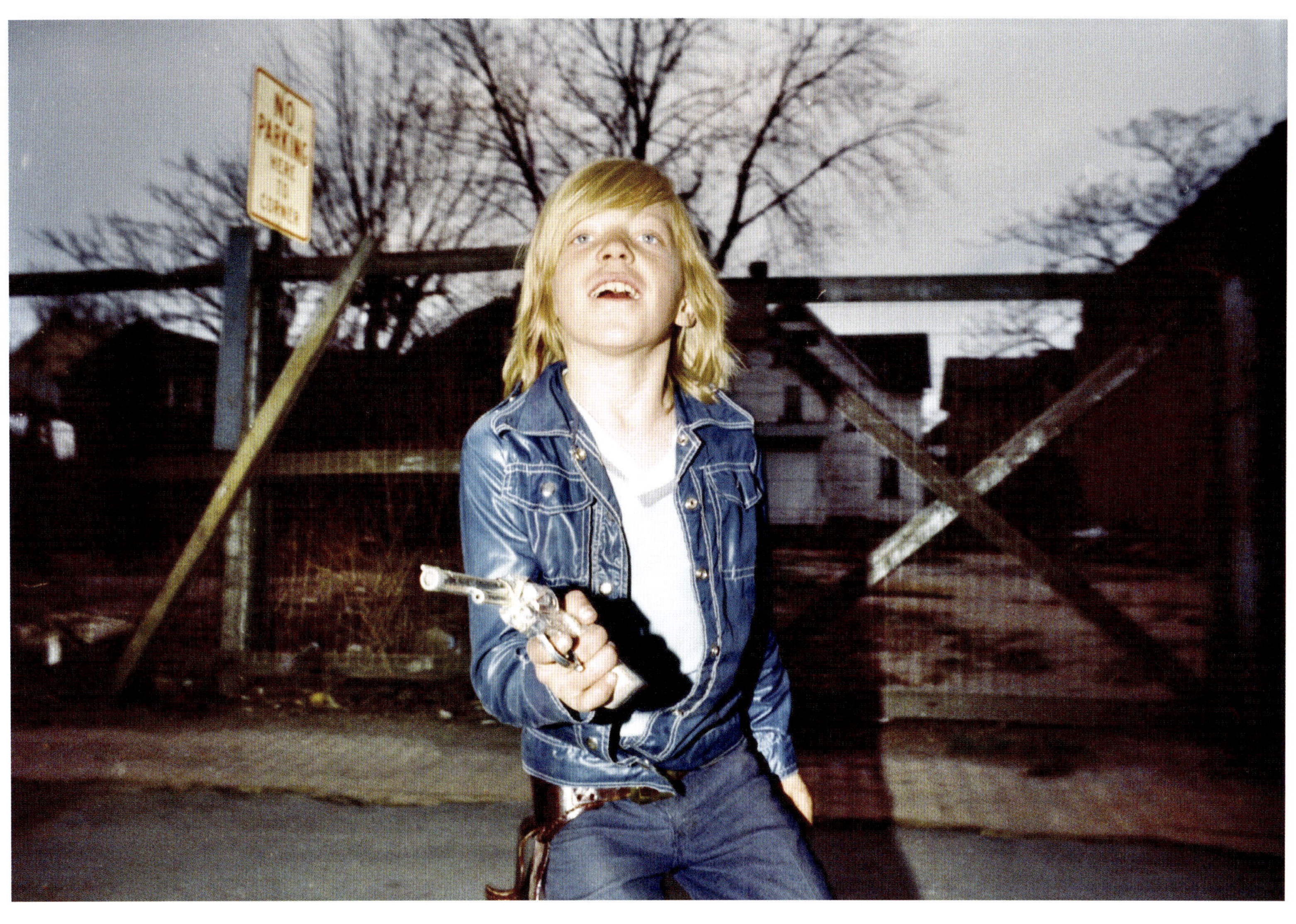
NO
PARKING

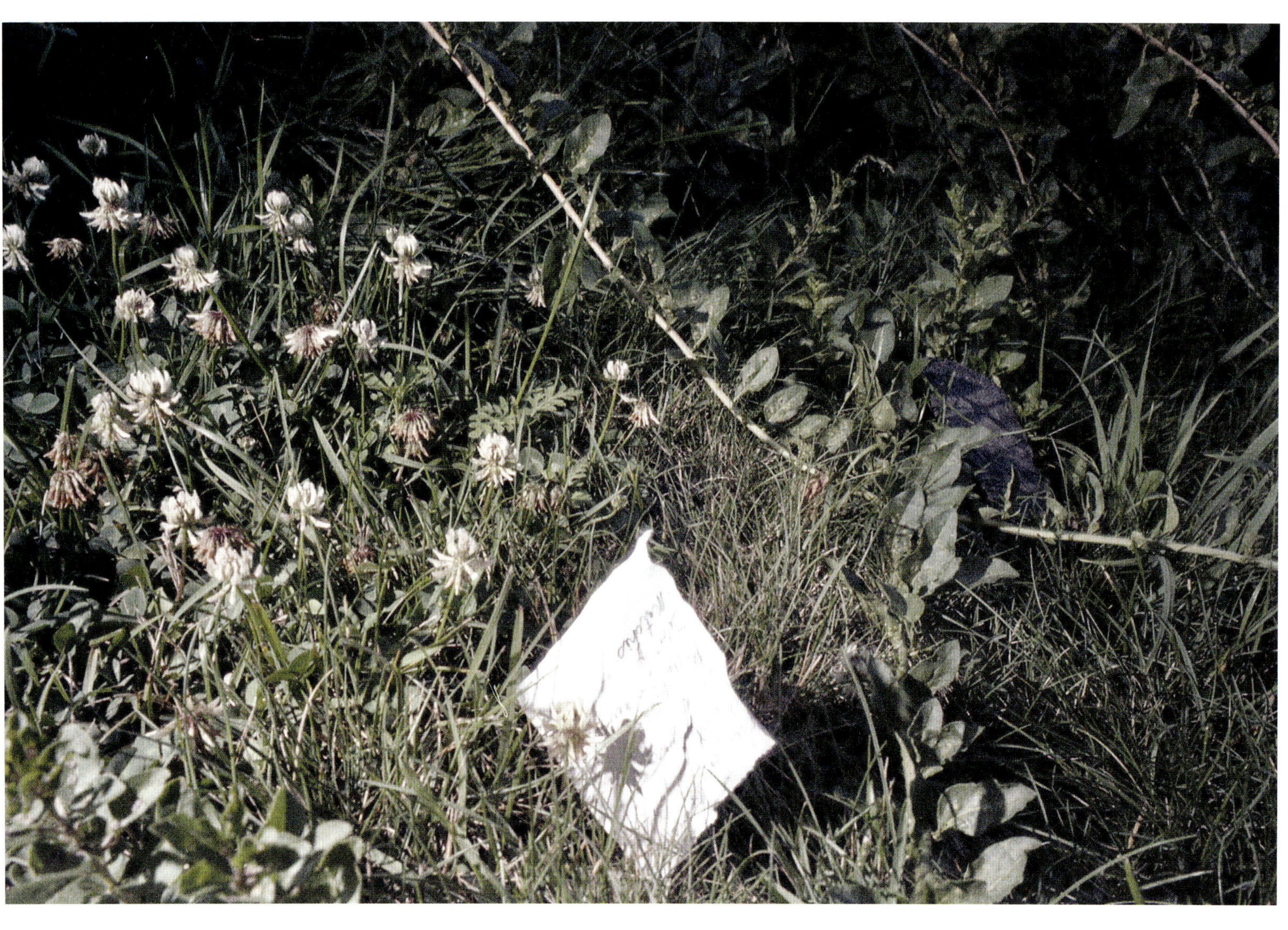

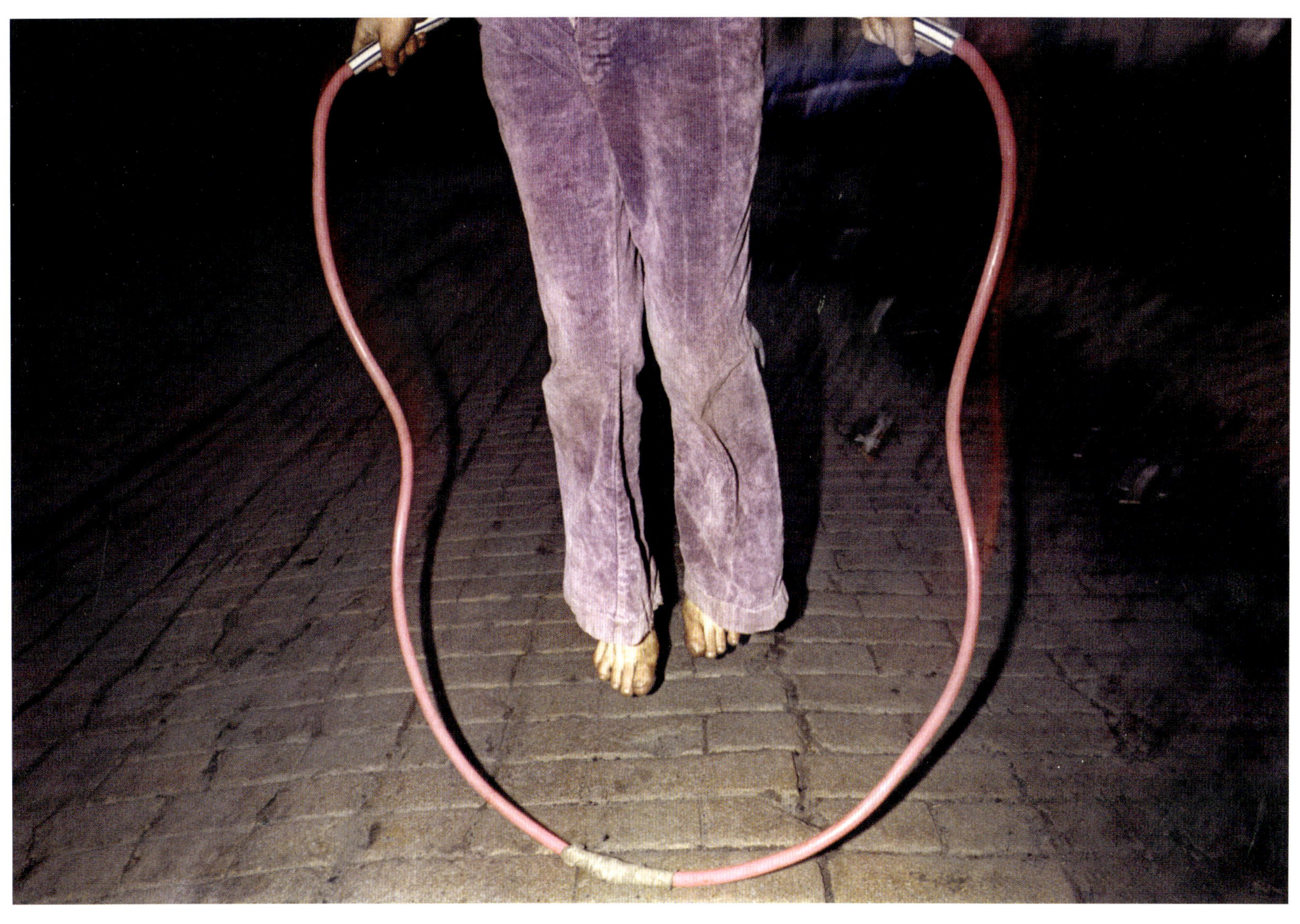

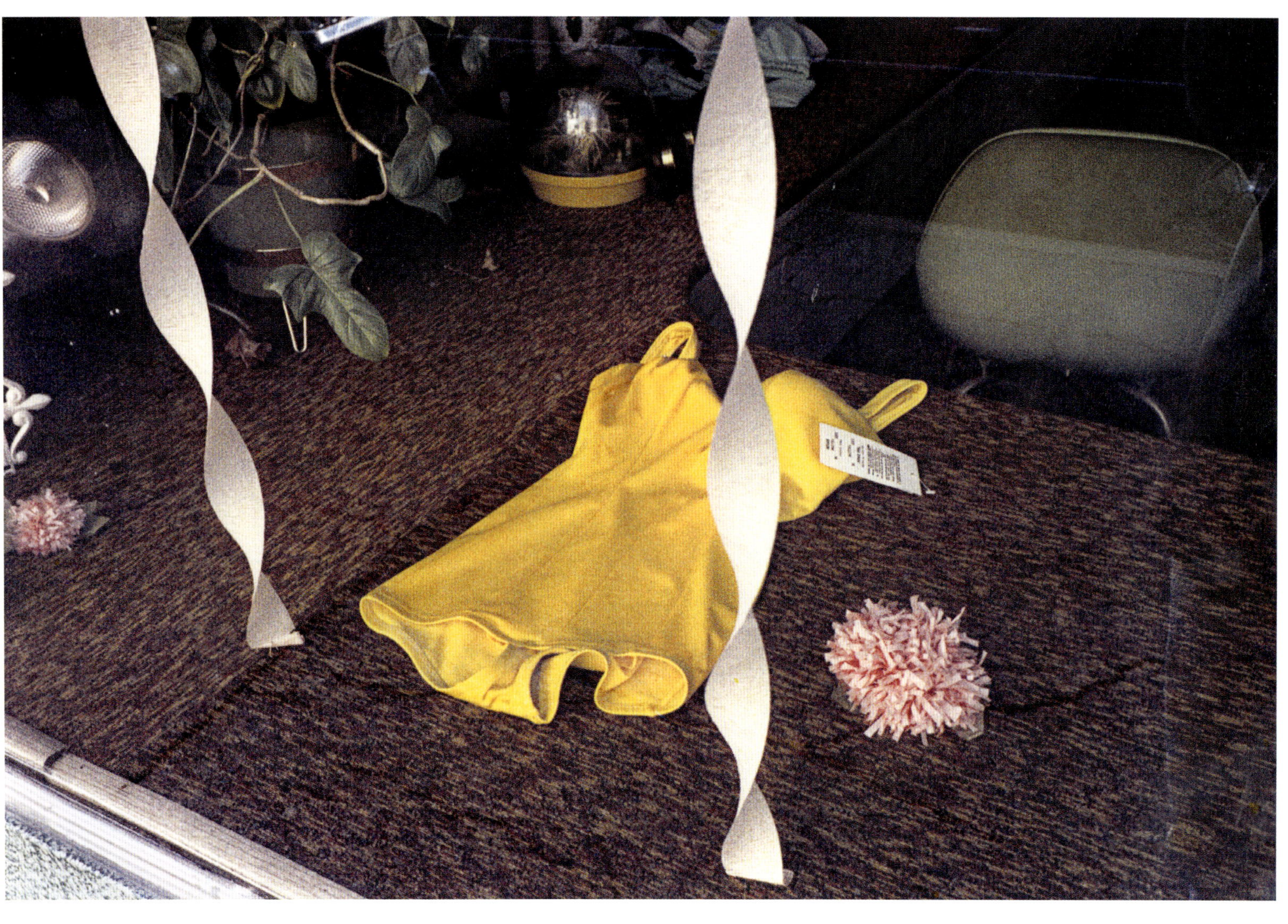

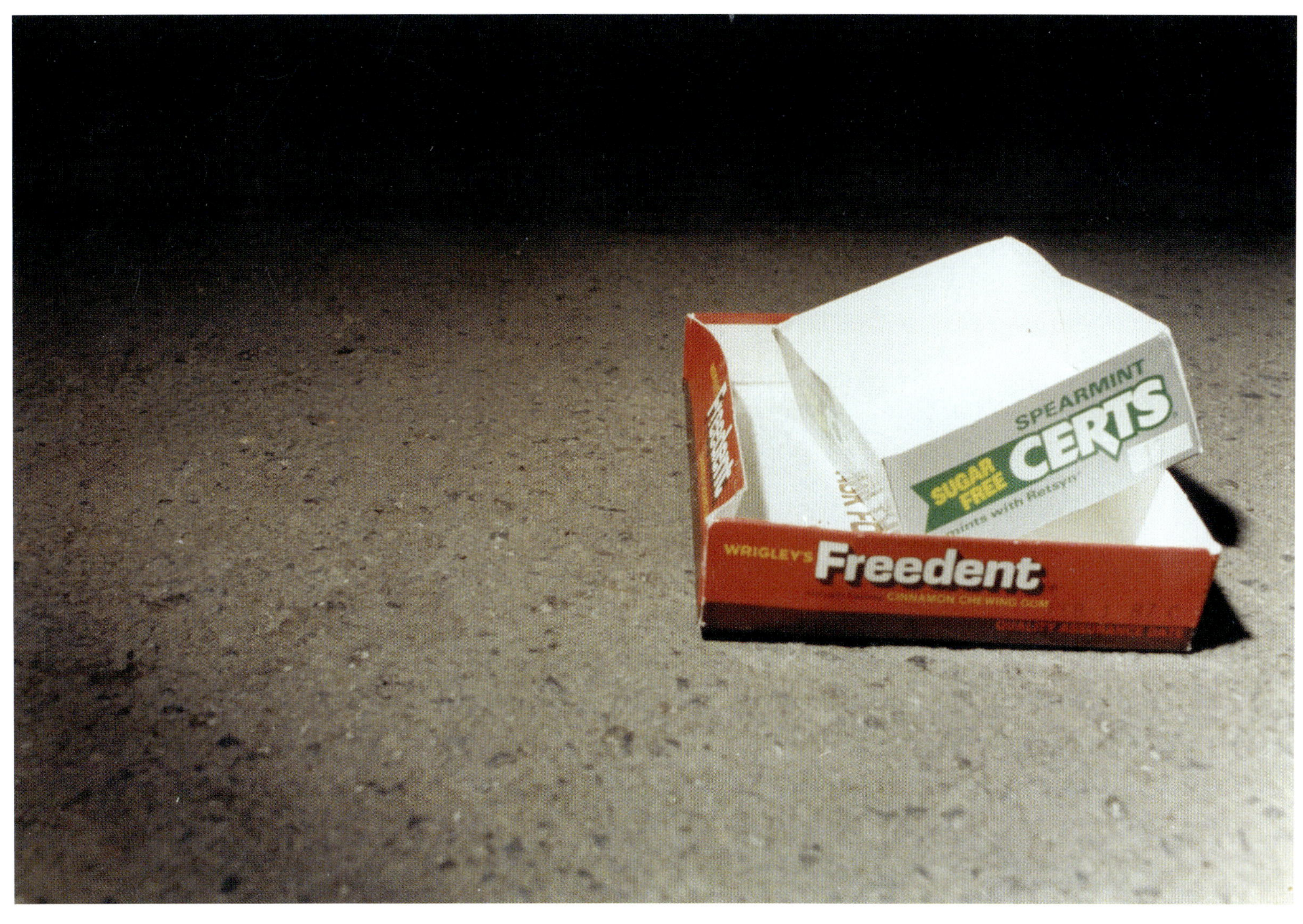
SPEARMINT
SUGAR FREE
CERTS
with Retsyn
WRIGLEY'S
Freedent
CINNAMON CHEWING GUM

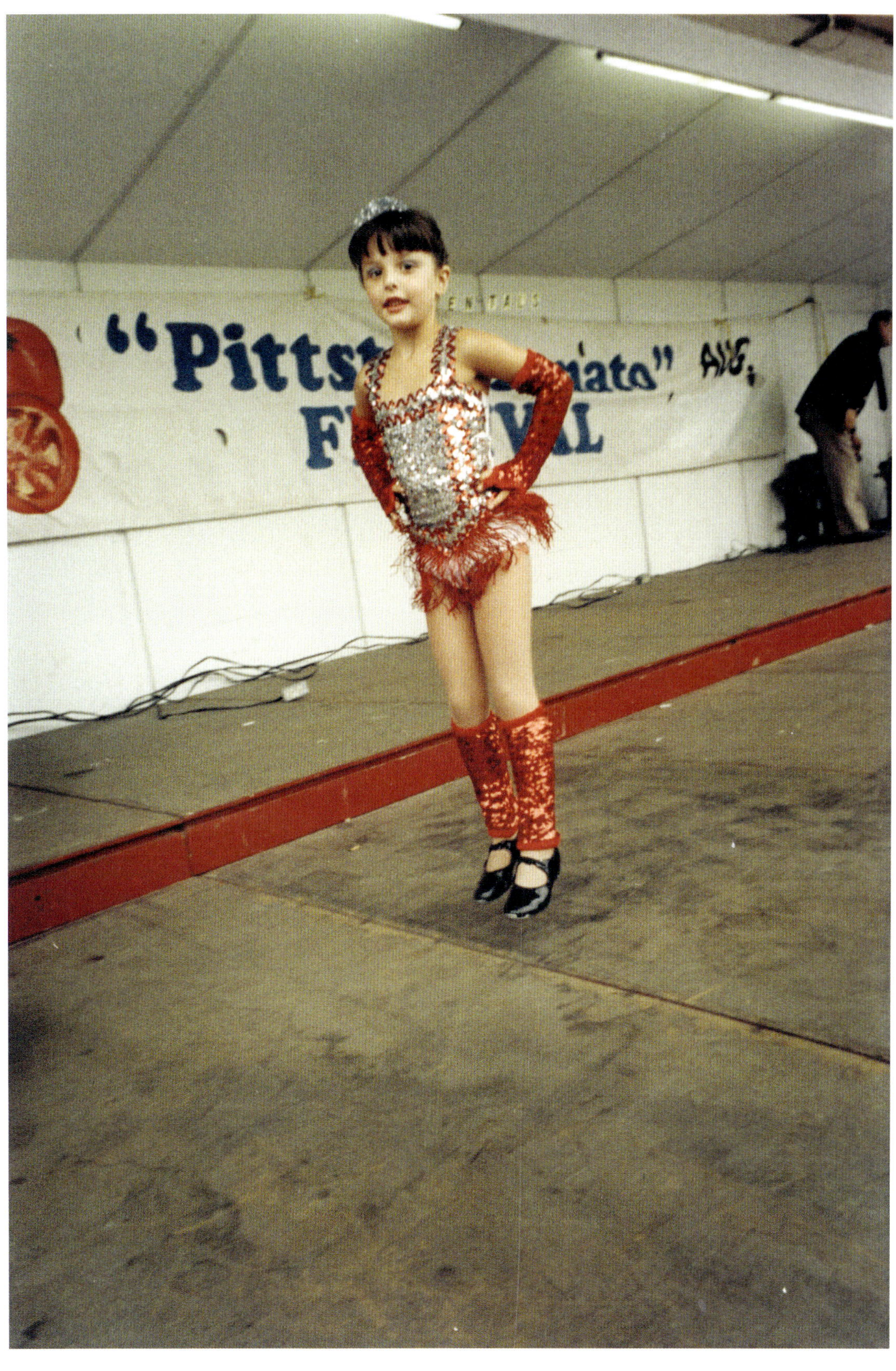
“Pittst
ato” AUG.

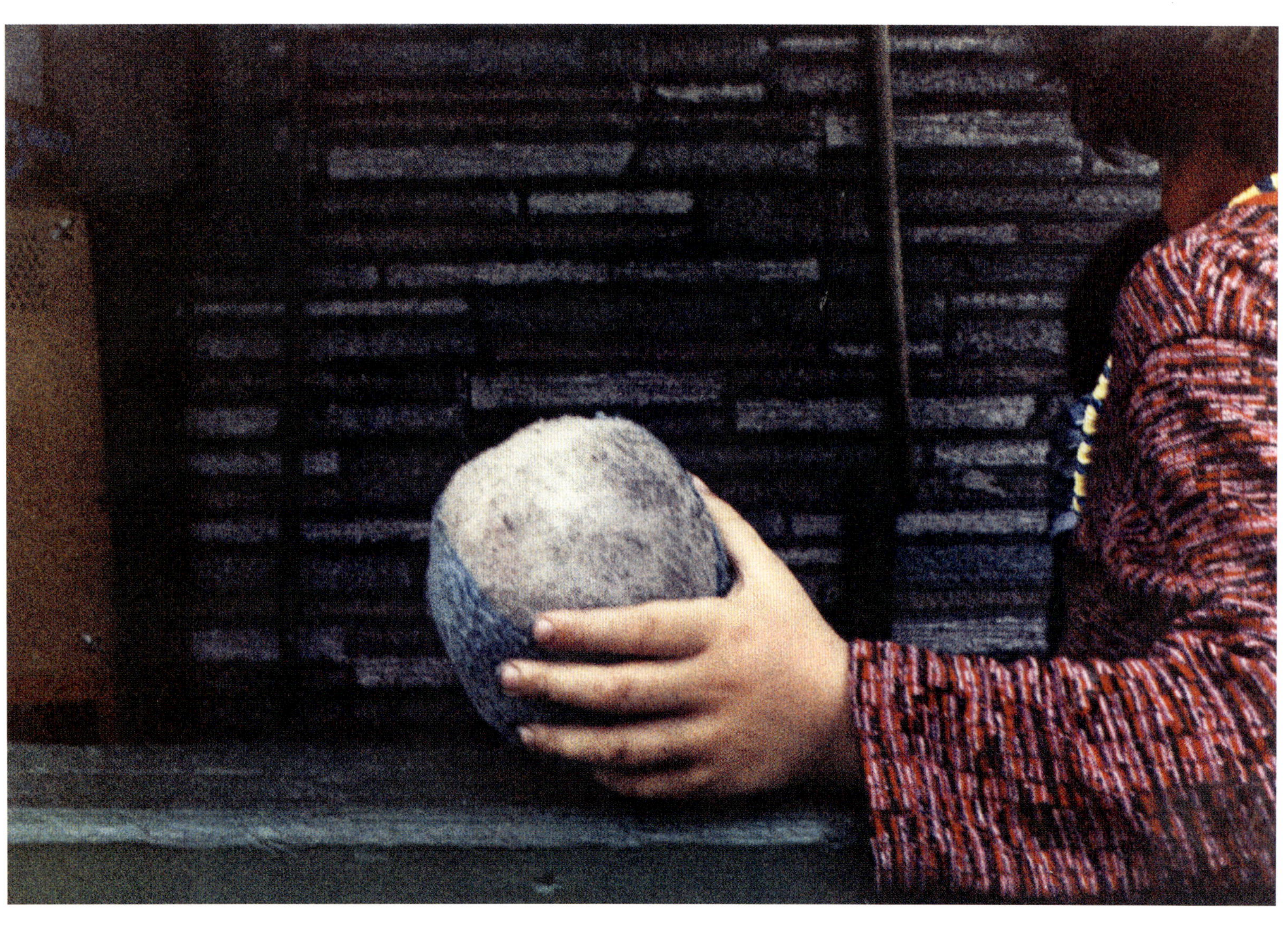

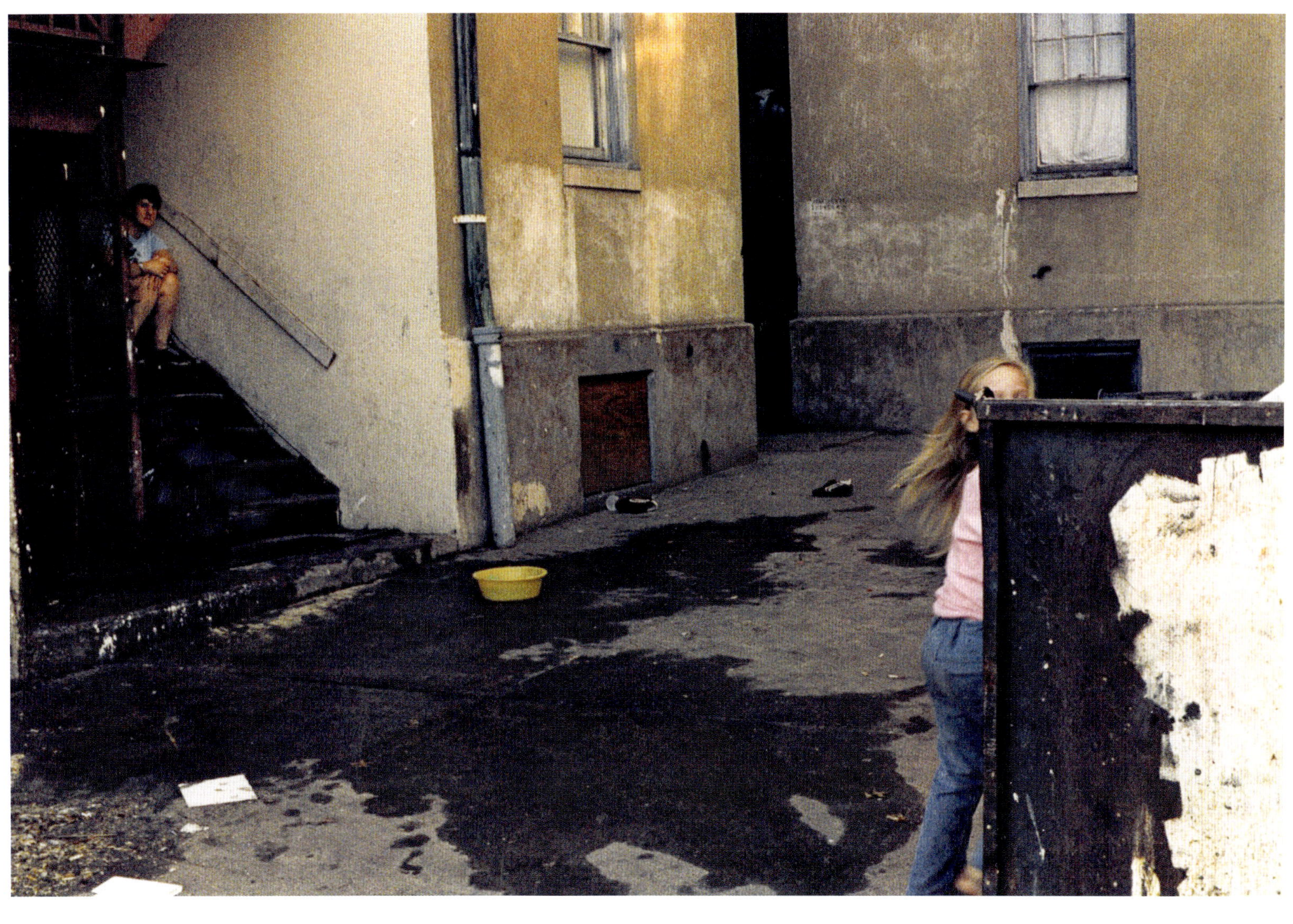

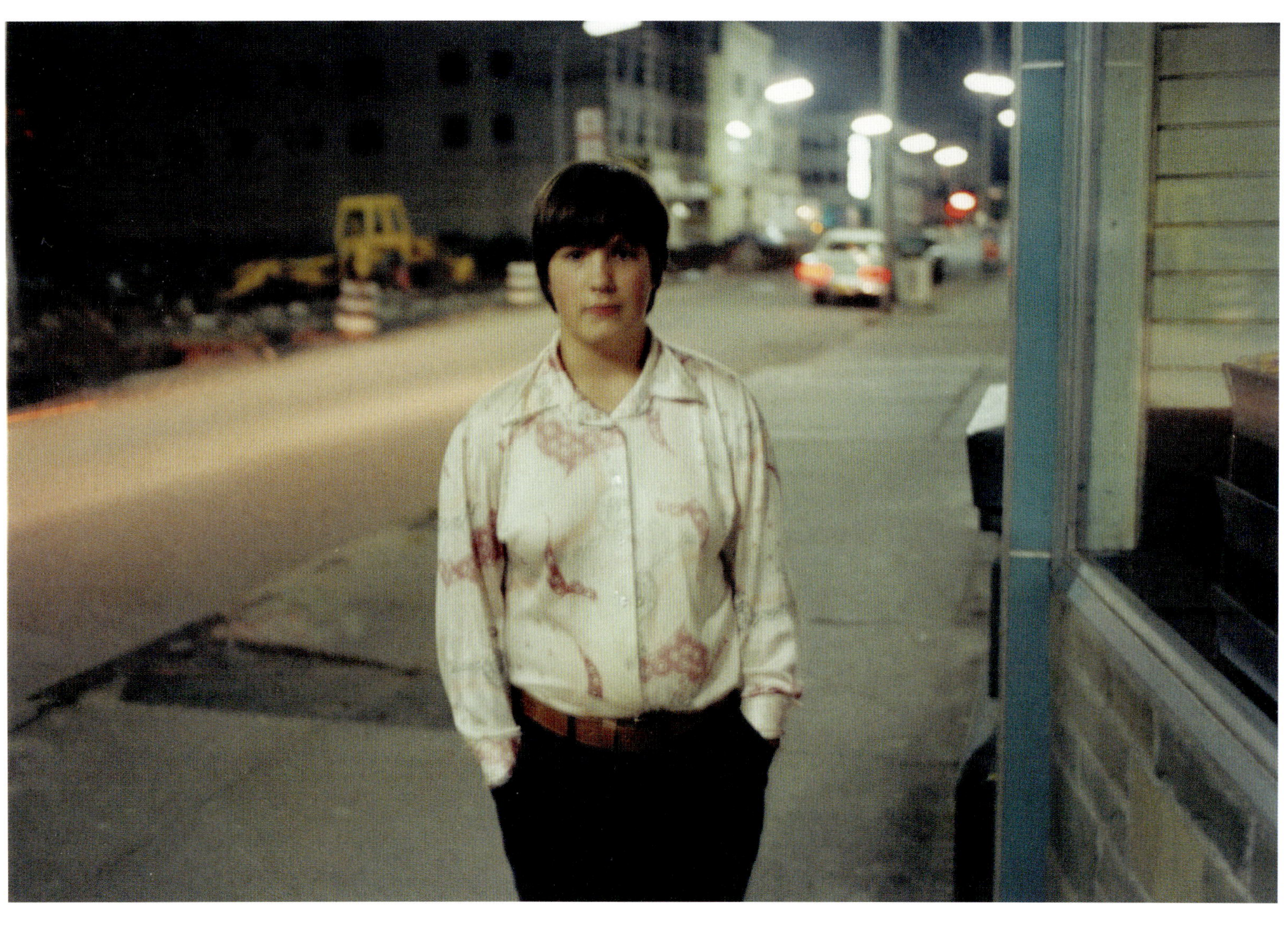

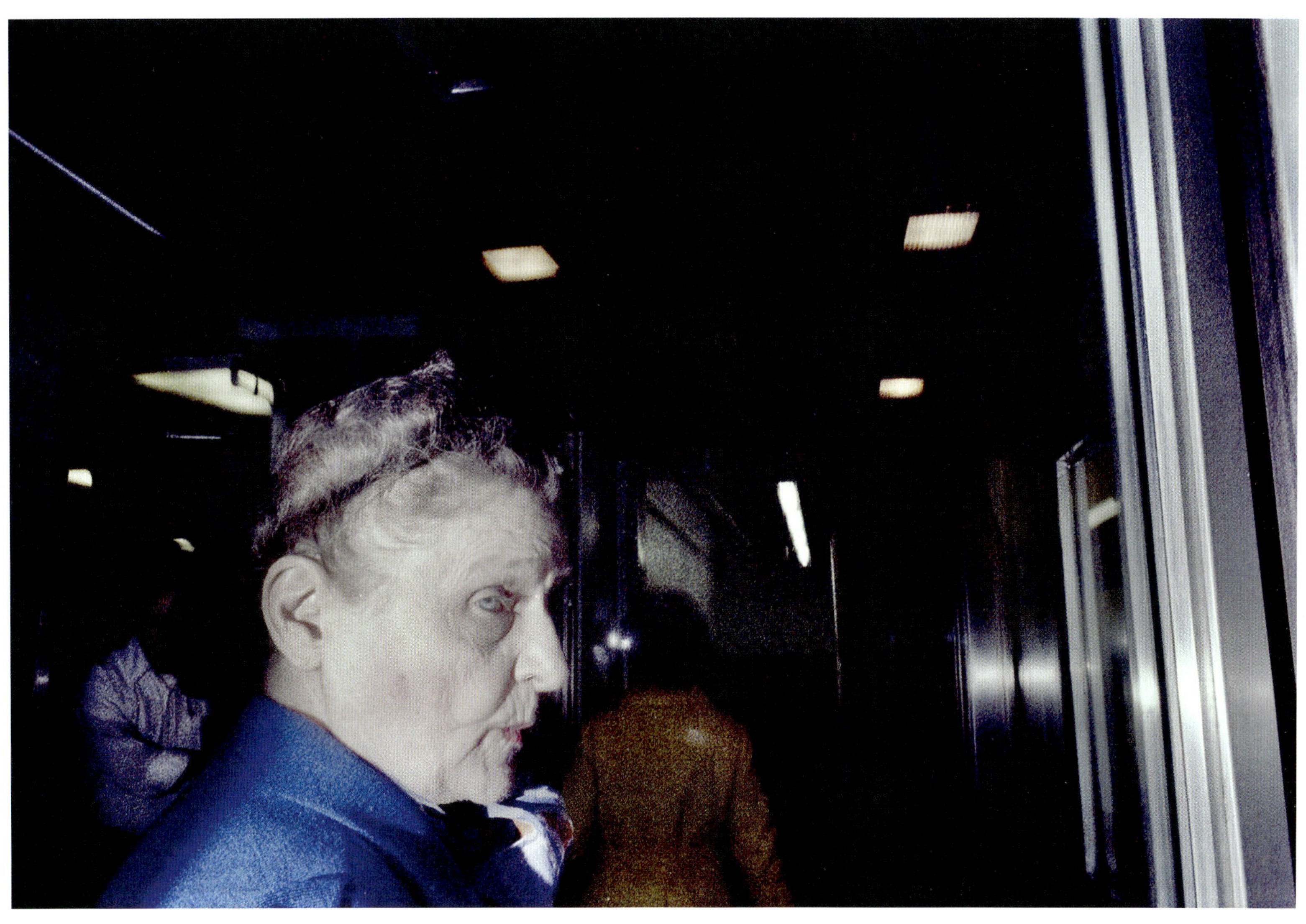

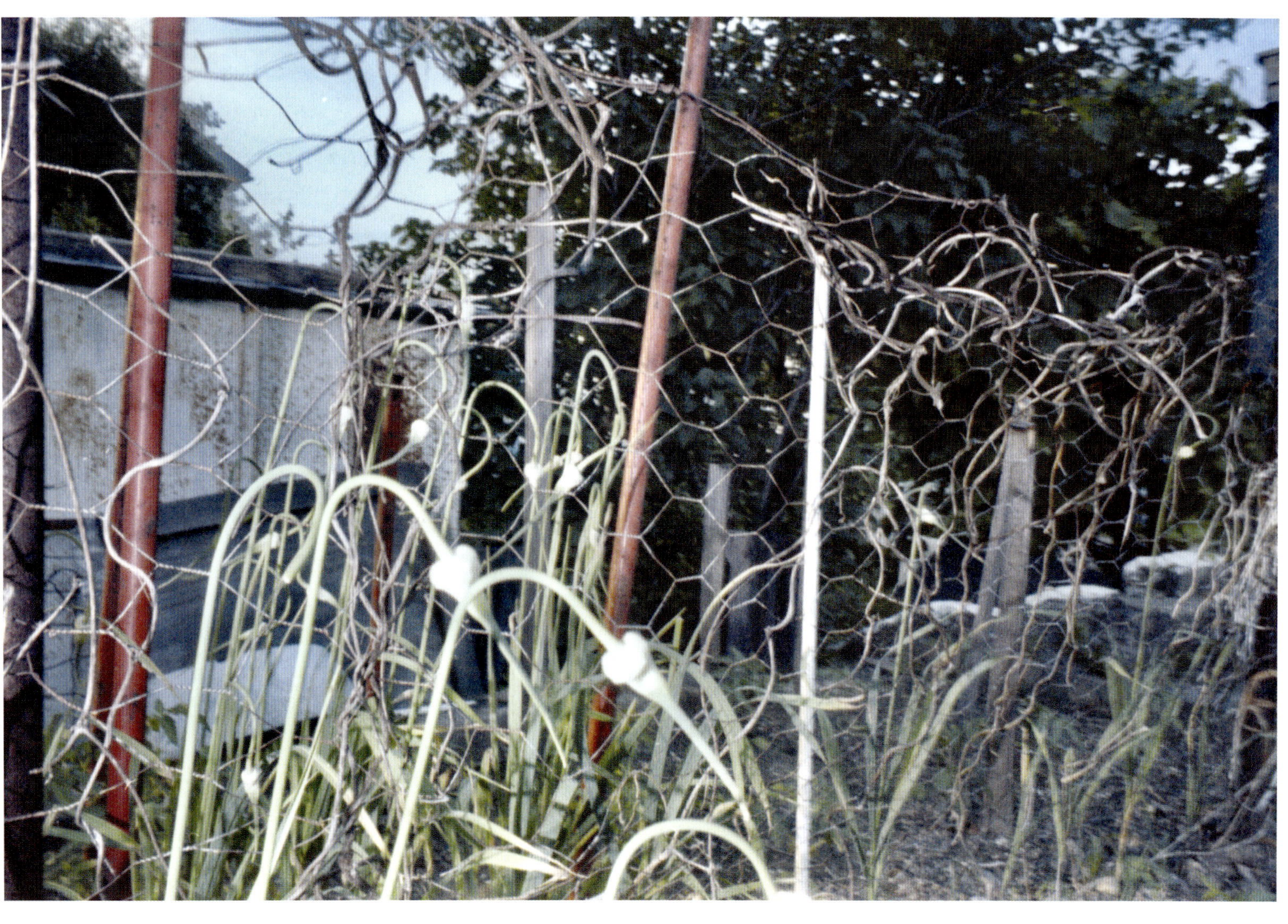

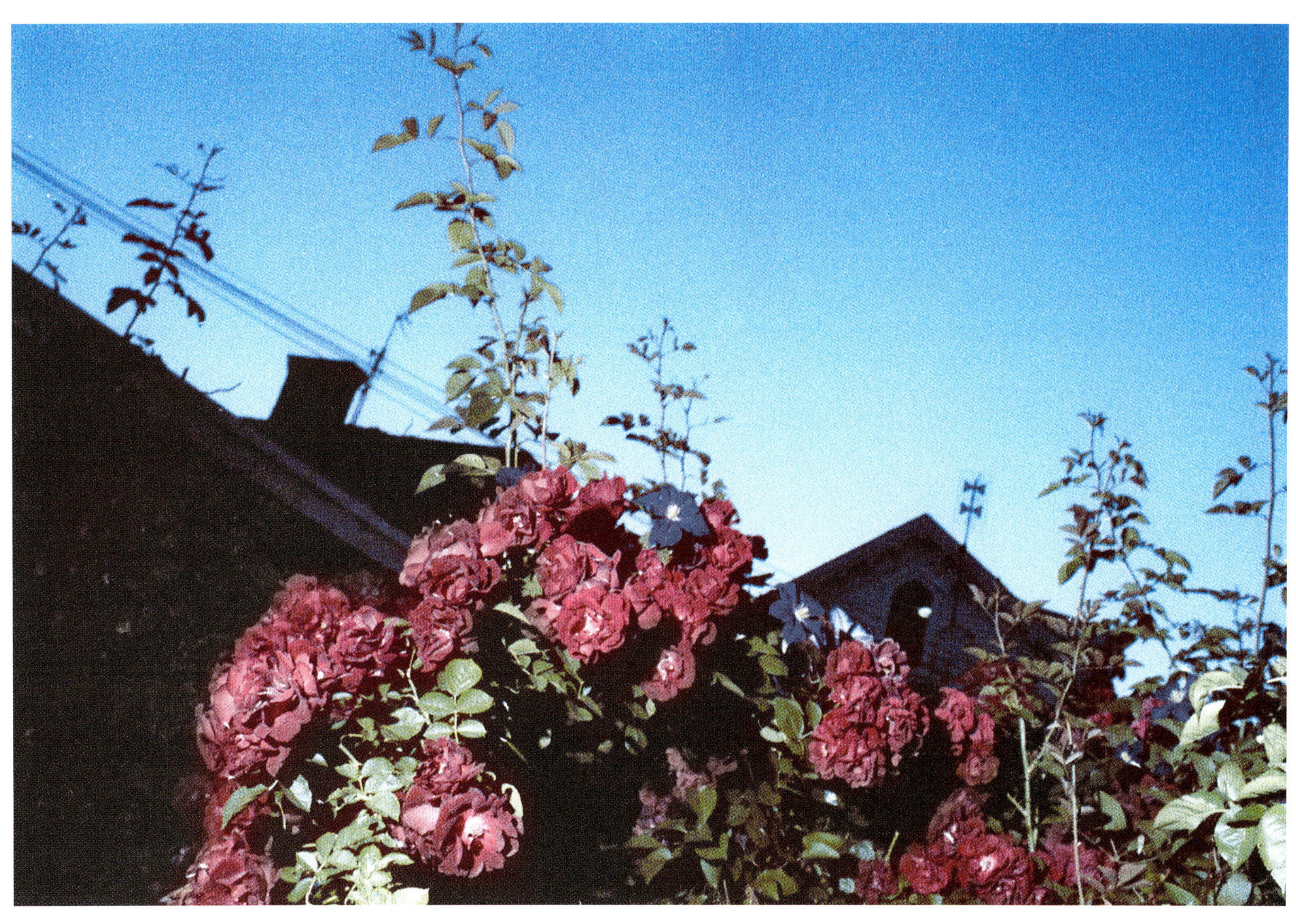

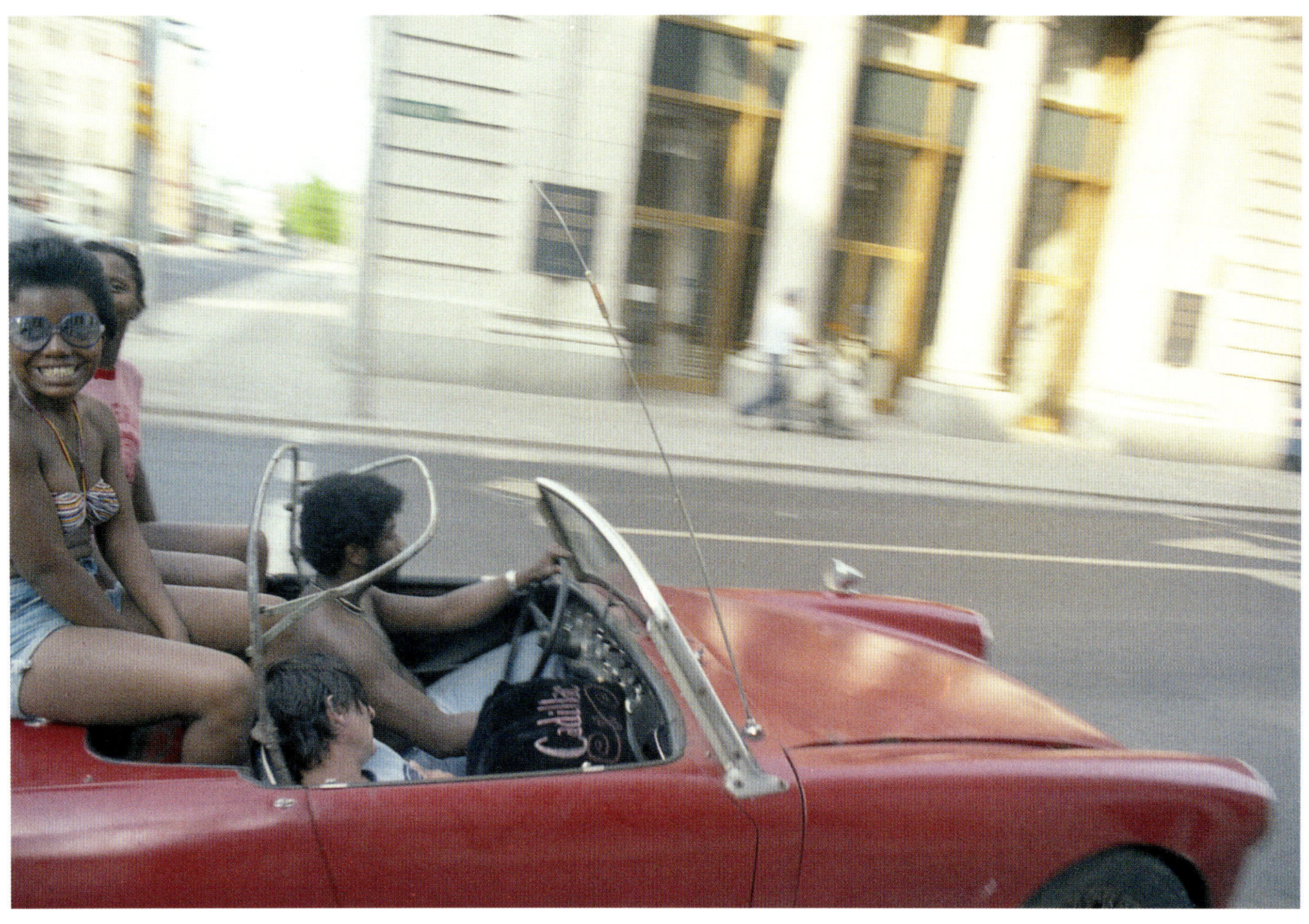

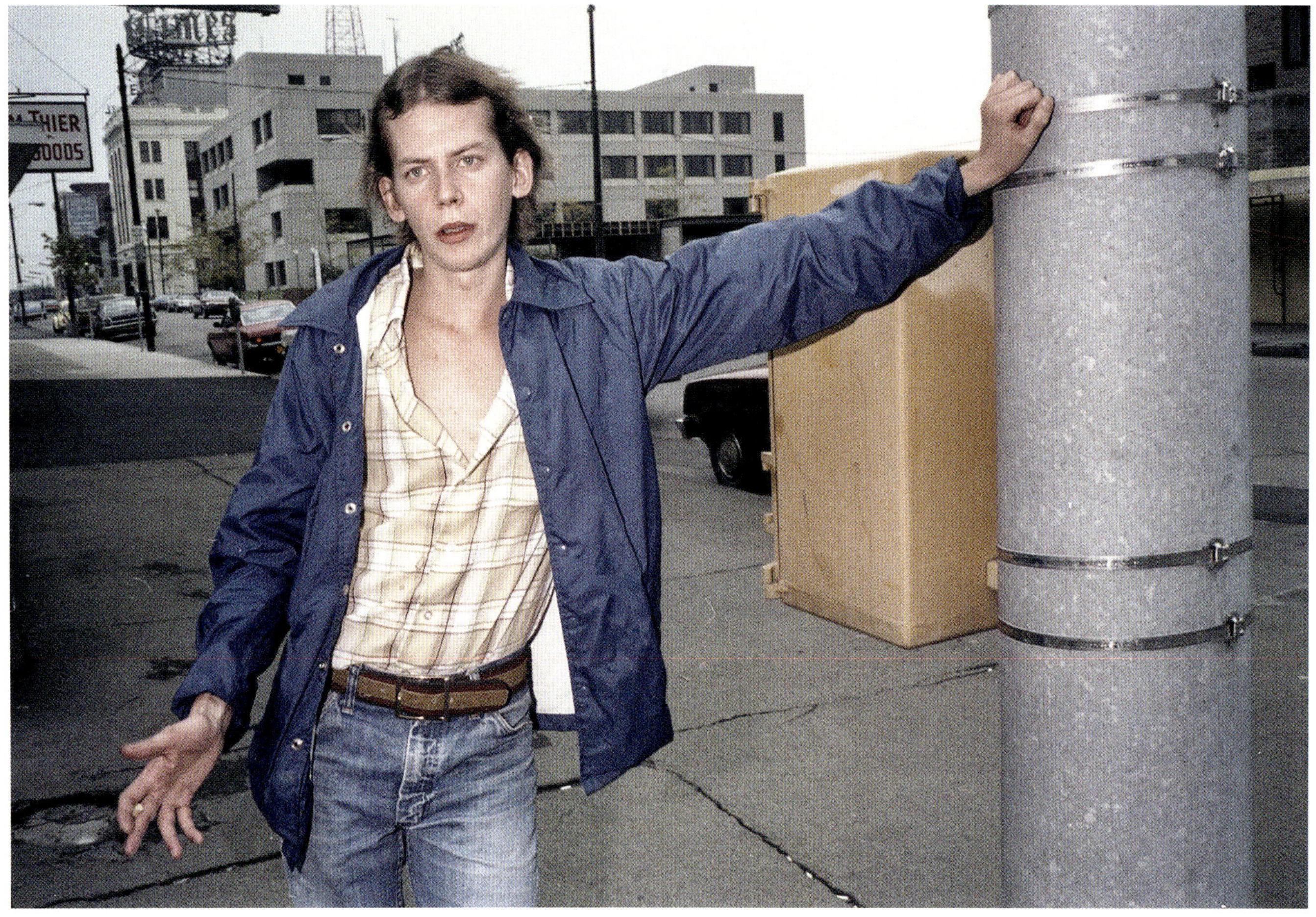

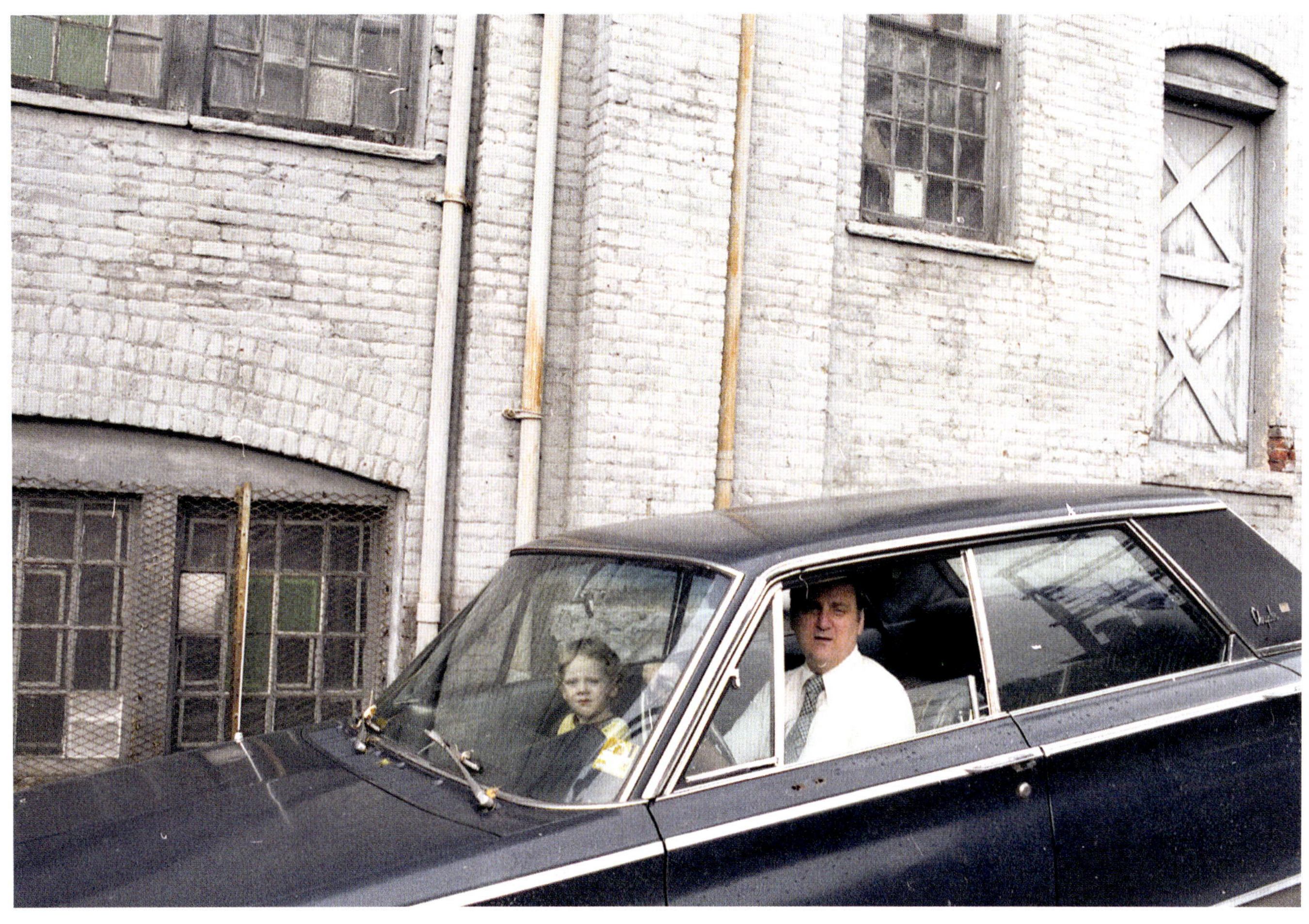

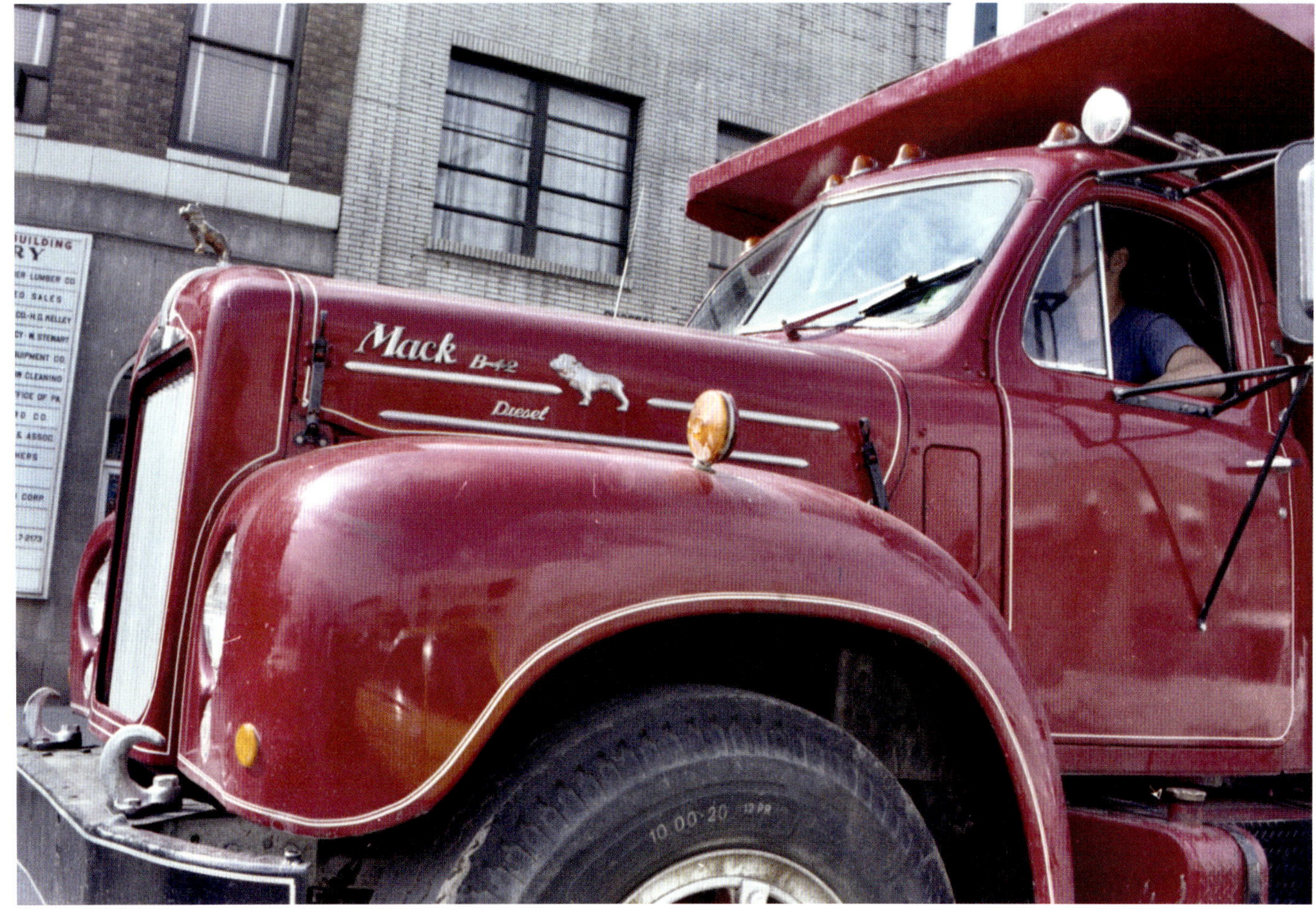
Mack B-42
Diesel
10.00-20

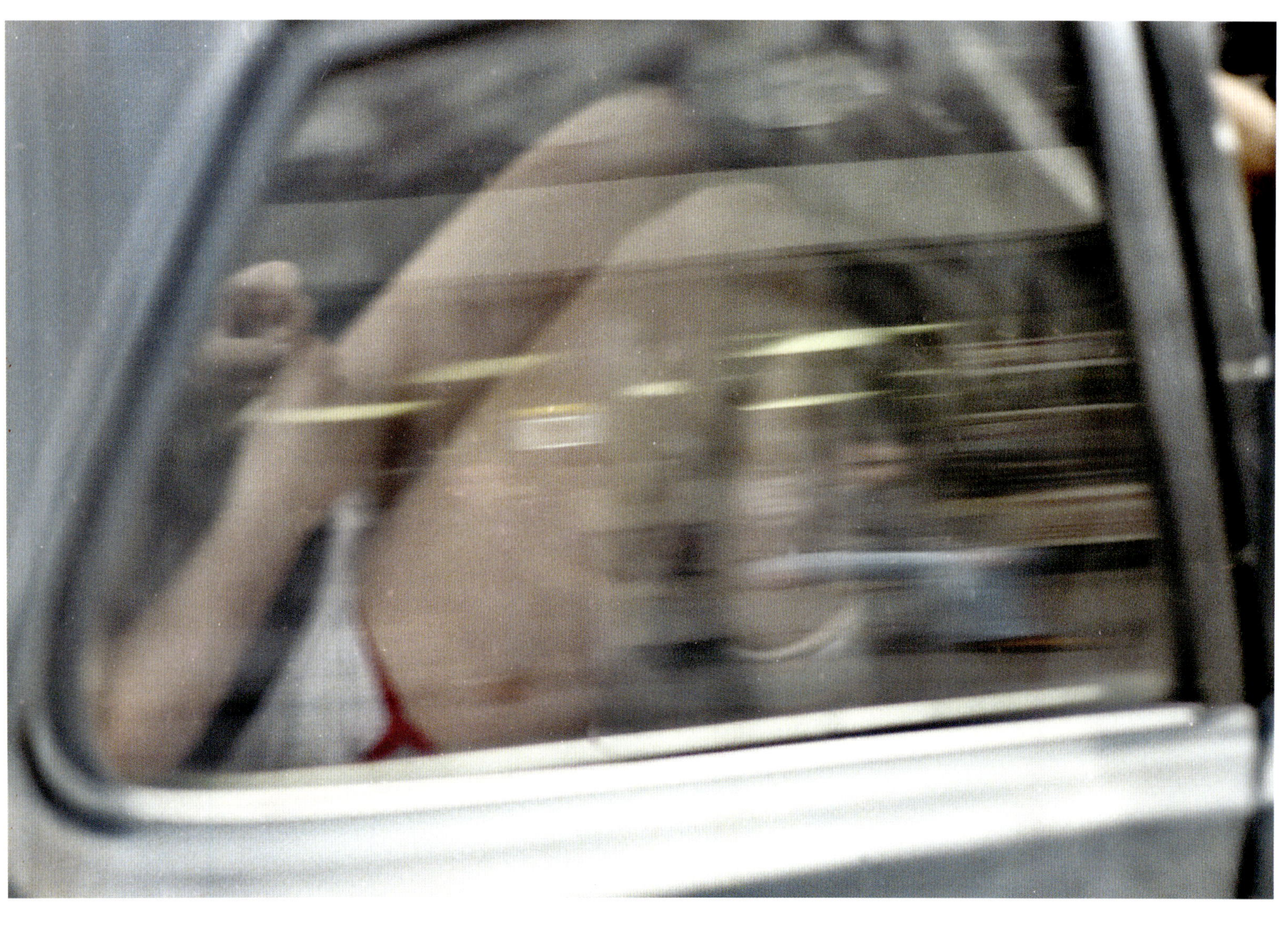

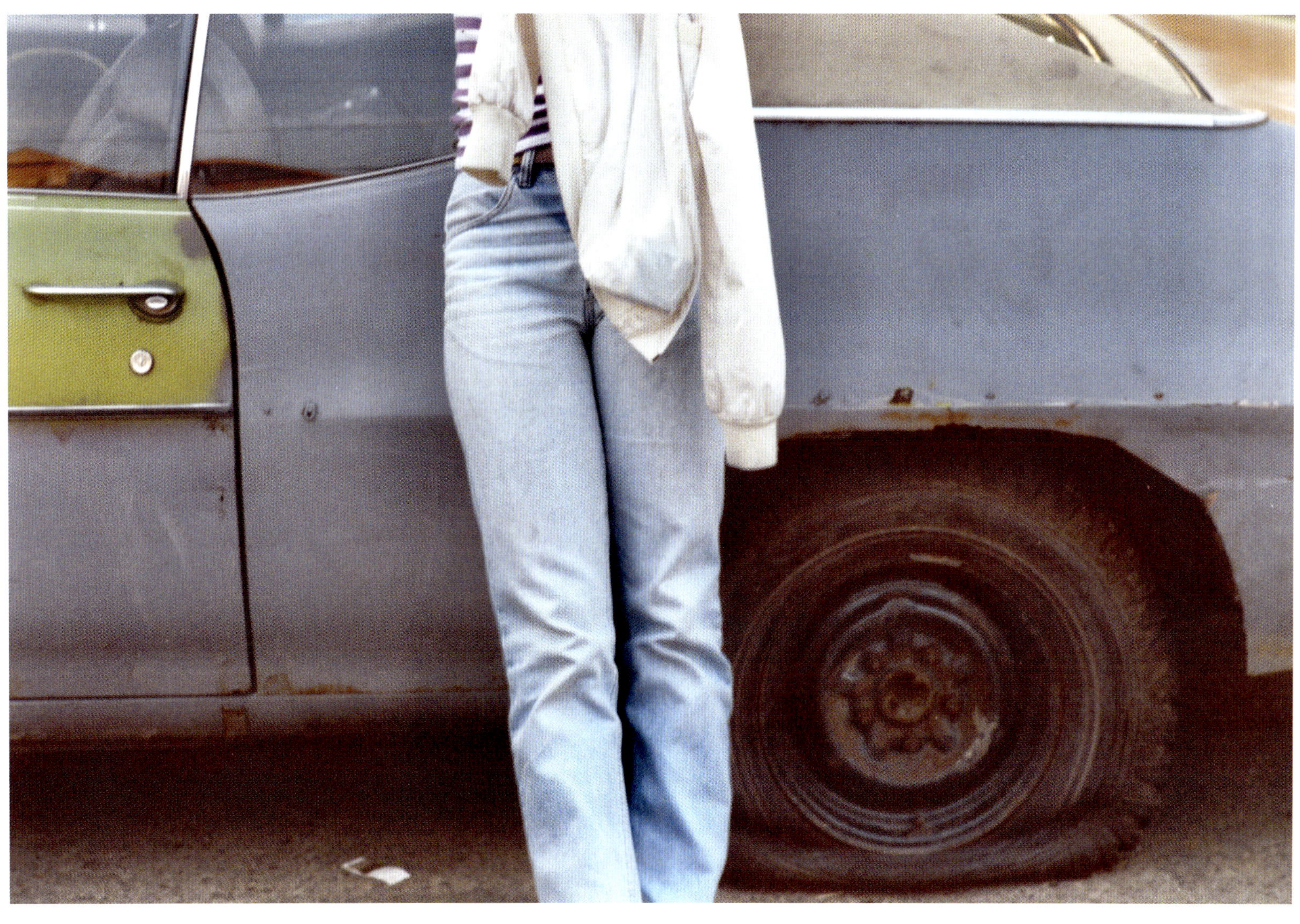

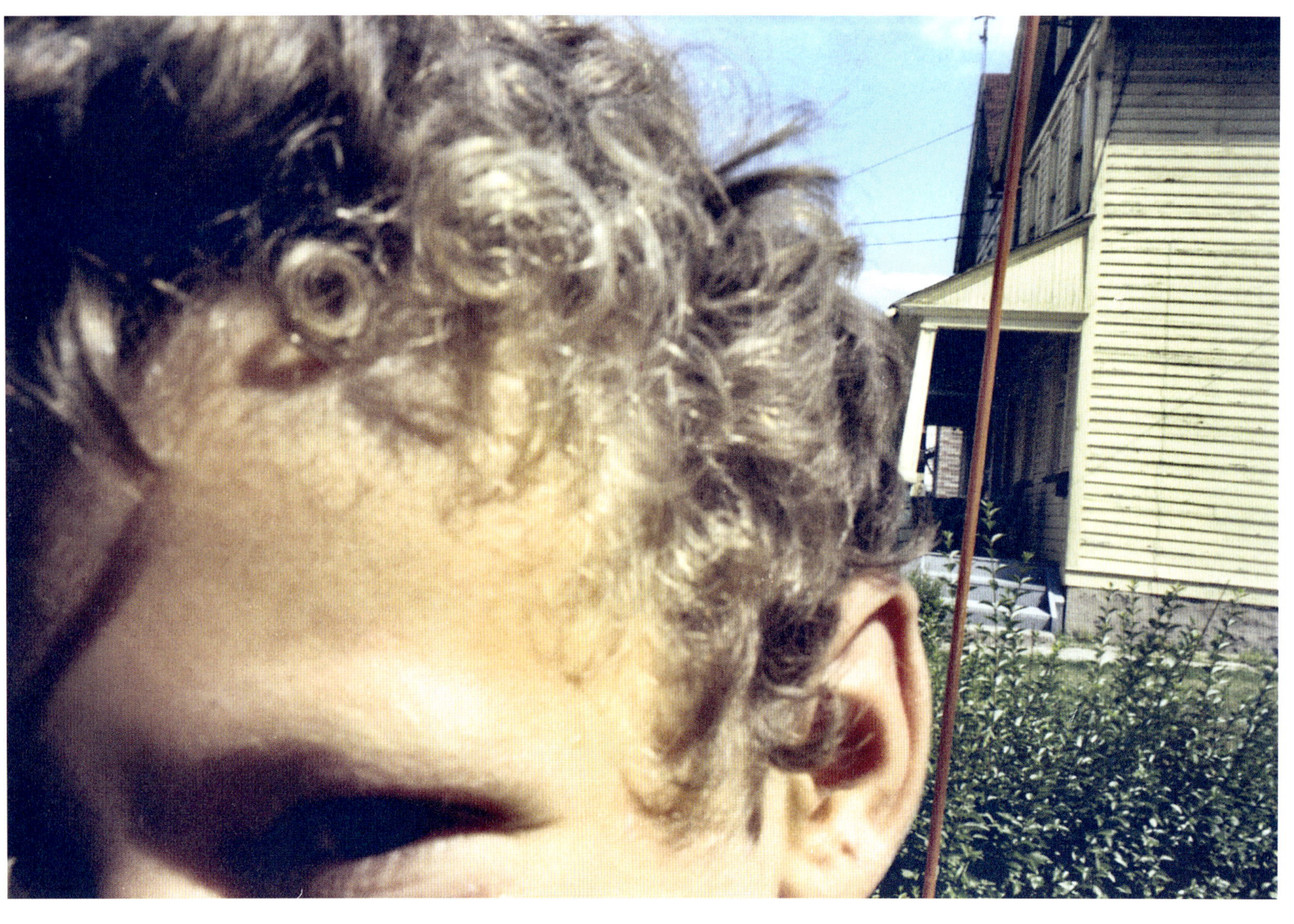

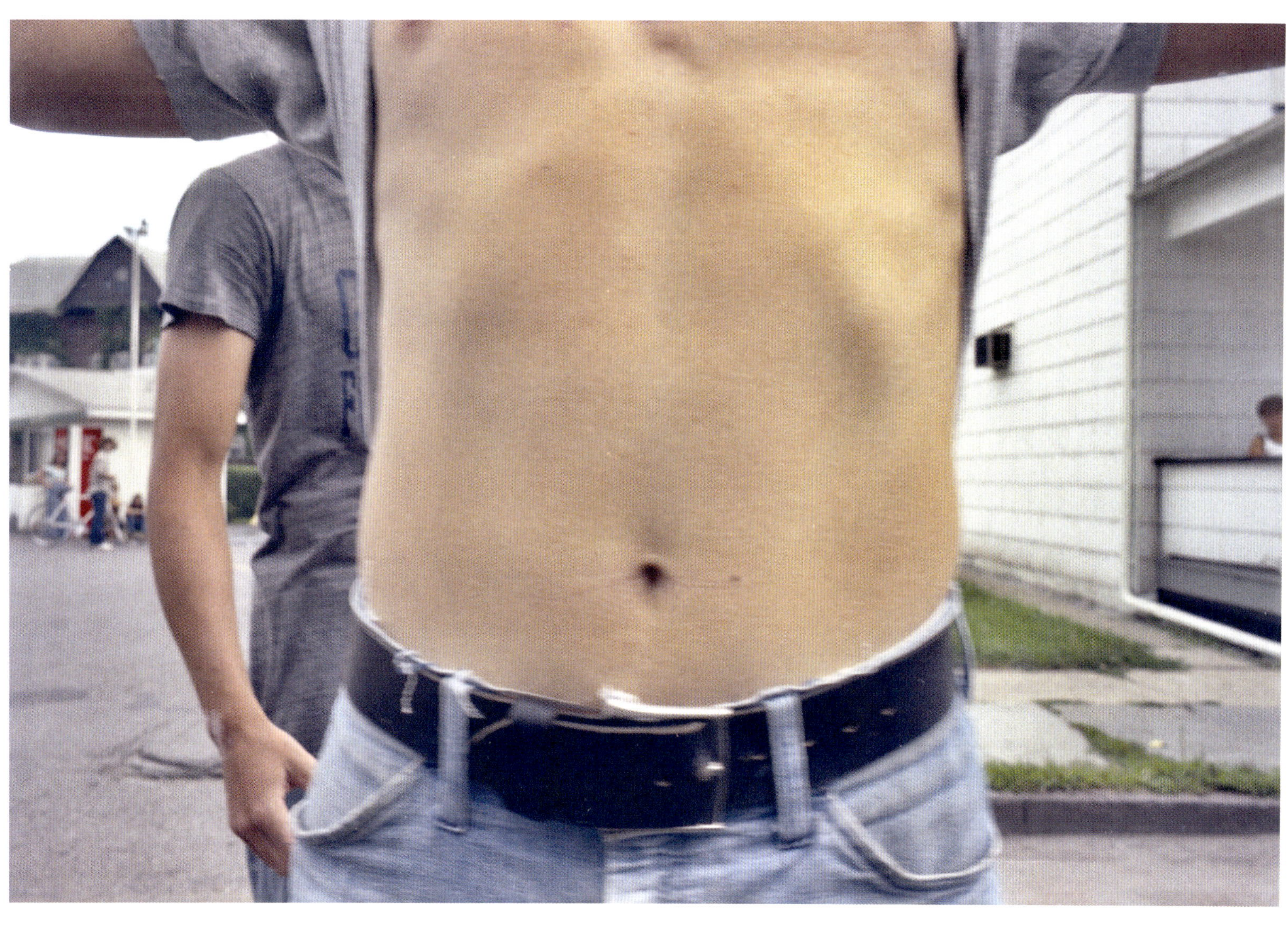

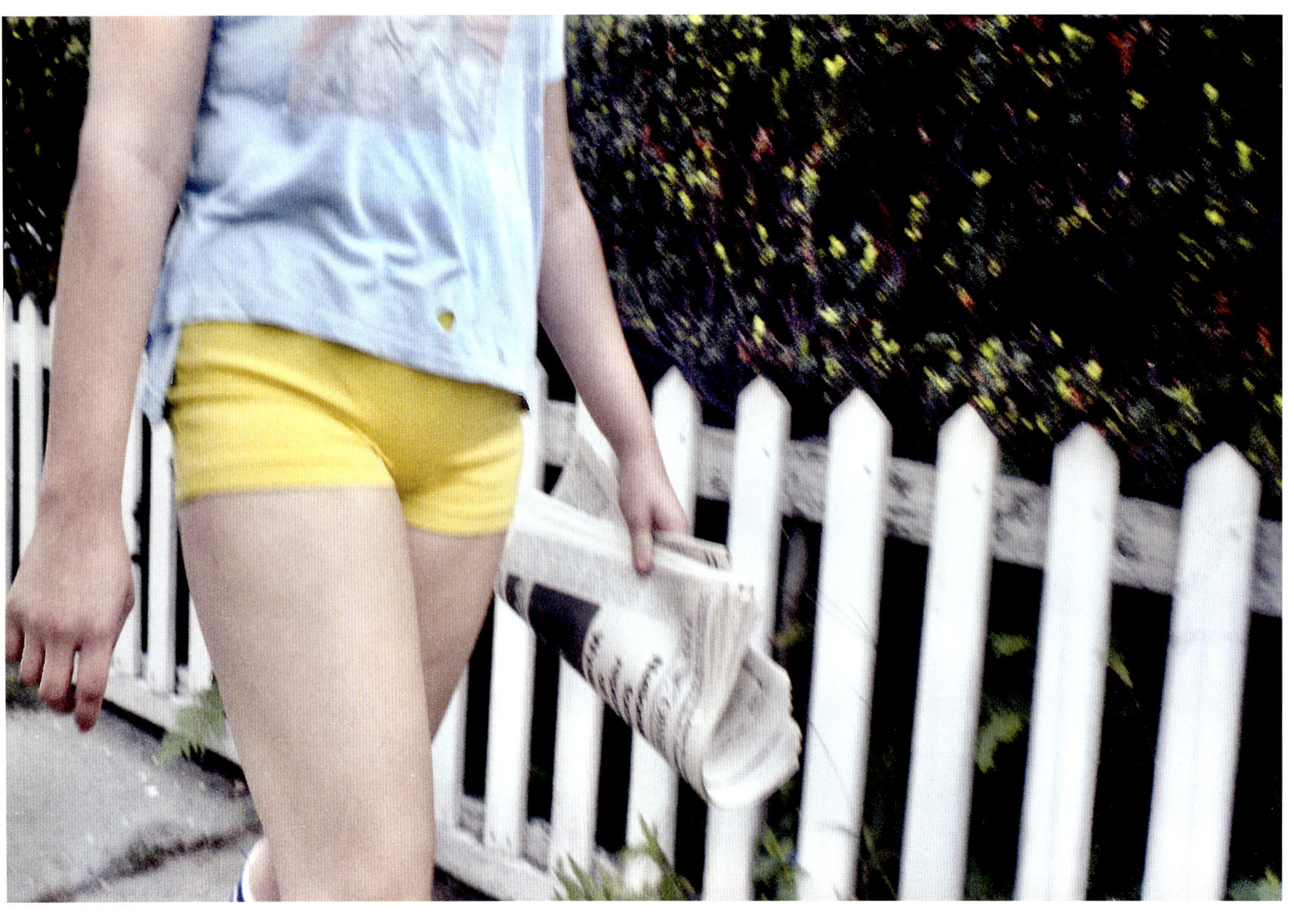

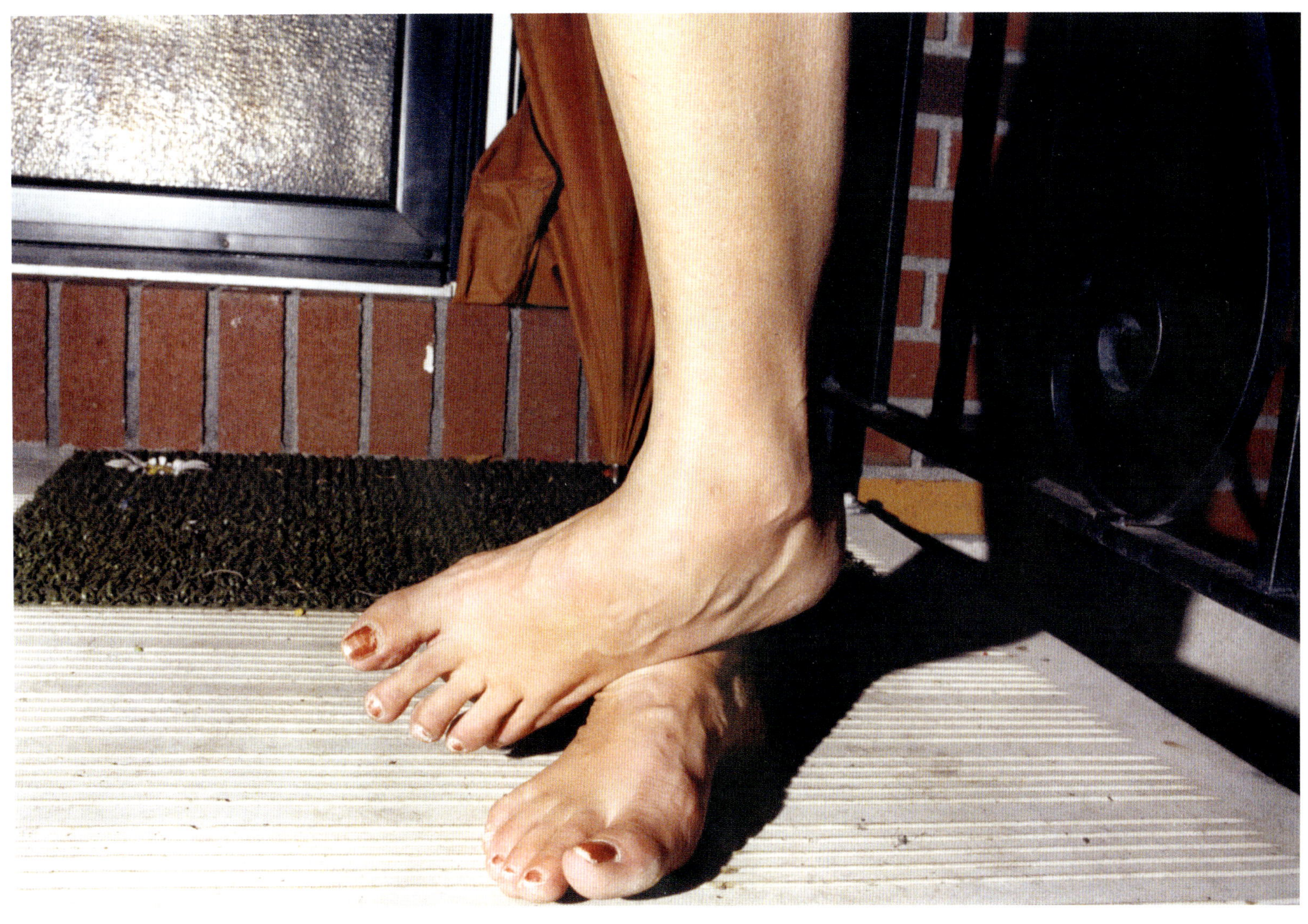

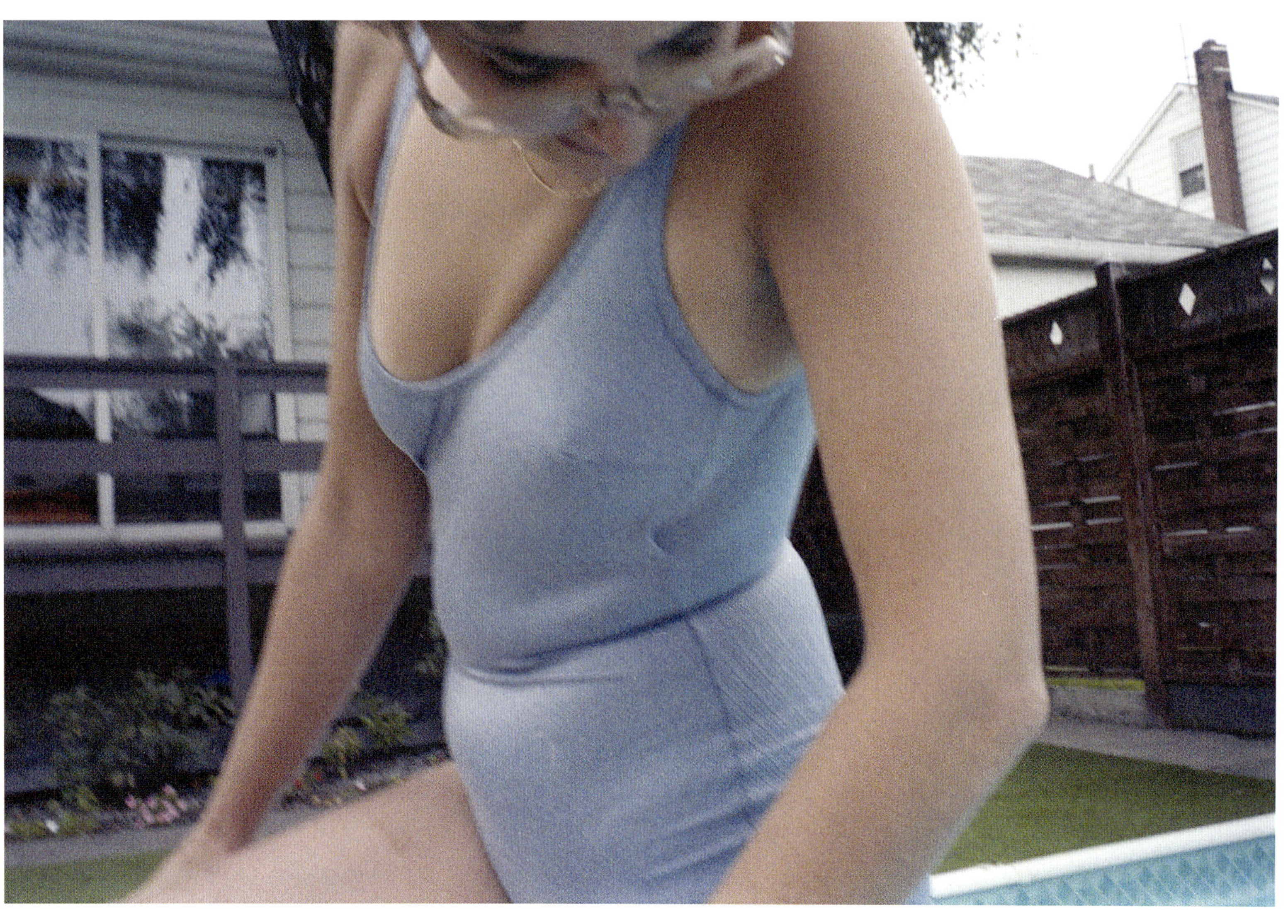

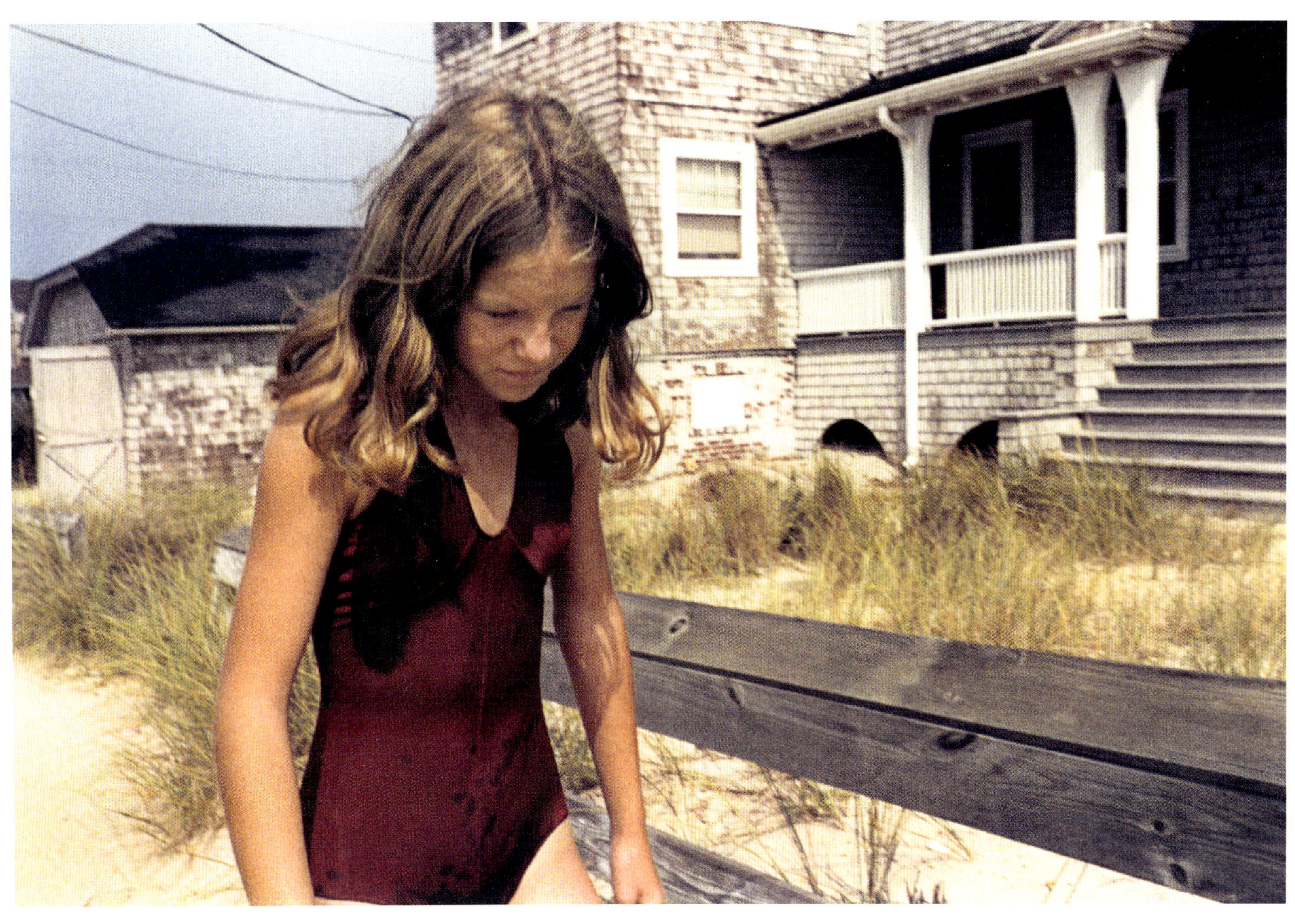

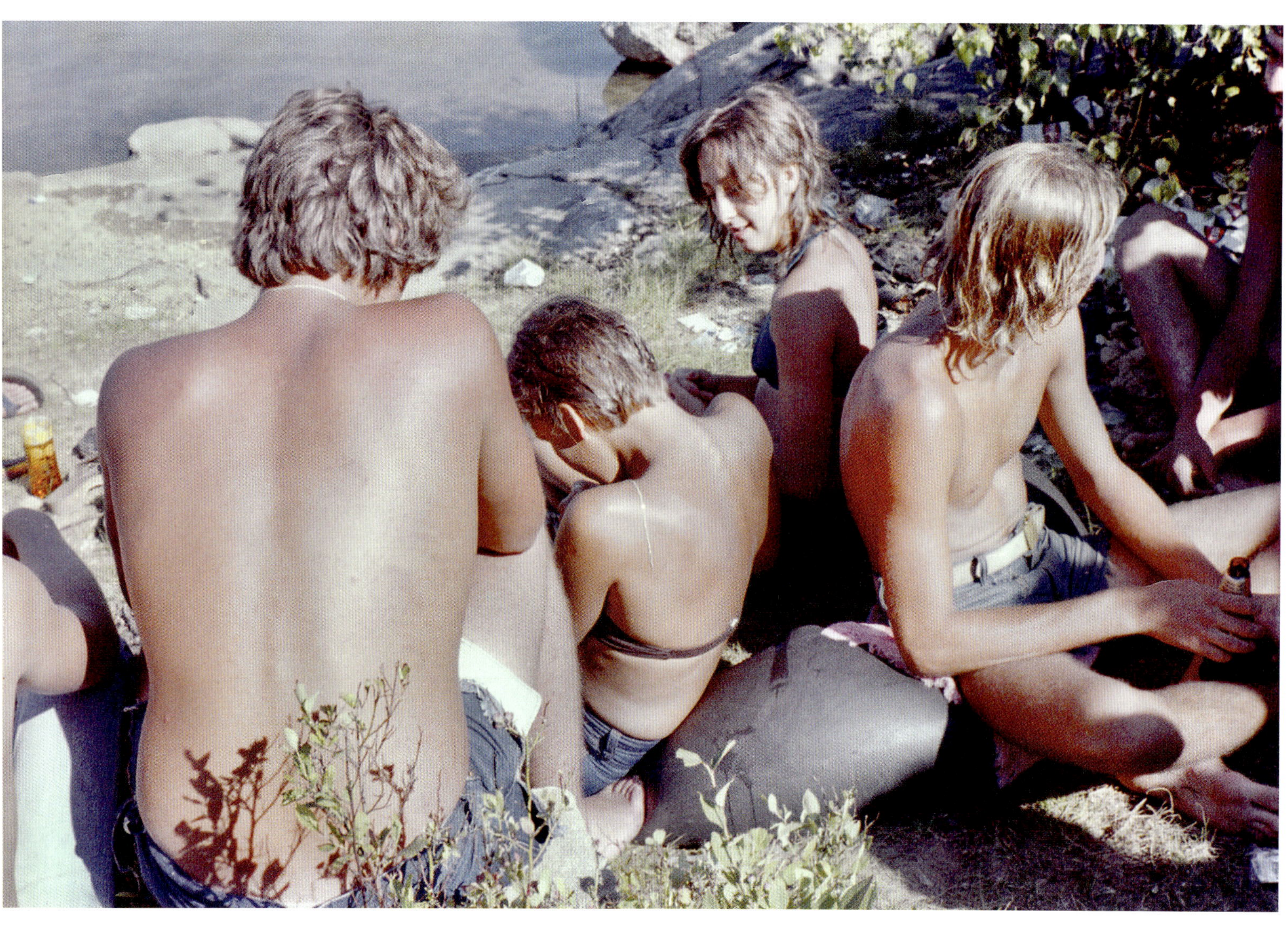

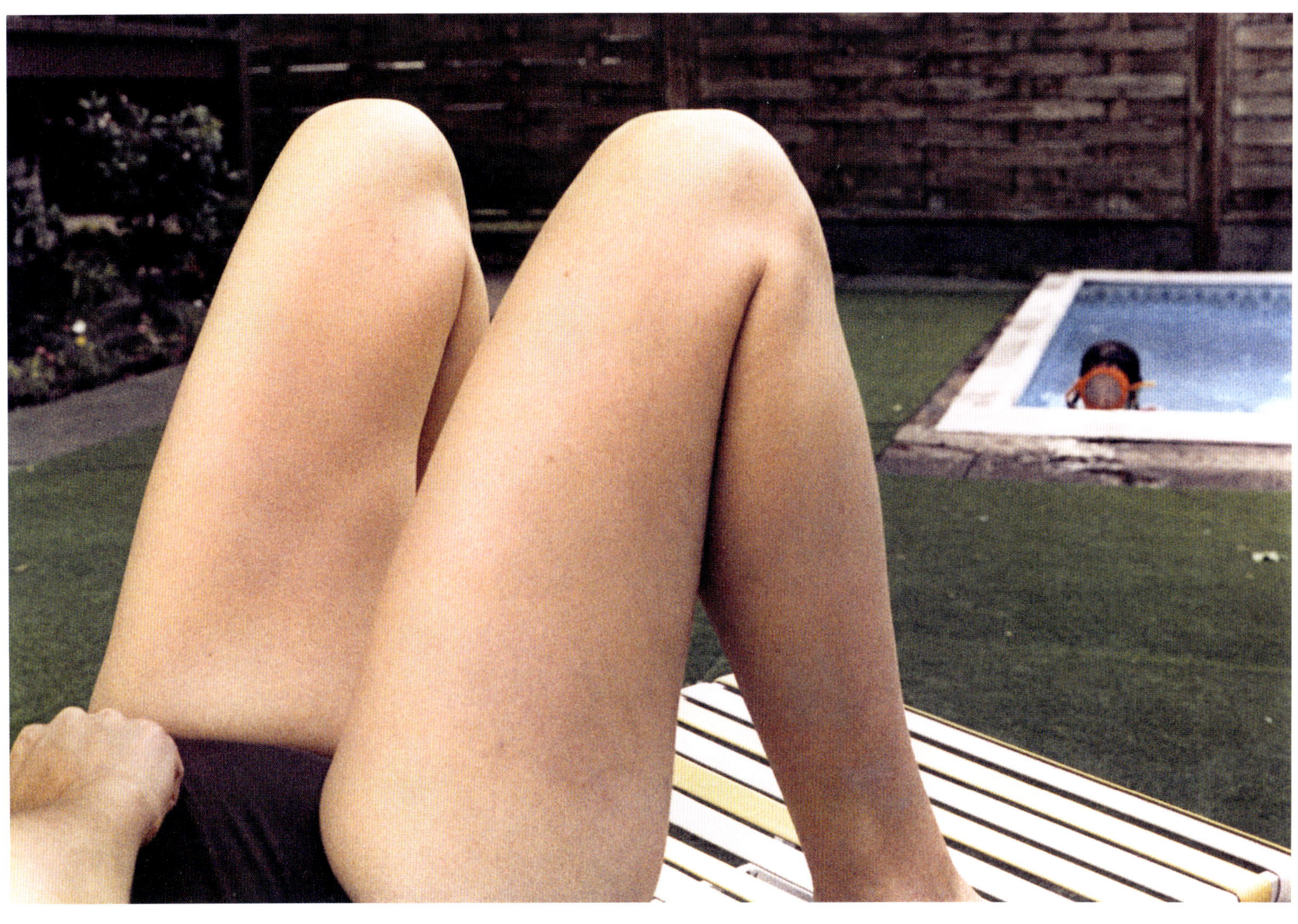

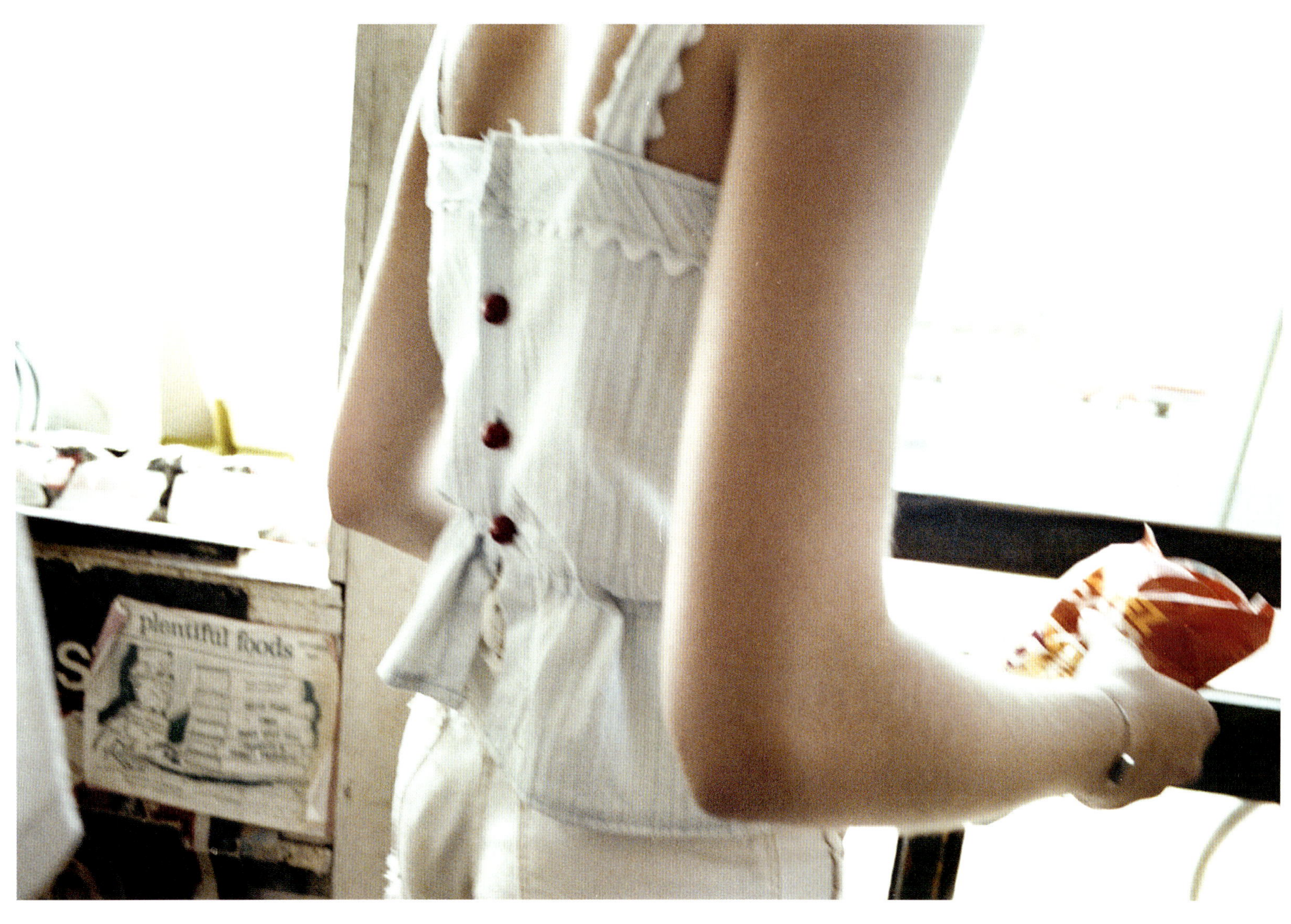
plentiful foods

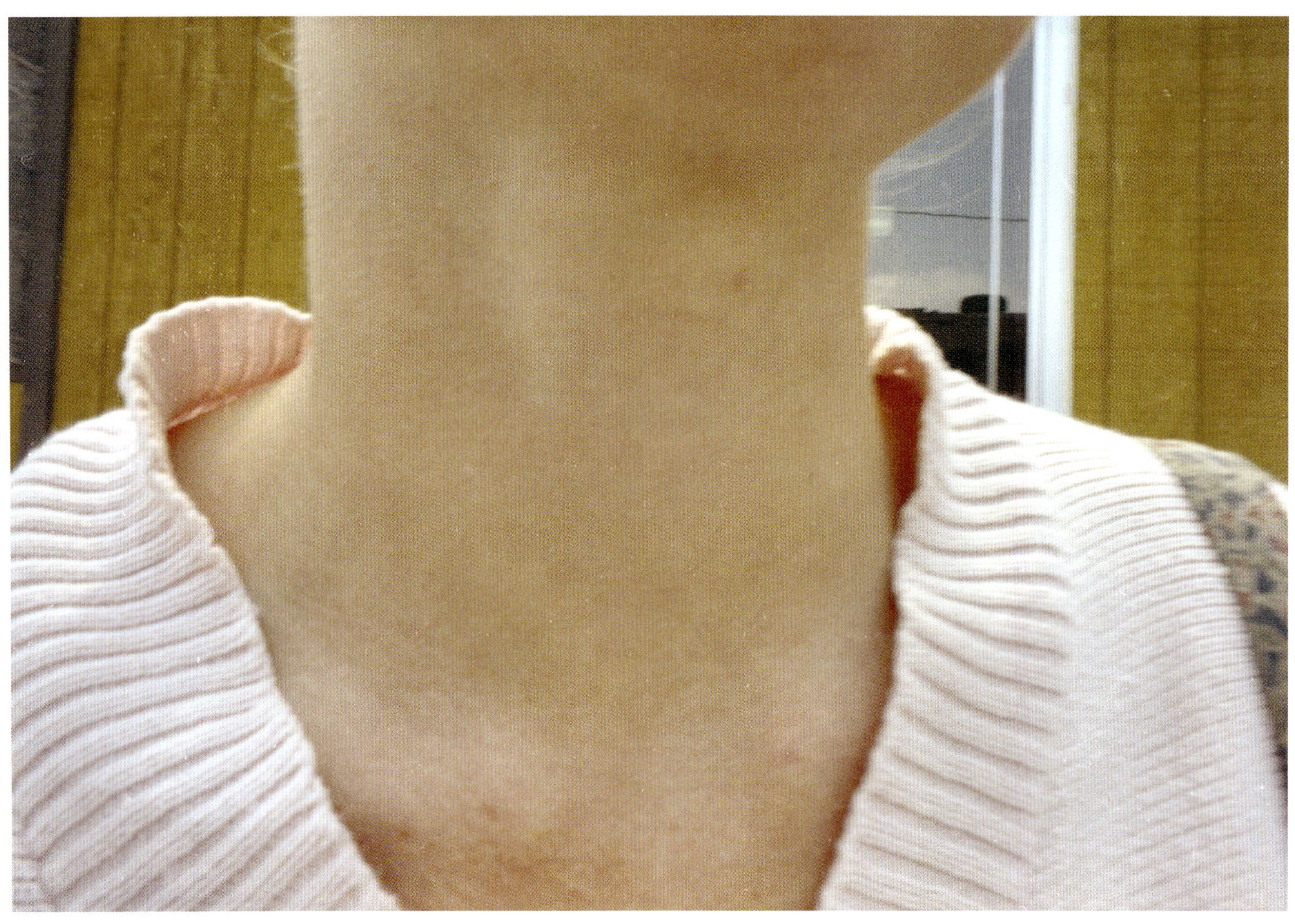

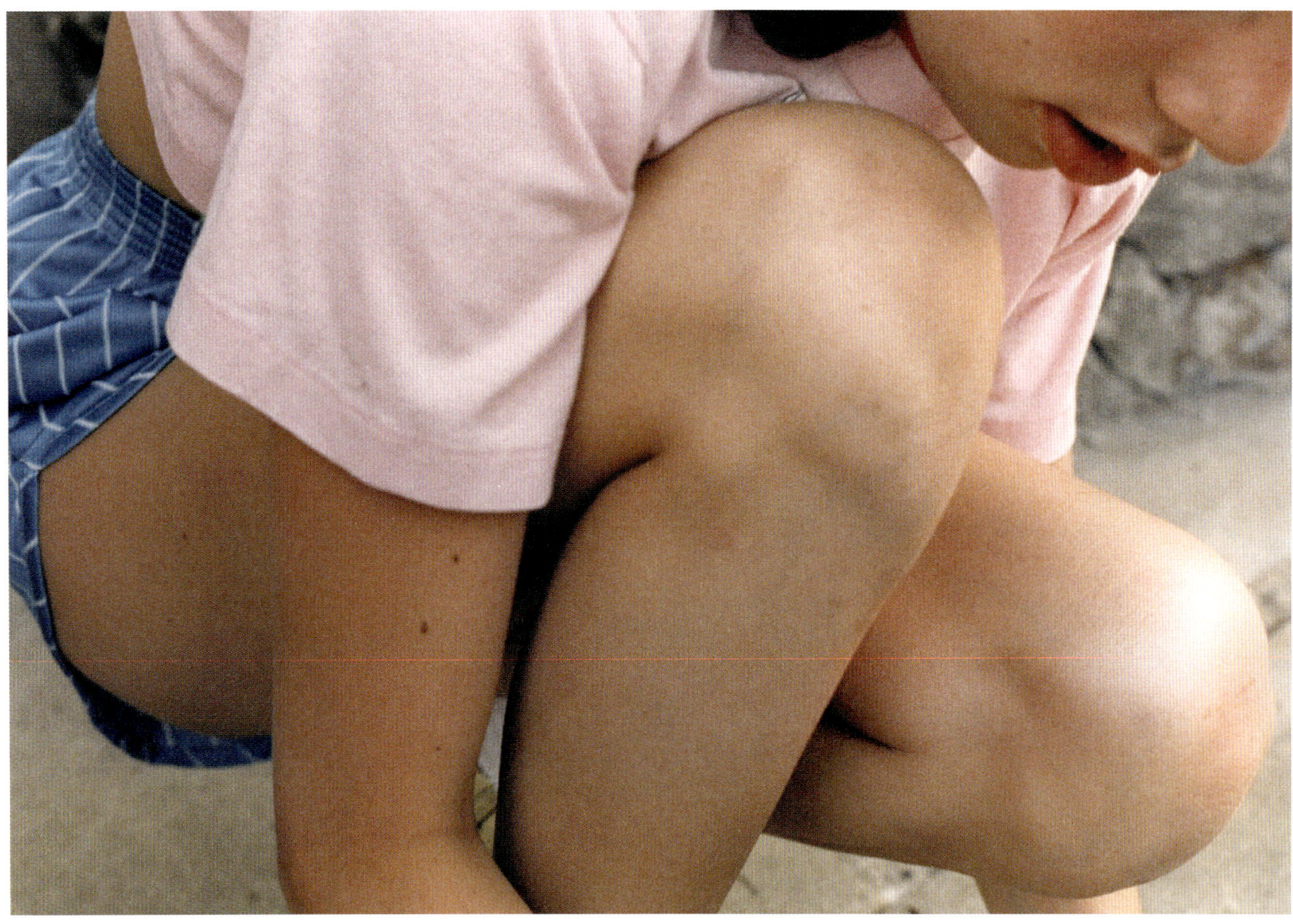

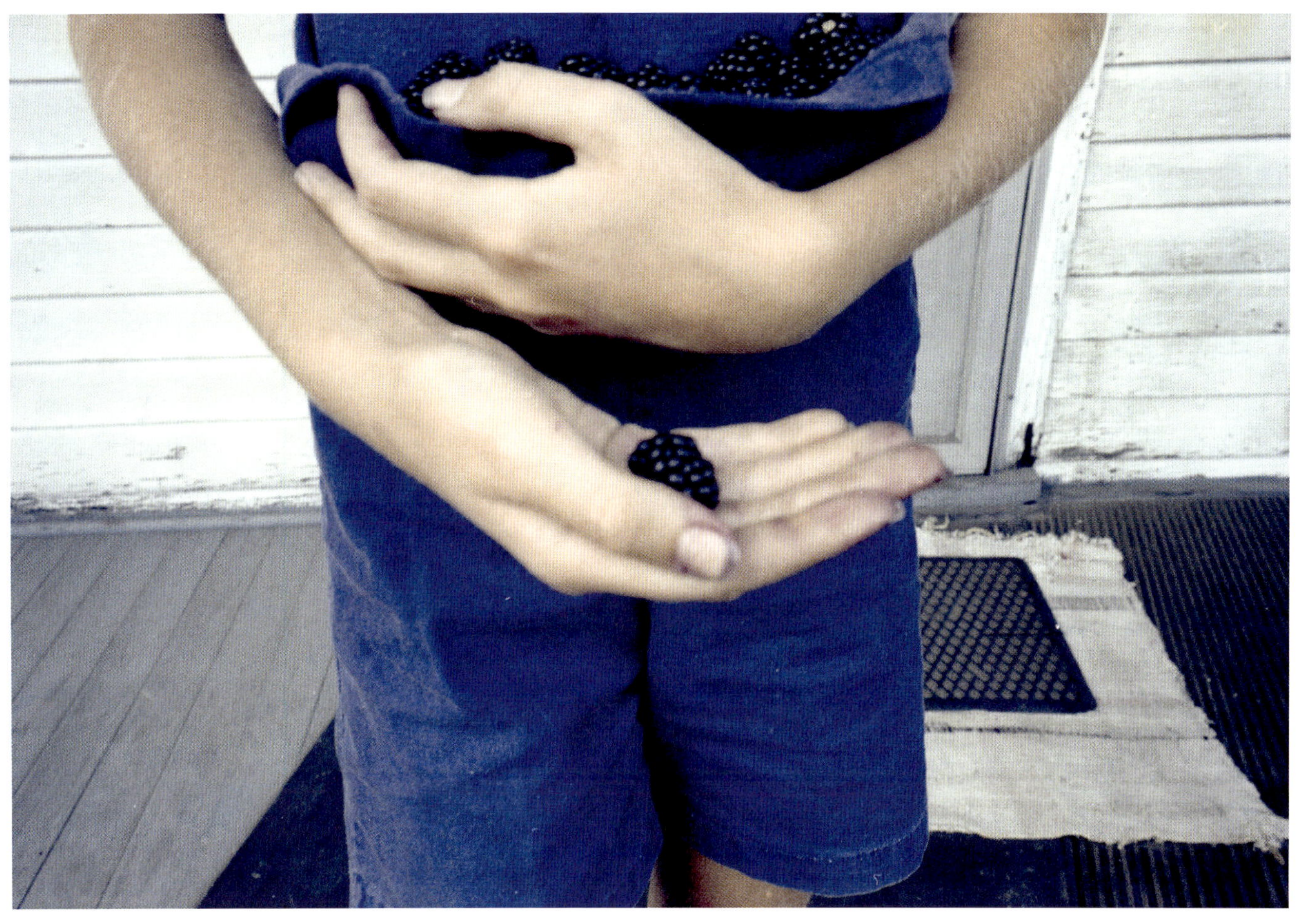

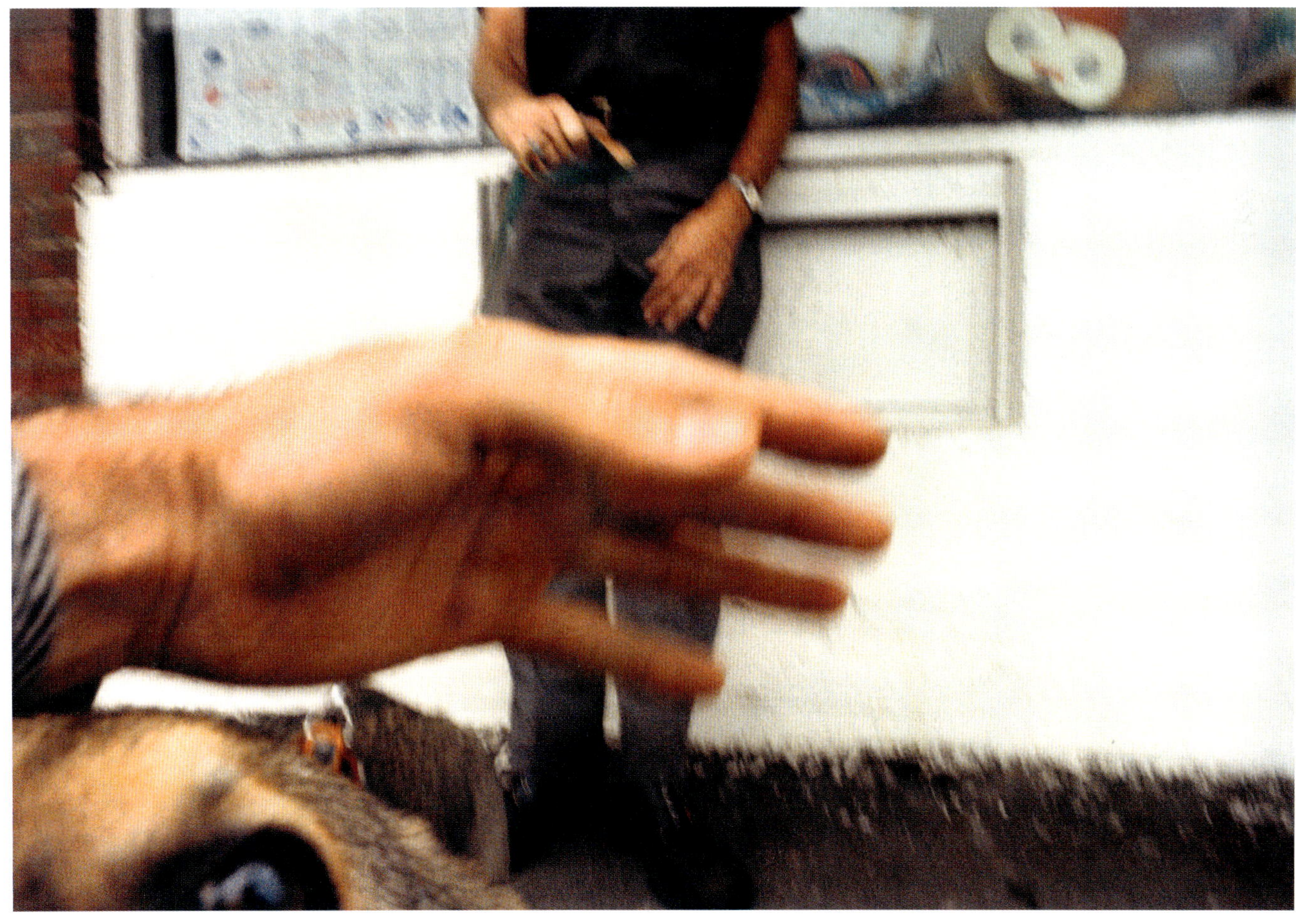

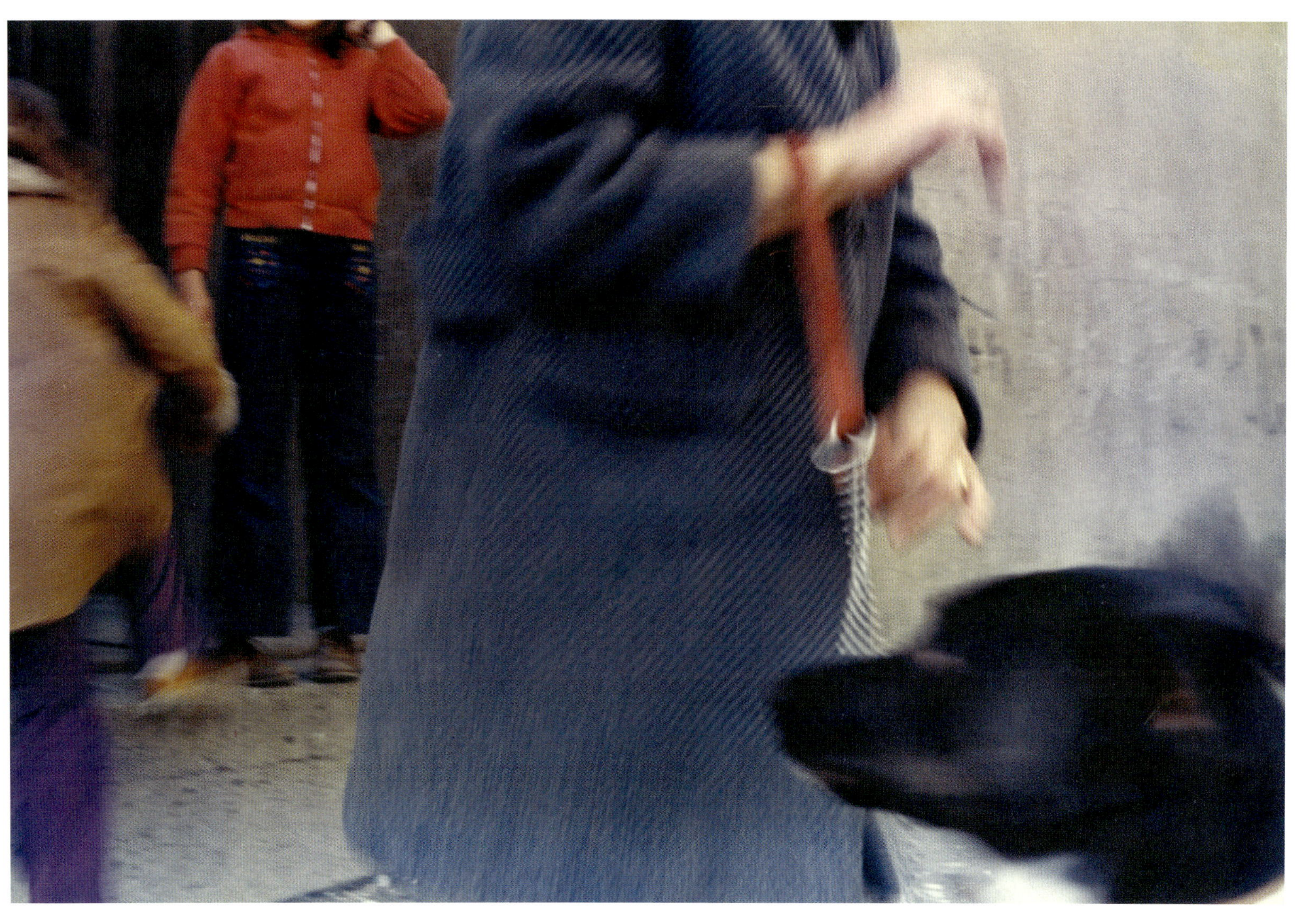

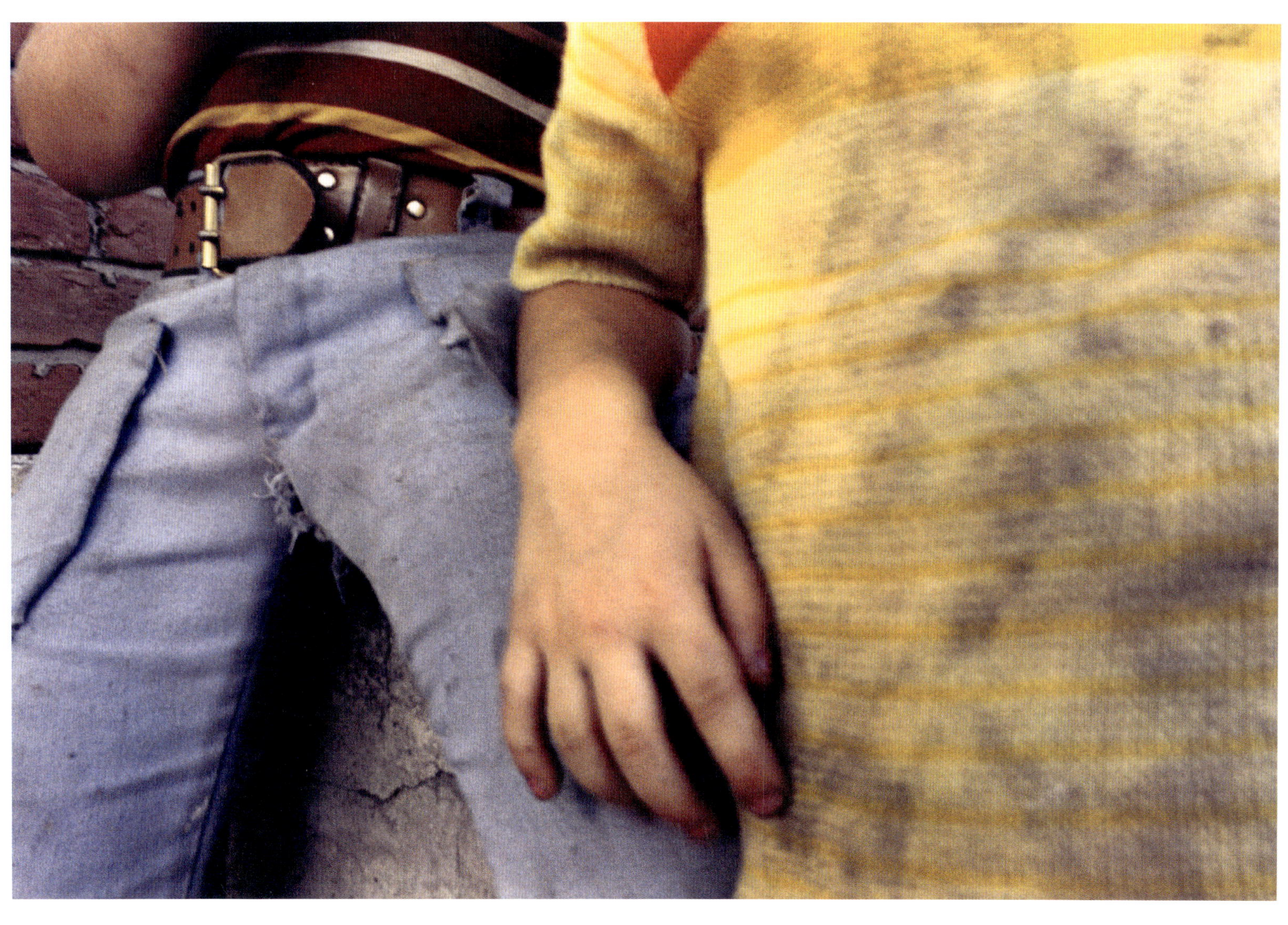

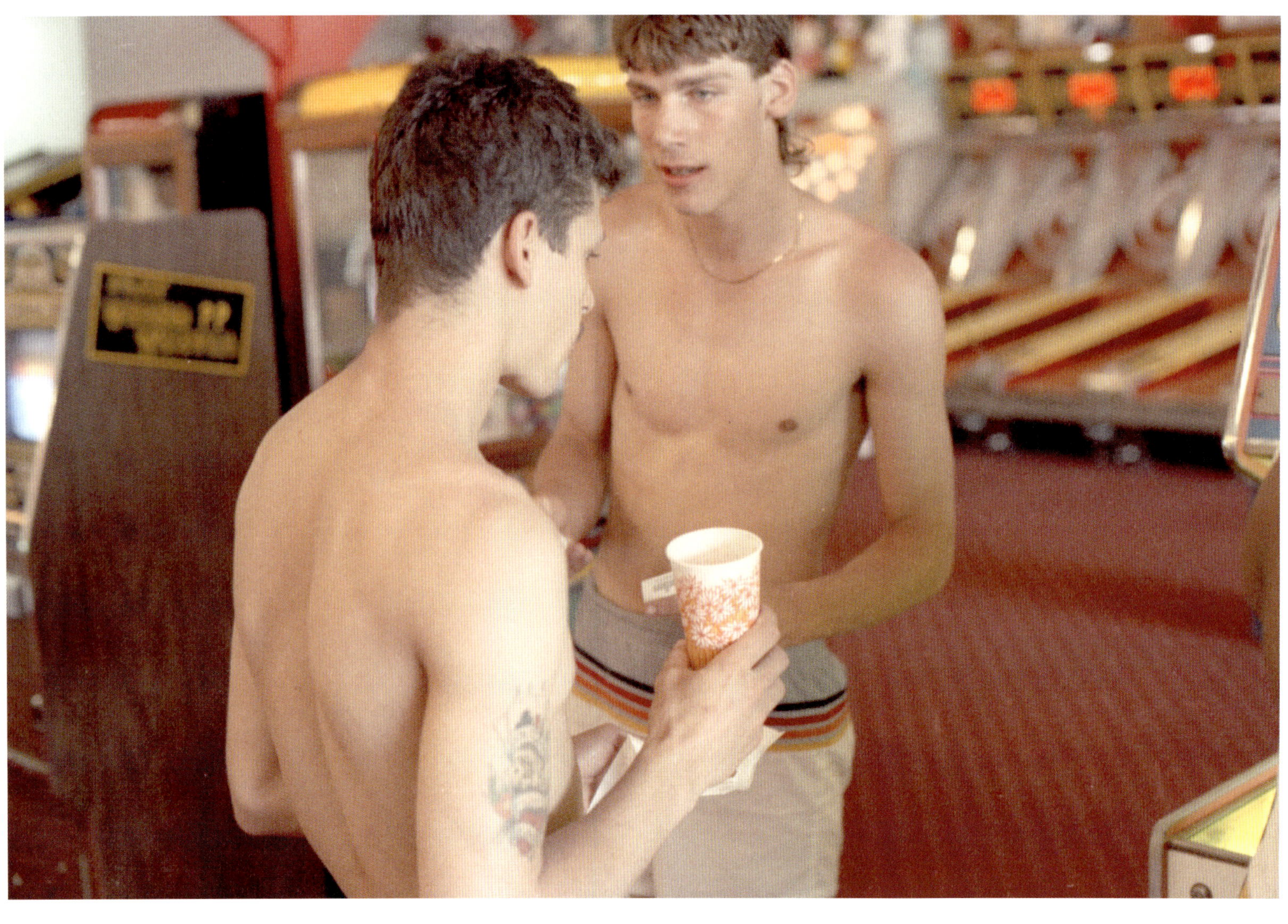

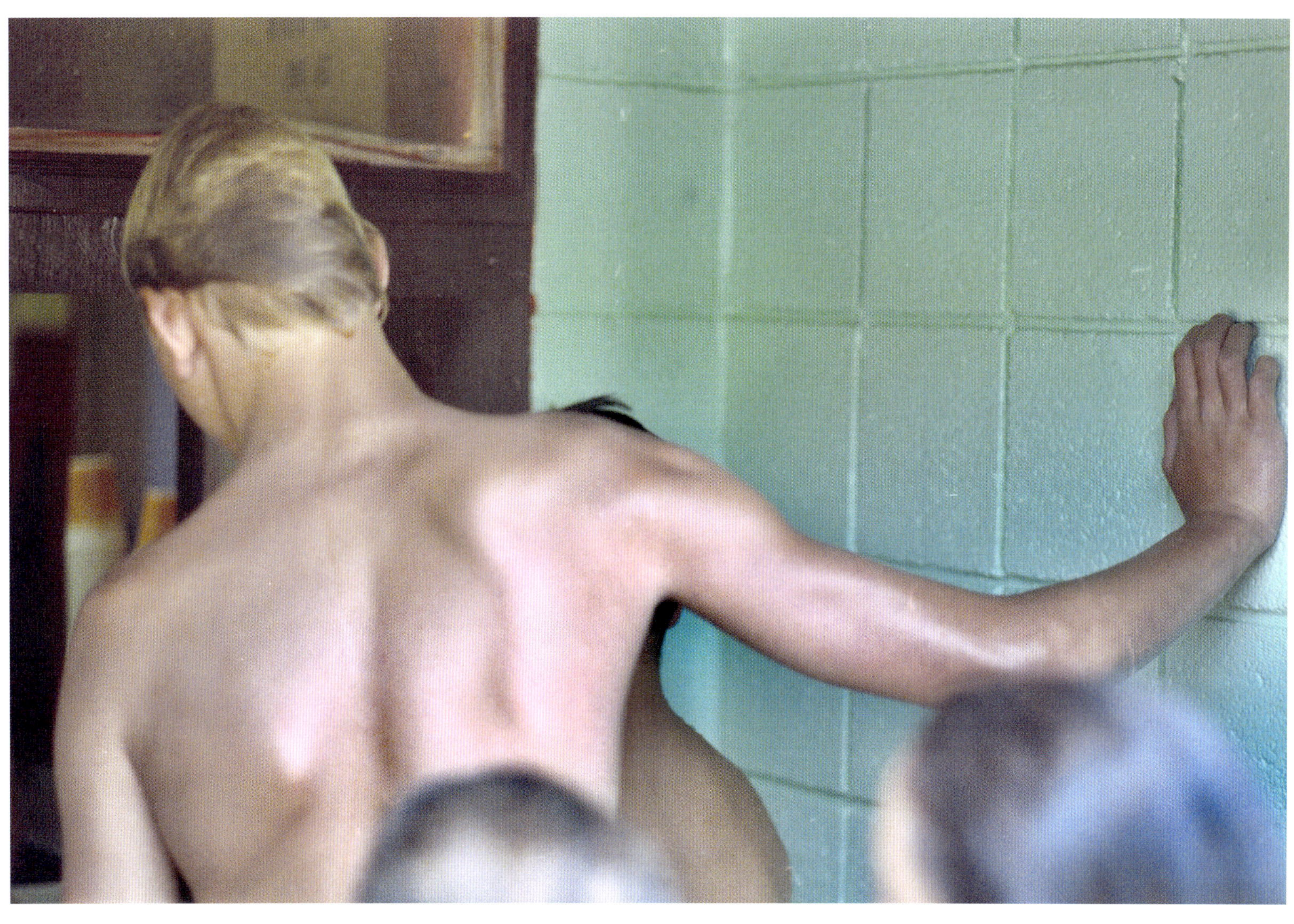

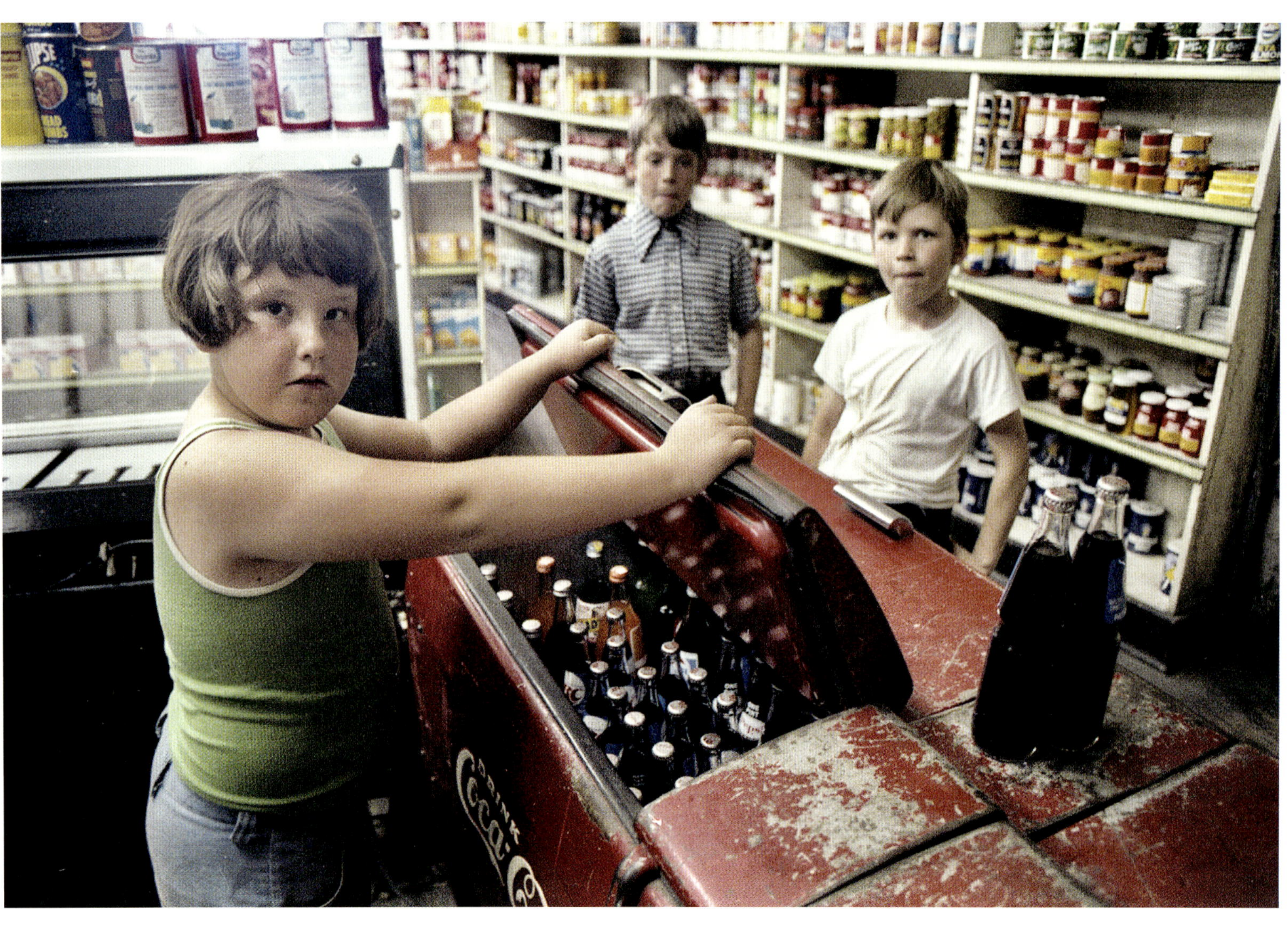
DRINK
Coca

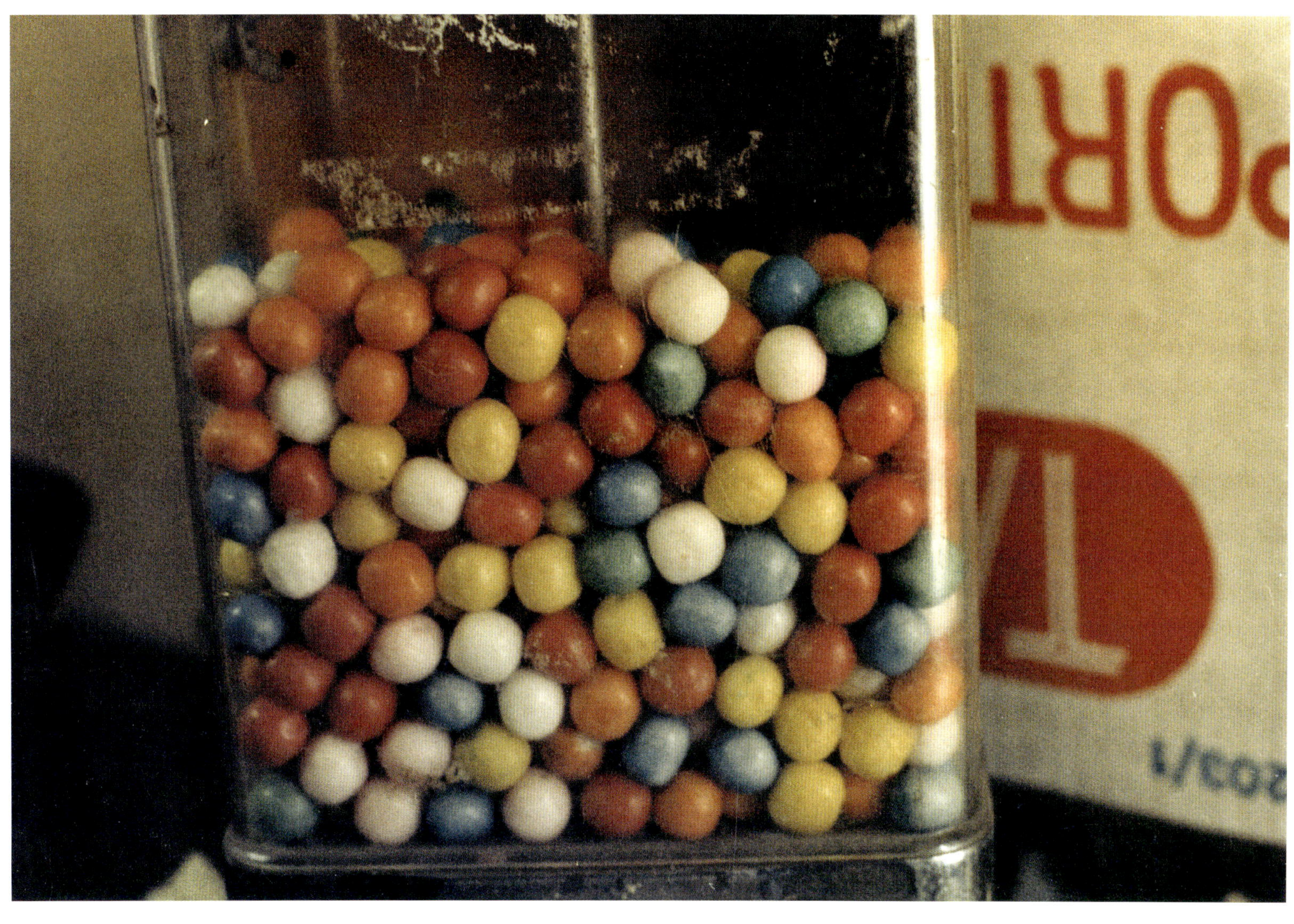

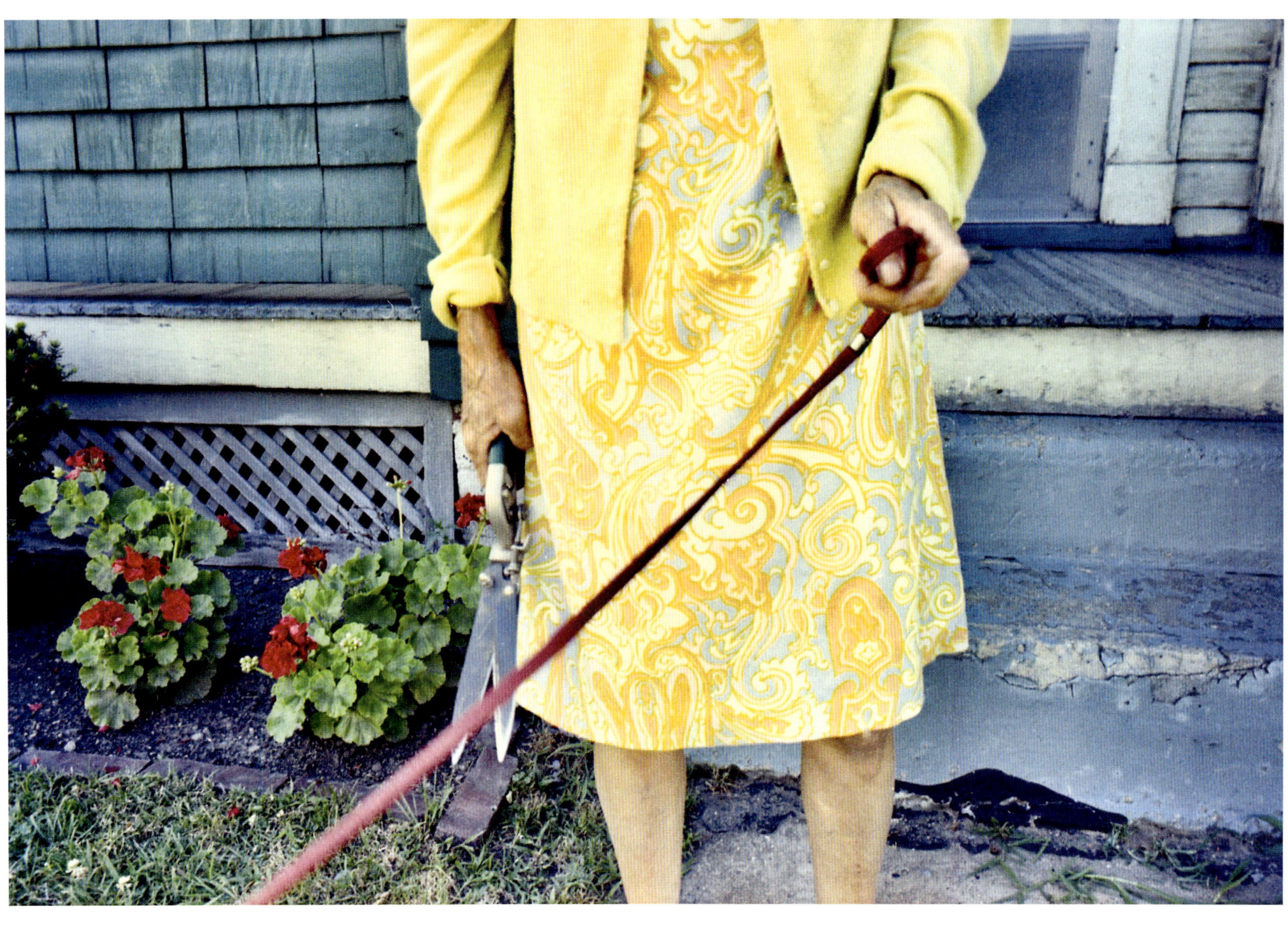

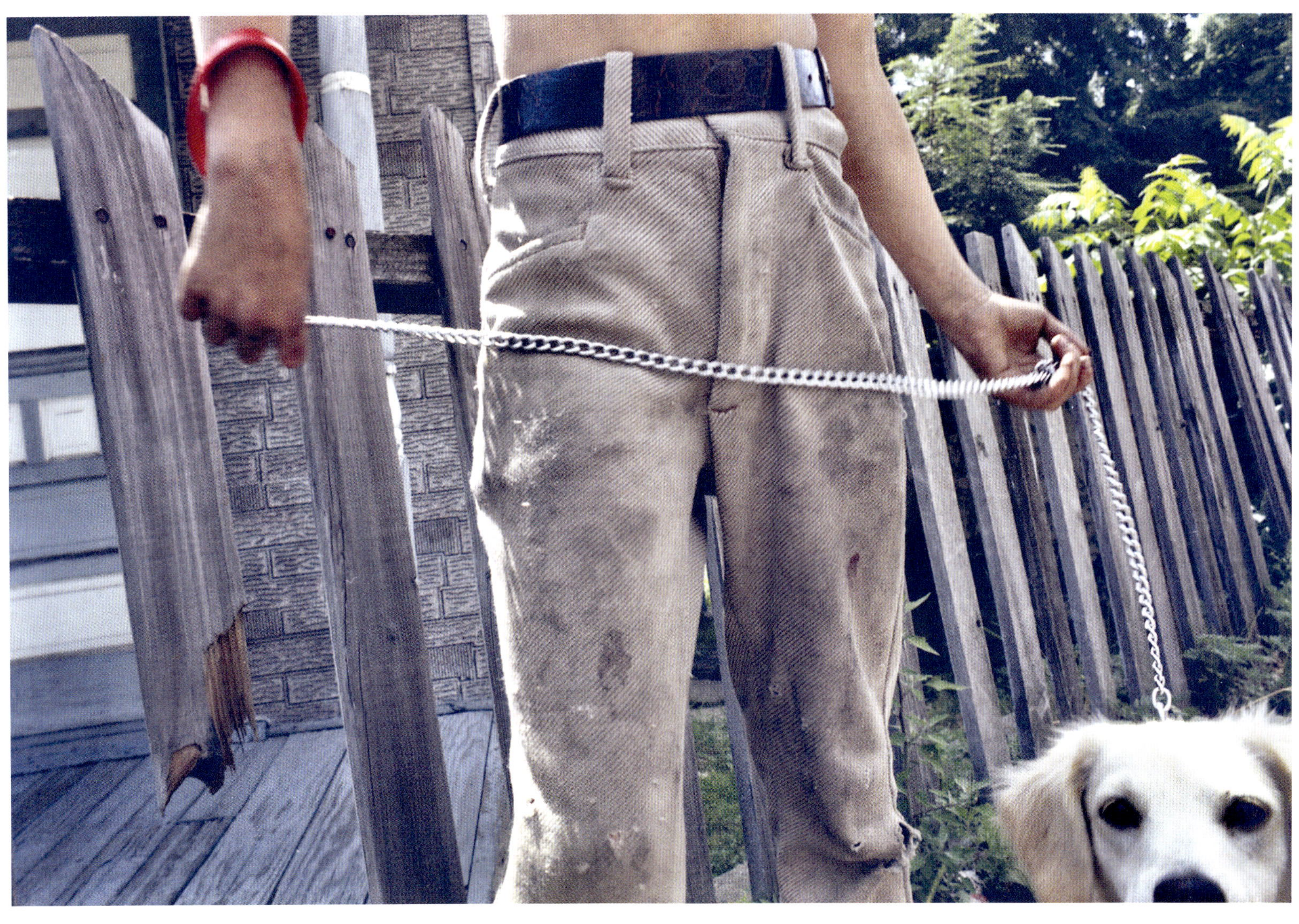

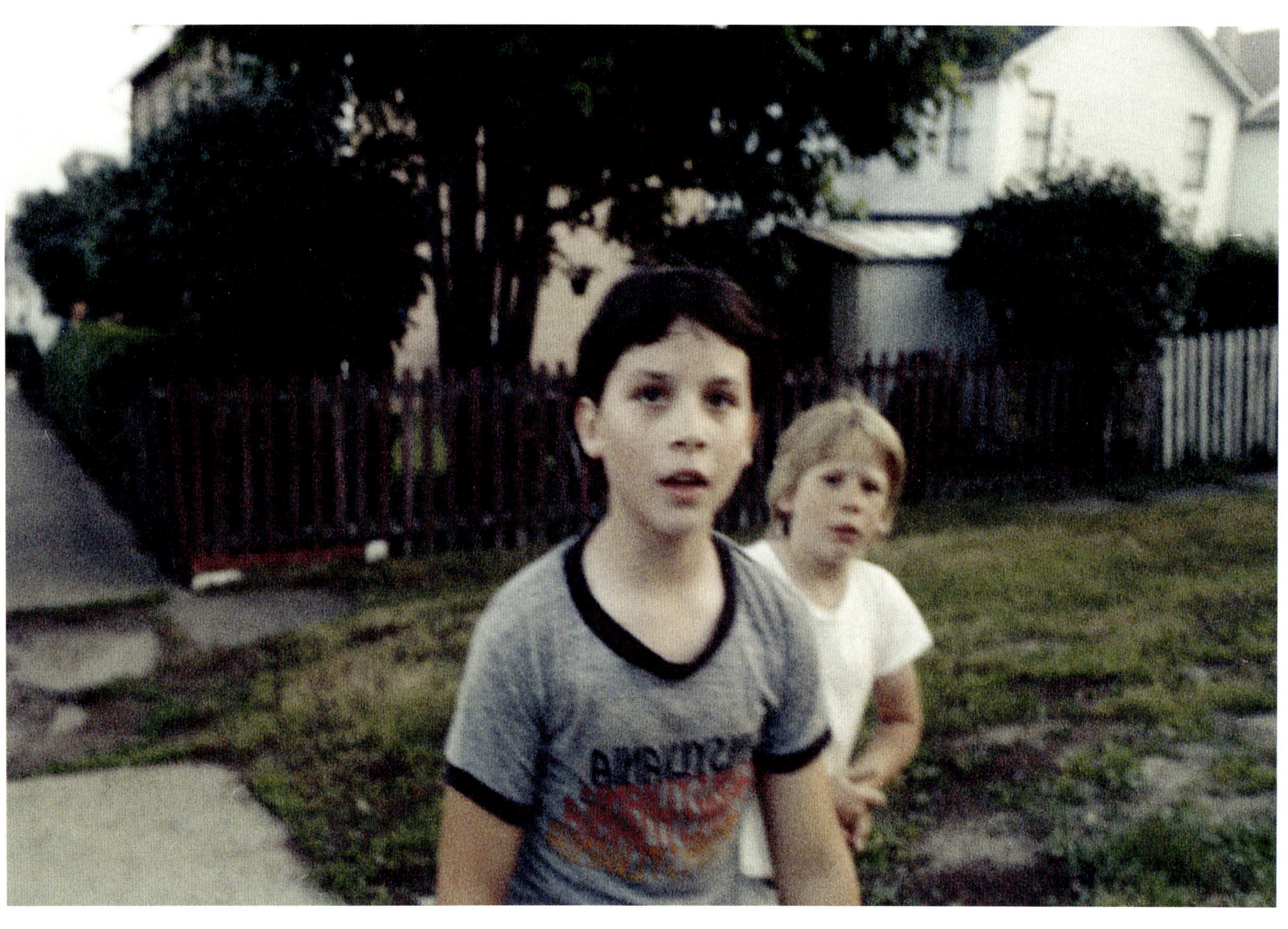

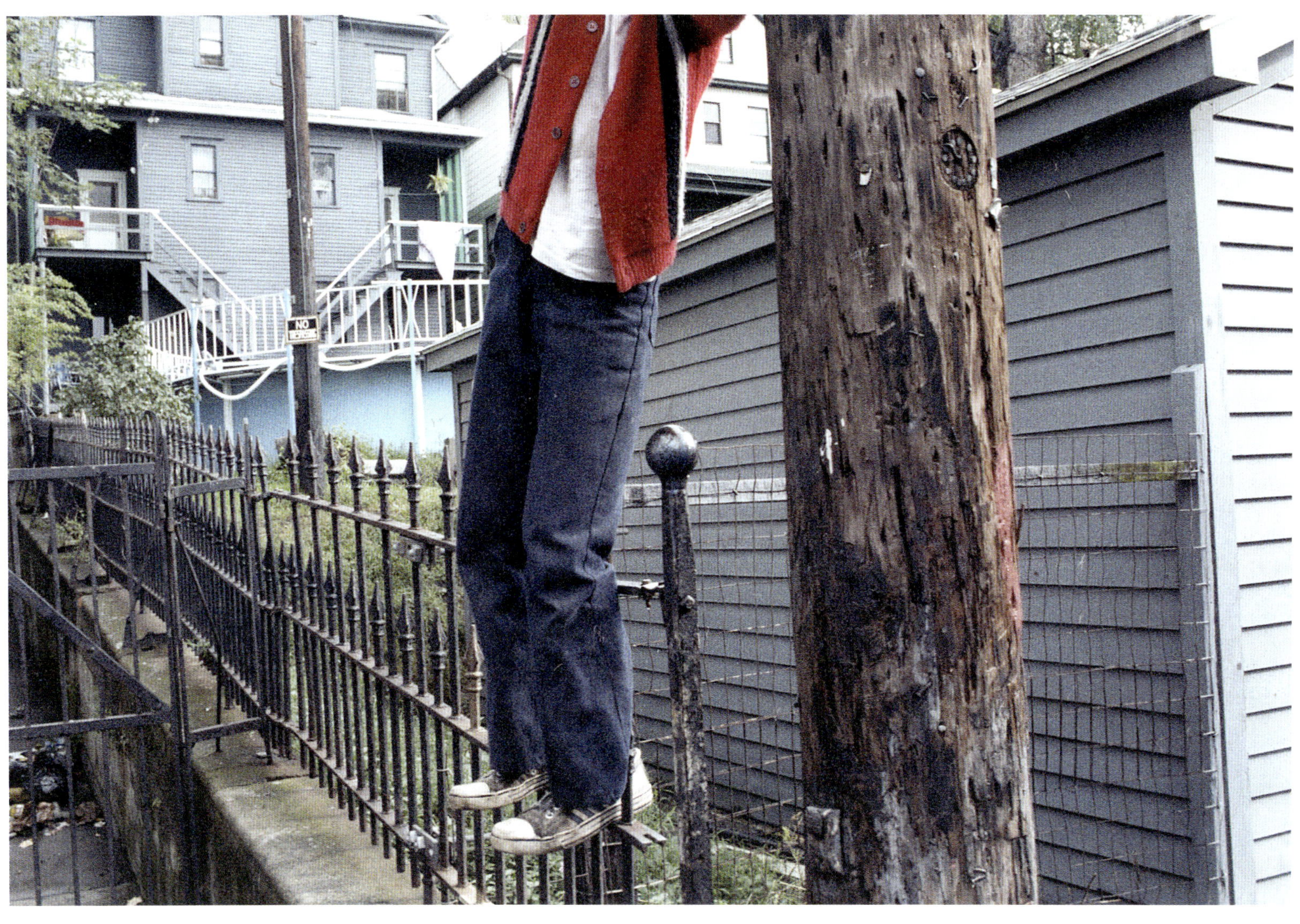
NO

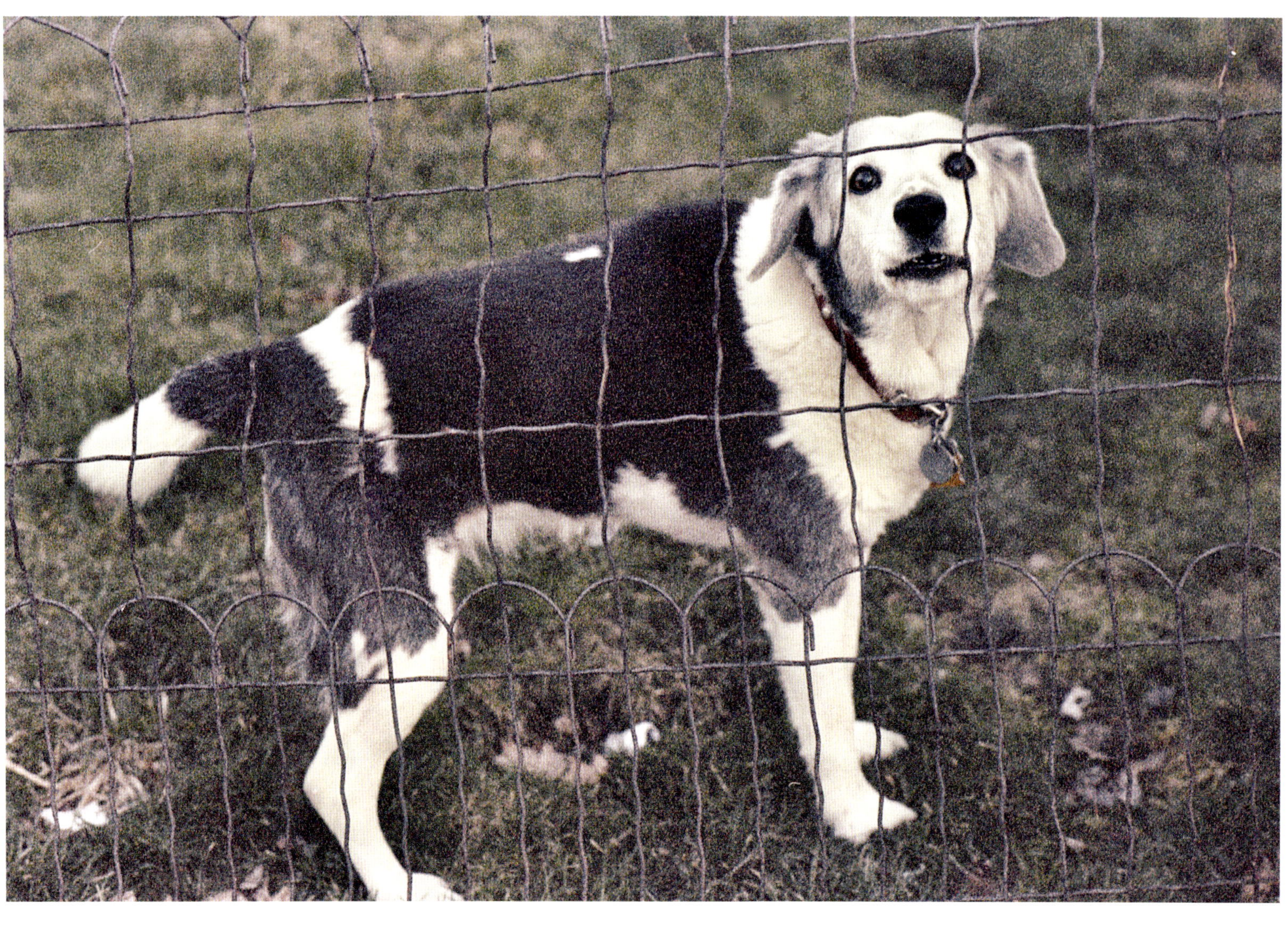

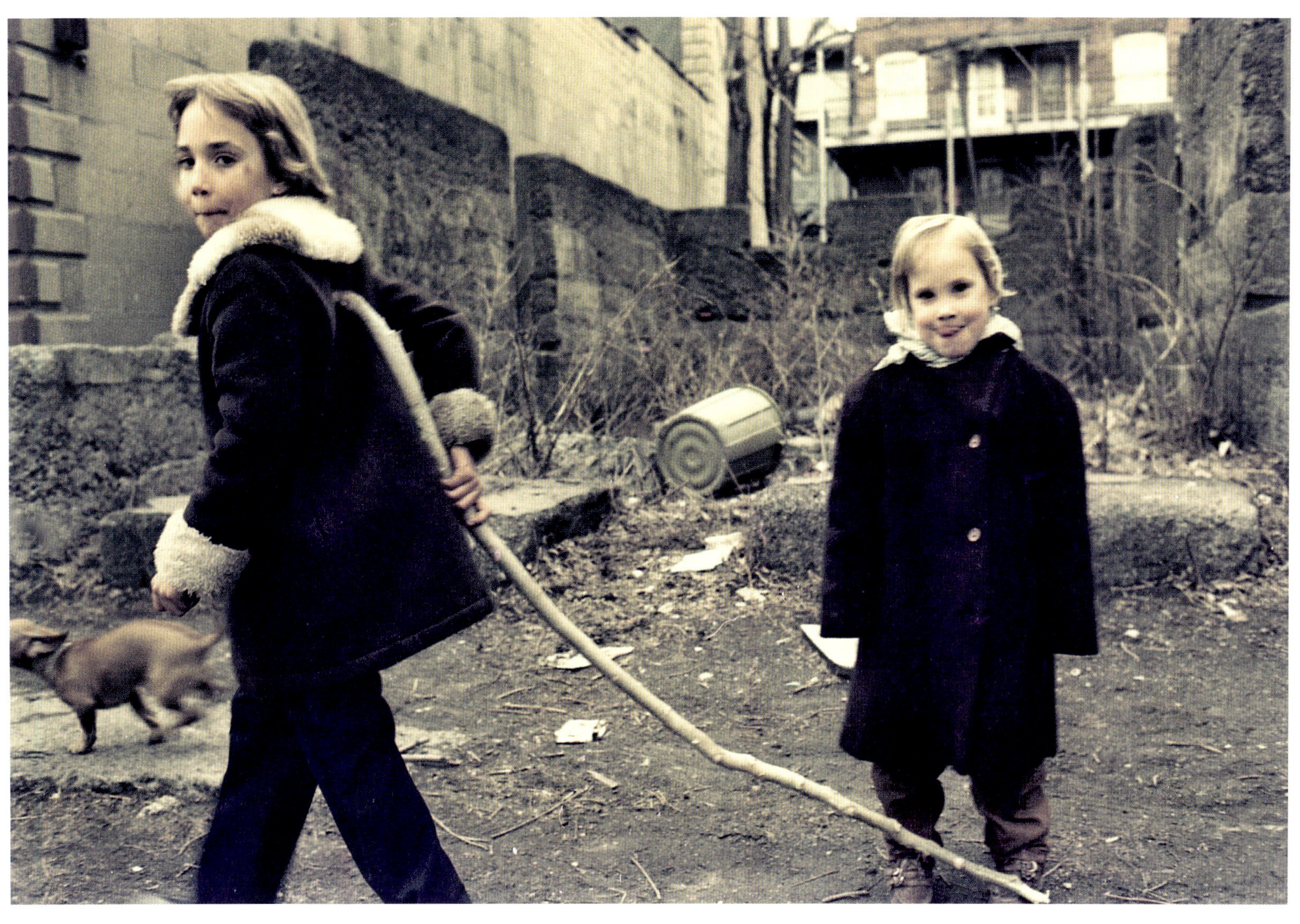

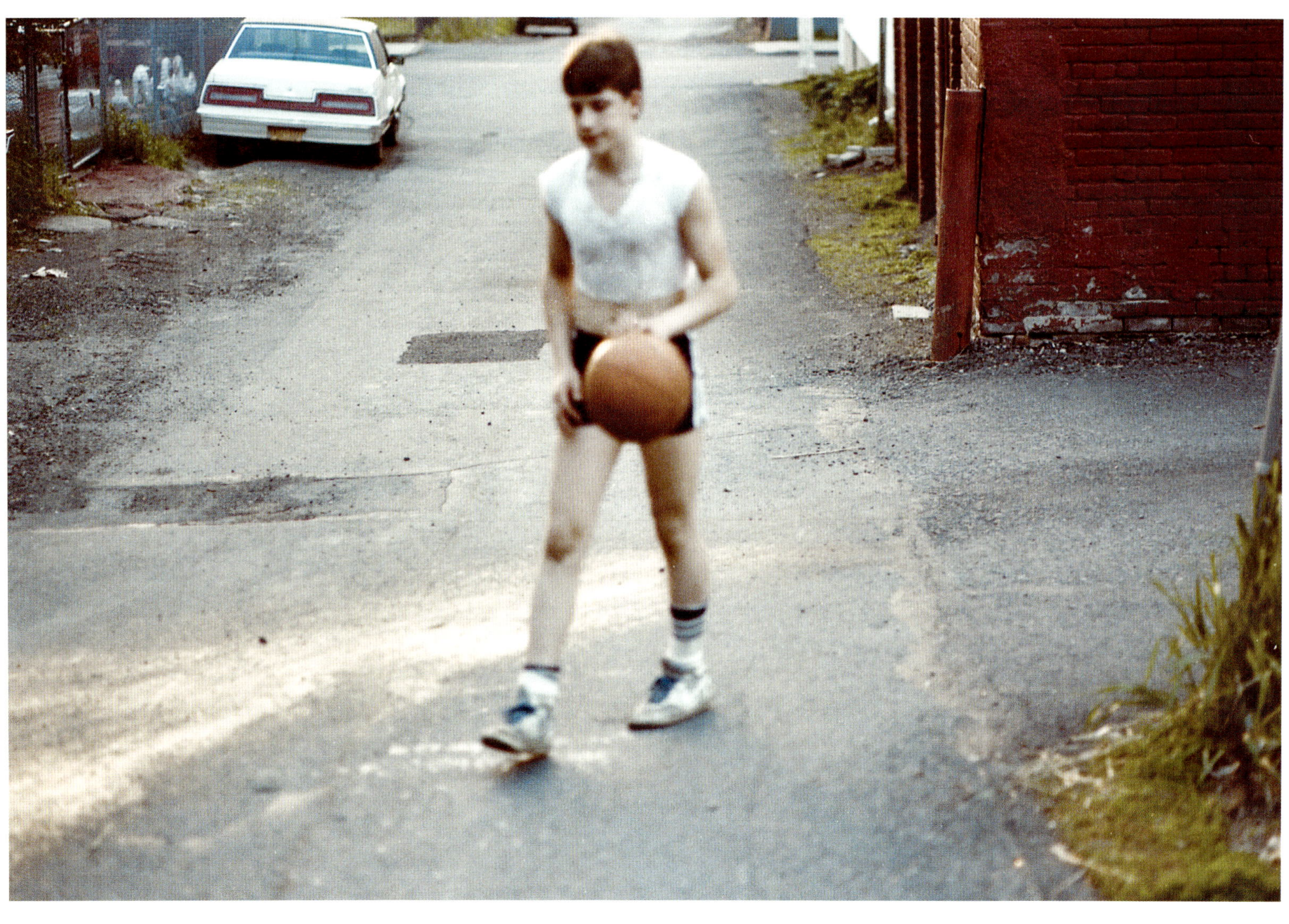

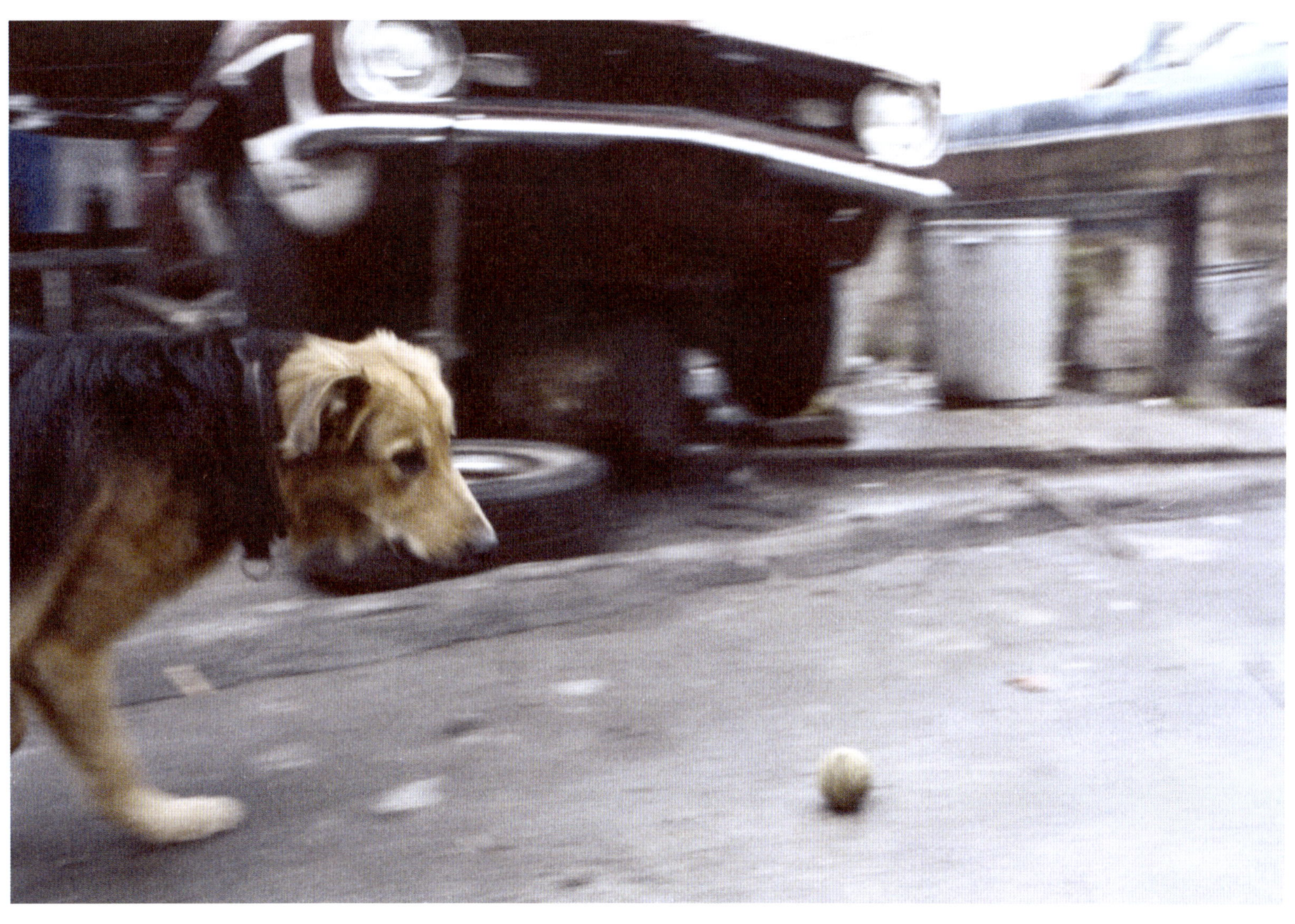

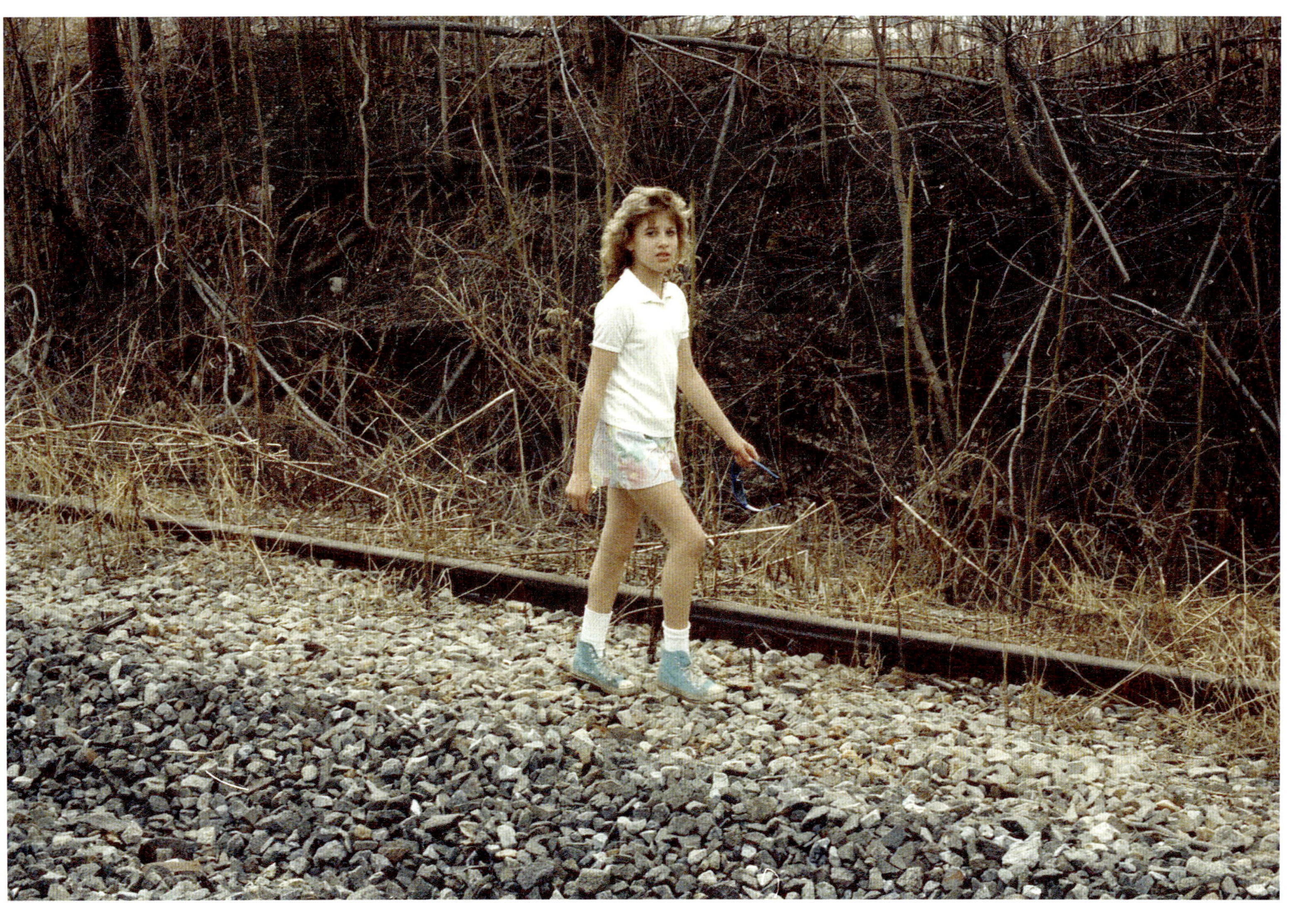

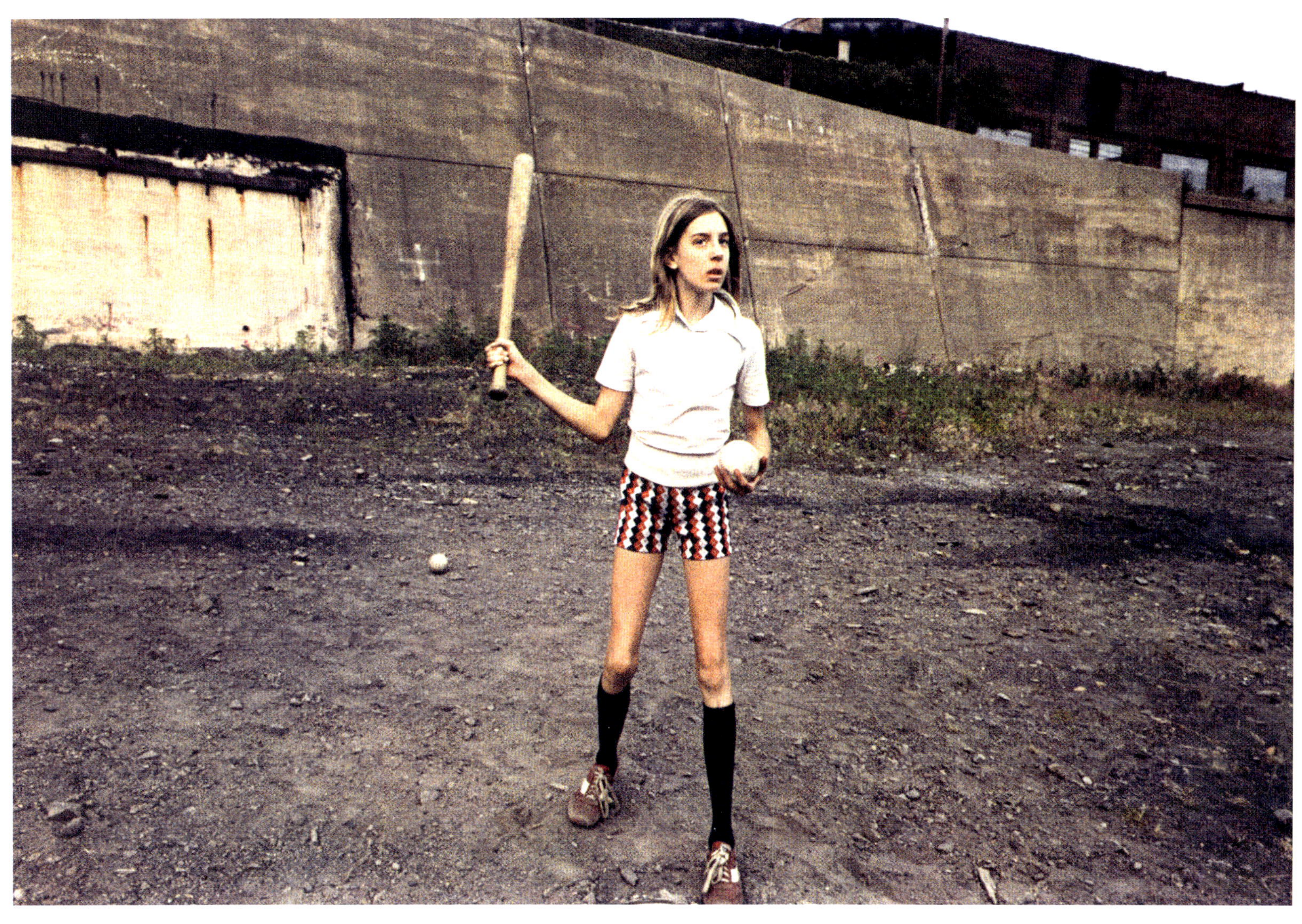

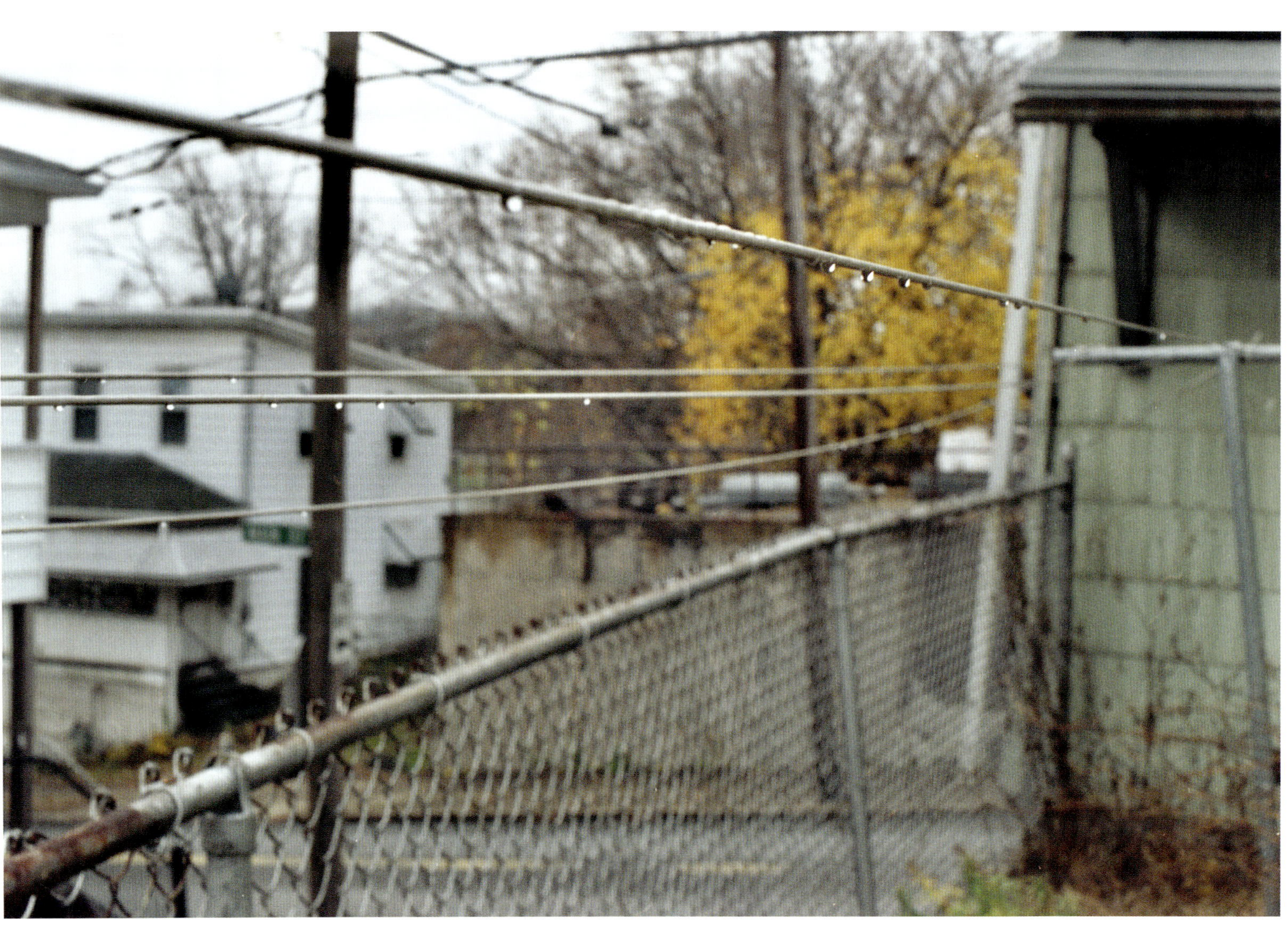

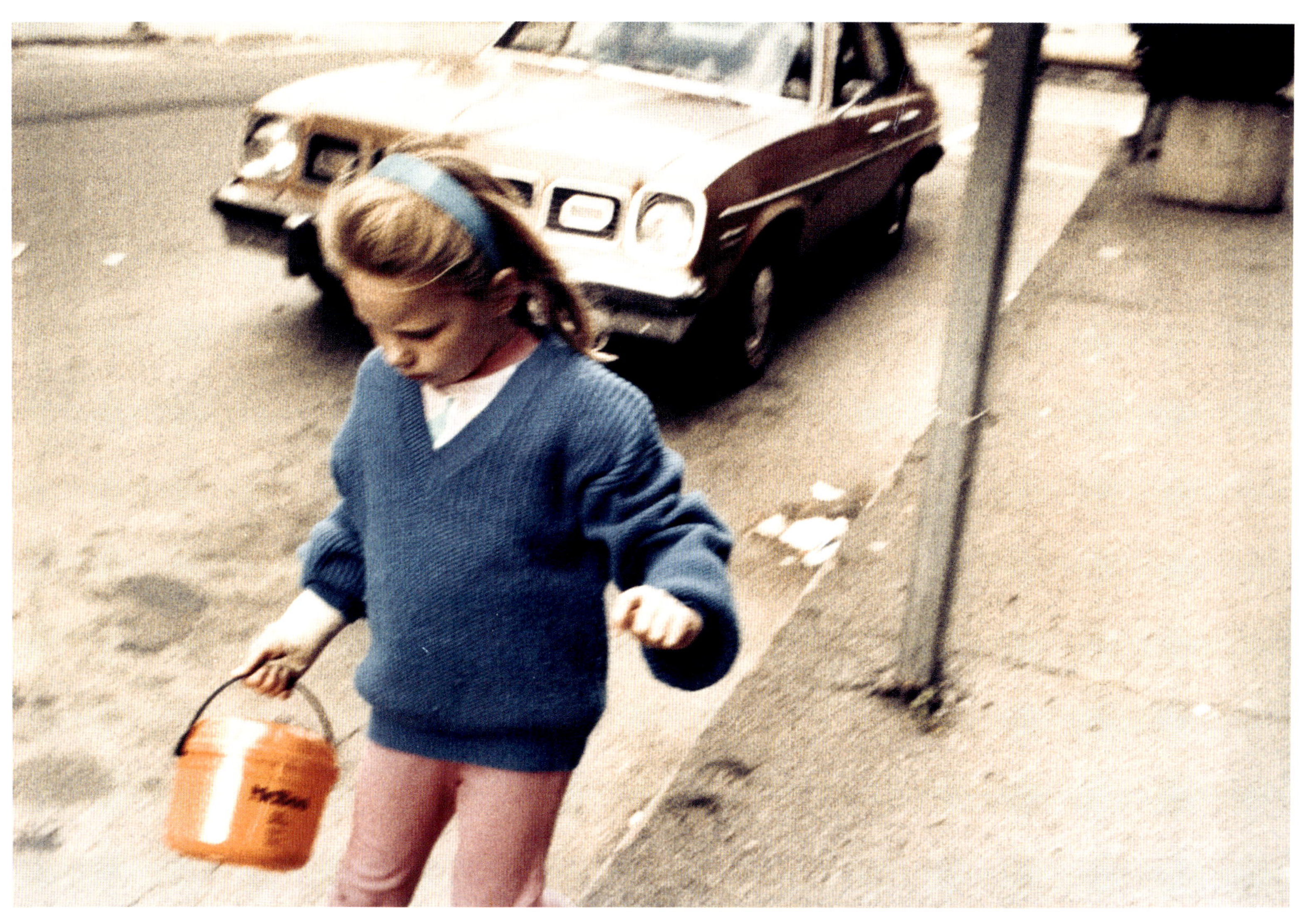

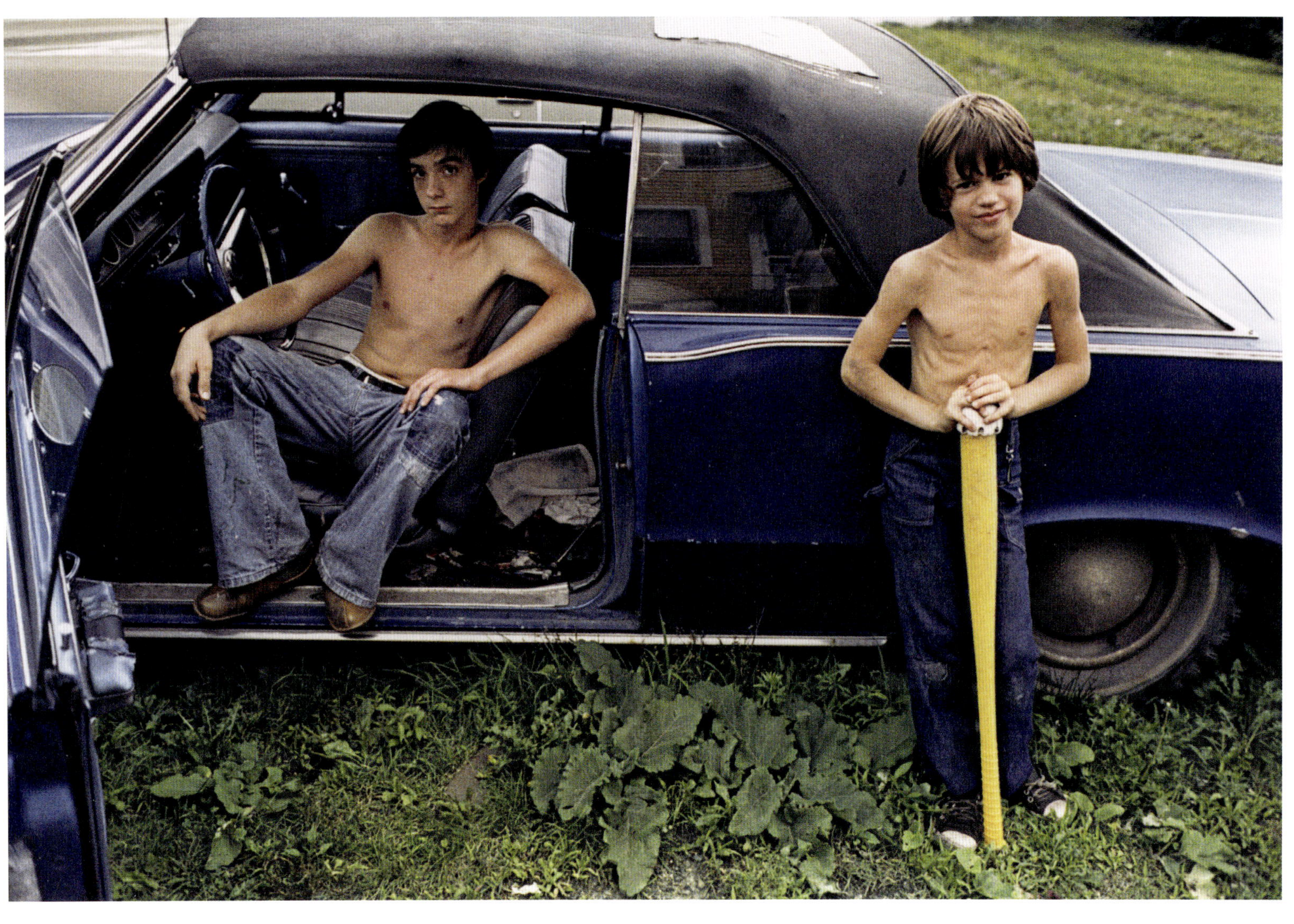

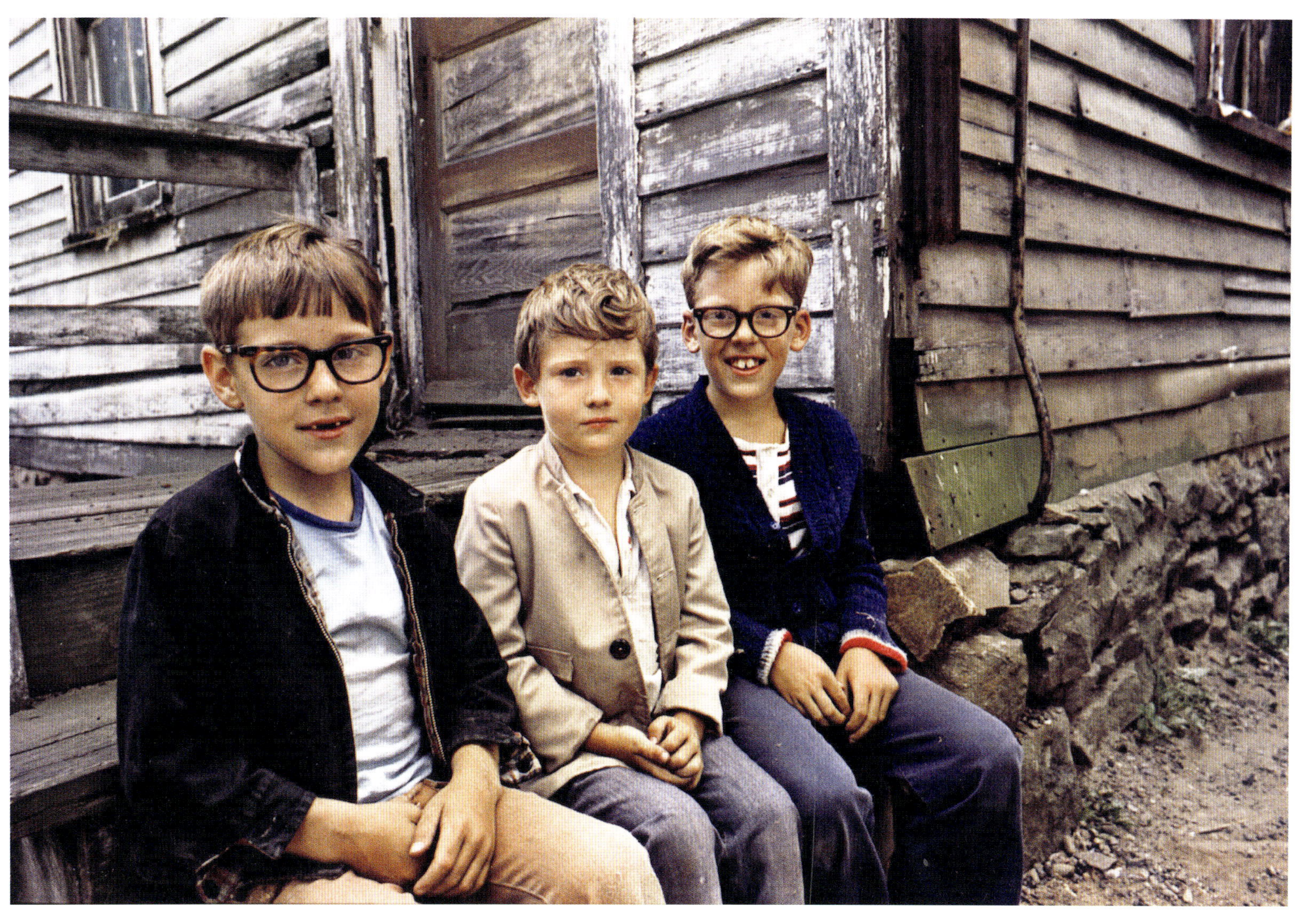

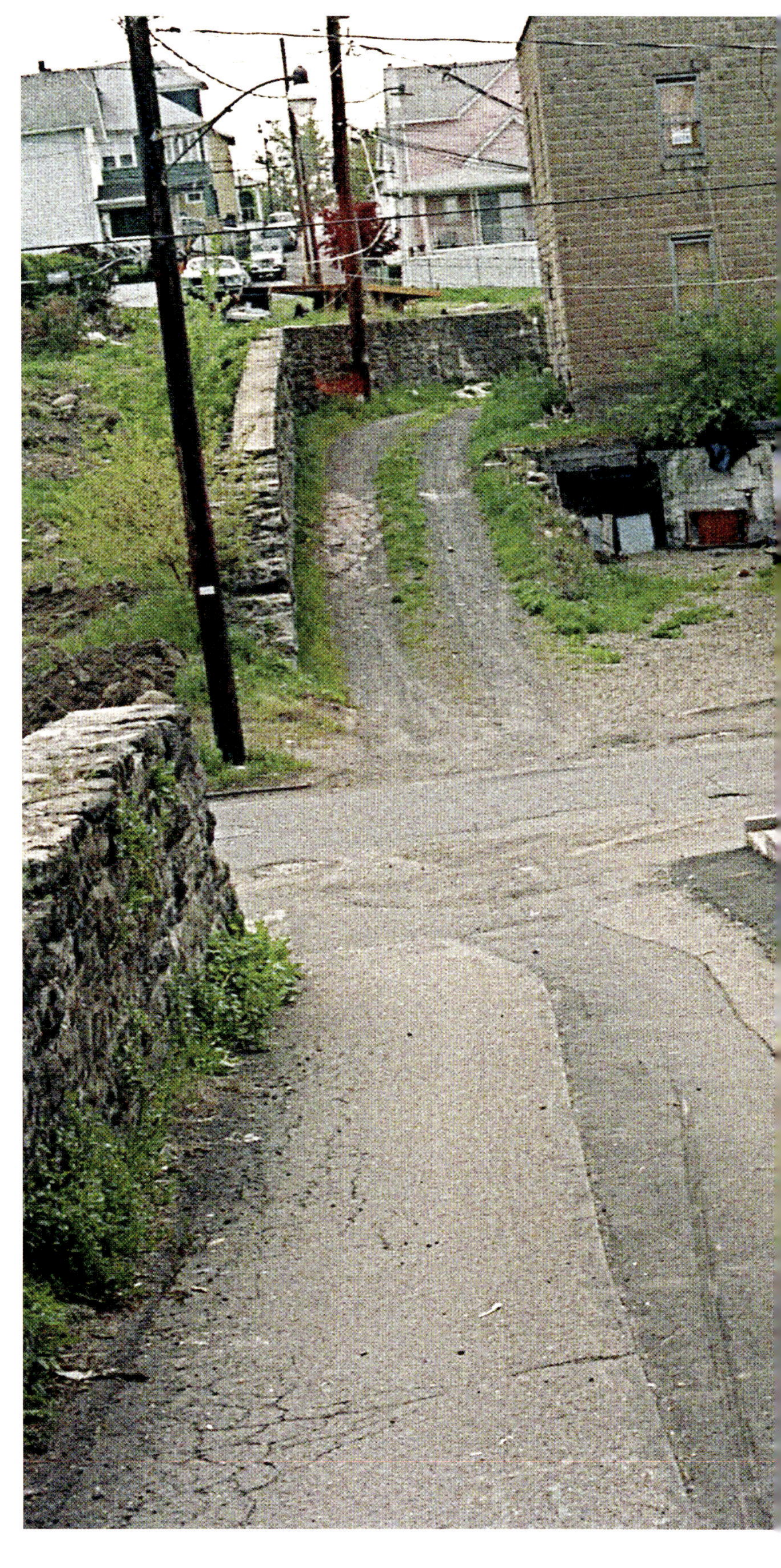

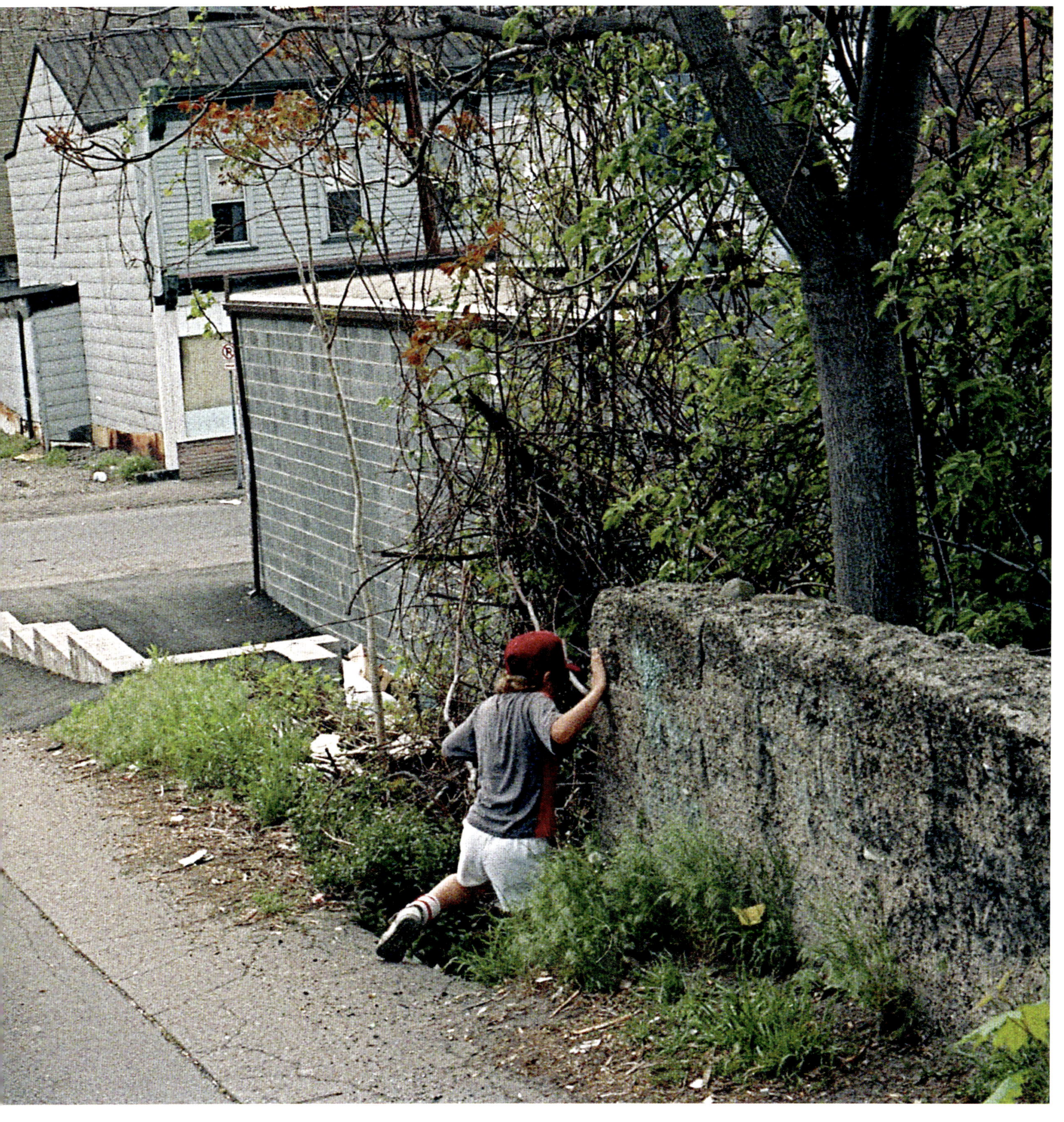

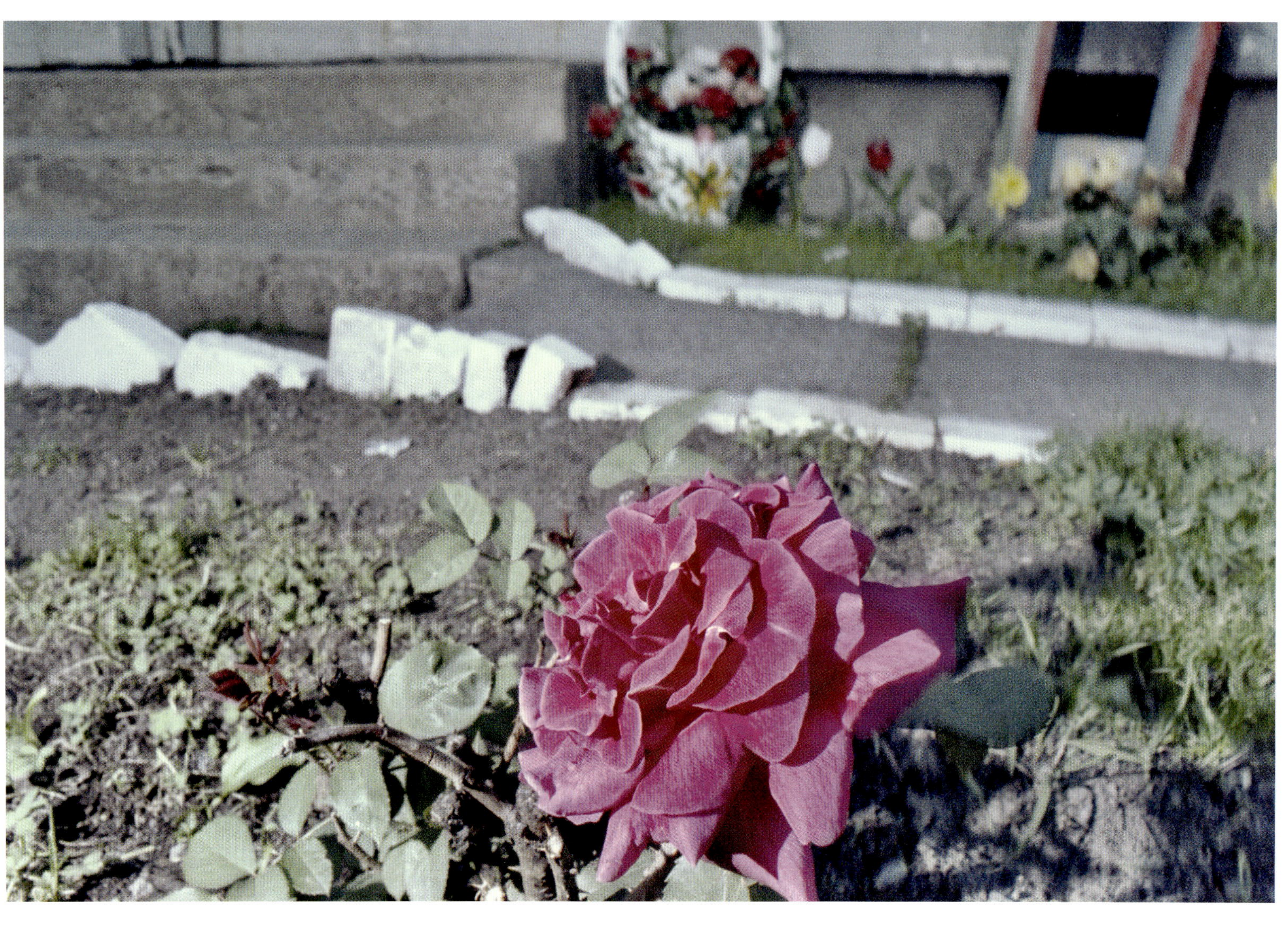

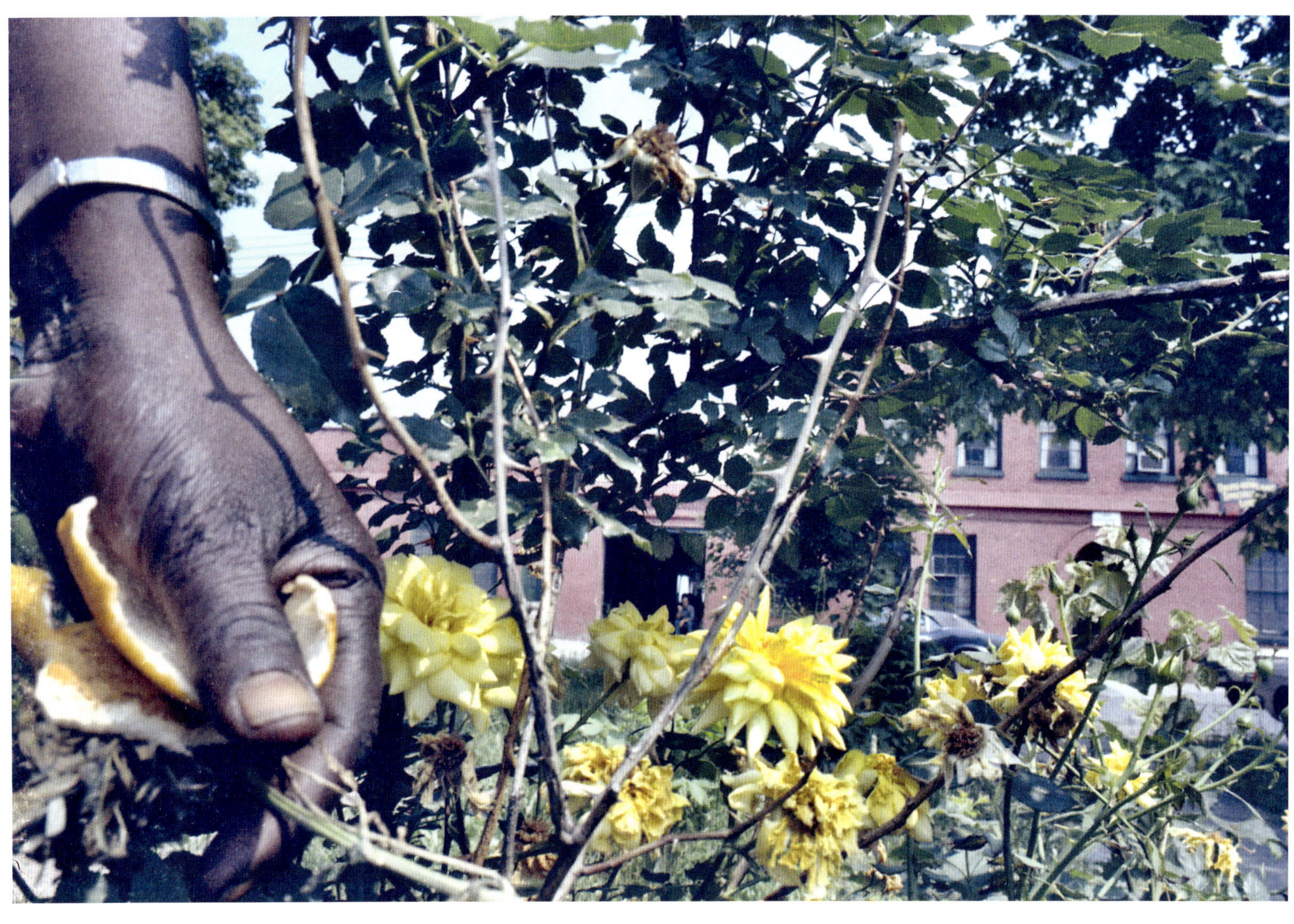

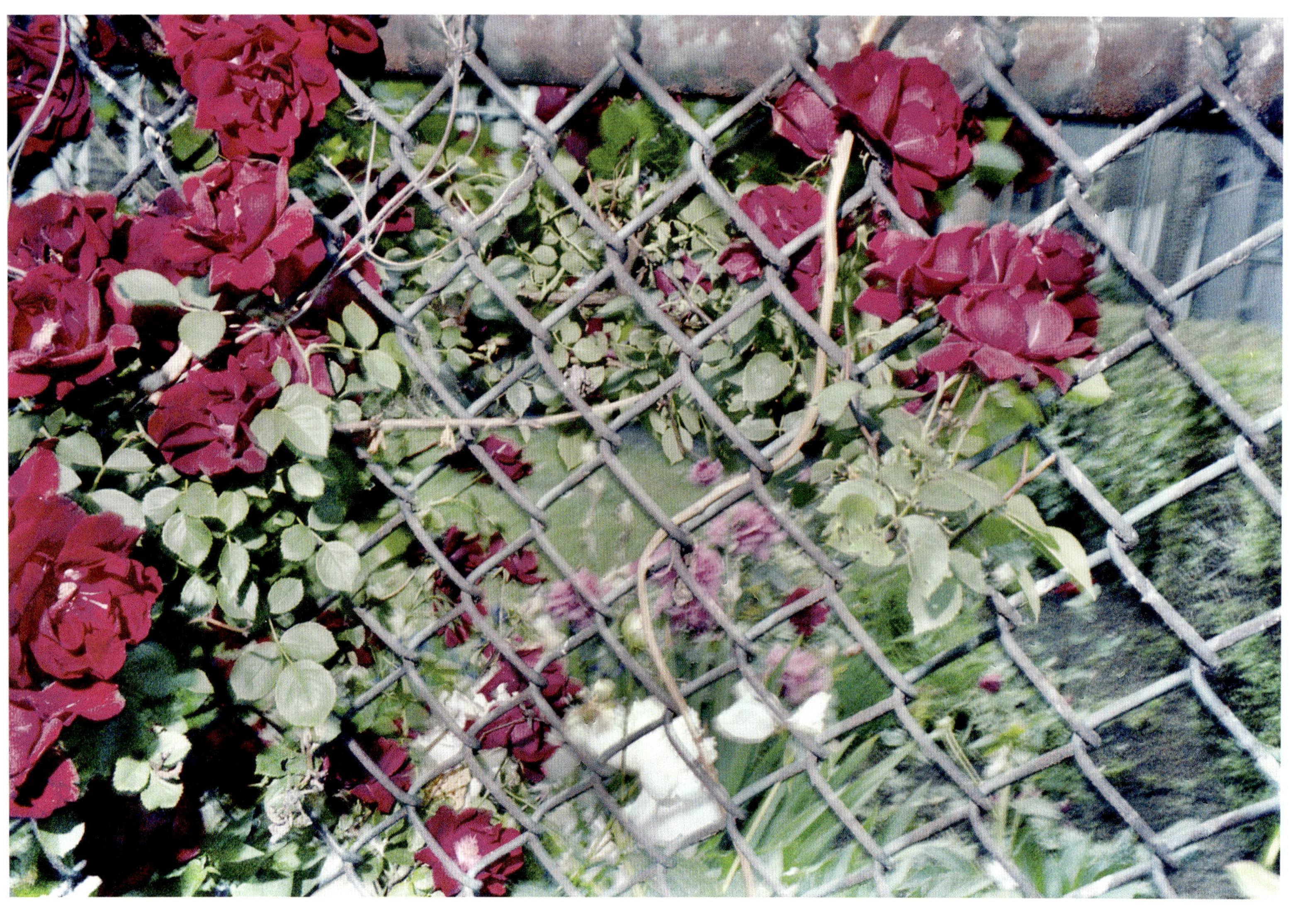

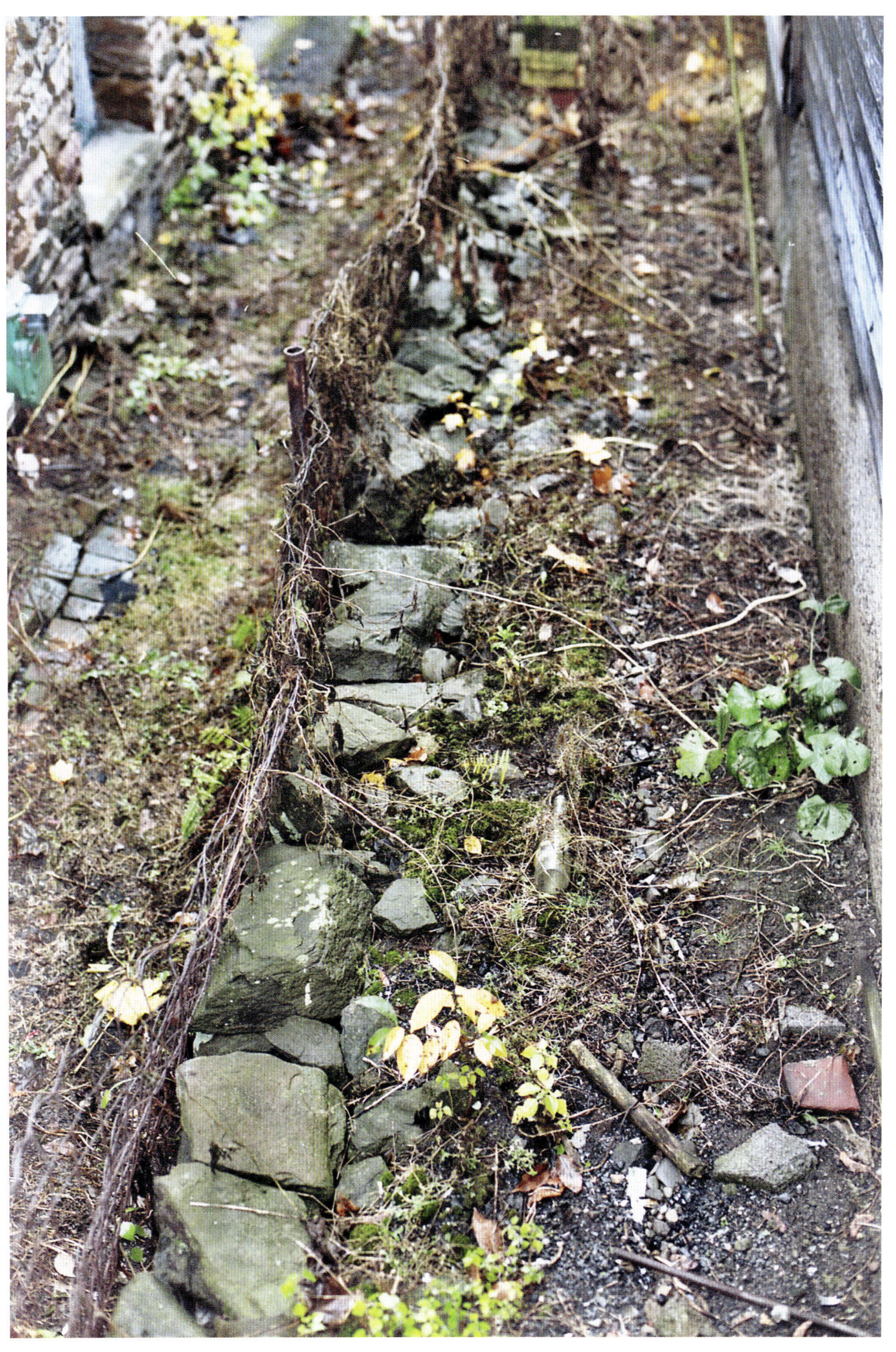

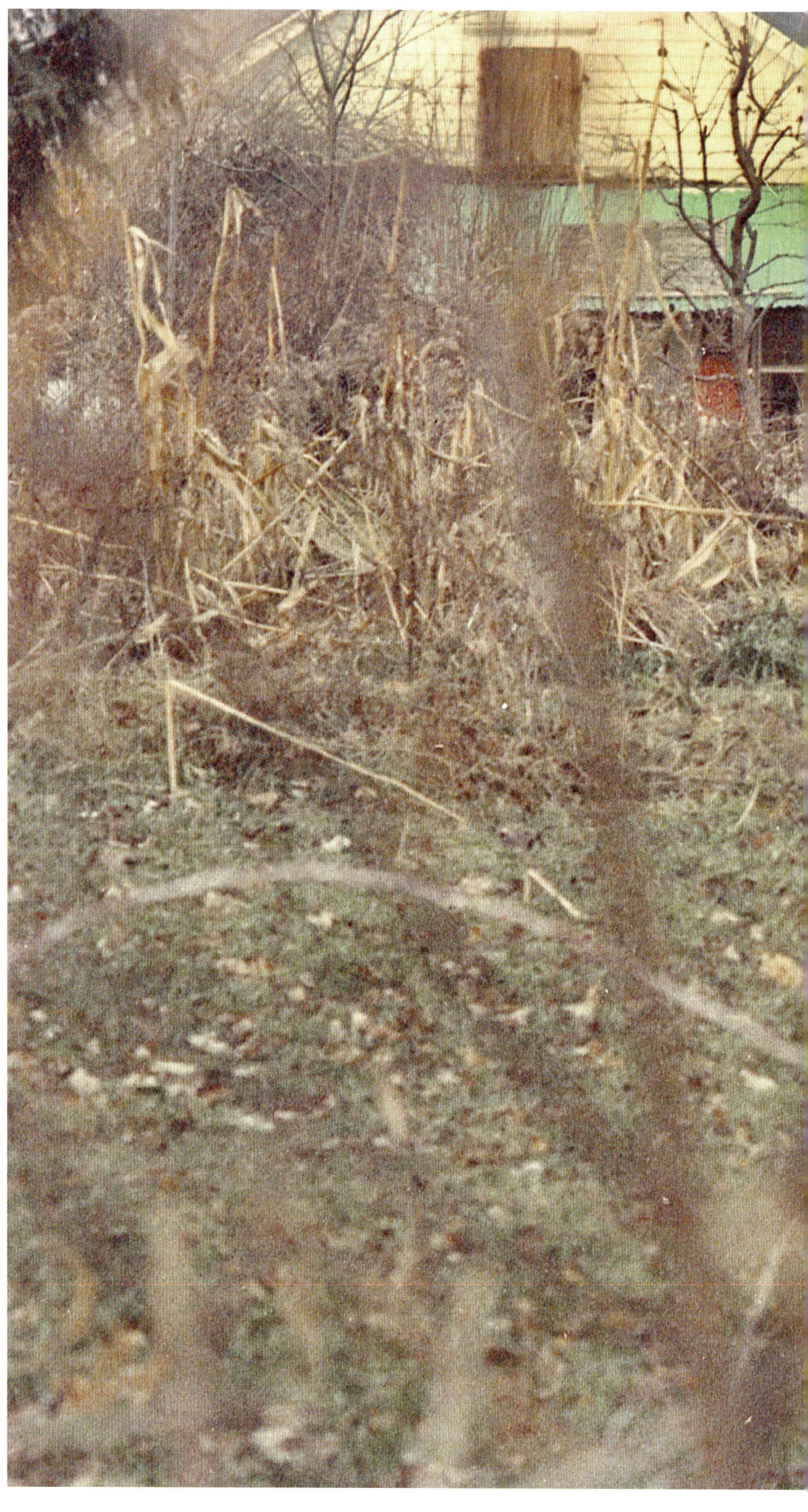

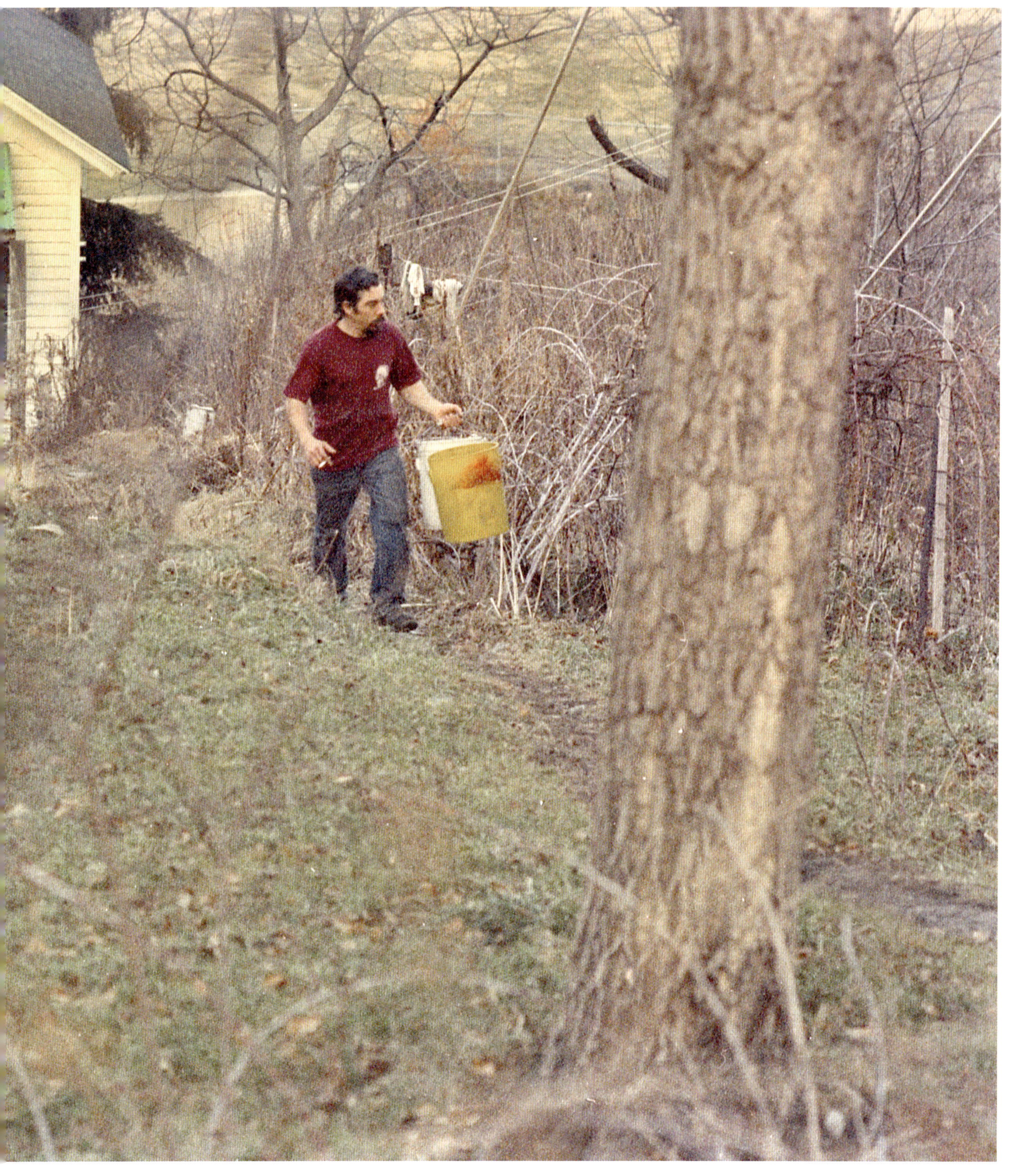

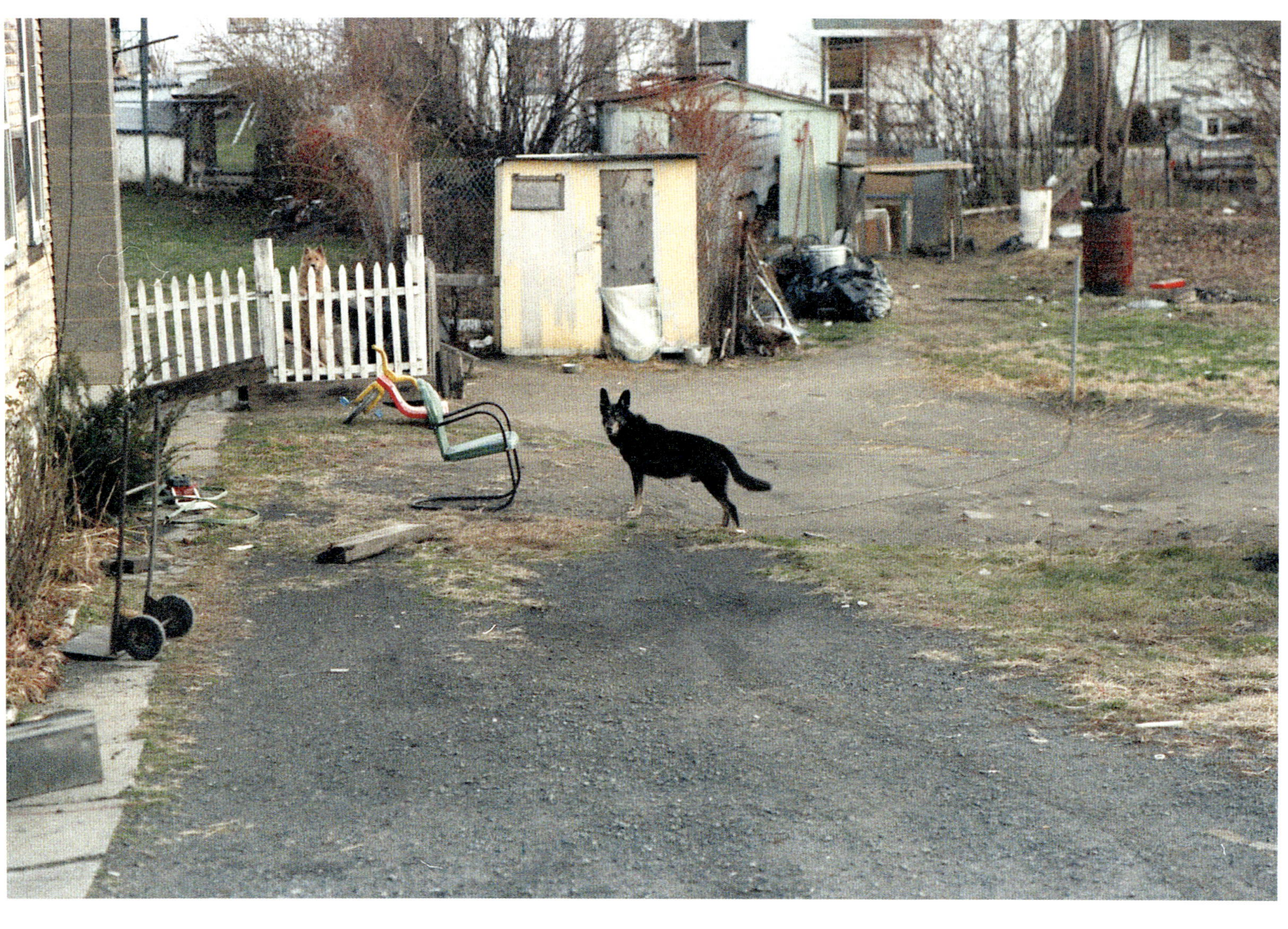

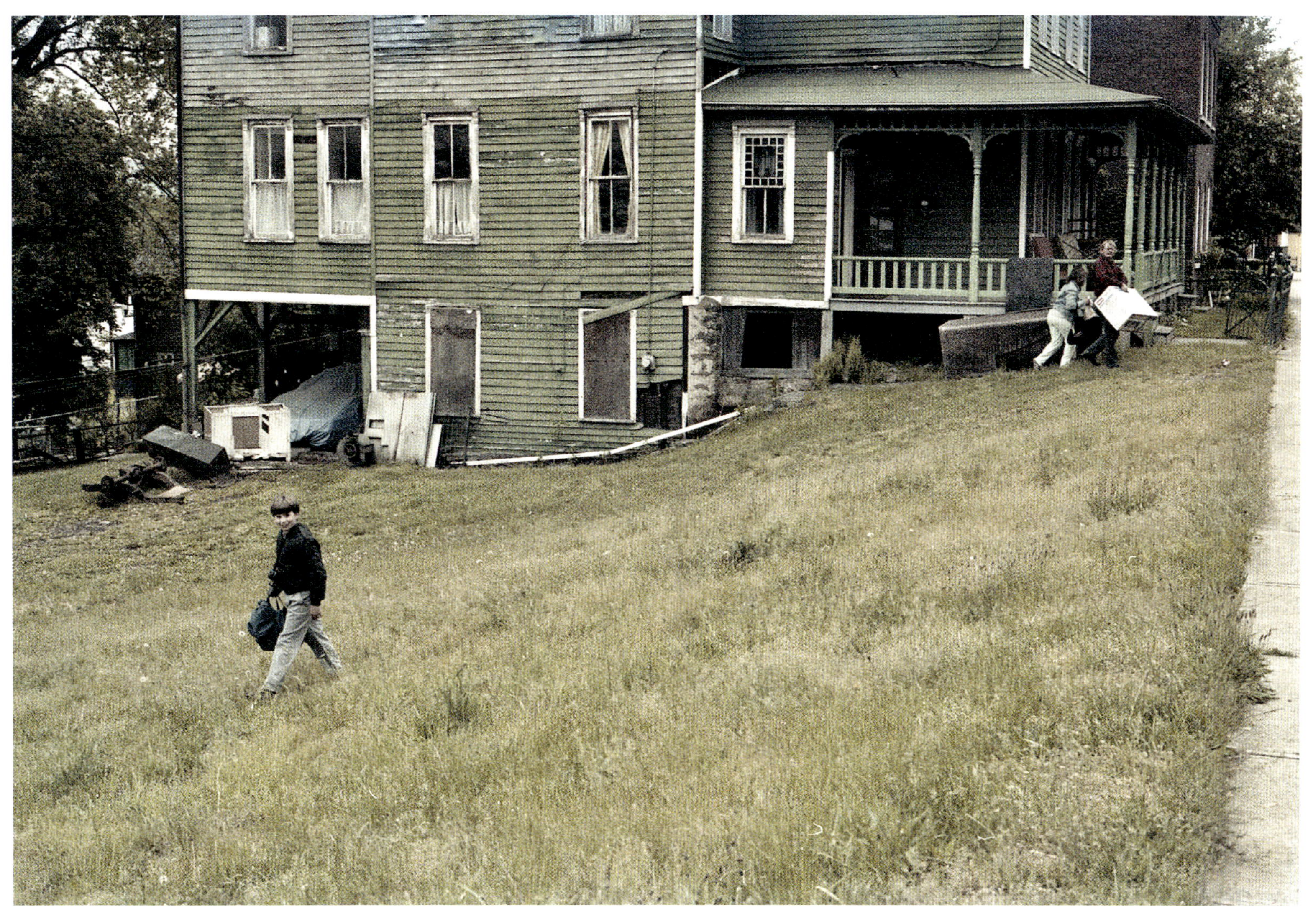

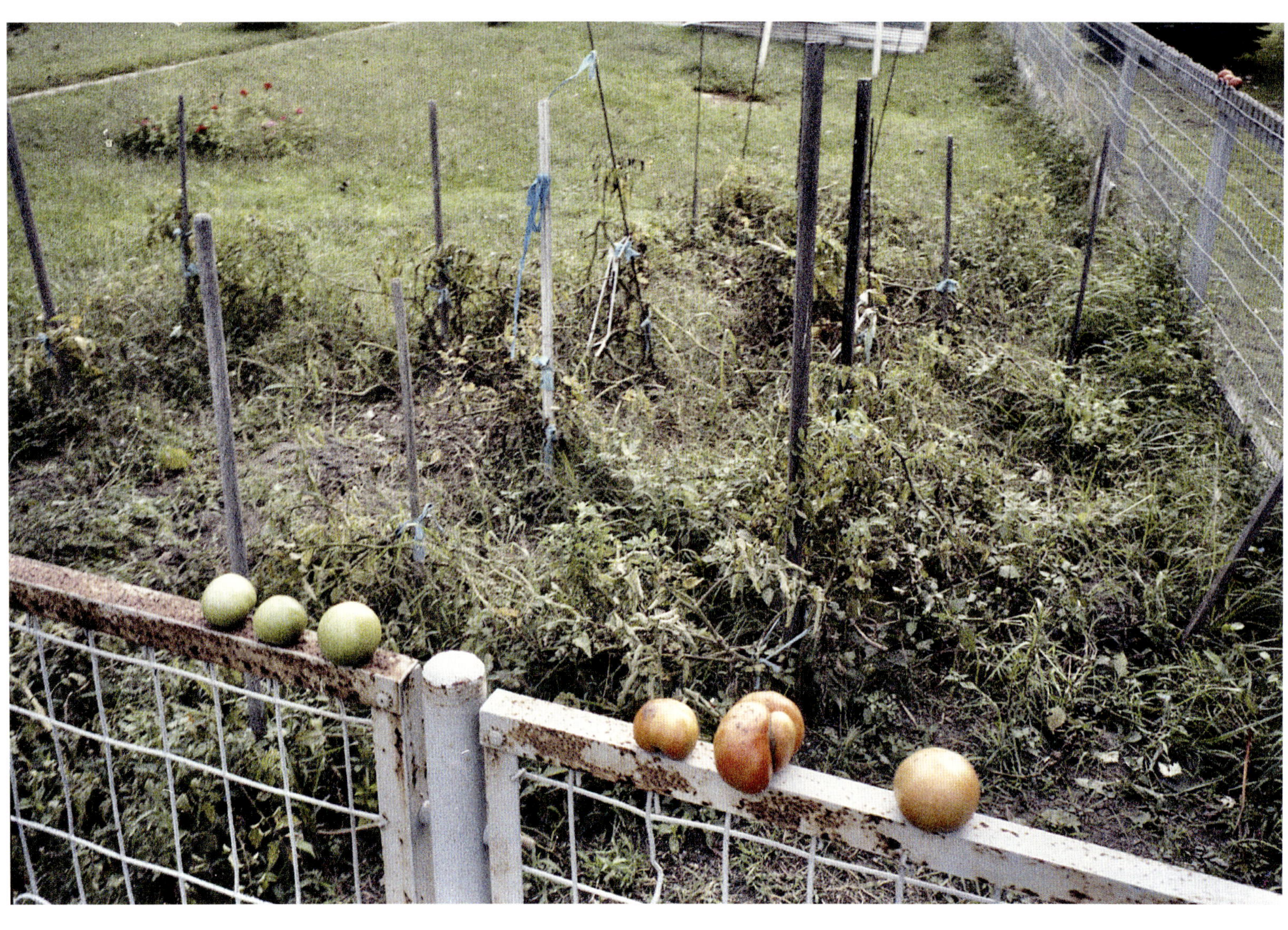

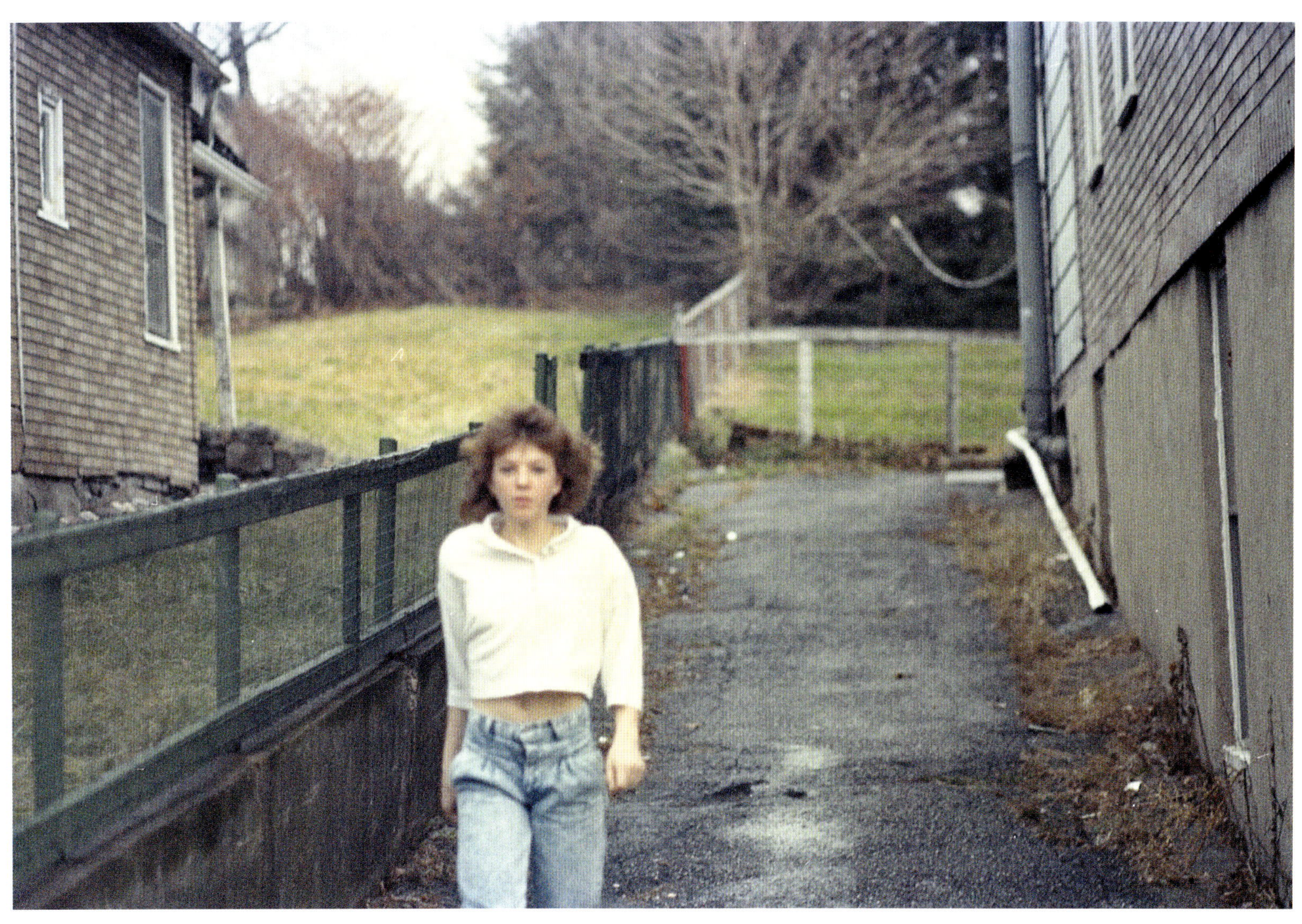

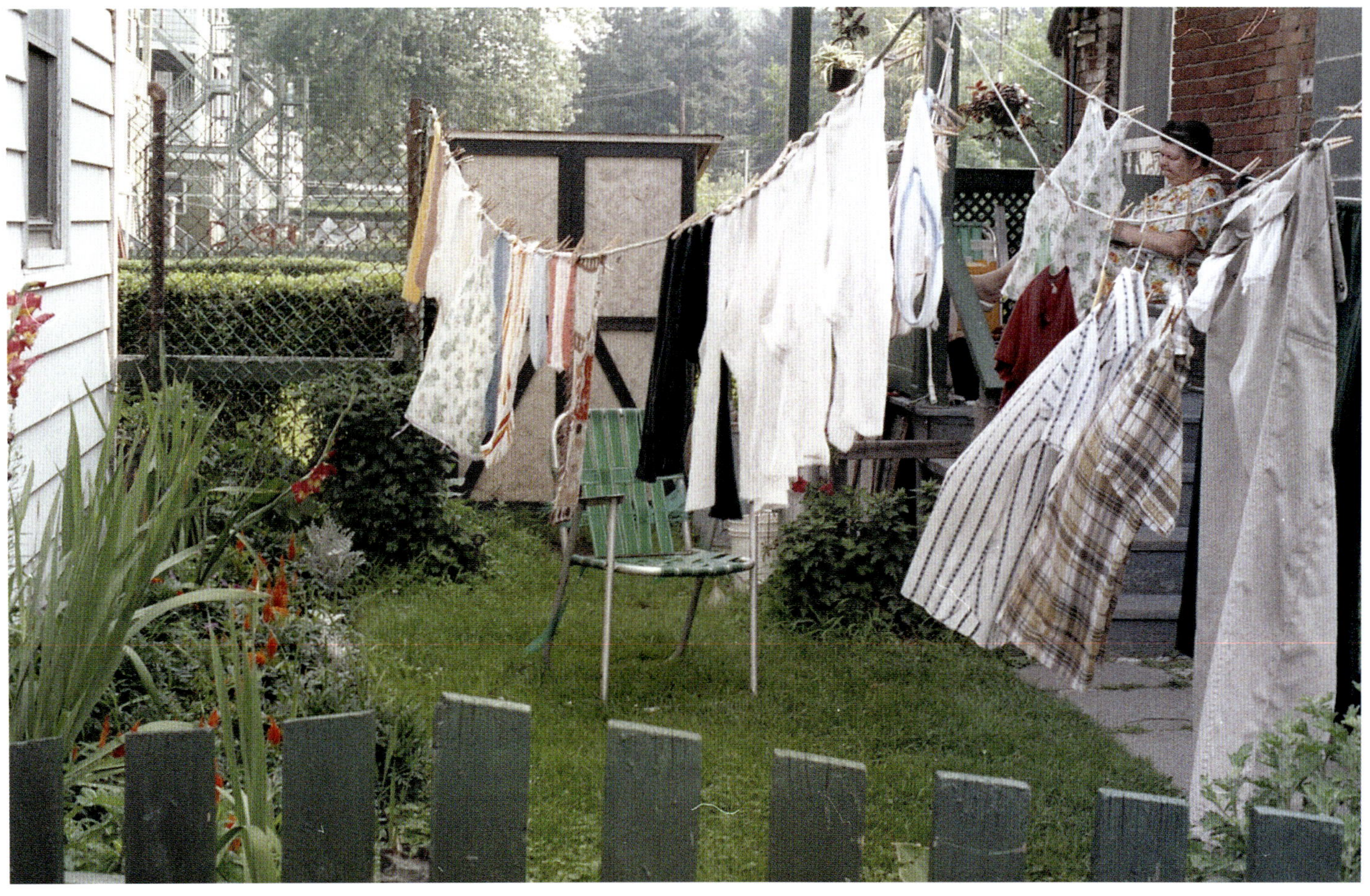

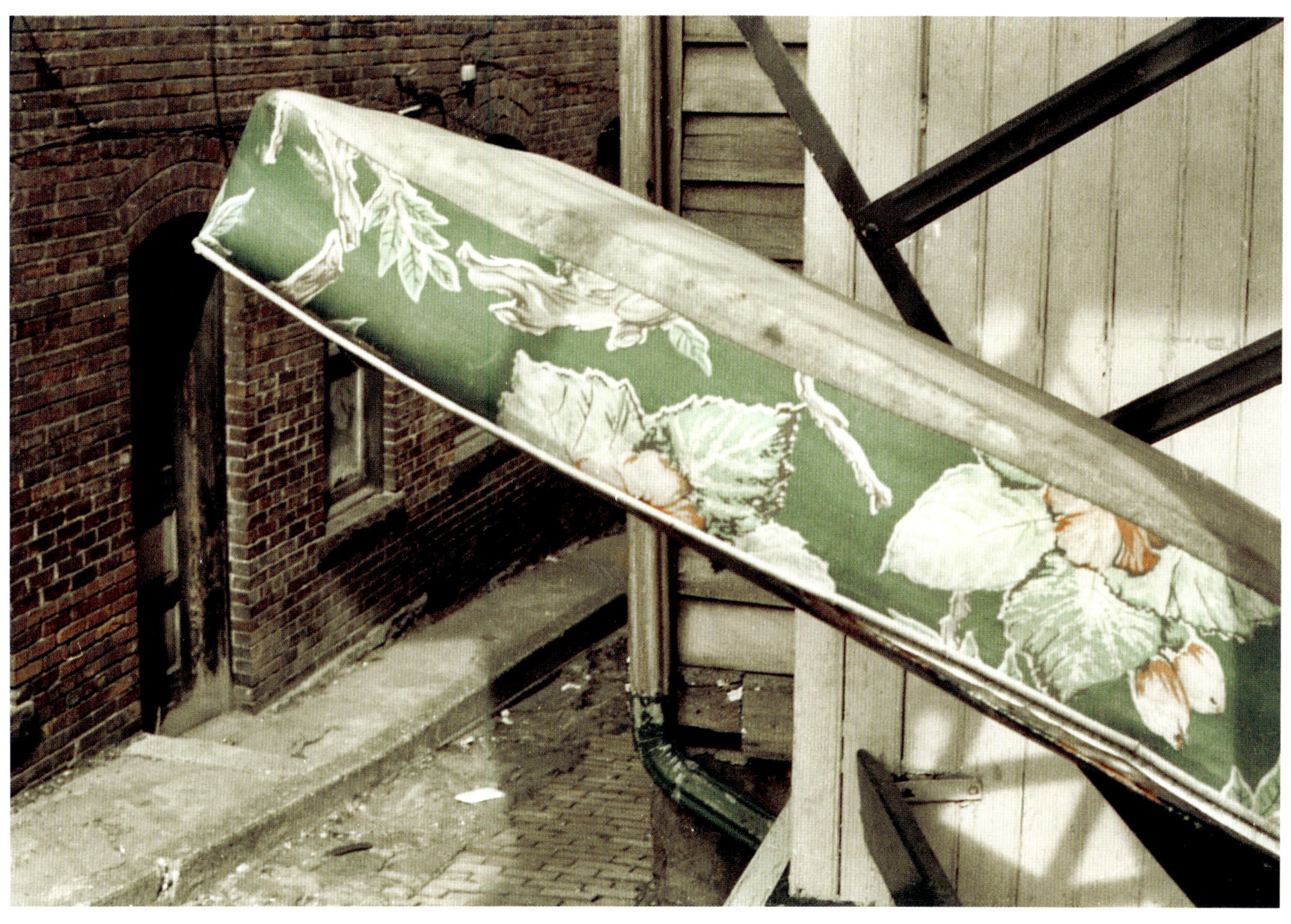

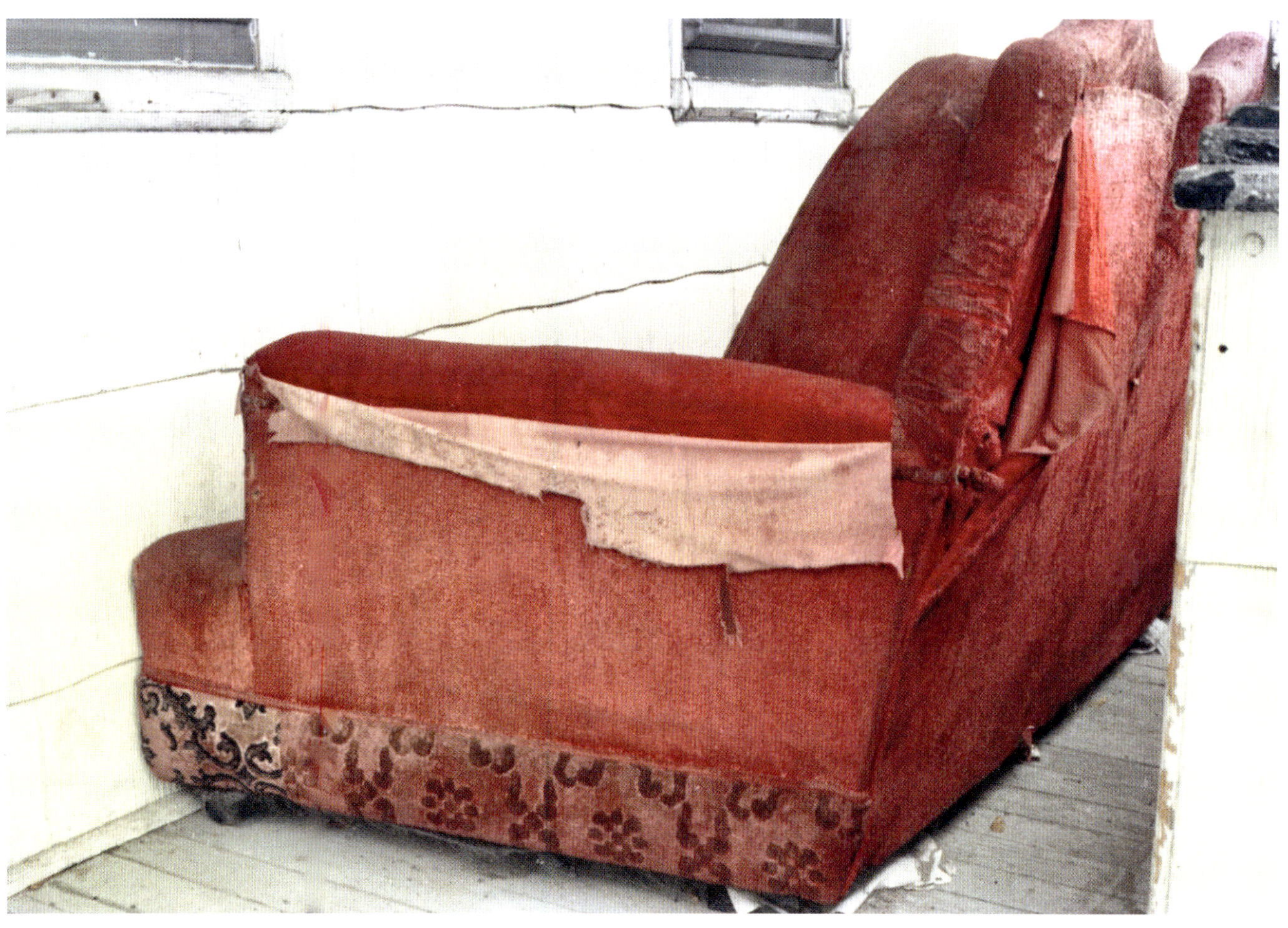

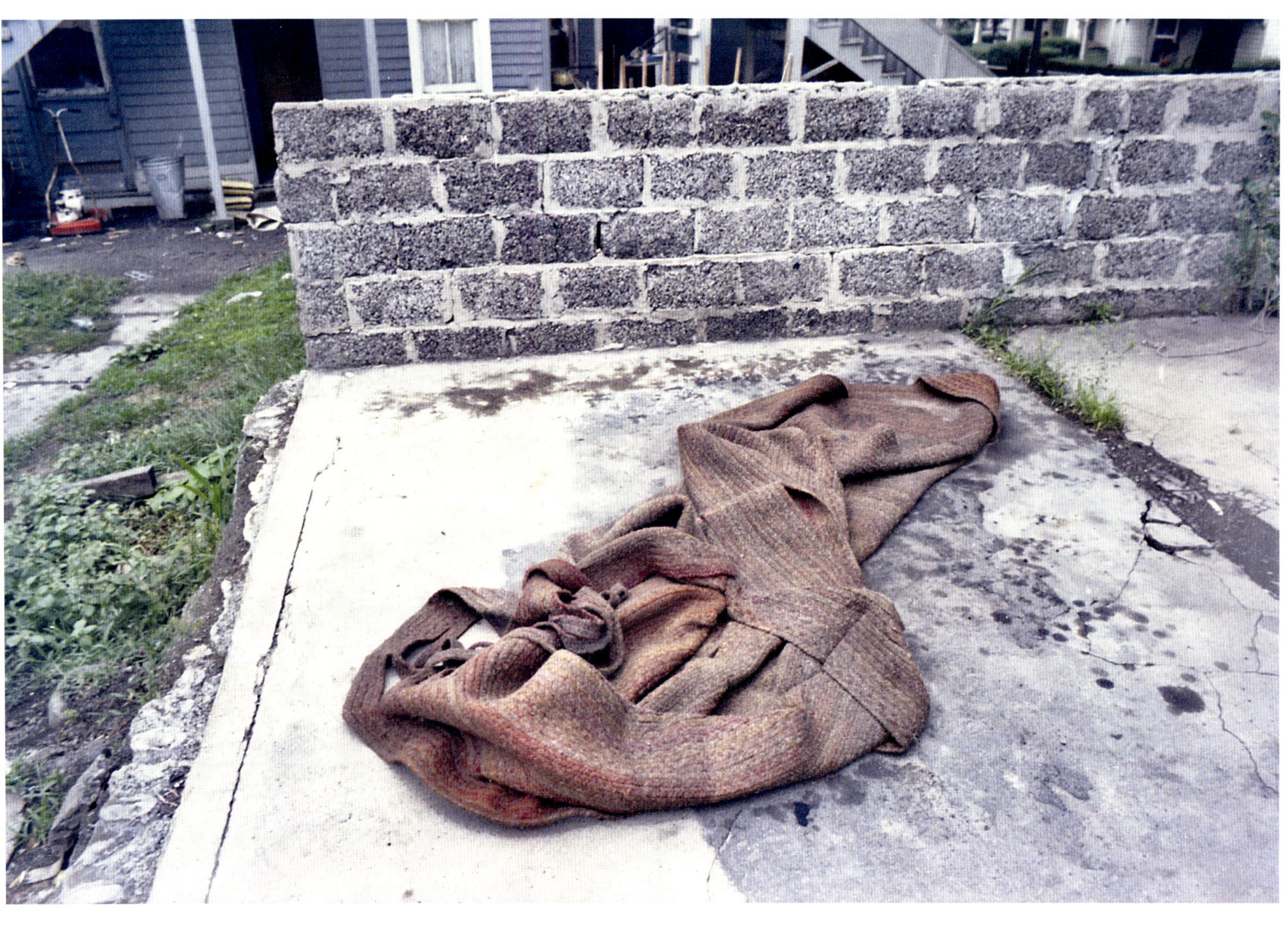

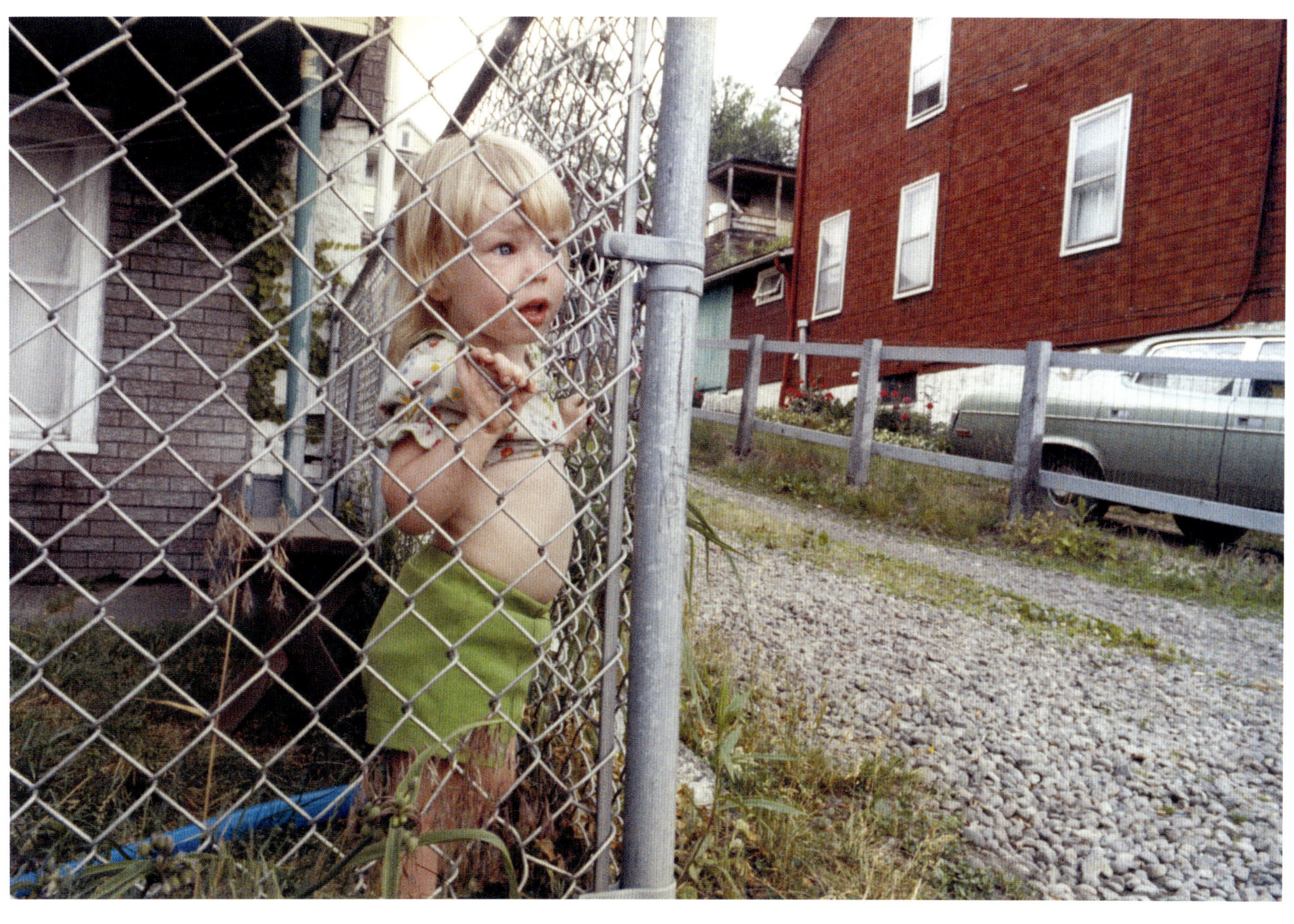

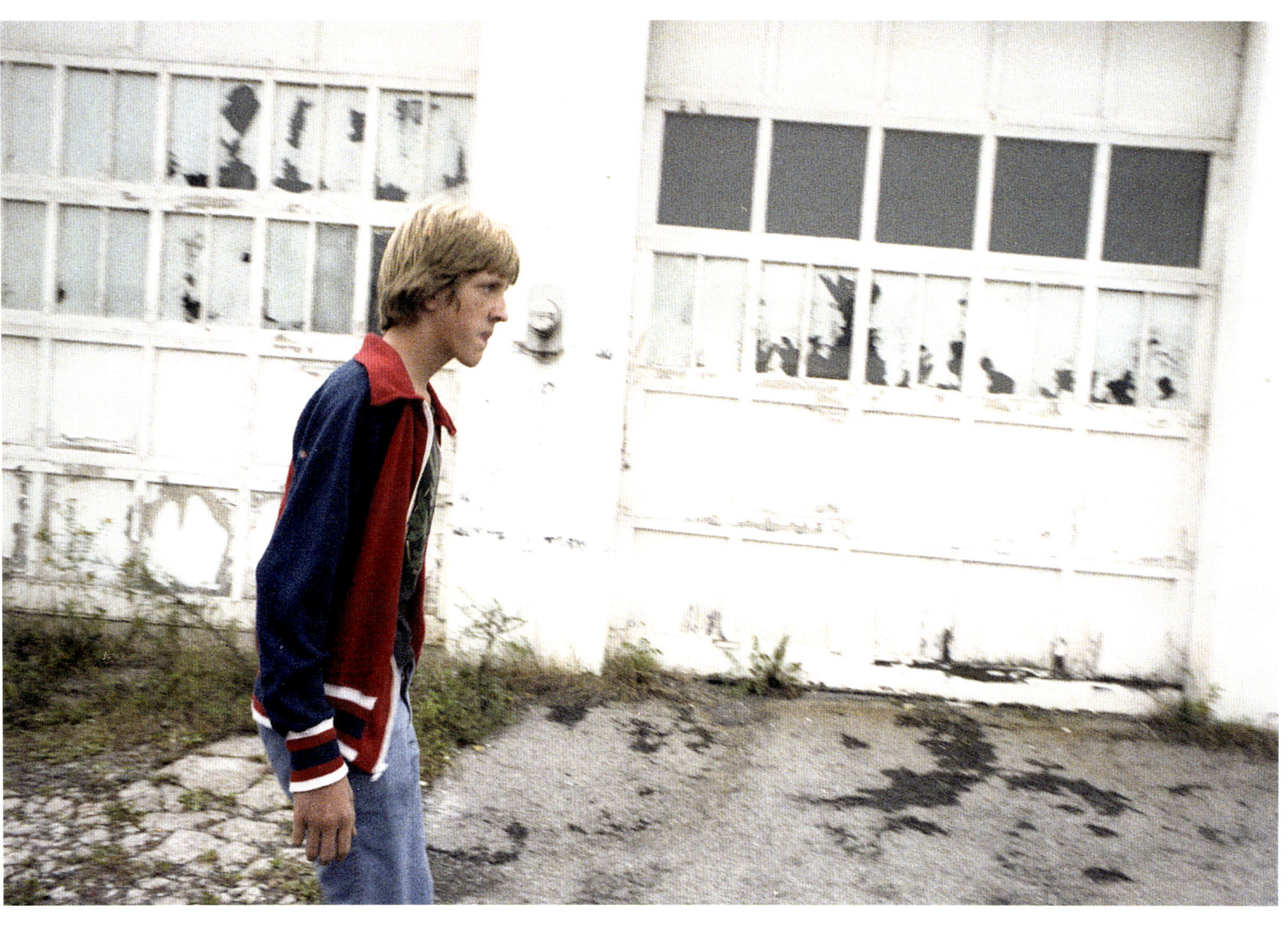

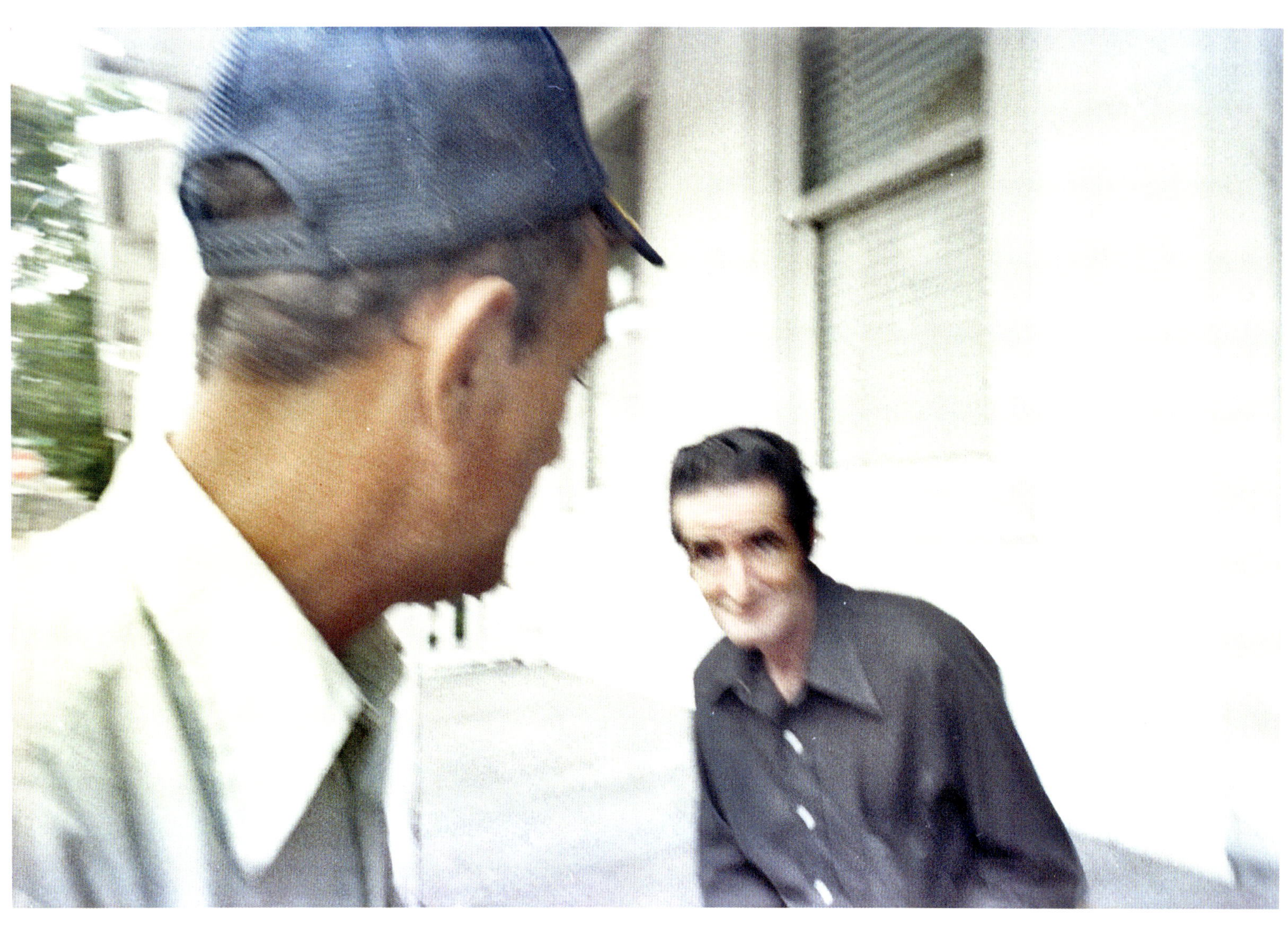

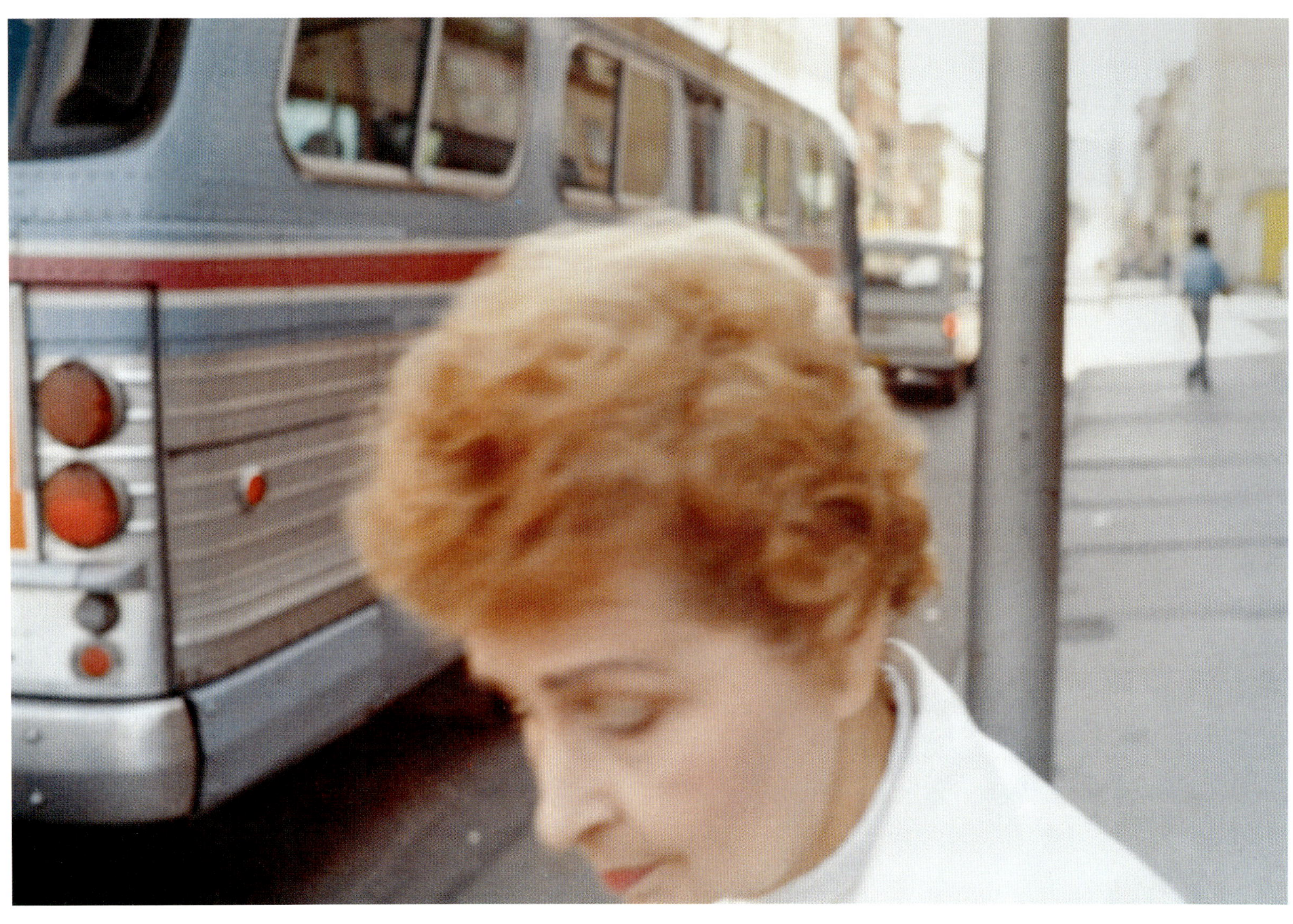

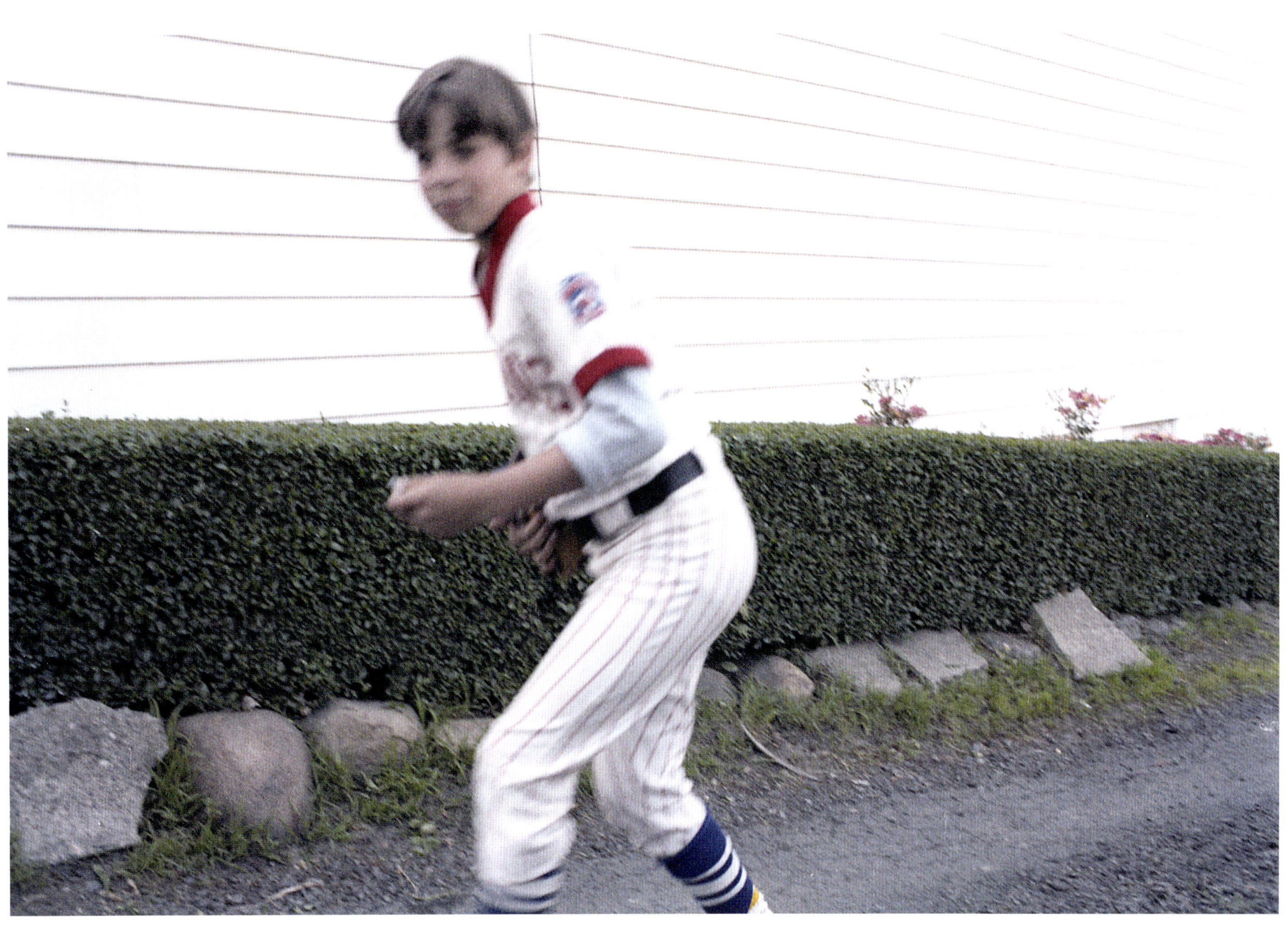

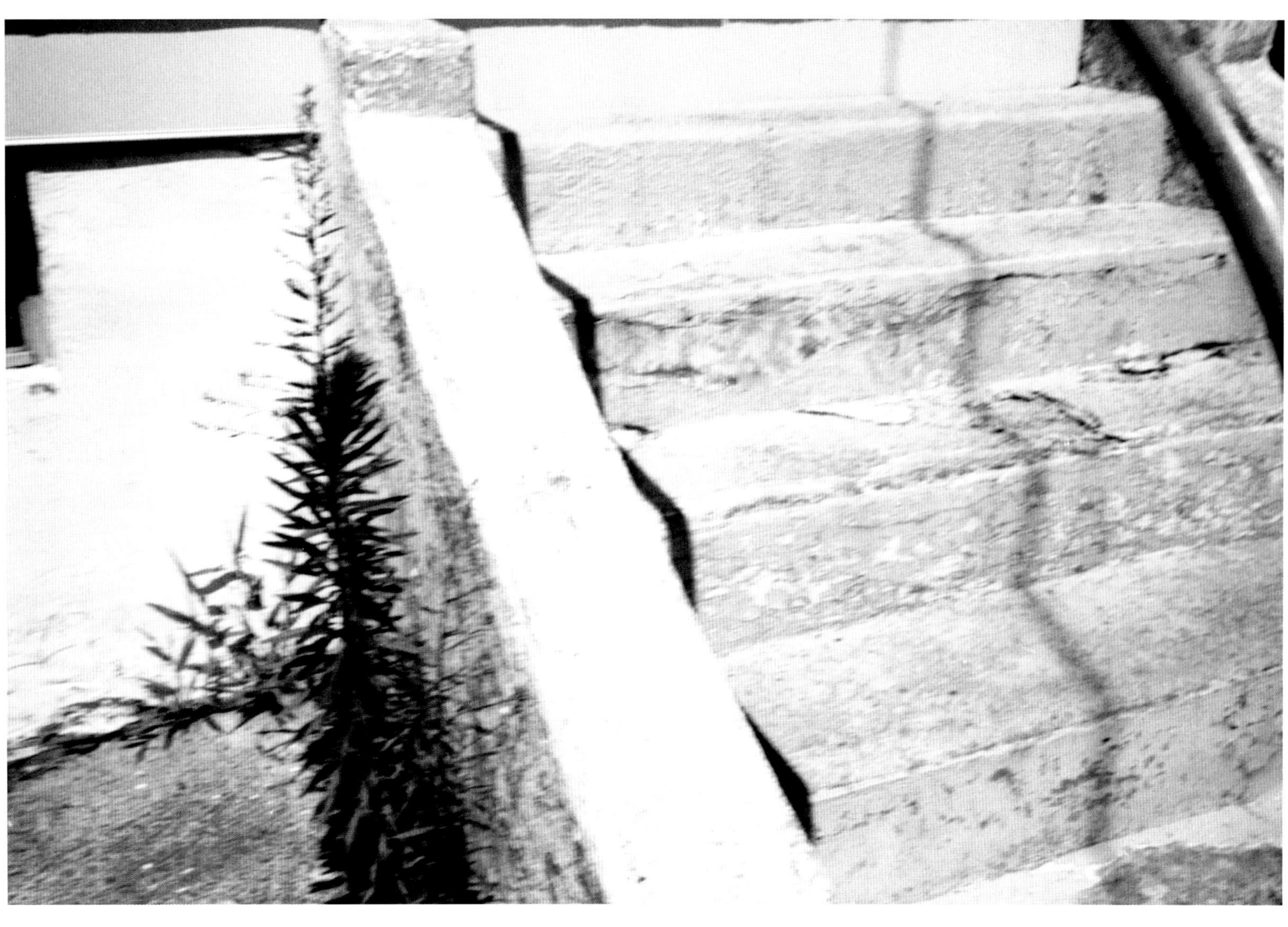

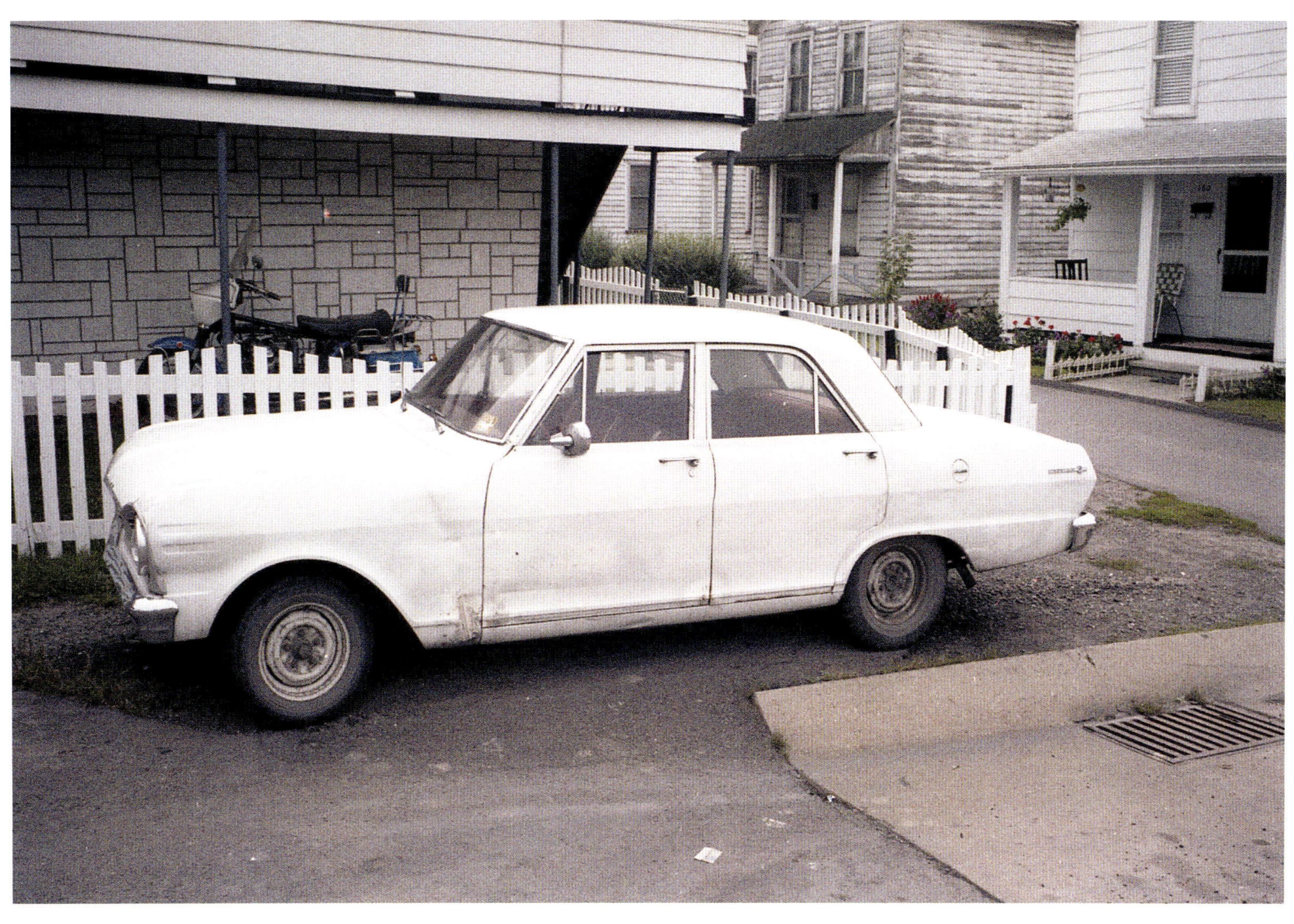

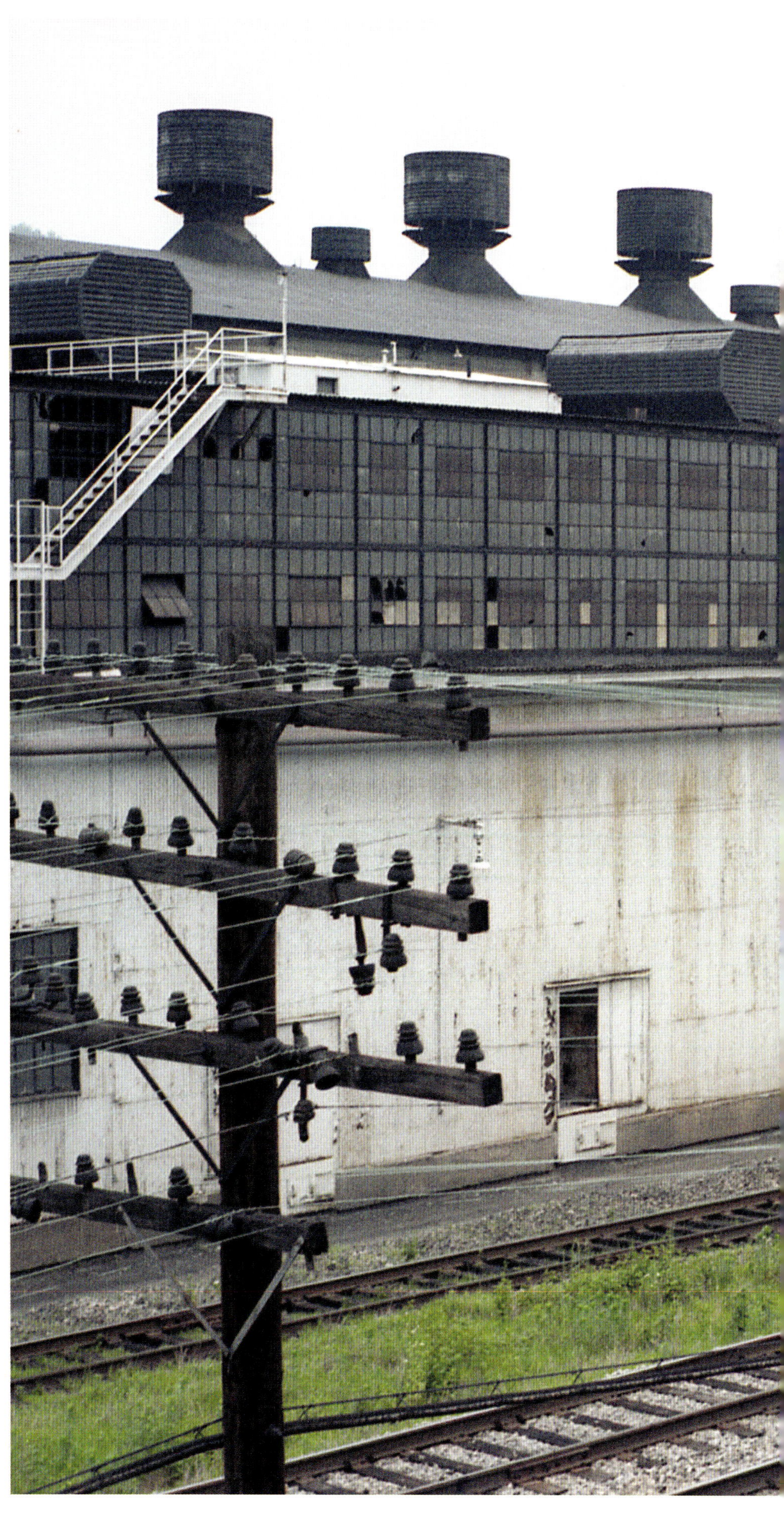

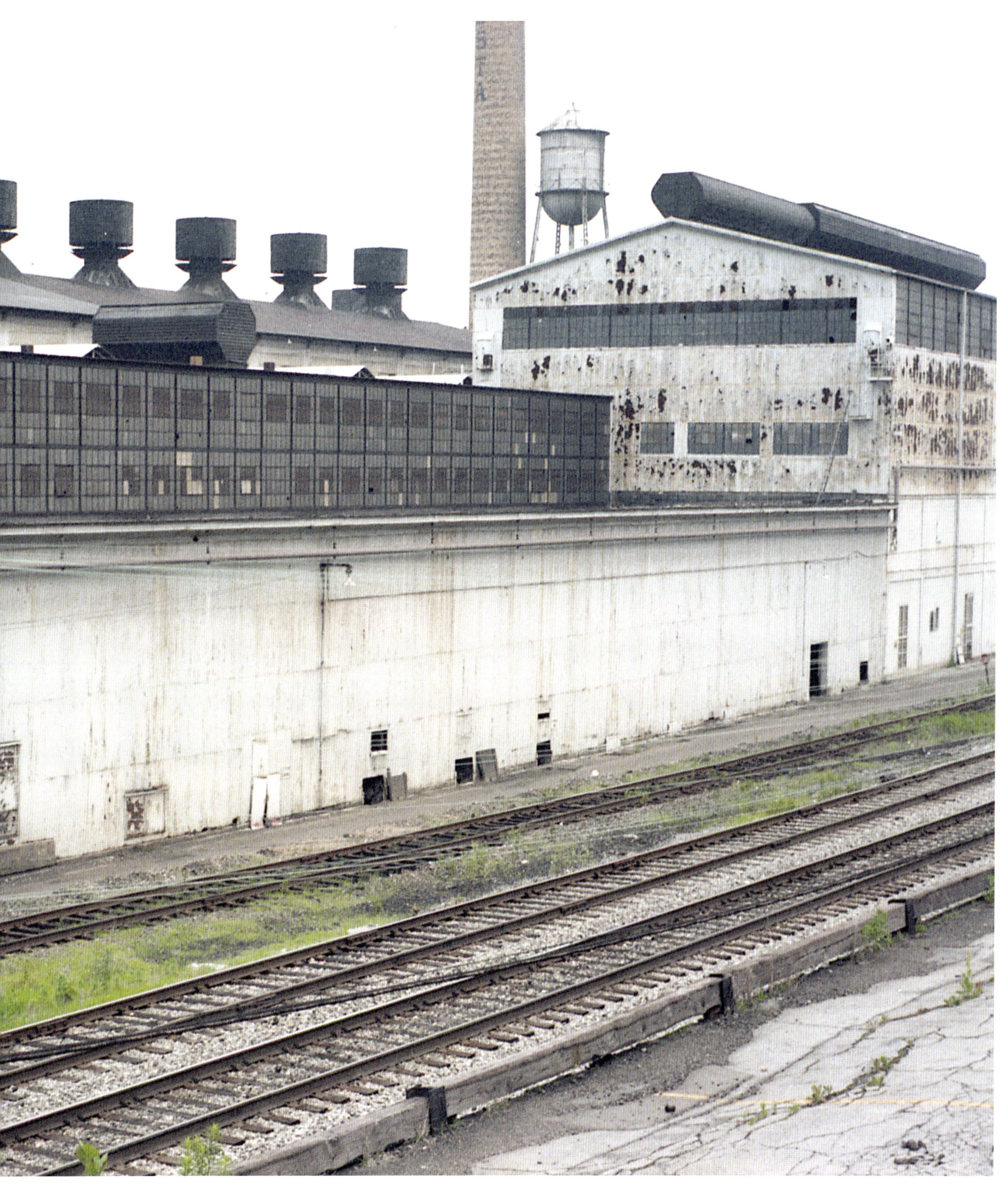

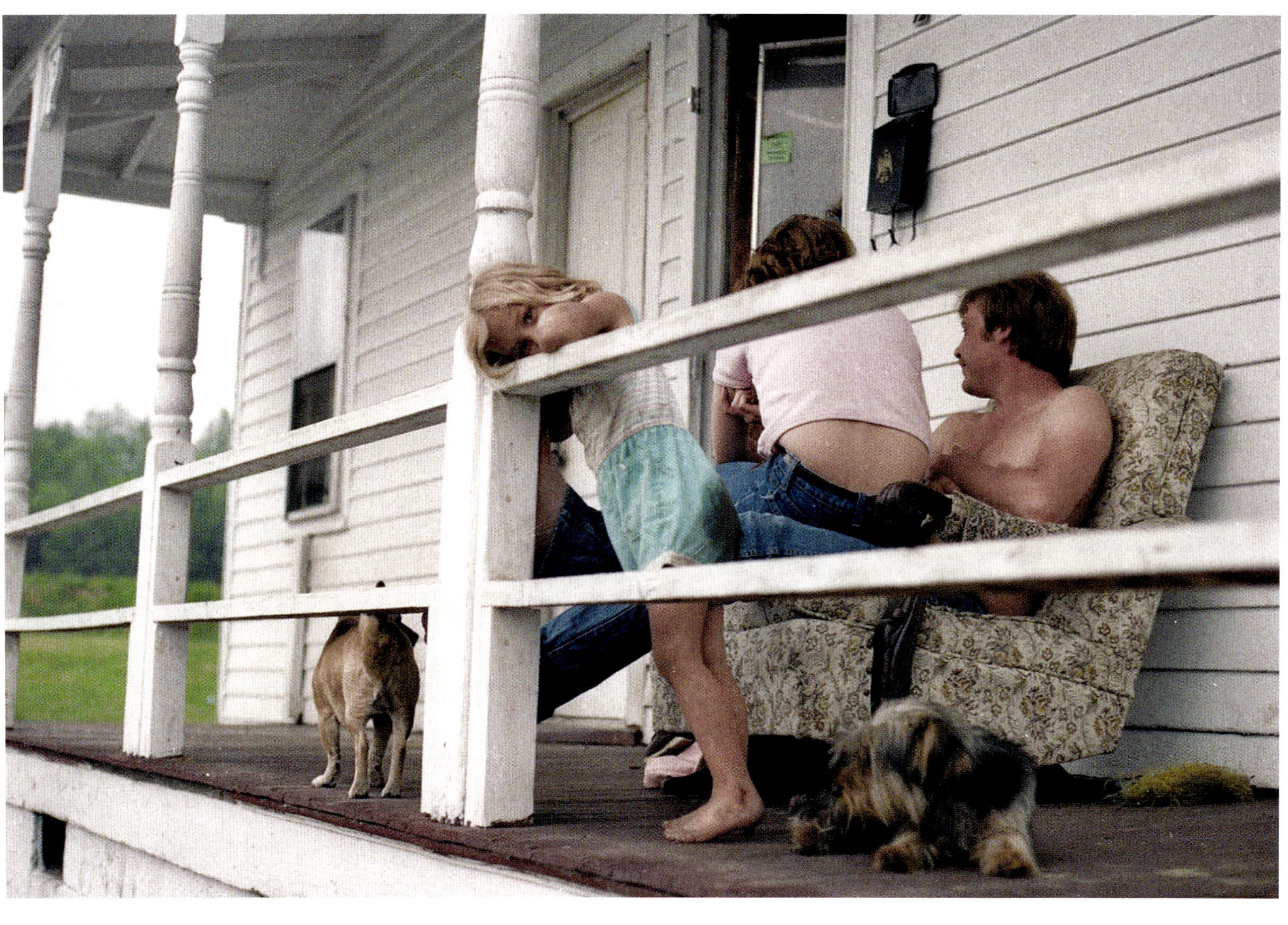

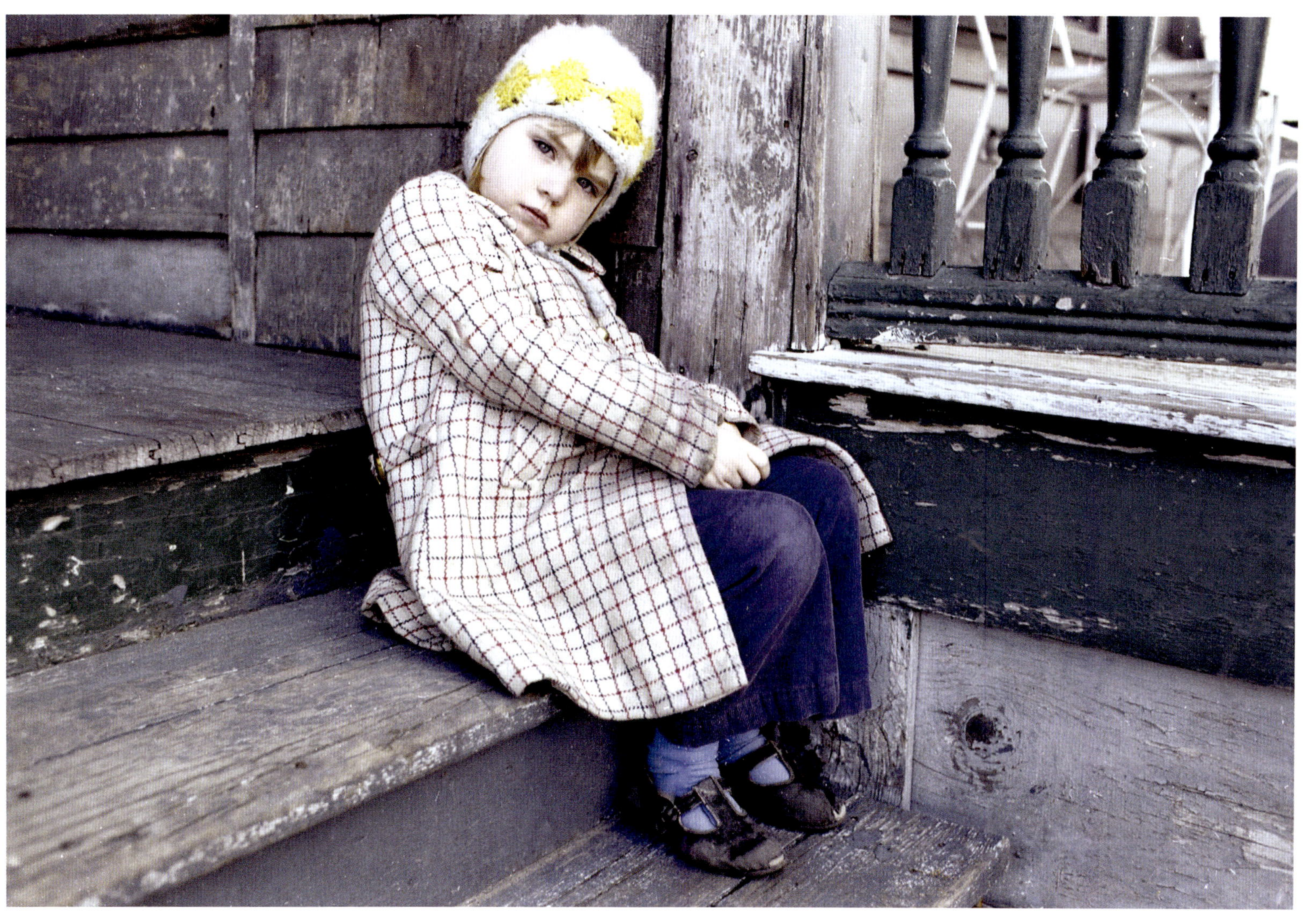

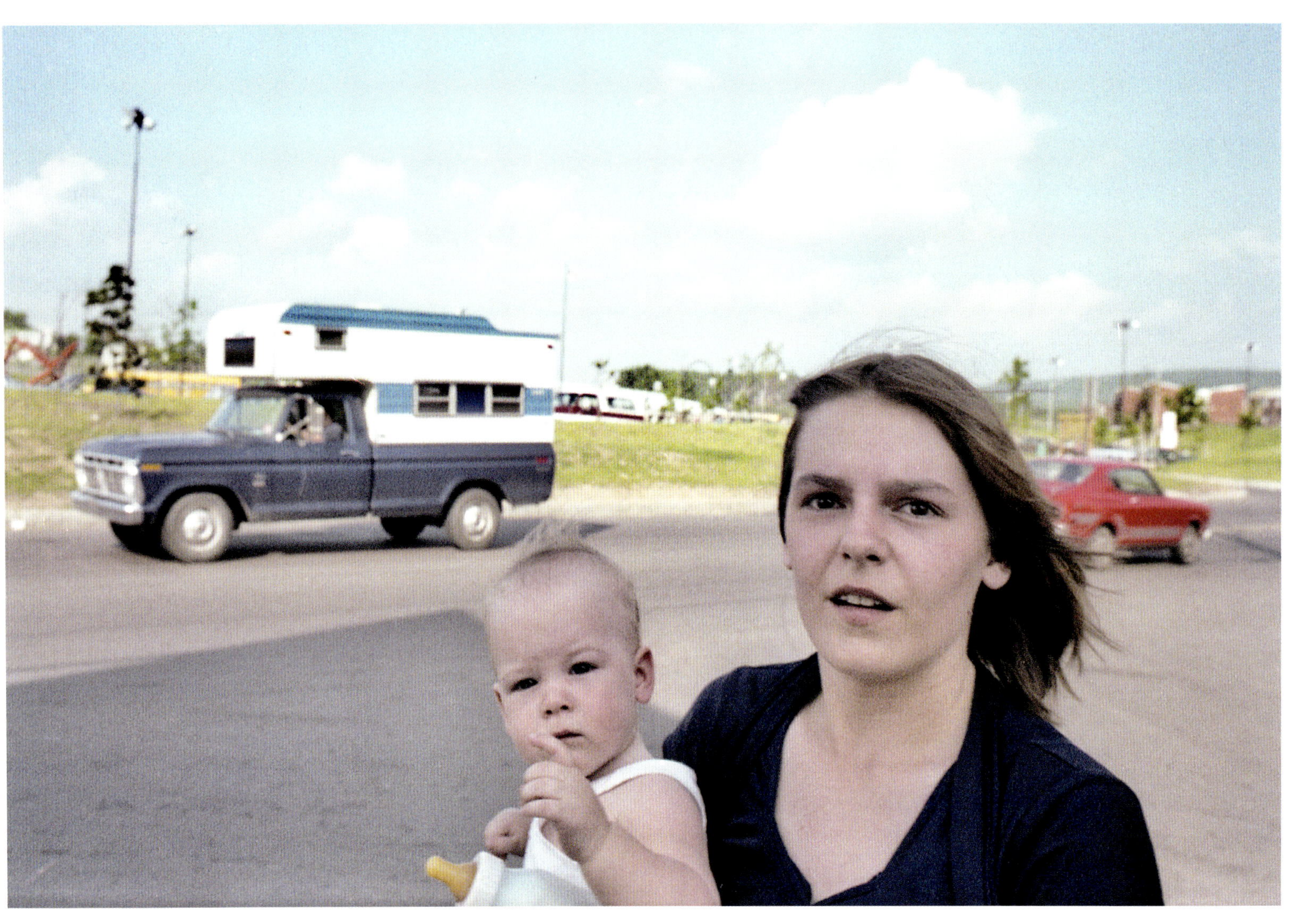

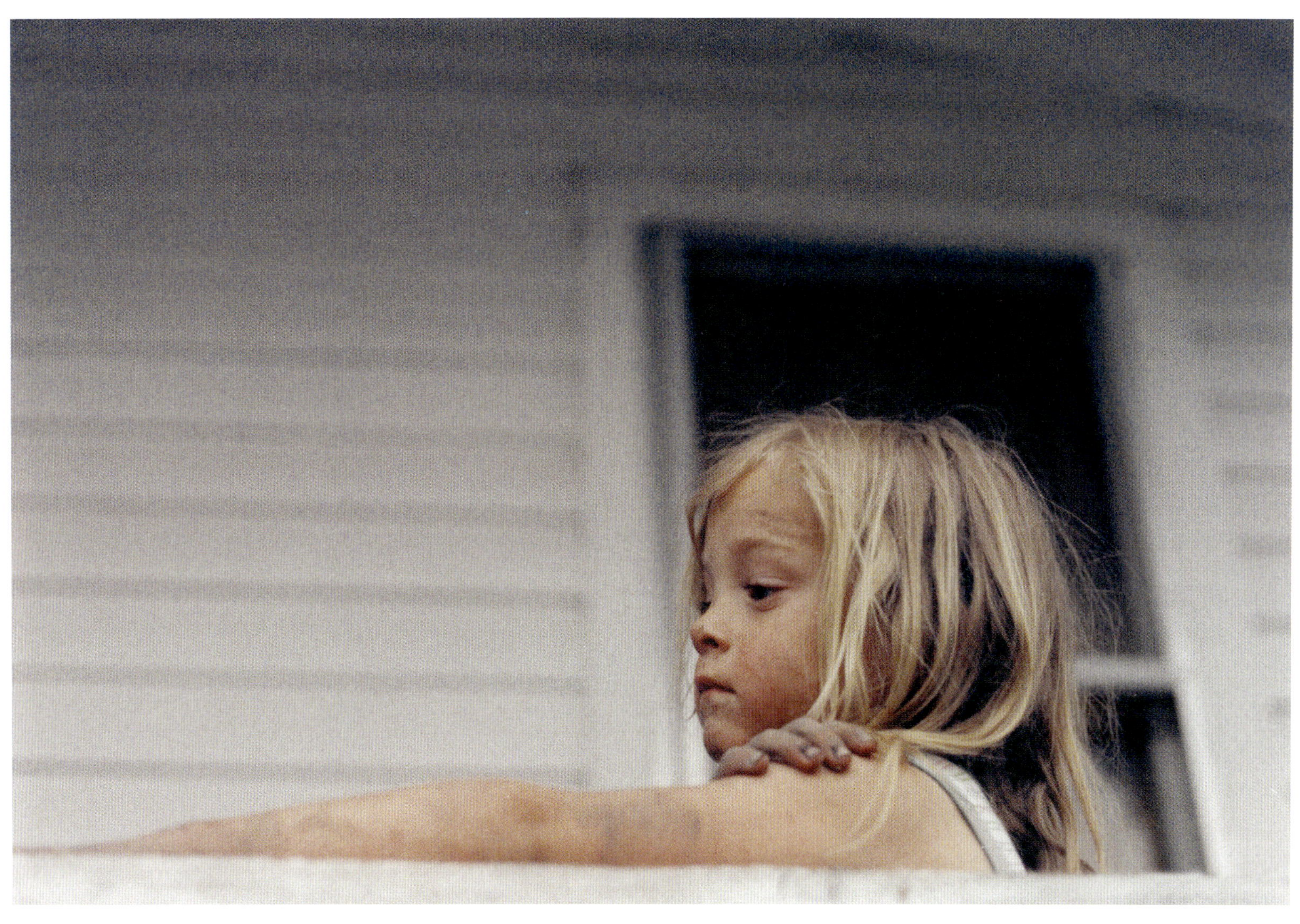

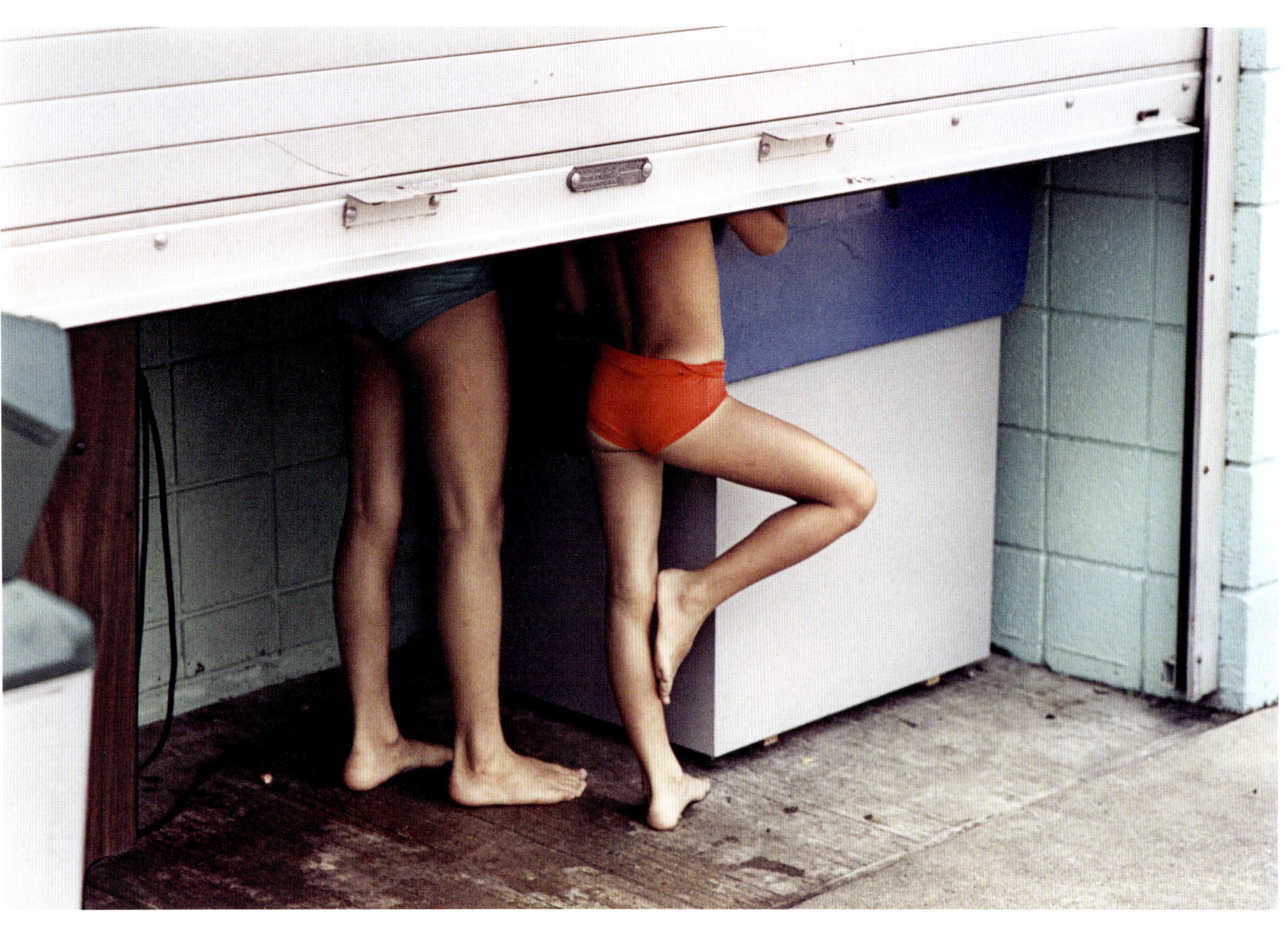

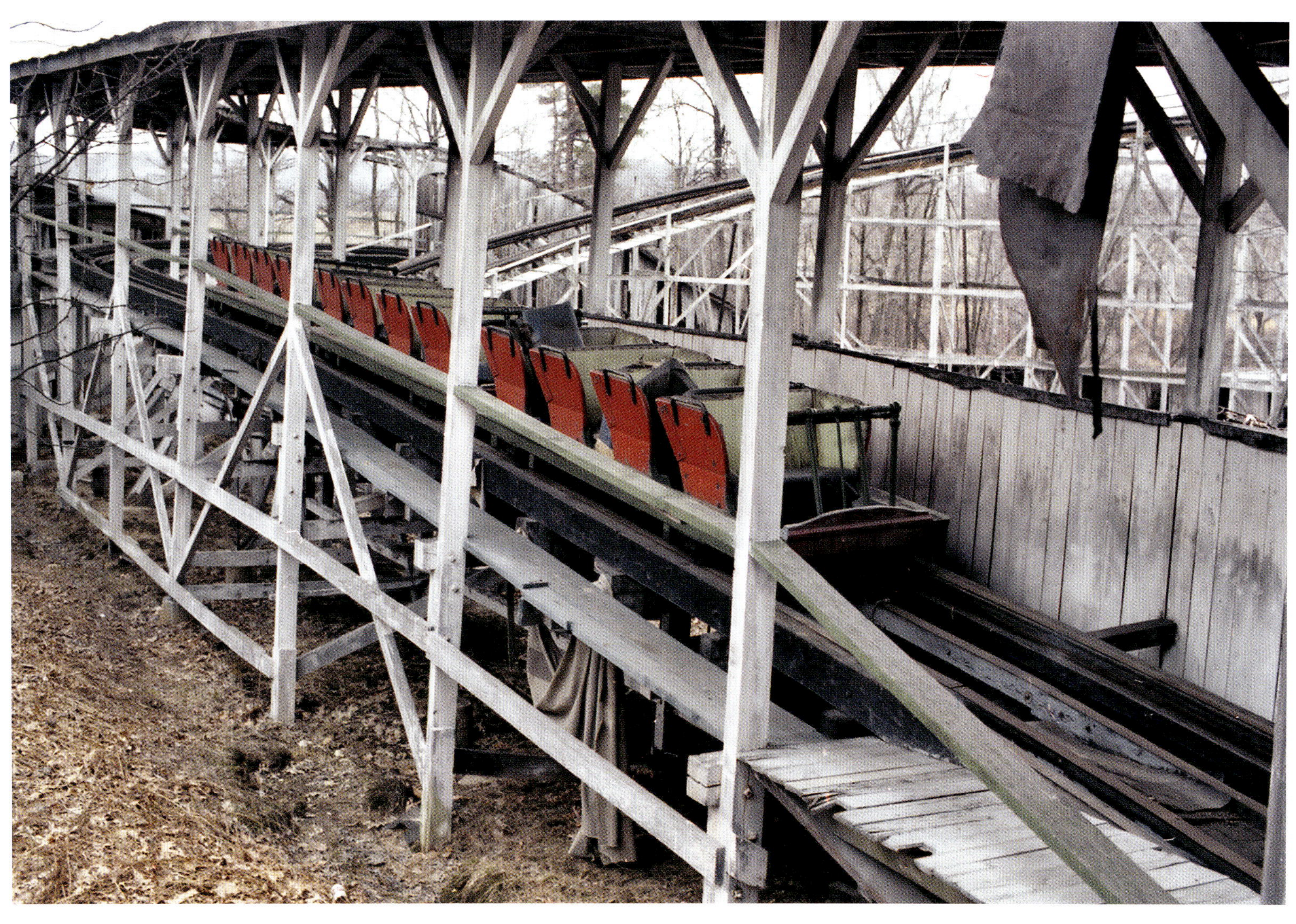

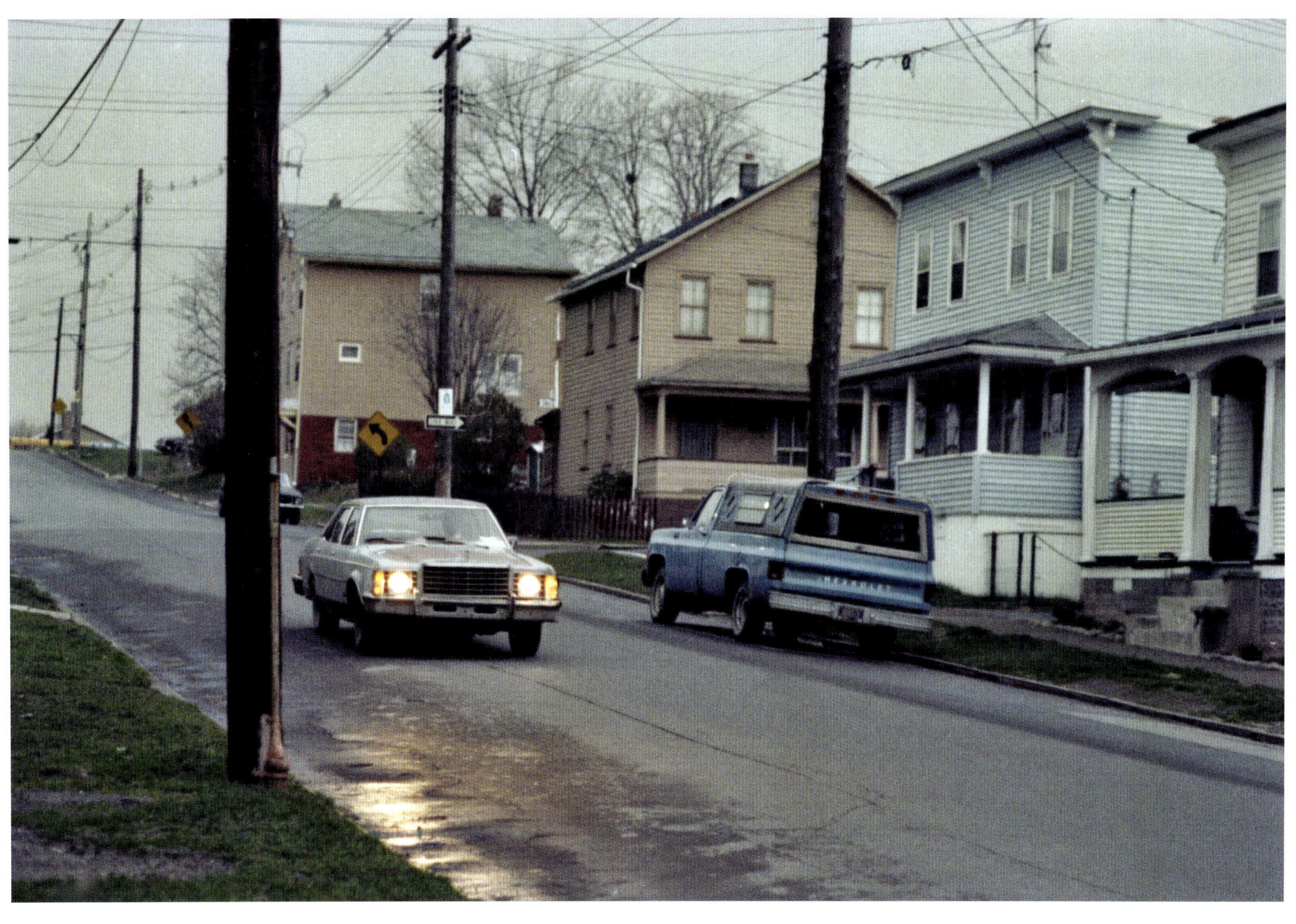

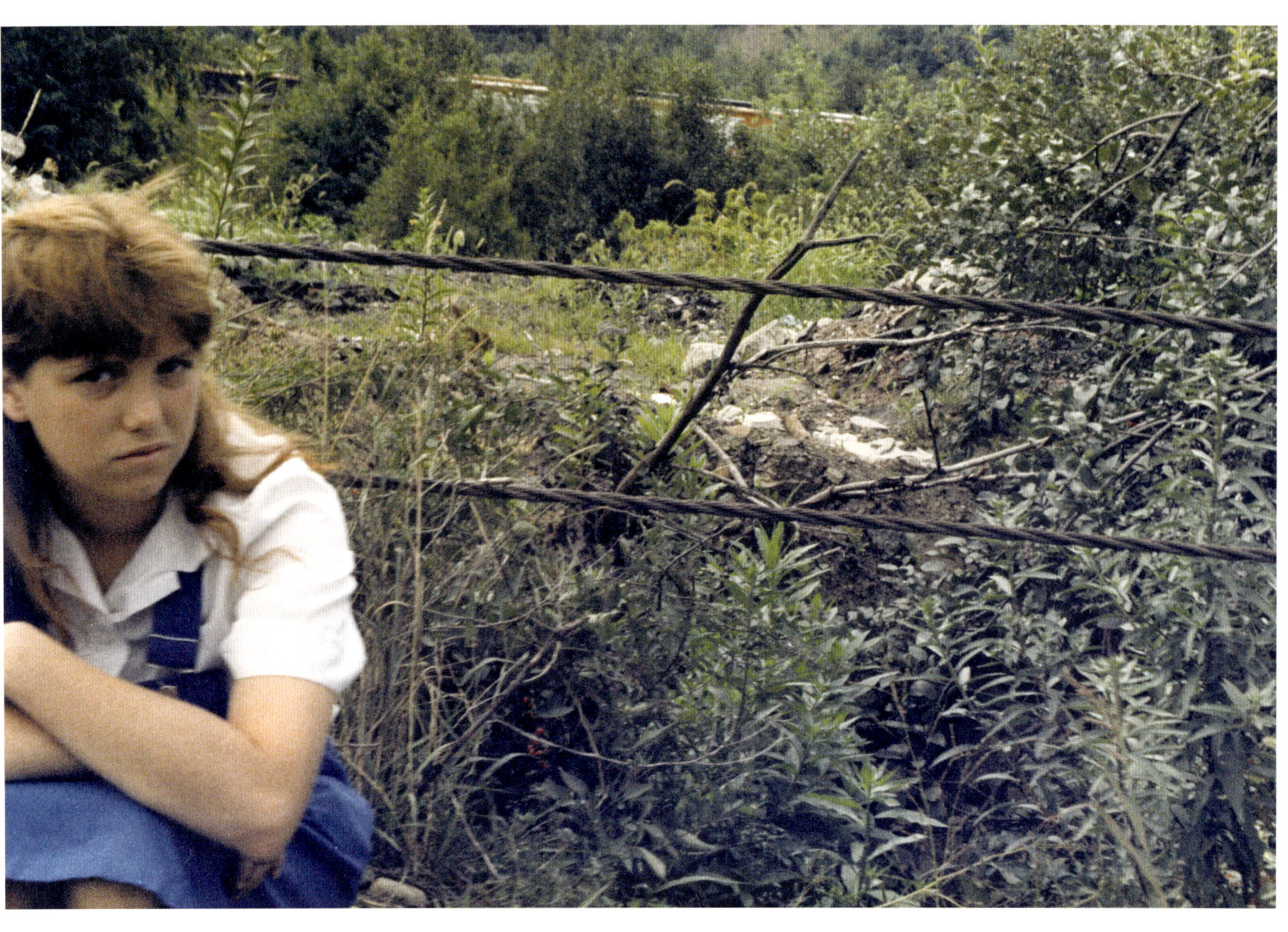

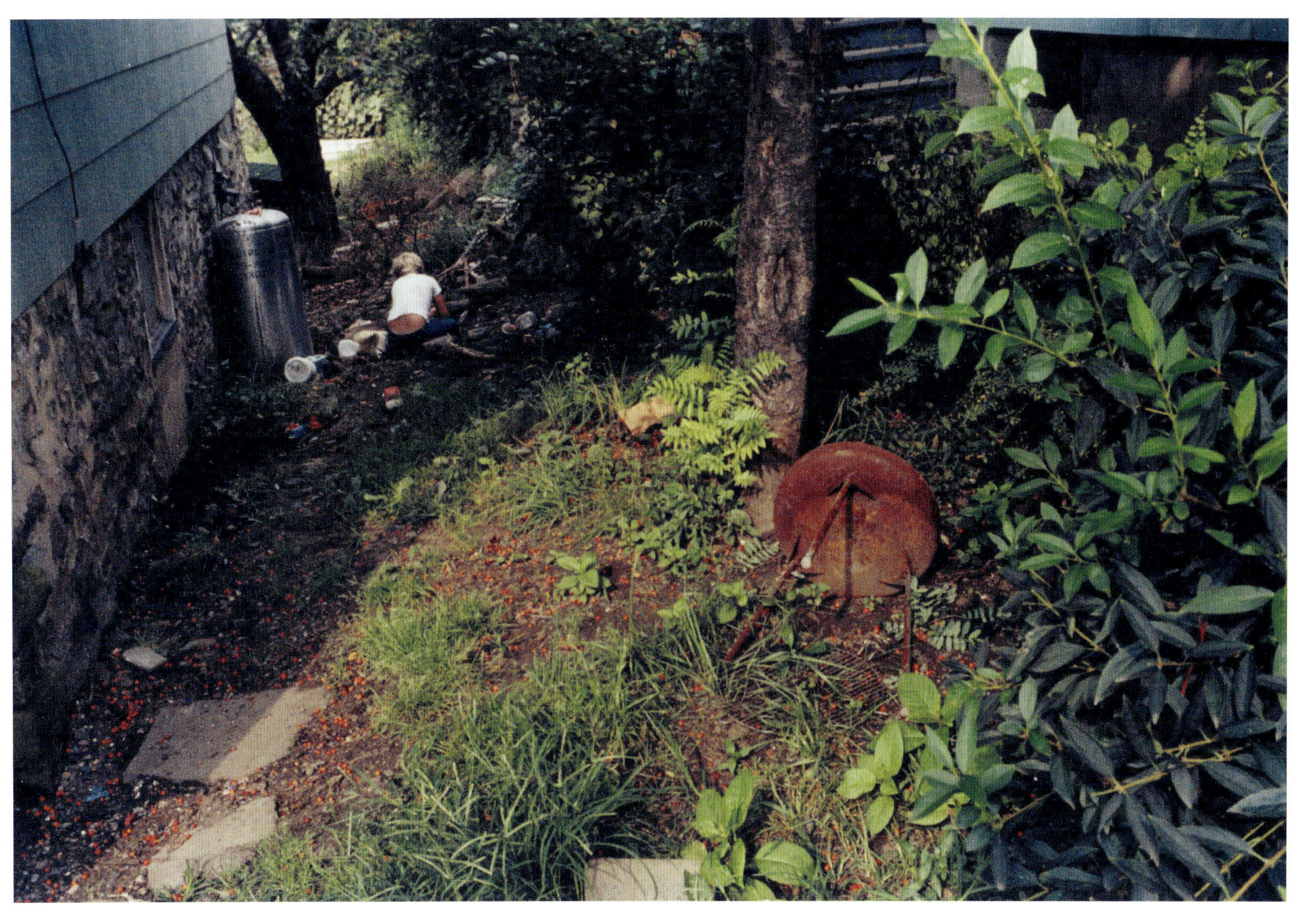

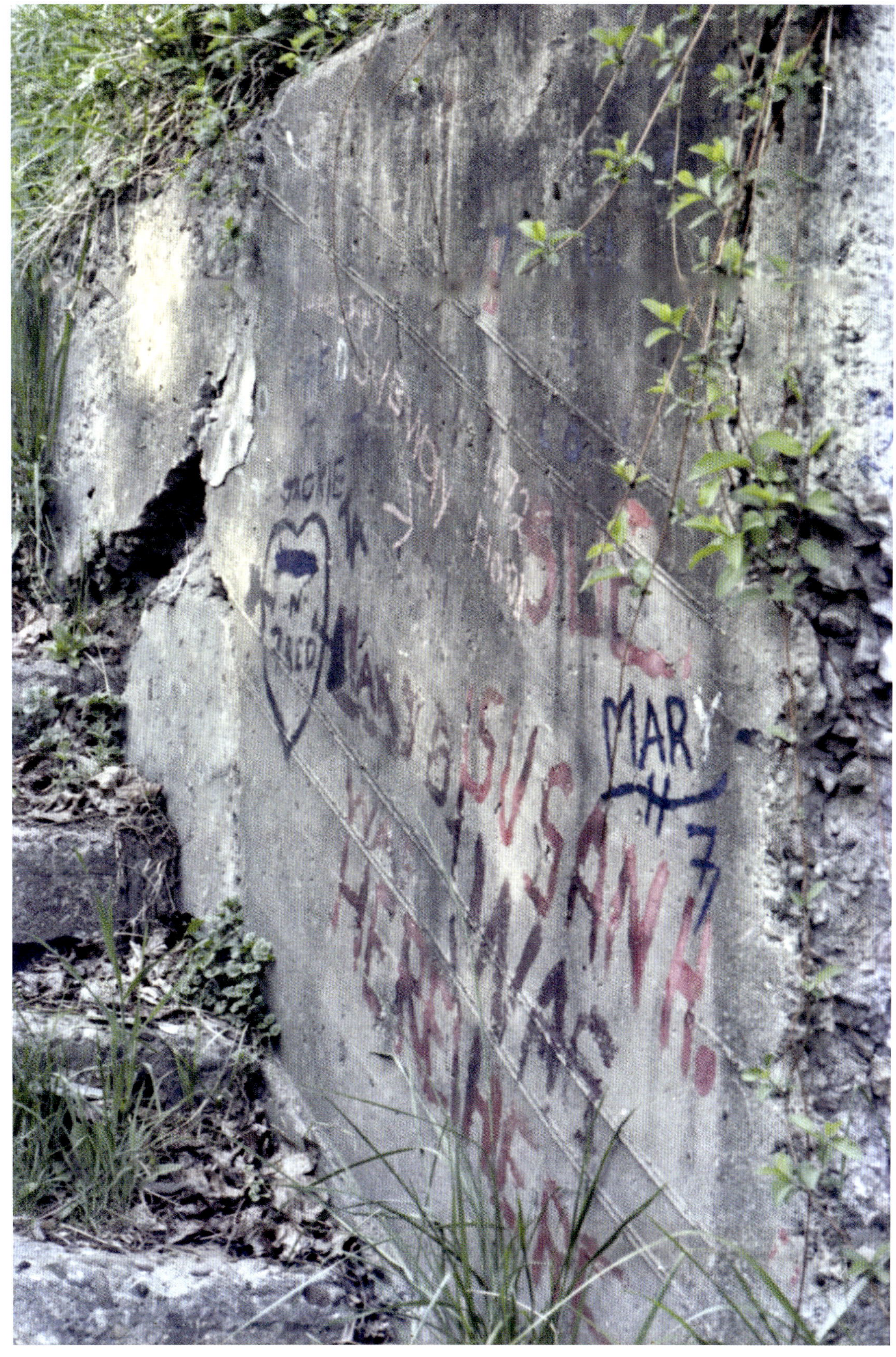
MARY
SUSAN H.

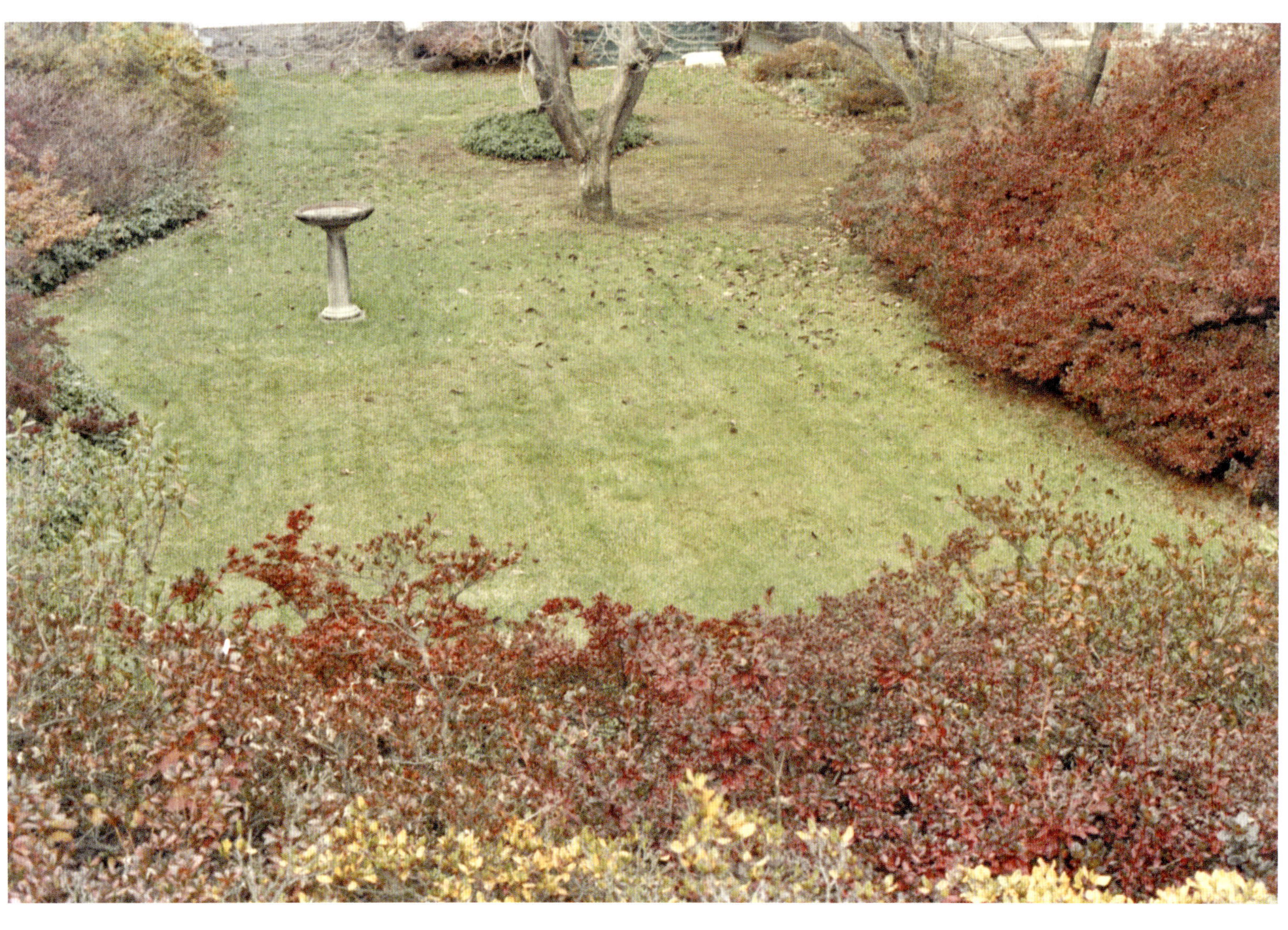

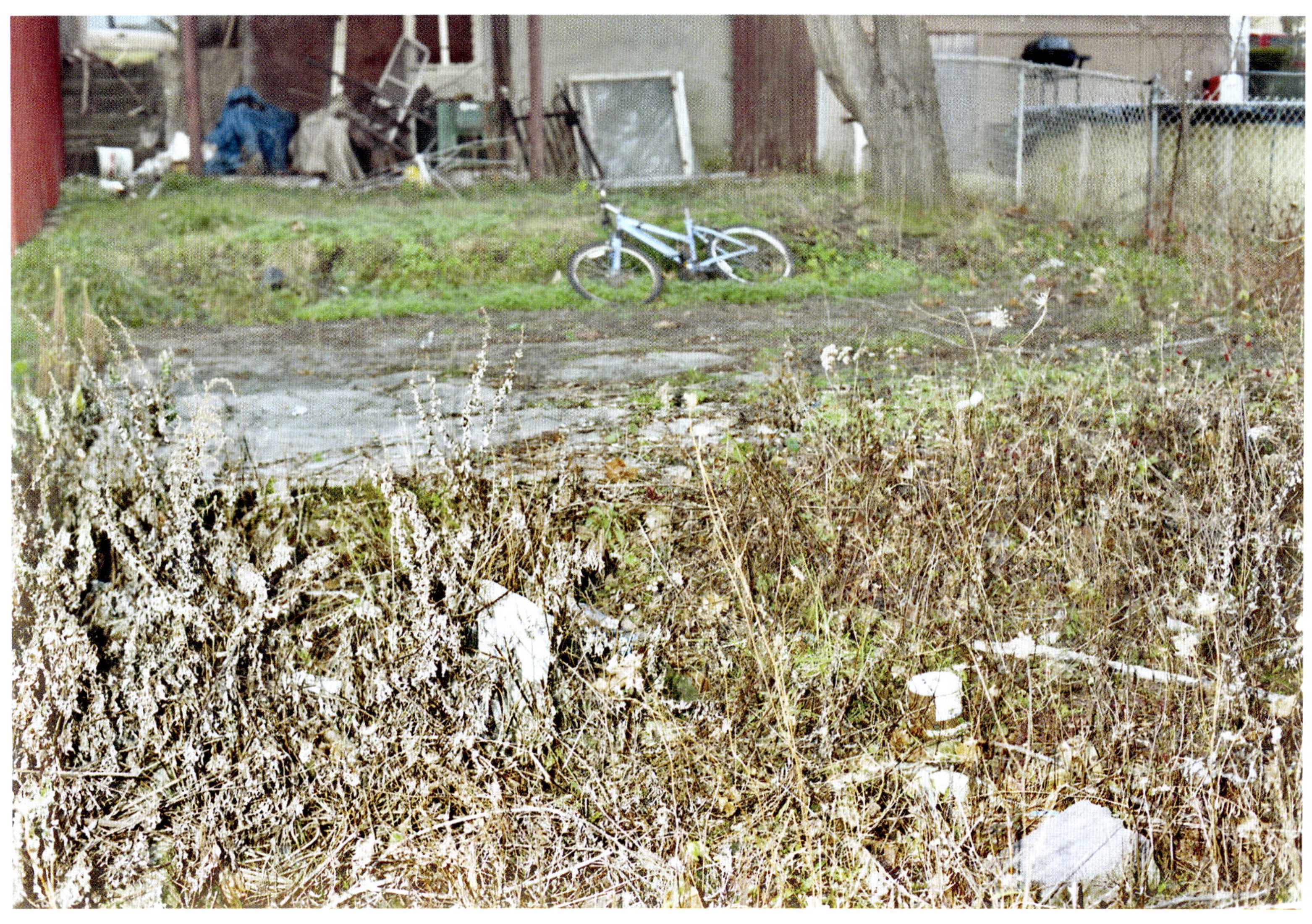

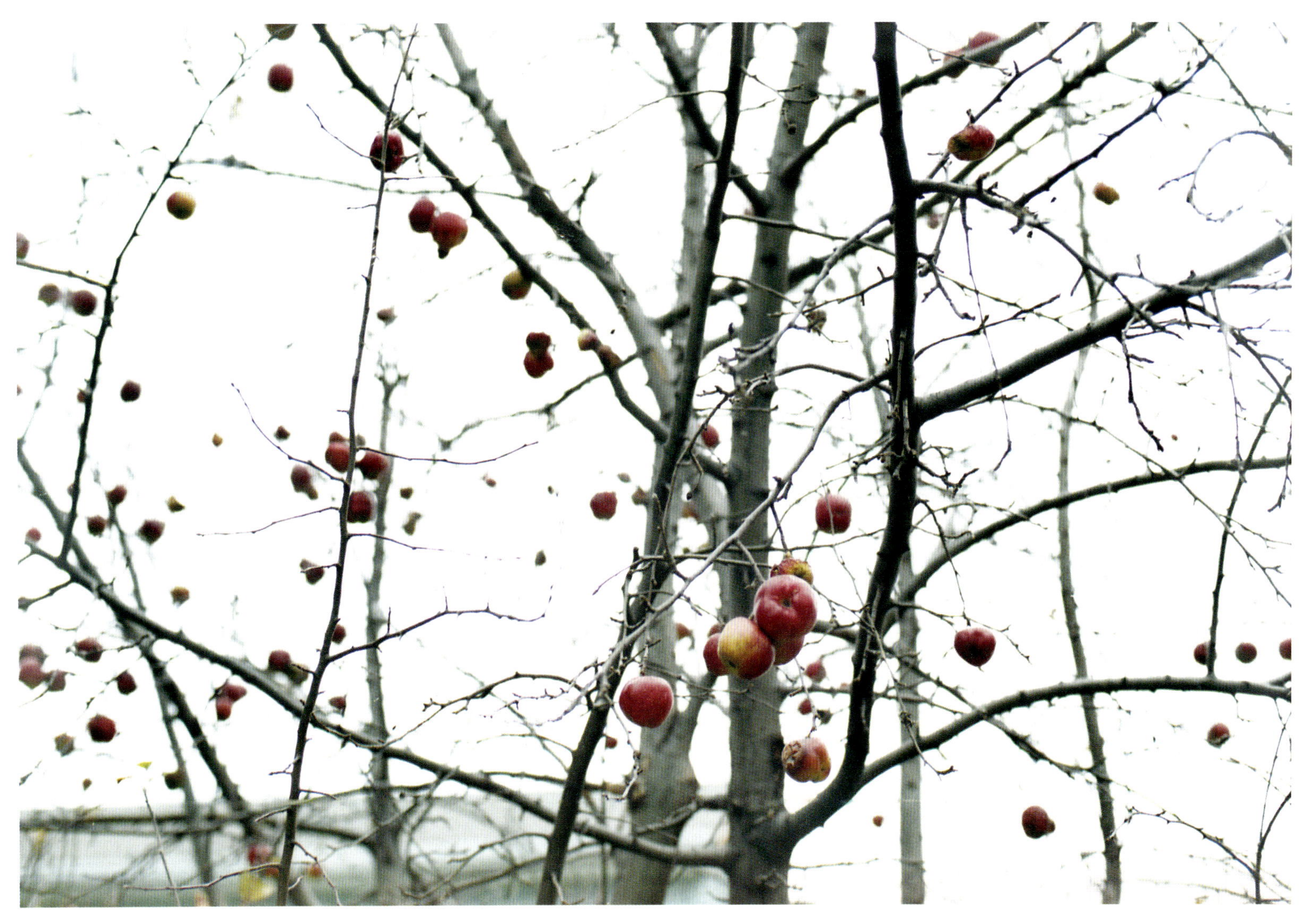

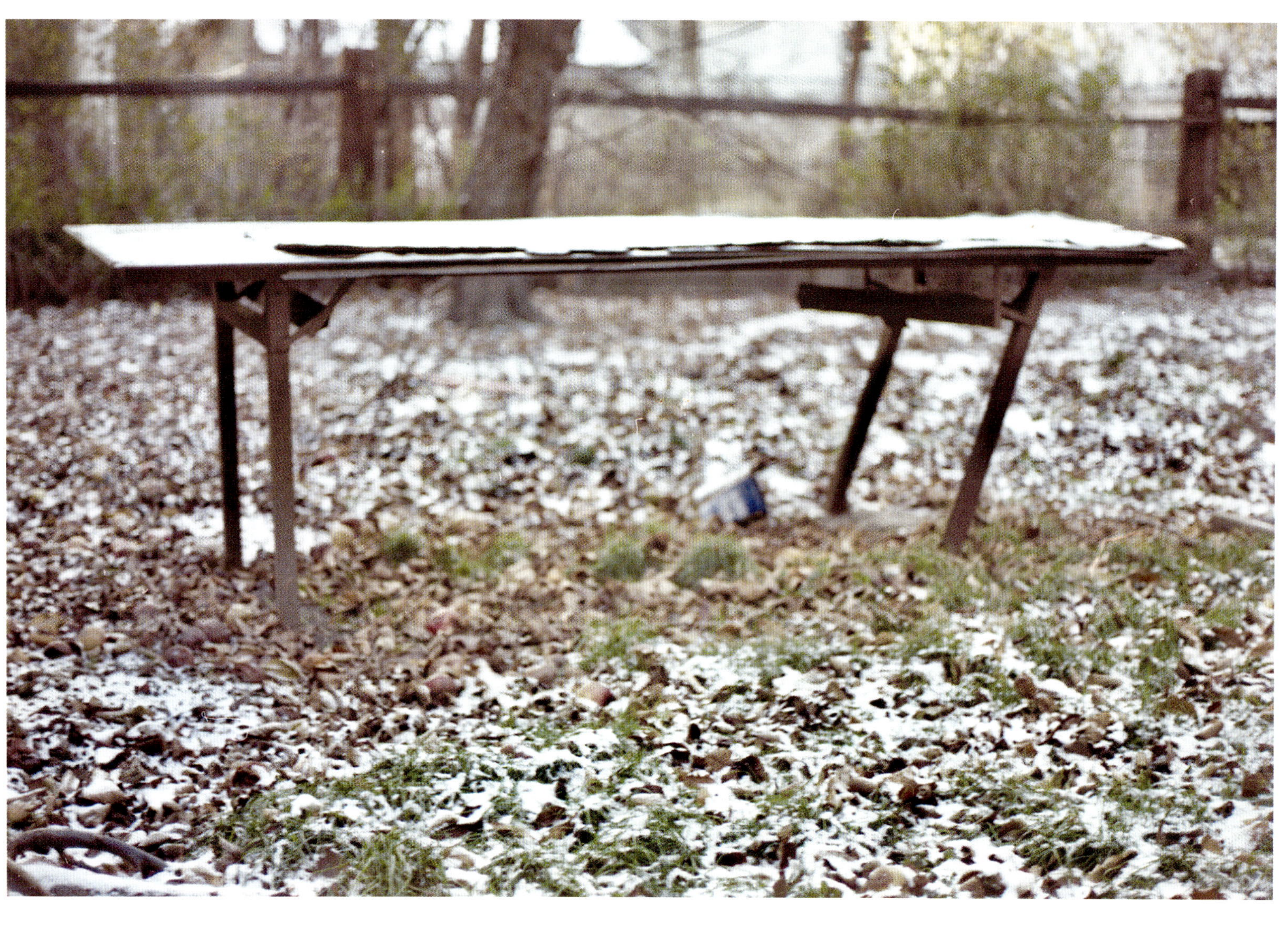

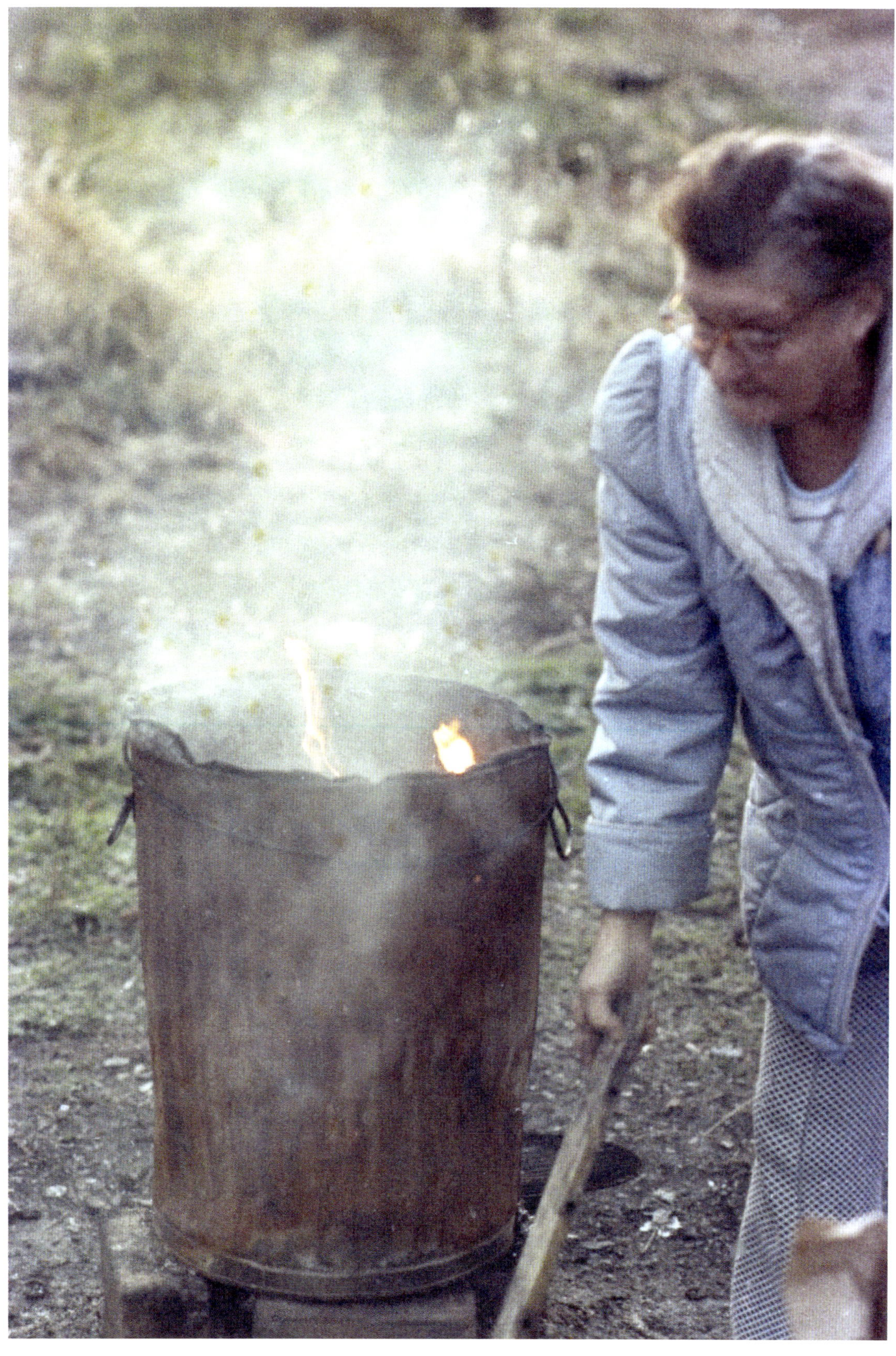

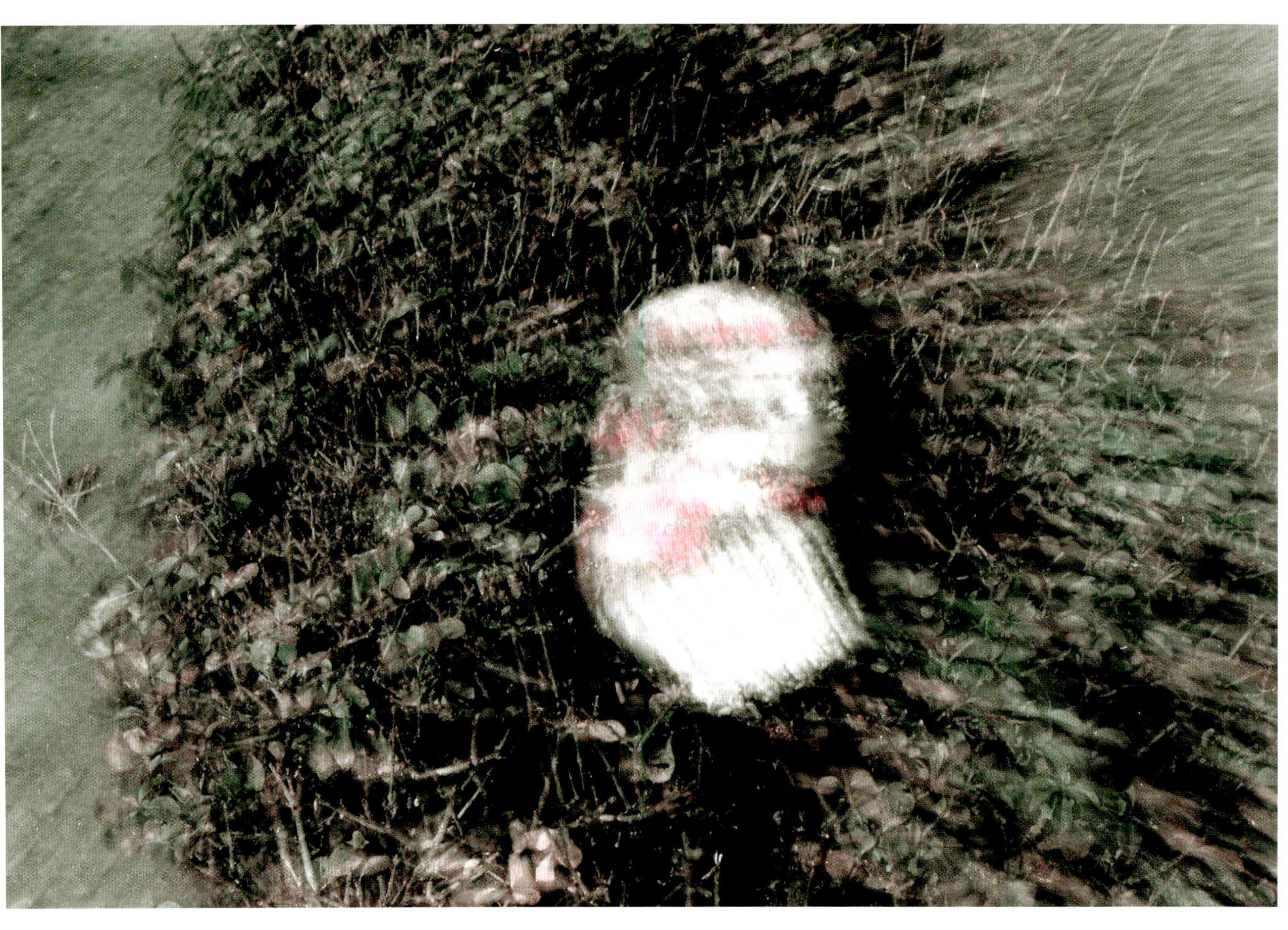

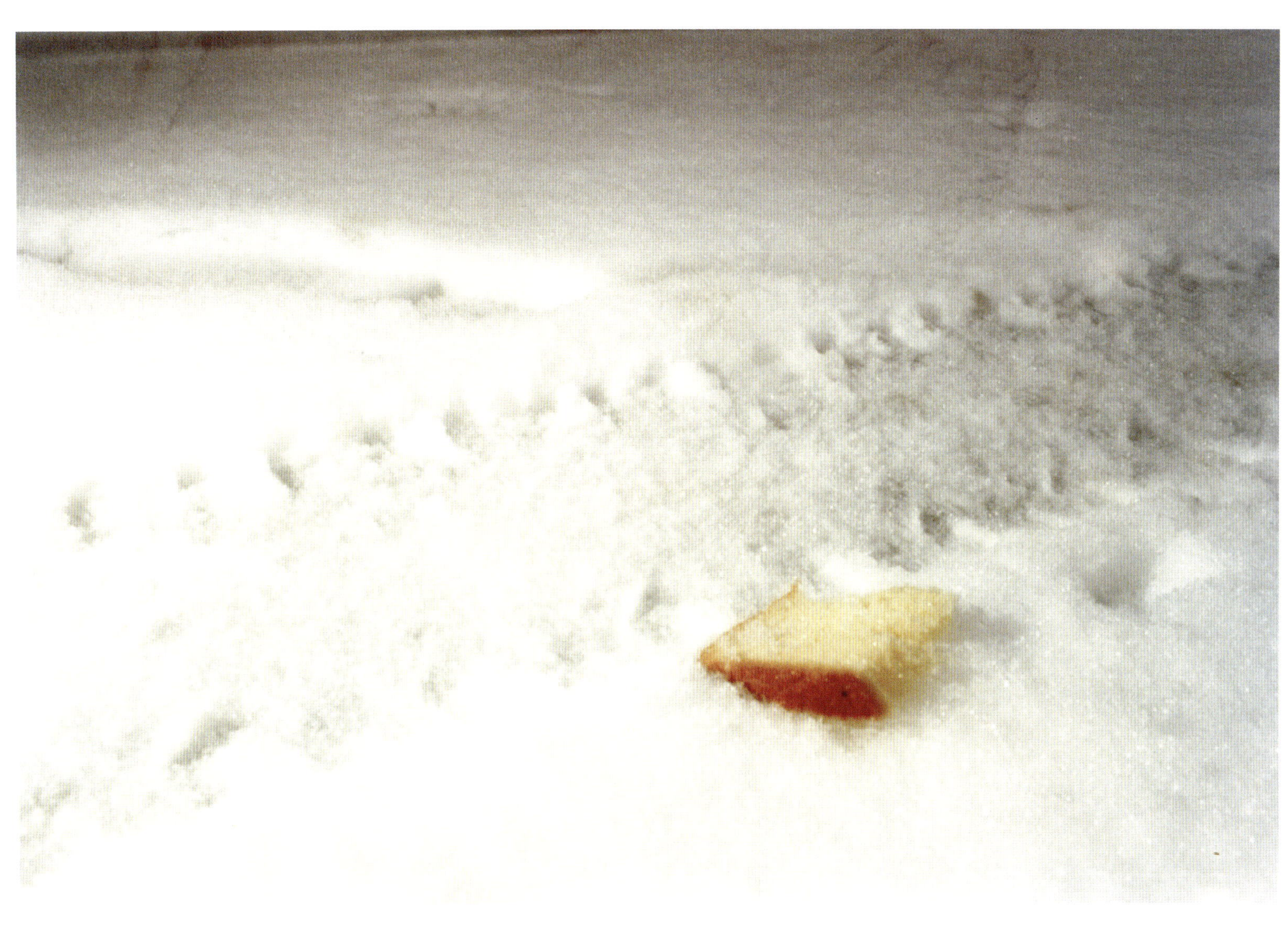

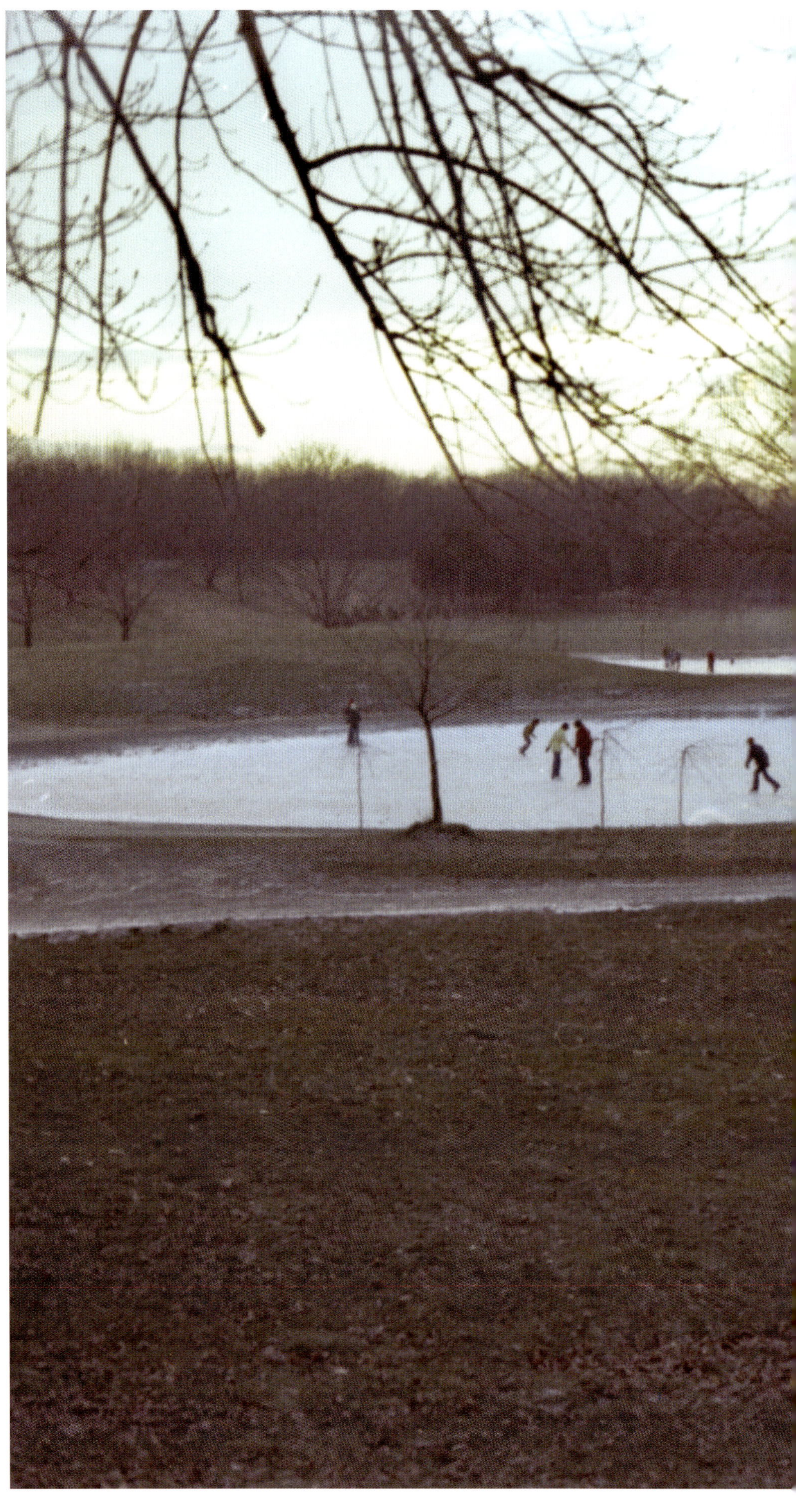

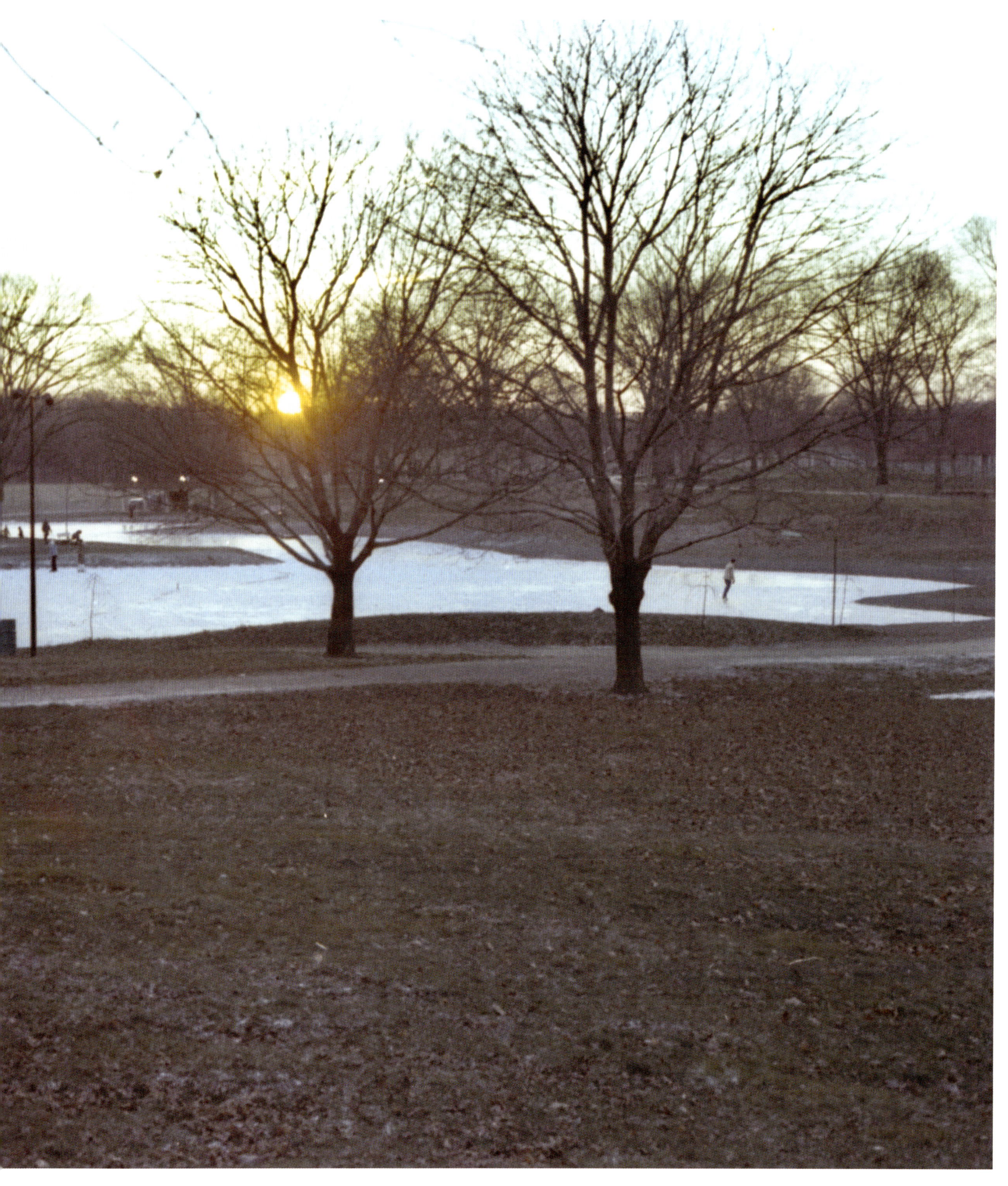

INTERVIEW BETWEEN MARK COHEN AND PHILLIP PRODGER, PHILADELPHIA, FEBRUARY 2025

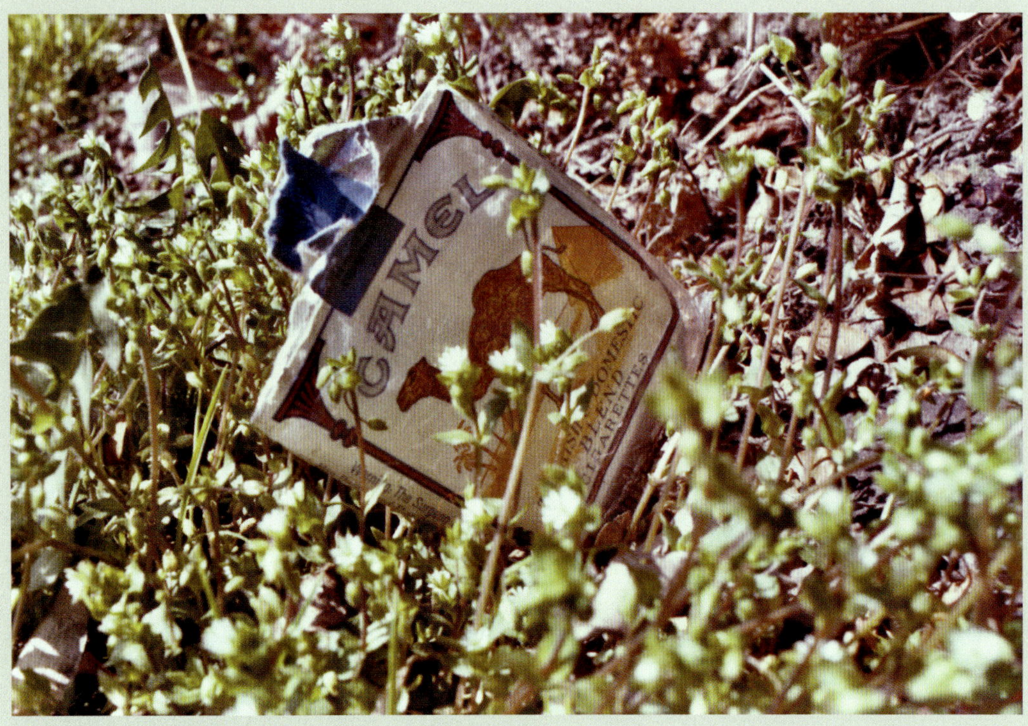

Phillip Prodger: I thought that to start things off I would ask what it was like growing up in Wilkes-Barre.

Mark Cohen: It was pretty normal.

PP: You spent your whole life in Wilkes-Barre, until you moved to Philadelphia, right?

MC: Yes.

PP: How did you feel living there? Did you yearn to be somewhere else?

MC: I never felt like I was part of the community ever, anywhere. It was just the United States of America. I lived in a little town called Forty Fort, which is a little suburb of Wilkes-Barre. I got there when I was six years old from an even more remote suburb called Plymouth. I went to grade school in Wilkes-Barre. It was perfectly normal-seeming.

I think by about the age of ten or twelve, I had been to New York. I was trying to remember if I had actually been to the Museum of Modern Art to see the *Family of Man* show. I would have had to have been ten or twelve to have done that. My father had a camera and a photo album. I remember seeing what my parents looked like ten years before I was born. You can get a magical photography vibe at a very young age when you look at pictures of your parents in a photo album with deco edges and photo corners around it.

By the time I was in high school I had already been developing film and making prints, and I knew how to make test strips. And I kept trying different cameras. I went from a plastic camera to square roll film, then I wanted a 35mm camera.

I would get on the bus and go to Public Square in Wilkes-Barre, and go to the magazine stand where I would read *Modern Photography* and *Popular Photography* and *US Photography*, and they all had annuals. By the time I was in tenth or eleventh grade I was way into photography.

PP: How did you learn to develop and print?

MC: I had an uncle, Uncle Lenny, who showed me how to make a test strip with an enlarger. Well, once you know how to make a test strip, then you can really adjust the kind of saturation that you'll get on a print, and that was a very key thing. I mean, you only have to show somebody that once.

When I was teaching at Wilkes College, the first thing I would show people is how to make a test strip, and they could make prints right away.

PP: So in those early days, when you were in tenth or eleventh grade, did you have an enlarger at home?

MC: I had a darkroom in the basement. I got into this hobby of photography. When I was twelve a cousin of mine gave me a camera. Then, when I was growing up, a friend of my father's brought a Leica 3F, three lenses, and all this stuff to my house. It was in a fancy leather case, and he said he'd come back for it later, but I could use it. I later found out that he believed you have to give a kid good equipment if he's going to learn how to do anything well. And so I had this good equipment, and then, later on, I got my own. He had left the camera with me for two years.

I was in high school when I saw [Cartier-Bresson's] *Decisive Moment* book and that set the format for me, because [like him] I don't crop pictures. And I thought Cartier-Bresson was exceptional. I don't know where I saw the book. I didn't have it; I must have seen it somewhere. In about 1959 or '60 I saw that book. And it's still pretty fantastic.

PP: Now that you live in Philadelphia, do you miss Wilkes-Barre?

MC: Not really, because I felt that I had seen it. There was only so many times I could go to Public Square and take pictures of people getting off the bus, and I could always go there and take pictures. I actually moved to downtown Wilkes-Barre and I could just walk out of the house and go by various routes, and the whole thing was like a set. I felt that I had artistic license to do pretty much whatever I wanted to do.

As soon as I could drive, I started to go to New York. But Wilkes-Barre was like the Big Easy, you know.

PP: No, what do you mean?

MC: I had a teaching job at the college. I had a pretty good photography business there, doing portraits of children.

PP: You were set up.

MC: Yeah, and I had space there. I had a great house, with plenty of room. I had a whole downstairs that I could use, a spacious darkroom, and a room to keep prints.

PP: Going to Public Square, or other areas that you used to visit, did you find that at a certain point you started to get recognized?

MC: Yes, because I traveled all over. One neighborhood was called the Heights. The cover picture of our book [*Girl Jumping Rope*] is made up there, and I would go up to that area two or three times a week, because it had a very rich set of possibilities. It was a working-class neighborhood, and these kids would play in the street. You see those kinds of streets in lots of places. I guess they're in Scranton and Pittsburgh, too, but in Wilkes-Barre they had a whole atmosphere, with wire fences and the street, and it became a part of my visual vocabulary at the time. Same with the buses on Public Square. These things all coalesced into "the city." It could have been Toledo or any other small American city.

PP: Was that important to you, to make it more general in that way?

MC: I guess it was, unconsciously. I didn't want to make a book about Wilkes-Barre. I'm taking pictures in Philadelphia now, and I see there's so many people that seem to want to do books of architectural details. But I wasn't trying to identify a specific set of buildings. I was trying to establish myself as an observer of the life on the street, in the store, in and out of stores. There's a picture I have of a kid taking a soda out of a Coca-Cola cooler.

After a while, people would see me walking on the street, and they would say: "Hey, photo man!" They would recognize me as somebody taking pictures in Wilkes-Barre. I wasn't crazy about that.

PP: Did your relationship with the subjects change when that happened?

MC: No. I rarely encountered the same people twice. If you go to Public Square ten times in a month and take ten pictures, the chances of overlapping with the same person are very small. And I'm trying to take a picture of a button sometimes.

PP: How did you go about choosing what you were going to photograph?

MC: I didn't have a plan. I walked out of the house. I took a lot of pictures of fences. I took a lot of pictures of a lot of different subjects. I even took pictures of detritus and stuff that was laying around, and chalk marks on the street and graffiti.

PP: Did your subjects ever complain about being photographed?

MC: Oh yeah, lots of times. I had all kinds of altercations with the subjects.

PP: You mean it got physical?

MC: Sometimes it would get physical. When you take a picture of a person, you're singling them out, and you're trespassing into their space. Especially when you're using a 28mm lens. You're invading space.

PP: And that didn't concern you at all?

MC: Well, I was careful, you know what I mean. I would keep my distance when I had to, and I would gauge the situation and move away quickly. People might yell, and then I would duck around the corner or something like that. But it didn't happen that much.

PP: How do you respond to people who criticize your work saying that it's an invasion of privacy?

MC: There's cameras all over. You can't walk down the street without being photographed. If you walk by a bank you're on tape. There are cameras everywhere you look.

And what are the damages? If I take a picture of kids running down the street, or I take a picture of a knee and I put it in a book—I'm not identifying the place or who it is, it's just a picture of a knee.

PP: Okay, but how would you feel about being photographed in that way?

MC: I object to it.

There are some people in Philadelphia who recognize me and come to take my picture because they heard about what I do. So they say, oh, that's smart, we'll get his picture. It has happened a few times. I'm not crazy about it. It's an invasion, but it has to happen. I'm not the first guy to do that. I'm not.

PP: Photographing the way that you do, you obviously generate a lot of pictures, which you may or may not use later. So that means that a lot of what you do is based on editing.

MC: Right.

PP: When you go back and look at strips of negatives, how do you decide what's worth printing?

MC: I would usually shoot three rolls of film at a time. So that's a hundred negatives. And I processed these films, cut them into strips of six, and laid them out on a light table. I had developing trays all set up and everything, and in 1972, '73, and '74, I would make around eight prints at a time from eight different negatives. Then I would choose just one of them to make a final print.

I could see the negatives, and I learned to look at them. I didn't even use a magnifying glass back then. I could see the negatives I wanted to print. Now I use a magnifying glass.

PP: What are you responding to? What excites you about a particular negative over the others?

MC: Before the film was developed, I may have had some interaction that I remembered with the subjects of the film, with the people, or with something I saw, like a still life or a landscape. So I might have remembered something like that. And then, when I'd see the negatives that were related to that, it might have been only one picture.

It would have to have a certain kind of visual impact and a certain composition, and it had to work in the frame because I printed everything full frame, and that's how I picked out the negatives. I could imagine it on the wall. I could look at a negative and pre-visualize a print.

PP: So, in a sense, the pictures that you decide to print are memories of your experience being out in the world.

MC: Yes, to some degree.

Back then, I would be looking at something that might have happened four hours ago. Now I'm looking at negatives from thirty, forty, fifty years ago that I have no recollection of where they were taken, or that I don't remember taking. But when I started, I could have an exhibition three months after the negatives were made.

PP: I'm going to switch gears a little and talk about that period in the early 1970s when you were first starting to become known. Who were some of your contemporaries you were watching, and whom did you admire at that time.

MC: At that time it would have been Lee Friedlander, Garry Winogrand, and Diane Arbus. Arbus was older, but she was almost a contemporary of mine. Also William Klein, who, you know, is a great photographer, and Josef Koudelka. Other than Arbus, they were all 35mm people. Those were most inspiring to me.

PP: How did you get to know their work?

MC: You know, you could get them. They were on the newsstand.

I would apply to be in the same magazines. I would send eight-by-ten glossies to an editor in New York. And if I could get a picture in there, I thought that was great. I got some pictures in the annuals. It was something I was doing in an isolated way. But I knew what was going on.

PP: Can you tell me a little bit about what was happening specifically in color in the early 1970s, when you started working with it.

MC: I knew about Ernst Haas, but color was completely absorbed by Eggleston.

Eggleston had such a big footprint because John Szarkowski made the book *William Eggleston's Guide*, and suddenly everybody's making color pictures.

They noticed me after I did the Eastman House project [in 1976]. And then Sally Eauclaire put me in her book [*The New Color Photography*, 1981] with four or five pictures. She came to Wilkes-Barre, and we talked these things over.

I'm trying to think how I went from there. Those pictures were like '77, or '78, but in the early seventies I had a commercial photography studio, and I did a lot of color pictures, portraits of children in color, and I had a real good lab, and they did the processing for me and made contact sheets.

PP: Is photographing in color different than in black and white?

MC: Oh, it's a lot different. It's similar in some ways, and it's different in others. Because a lot of times I'd see a color picture—colors will emerge from the scene, you know. I used to work in color in the darkroom. I could make test strips of color negatives and see the amazing number of colors in the grain of a Type-C test strip.

You see something like that now when you scan color negatives. But when you're taking pictures in color, it's different. I always saw color, but when you're only using black-and-white film, you don't think about that. Adding color is like adding flash to a picture.

PP: How do you mean?

MC: If you start using flash, that disturbs the scene. And in the same way, adding color disturbs the scene too, or if it doesn't disturb it, it enhances it somehow.

PP: Which came first for you, color or flash?

MC: Flash. But I was already thinking about color [in the late 1960s]. I'd take color slides, and, well, maybe I could get a picture in *National Geographic*, so I wouldn't go to Spain without taking some Kodachrome. Maybe I could sell one of these, but I took black-and-white pictures all the time, because I could handle that material in the darkroom. Pre-digital, there was a certain value to the trays and the lenses and optics.

PP: How did you choose the materials you were using? You made some decisions that were different from most of your peers at that time—shooting color negative film, for example.

MC: One of the first things I did when I started with color was try to get a 400-speed color film [the same as the black-and-white film he used]. Here comes somebody—I want to get their picture. So I walk by real quick at f22, and make a picture, or use the flash or something like that. If my films are the same speed, I don't have to use a meter or anything. Kodachrome [which is much slower], that's a different thing. Think about how slowly you have to work with an 8 × 10 camera. And the false reverence that accrues, you know, and how much curators love to see a contact print of an 8 × 10 negative. They think they're at the zenith of their imagination. It's so crazy! And now the iPhone does the same thing an 8 × 10 can. But I made 8 × 10 negatives of things in black and white, and they're great—incredibly seductive. But that's why I got color negative film. There are a lot of films that came out at 400. There was a Kodacolor 400, an Ektacolor, and a Vericolor 400.

PP: So, are you saying that you switched back and forth between color and black and white sometimes?

MC: Sometimes I did that, and sometimes I tried to do it in such a way that I didn't know which film was in [the camera]. I thought it'd be cool not to know what kind of film I'm shooting.

PP: But you said that photographing in color or in black and white is different.

MC: I'm much older now. I've given it a lot more thought than the first time I did it. I just thought it would be cool to not know, because I considered the issue of taking the picture and being on the street much more important. The barrier with color was always the price of the sixteen-by-twenties in print.

PP: Why was it important to print so big?

MC: Somebody wrote a review in the *New York Times* and said that these pictures are as big as a two-page spread in *Life* magazine. That was influential. I thought, when you hold it in your hand, it doesn't have the preciousness of an eight-by-ten on an editor's desk, you know, with the green eyeshade looking down at it.

I was in a big group show in 1968, and I realized that if I had sixteen-by-twenties on the wall, I would be given a lot more space. So when I got back, I started printing that size. The show I had at MoMA was half eleven-by-fourteens and half sixteen-by-twenties

PP: One last question. You're often described as a street photographer. What do you think about that? And what is a street photographer, anyway?

MC: I took some pictures to [well-known photojournalist] Arthur Rothstein once when I was very young, before I could drive I think, maybe around sixteen or seventeen. I didn't realize who he was. "These pictures are good," he said, "but they don't tell a story." I didn't have a story or anything. I just had some miscellaneous pictures. But that was all a long time ago.

A street photographer is a photographer who works on Fifth Avenue in New York. That's what a street photographer does. There are a lot of people around, so you can do whatever you want. I'm like an alley photographer. I go everywhere to take pictures. If you walk down a remote alley somewhere at twilight, and there's like a little stream or a fence, or something going on, that's a great time to take pictures.

TITLES OF WORKS

ACKNOWLEDGMENTS

Mark Cohen and Phillip Prodger would like to thank Curt Holtz and Corinna Pickart at Prestel for their vision and expert production of this book, Melanie Mues for her beautiful design, and Jonathan Fox for proofreading the text.

Mark Cohen also thanks The John Simon Guggenheim Memorial Foundation.

Phillip Prodger thanks copyeditor and collaborator Claudia Sorsby for her help with the text. Special thanks, as always, to April and Leo.

produktsicherheit@penguinrandomhouse.de
(the above information is mandatory according to GPSR)

A Library of Congress Control Number is available. A CIP catalogue record for this book is available from the British Library.

Editorial direction: Curt Holtz
Copyediting: Claudia Sorsby, Jonathan Fox
Design and typesetting: Melanie Mues, Mues Design, London
Production: Corinna Pickart
Origination: Schnieber Graphik GmbH
Printing and binding: Livonia Print, Riga
Paper: Magno Volume

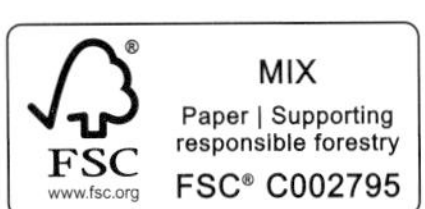

Penguin Random House Verlagsgruppe FSC® N001967

Printed in Latvia
ISBN 978-3-7913-9354-4
www.prestel.com